Modality Across Syntactic Categories

OXFORD STUDIES IN THEORETICAL LINGUISTICS

GENERAL EDITORS: David Adger and Hagit Borer, Queen Mary, University of London

ADVISORY EDITORS: Stephen Anderson, Yale University; Daniel Büring, University of Vienna; Nomi Erteschik-Shir, Ben-Gurion University; Donka Farkas, University of California, Santa Cruz; Angelika Kratzer, University of Massachusetts, Amherst; Andrew Nevins, University College London; Christopher Potts, Stanford University; Barry Schein, University of Southern California; Peter Svenonius, University of Tromsø; Moira Yip, University College London

RECENT TITLES

48 Syntax and its Limits
edited by Raffaella Folli, Christina Sevdali, and Robert Truswell

49 Phrase Structure and Argument Structure
A Case Study of the Syntax-Semantics Interface
by Terje Lohndal

50 Edges in Syntax
Scrambling and Cyclic Linearization
by Heejeong Ko

51 The Syntax of Roots and the Roots of Syntax
edited by Artemis Alexiadou, Hagit Borer, and Florian Schäfer

52 Causation in Grammatical Structures
edited by Bridget Copley and Fabienne Martin

53 Continuations and Natural Language
by Chris Barker and Chung-chieh Shan

54 The Semantics of Evaluativity
by Jessica Rett

55 External Arguments in Transitivity Alternations
by Artemis Alexiadou, Elena Anagnostopoulou, and Florian Schäfer

56 Control and Restructuring
by Thomas Grano

57 The Interaction of Focus, Givenness, and Prosody
A Study of Italian Clause Structure
by Vieri Samek-Lodovici

58 The Morphosyntax of Gender
by Ruth Kramer

59 The Morphosyntax of Imperatives
by Daniela Isac

60 Sentence and Discourse
edited by Jacqueline Guéron

61 Optimality-Theoretic Syntax, Semantics, and Pragmatics
From Uni- to Bidirectional Optimization
edited by Géraldine Legendre, Michael T. Putnam, Henriëtte de Swart, and Erin Zaroukian

62 The Morphosyntax of Transitions
A Case Study in Latin and Other Languages
Víctor Acedo-Matellán

63 Modality Across Syntactic Categories
edited by Ana Arregui, María Luisa Rivero, and Andrés Salanova

For a complete list of titles published and in preparation for the series, see pp. 346–348.

Modality Across Syntactic Categories

Edited by
ANA ARREGUI, MARÍA LUISA RIVERO,
AND ANDRÉS SALANOVA

OXFORD
UNIVERSITY PRESS

Great Clarendon Street, Oxford, OX2 6DP,
United Kingdom

Oxford University Press is a department of the University of Oxford.
It furthers the University's objective of excellence in research, scholarship,
and education by publishing worldwide. Oxford is a registered trade mark of
Oxford University Press in the UK and in certain other countries

© editorial matter and organization Ana Arregui, María Luisa Rivero, and Andrés Salanova 2017
© the chapters their several authors 2017

The moral rights of the authors have been asserted

First Edition published in 2017
Impression: 1

All rights reserved. No part of this publication may be reproduced, stored in
a retrieval system, or transmitted, in any form or by any means, without the
prior permission in writing of Oxford University Press, or as expressly permitted
by law, by licence or under terms agreed with the appropriate reprographics
rights organization. Enquiries concerning reproduction outside the scope of the
above should be sent to the Rights Department, Oxford University Press, at the
address above

You must not circulate this work in any other form
and you must impose this same condition on any acquirer

Published in the United States of America by Oxford University Press
198 Madison Avenue, New York, NY 10016, United States of America

British Library Cataloguing in Publication Data
Data available

Library of Congress Control Number: 2016942731

ISBN 978-0-19-871820-8

Printed in Great Britain by
Clays Ltd, St Ives plc

Links to third party websites are provided by Oxford in good faith and
for information only. Oxford disclaims any responsibility for the materials
contained in any third party website referenced in this work.

Contents

General preface	vii
List of abbreviations	viii
List of contributors	xi

1. Introduction   1
   Ana Arregui, María Luisa Rivero, and Andrés Salanova

Part I. Low modality

2. Epistemic indefinites: On the content and distribution of the epistemic component   11
   Luis Alonso-Ovalle and Paula Menéndez-Benito

3. Modal indefinites: Where do Japanese *wh-ka*s fit in?   30
   Luis Alonso-Ovalle and Junko Shimoyama

4. Modality in the nominal domain: The case of adnominal conditionals   49
   Ilaria Frana

5. The non-modality of opinion verbs   70
   David-Étienne Bouchard

6. Sublexical modality in defeasible causative verbs   87
   Fabienne Martin and Florian Schäfer

7. Straddling the line between attitude verbs and necessity modals   109
   Aynat Rubinstein

8. *May* under verbs of hoping: Evolution of the modal system in the complements of hoping verbs in Early Modern English   132
   Igor Yanovich

Part II. Middle modality

9. In an imperfect world: Deriving the typology of counterfactual marking   157
   Bronwyn M. Bjorkman and Claire Halpert

10. Dimensions of variation in Old English modals   179
    Remus Gergel

Part III. High modality

11 Aspect and tense in evidentials   211
    Ana Arregui, María Luisa Rivero, and Andrés Salanova

12 Past possibility cross-linguistically: Evidence from twelve languages   235
    *Sihwei Chen, Vera Hohaus, Rebecca Laturnus, Meagan Louie,
    Lisa Matthewson, Hotze Rullmann, Ori Simchen, Claire K. Turner,
    and Jozina Vander Klok*

13 A modest proposal for the meaning of imperatives   288
    Kai von Fintel and Sabine Iatridou

References   320
Index   343

General preface

The theoretical focus of this series is on the interfaces between subcomponents of the human grammatical system and the closely related area of the interfaces between the different subdisciplines of linguistics. The notion of 'interface' has become central in grammatical theory (for instance, in Chomsky's Minimalist Program) and in linguistic practice: work on the interfaces between syntax and semantics, syntax and morphology, phonology and phonetics, etc., has led to a deeper understanding of particular linguistic phenomena and of the architecture of the linguistic component of the mind/brain.

The series covers interfaces between core components of grammar, including syntax/morphology, syntax/semantics, syntax/phonology, syntax/pragmatics, morphology/phonology, phonology/phonetics, phonetics/speech processing, semantics/pragmatics, and intonation/discourse structure, as well as issues in the way that the systems of grammar involving these interface areas are acquired and deployed in use (including language acquisition, language dysfunction, and language processing). It demonstrates, we hope, that proper understandings of particular linguistic phenomena, languages, language groups, or inter-language variations all require reference to interfaces.

The series is open to work by linguists of all theoretical persuasions and schools of thought. A main requirement is that authors should write so as to be understood by colleagues in related subfields of linguistics and by scholars in cognate disciplines.

Human language, allowing us to consider circumstances that go beyond the actual. The philosophical tradition typically examines modality as a sentence level phenomenon. In this volume, the editors take a more linguistic tack, using the layers of sentential and nominal structure discovered in syntactic (especially cartographic) investigation as contours in an exploration of modality and spreading the empirical domain well beyond European languages. This opens up questions of which kinds of modal meanings are available at different levels of syntactic structure and the various contributions collected here show how syntax specializes the expression of modality in intriguingly similar ways across unrelated languages. As a whole, the book opens up a new research programme bringing the work of syntacticians, semanticists, and philosophers closer together in a crucial area of linguistic research.

David Adger
Hagit Borer

List of abbreviations

Terminology

A	adjective
AC	adnominal conditional
ACC	accusative
ACH	Agent Control Hypothesis
AdjP	adjectival phrase
AOR	aorist
Asp	aspect
B	b-stem
CC	conceptual cover
CF	counterfactual
CP	complementizer phrase
COND	conditional
CoS	Change of State
CQ	concealed question
DAT	dative
DP	determiner phrase
DUR	durative
EAT	Evidence Acquisition Time
e-IaD	endorsing IaD
EV	epistemic/evidential modal
FEM	feminine
FLV	future less vivid
FUT	future
HAB	habitual
IaD	Imperative and Declarative
IFA	Intensional Functional Application
IMPERF, IMPF, IMPV	imperfective
INDEF	indefinite
INSTR	instrumental
IP	inflectional phrase

LF	Logical Form
LOC	locative
MB	modal base
MD	modal head
MOD	modal
N	noun
n-IaD	non-endorsing IaD
NC	non-culminating
NEG	negation
NONPST	non-past
NP	noun phrase
obj.	object
P	preposition
PA	Palestinian Arabic
PERF, PFV	perfective
PL	plural
PP	prepositional phrase
PREF	prefix
PrefP	prefix phrase
PRES	present
PROG	progressive
PST	past
PTCP	participle
PPT	predicate of personal taste
RM	renarrated mood
RP	resultative morpheme
SG	singular
subj.	subject
SUBJ	subjunctive
TDL	to-do list
T	tense
T.O.	temporal orientation
T.P.	temporal perspective
TP	tense/topic phrase
V	verb

VB	verbal head
VoiceP	voice phrase
vP	little voice phrase
VP	verb phrase
VPE	verb-phrase ellipsis

Corpora

BNC	British National Corpus
CASO	Corpus of American Soap Operas
CLMEP	A Corpus of Late Modern English Prose
COCA	Corpus of Contemporary American English
PCEEC	Parsed Corpus of Early English Correspondence
YCOE	York–Toronto–Helsinki Parsed Corpus of Old English Prose

List of contributors

LUIS ALONSO-OVALLE is Associate Professor at the Department of Linguistics of McGill University. His research focuses on natural language semantics and its interfaces with pragmatics. His published work in these areas include articles in *Natural Language Semantics*, *Journal of Semantics*, and *Linguistics and Philosophy*. Prior to joining McGill University, he worked as Lecturer at the Massachusetts Institute of Technology and as Assistant Professor at the University of Massachusetts Boston. He holds a Licenciatura in Spanish Philology from the University of Oviedo (Spain), an MA in Hispanic Linguistics, and a Ph.D. in Linguistics, both from the University of Massachusetts Amherst.

ANA ARREGUI is Associate Professor of Linguistics at the University of Ottawa. Her research is in the domain of natural language semantics, with focus on modality, tense, and aspect. Her publications include articles in *Natural Language Semantics*, *Journal of Semantics*, and *Linguistics and Philosophy*. She holds a Licenciatura en Letras from the University of Buenos Aires and a Ph.D. in Linguistics from the University of Massachusetts Amherst.

BRONWYN M. BJORKMAN is Assistant Professor at Queen's University in Canada. She received her Ph.D. from MIT in 2011; prior to joining Queen's University in 2015 she was a Banting Postdoctoral Fellow at the University of Toronto. Her research focuses on variation in the representation of morphosyntactic categories, particularly in the domain of tense, aspect, and modality.

DAVID-ÉTIENNE BOUCHARD obtained his Ph.D. in Linguistics from McGill University in 2013, where he received the Arts Insight Award for best dissertation in the Faculty of Arts. His work focuses on the syntax and semantics of non-canonical degree constructions and the place of subjectivity in semantic theory, both in English and in Québec French.

SIHWEI CHEN obtained her MA on Atayal voice and argument structure from the National Tsing Hua University (Taiwan) in 2007, where she studied Chinese linguistics and began doing fieldwork on Atayal (Austronesian). She is currently a Ph.D. candidate at the University of British Columbia. Before attending UBC, she worked as a research assistant at the Academia Sinica. Since 2005, she has worked on a variety of topics in Atayal. Her research interests have been in the area of syntax and semantics, recently on issues of tense, aspect, modality, quantifier scope, and definiteness.

ILARIA FRANA completed her Ph.D. in Linguistics from the University of Massachusetts Amherst in 2010. Since then, she has taught at the University of Connecticut, the University of Massachusetts Amherst, and the University of Göttingen. Her research addresses questions in semantics and pragmatics, primarily through an exploration of intensional constructions. Specific topics include epistemic biases in polar questions, adnominal conditionals, concealed questions, and specificational clauses. She is currently preparing a research monograph on concealed questions (Oxford University Press, forthcoming).

REMUS GERGEL earned his doctorate from Tübingen with work on modals and ellipsis (de Gruyter, 2009). He has worked on the syntax–semantics interface as a research fellow at the English Department, and in cross-linguistic projects of two collaborative research centers in Tübingen, as a postdoctoral researcher at the University of Pennsylvania, as a temporary professor at the University of Göttingen, and as professor at the University of Graz and Saarland University. His research includes topics in syntactic and semantic variation and change, modality, decomposition, focus, and gradable constructions.

CLAIRE HALPERT is Assistant Professor of Linguistics at the University of Minnesota, Twin Cities. She joined the University of Minnesota faculty after receiving her Ph.D. from MIT in 2012. Her research focuses on the syntax and morphology of Bantu languages.

VERA HOHAUS is a researcher and lecturer in semantics at Eberhard Karls Universität Tübingen, where she completed her Ph.D. in 2015. Her research interests include the cross-linguistic representation of scalarity in the grammar, the architecture of tense and modality at Logical Form as well as the grammar of alternatives across languages.

SABINE IATRIDOU is Professor of Linguistics at Massachusetts Institute of Technology and Fellow of the Linguistic Society of America. Her areas of research are syntax and semantics.

REBECCA LATURNUS is a Ph.D. student at New York University. She began fieldwork as an undergraduate at the University of British Columbia in 2010, working closely with consultants on a variety of topics in Ktunaxa. Since graduating from UBC in 2012, Rebecca's research interests have shifted several times, most recently to focus on issues of cross-language and talker-specific perception and theories of phonological representation. Though she is no longer actively involved in fieldwork, she remains interested in language documentation, revitalization, and language policy.

MEAGAN LOUIE began doing fieldwork on Blackfoot (Algonquian) as an undergraduate student at the University of British Columbia in 2006. She went on to major in linguistics, receiving an MA from the University of Toronto (2008), and then returning to UBC to complete her doctorate (2015). Her research interests are in the domain of formal semantics and pragmatics; she has worked on issues such as temporality, modality, conditionals, and distributivity. She is currently teaching at the Department of Linguistics at Srinakharinwirot University in Bangkok.

FABIENNE MARTIN received her Ph.D. from the Université libre de Bruxelles in 2006, and has worked since then as a postdoctoral researcher at the Universität Stuttgart. She works on the interface between lexical semantics and tense, aspect and modality, with a focus on Romance languages.

LISA MATTHEWSON obtained her Ph.D. on Salish determiners and quantifiers at the University of British Columbia in 1996. She held a SSHRC postdoctoral fellowship at MIT and was Assistant Professor at the University of Massachusetts, Amherst, before returning to UBC, where she is currently Professor in Linguistics. Her research interests centre on semantic variation and universals, with specific attention to modality, tense, aspect, quantification, discourse particles, and presupposition. She has worked on St'át'imcets (Salish) since the early 1990s, on Gitksan (Tsimshianic) since 2010, and has recently begun investigating Niuean (Austronesian).

PAULA MENÉNDEZ-BENITO is a visiting researcher at the Universitat Pompeu Fabra. She received her Ph.D. in Linguistics (2005) from the University of Massachusetts Amherst. Her research focuses on natural language semantics and its interfaces with pragmatics. Her published work in these areas includes articles in *Natural Language Semantics* and *Journal of Semantics*.

MARÍA LUISA RIVERO is Emeritus Professor of Linguistics at the University of Ottawa, and Fellow of the Royal Society of Canada. Her research has focused on syntax and semantics, with recent work paying particular attention to aspect, modality, and tense with emphasis on languages of the Romance and Slavic families and those of the Balkan peninsula.

AYNAT RUBINSTEIN received a Ph.D. in linguistics from the University of Massachusetts Amherst in 2012 and is currently a Lecturer in the Department of Linguistics and the Department of Hebrew Language at The Hebrew University of Jerusalem. Her research concerns the context dependency and gradability of modals and expressions of attitude across languages. In recent years she has been involved in the creation of a new annotated corpus of English modal expressions at Georgetown University.

HOTZE RULLMANN is Associate Professor in the Department of Linguistics at the University of British Columbia (Vancouver, Canada). He received his Ph.D. from the University of Massachusetts Amherst in 1995. Before joining UBC, he was a postdoctoral researcher at the University of Groningen and the University of Alberta, and an assistant professor at the University of Calgary. His research has been mostly in the area of semantics, focusing on a variety of topics including comparatives, *wh*-questions, negation and polarity, focus particles, and modality.

ANDRÉS SALANOVA is Associate Professor of Linguistics at the University of Ottawa. He has worked on the structure of the Jê language Mẽbengokre since 1996, to which both his Campinas MA and MIT Ph.D. are devoted. As primarily a descriptive linguist, he has worked on topics ranging from synchronic and historical phonology to evidentiality.

FLORIAN SCHÄFER is a researcher at the collaborative research centre (Sonderforschungsbereich) SFB 732 "Incremental Specification in Context" at the University of Stuttgart. He studied General and Theoretical Linguistics at the University of Potsdam and finished his dissertation in 2007 at the University of Stuttgart. His main research interests are located in the theories of syntax, morphology, and lexical semantics, and the interaction of these modules of grammar.

JUNKO SHIMOYAMA is Associate Professor at the Department of Linguistics of McGill University. Her research focuses on syntax and its interface with semantics. Her published work in these areas include articles in *Natural Language Semantics*, *Journal of Semantics*, and *Journal of East Asian Linguistics*. Prior to joining McGill University, she worked as Lecturer at the University of Texas at Austin and as Assistant Professor at the Kyushu Institute of Technology in Fukuoka. She holds a BA and MA in English Linguistics from Ochanomizu University in Tokyo, and a Ph.D. in Linguistics from the University of Massachusetts Amherst.

ORI SIMCHEN is Professor of Philosophy at the University of British Columbia. He works mainly in the philosophy of language and metaphysics, with side interests in the philosophy of mind and the history of analytic philosophy. He is the author of two books, *Necessary Intentionality: A Study in the Metaphysics of Aboutness* (Oxford University Press, 2012) and *Semantics, Metasemantics, Aboutness* (Oxford University Press, forthcoming). He is also the author of various articles in journals including *Noûs*, *Journal of Philosophy*, *Notre Dame Journal of Formal Logic*, and *Philosophical Quarterly*.

CLAIRE K. TURNER completed her Ph.D. at the University of Surrey in 2011, on the morphology and semantics of aspect in SENĆOŦEN, a dialect of Northern Straits Salish. This was followed by an SSHRC Postdoctoral Fellowship at the University of British Columbia, where she investigated modality in the same language and in the Hul'q'umi'num' dialect of Halkomelem. She currently teaches phonology and applied linguistics in an ESL programme in Barbados, at the University of the West Indies, Cave Hill. She maintains a working relationship with SENĆOŦEN teachers and learners, having developed a web database of language examples and helped create teaching materials.

JOZINA VANDER KLOK a graduate of McGill University, is currently a researcher and lecturer at the University of British Columbia (UBC). Previously, she was a SSHRC (Social Sciences and Humanities Research Council of Canada) postdoctoral fellow at UBC and a postdoctoral fellow at the Jakarta Field Station, Max Planck Institute for Evolutionary Anthropology. She has conducted fieldwork on different dialects of Javanese (Austronesian) in Indonesia since 2010, and is committed to the language documentation of under-studied languages. Her research investigates the cross-linguistic articulation of syntax and semantics, focusing on tense, aspect, and modality.

KAI VON FINTEL is Andrew W. Mellon Professor of Linguistics at Massachusetts Institute of Technology and Fellow of the Linguistic Society of America. His areas of research are semantics, pragmatics, philosophy of language, and the intersections thereof. He has written influential articles on exceptives, negative polarity, generics, conditionals, quantification, epistemic modality, weak necessity, semantic universals, and other topics. His paper "CIA Leaks" (with Thony Gillies) was chosen as one of the ten best papers in philosophy in 2008.

IGOR YANOVICH is currently a postdoctoral fellow at DFG Center for Advanced Studies "Words, Bones, Genes and Tools" at the University of Tübingen. The Center brings together geneticists, archaeologists, paleoanthropologists, and linguists combining forces to uncover the secrets of the human (and hominid) past. Igor received his Ph.D. in linguistics and philosophy from Massachusetts Institute of Technology, and has since held a postdoctoral grant from the Alexander von Humboldt foundation in Germany and a research fellowship at Carnegie Mellon Philosophy. His research specialization is in formal semantics, historical linguistics, and formal and computational methods.

1

Introduction

ANA ARREGUI, MARÍA LUISA RIVERO,
AND ANDRÉS SALANOVA

1.1 Background and scope

Modality is a core research topic for most disciplines interested in language, including linguistics, philosophy, and psychology. Modal expressions are the features of language that make it possible to displace our conversations from actual circumstances to non-actual situations. The ability to construct and understand modal sentences underlies our capacity to discuss and reason about what is possible, obligatory, desirable, or prohibited, a defining characteristic of human communication.

Modality has been a traditional area of research in the study of language, but focus has been placed on sentence-level modality. Adopting a more general perspective, this book examines the construction of modal meanings across a range of syntactic categories in addition to the sentential type. The study of modal meanings across a range of syntactic categories opens new windows both on the role of syntactic structure in the organization of modal meanings and on the formal linguistic characterization of non-actual possibilities.

Drawing on novel data from an extensive set of Indo-European and non-Indo-European languages, including many that lack traditional descriptions, the chapters in this volume offer a cross-linguistic perspective on the encoding of modal meanings. By putting forward specific case studies across a range of languages, the chapters allow us to gain insights into features that are common across languages in the construction of modal meanings, as well as constraints that are language-specific. The broad range of syntactic and morphological configurations under study in this book succeed in giving readers a sense of the extremely rich diversity found in natural language under the "modal umbrella."

Traditional semantic accounts of modality have often been inspired by logic and philosophy. Very often based on the grammar of Germanic languages, such accounts commonly assume that very specialized linguistic elements are responsible

Modality Across Syntactic Categories. First edition. Ana Arregui, María Luisa Rivero, and Andrés Salanova (eds.).
This chapter © Ana Arregui, María Luisa Rivero, and Andrés Salanova 2017. First published 2017 by Oxford University Press.

for constructing modal meanings. Such elements are often thought to be located in a fixed syntactic position within the sentence, roughly above temporal projections associated with tense and aspect within the clause. There also appears to be a common underlying assumption that there is a basic dichotomy between the types of meanings that we might consider "modal" and other kinds. Recent research, however, casts doubt on these restrictive views. On the one hand, there is a growing body of cross-linguistic evidence based on a larger variety of language families that suggests that modal meanings arise in a very broad set of syntactic contexts, and not simply in fixed positions within the clause. On the other hand, recent theoretical proposals have developed highly articulated relations between syntax and interpretation and a more fine-grained modal ontology, including situations, events, facts, and information states, which lead to the prediction that modal meanings could be available for all syntactic categories and at all the different levels of syntactic structure. In principle, all categories that manipulate individuals, events, and situations would be able to access non-actual possibilities. This raises the chance that modality could be encoded in rather "unexpected" places, that is, in a broader range of constructions and associated with a larger set of categories than contemplated in past philosophical, logical, and grammatical traditions.

There exists a tradition of studies about the relation between types of modality and syntactic structure in some languages, most notably relating to (English) modals. Given more recent perspectives, however, the question becomes fully general, opening the door to research regarding restrictions on modality across multiple syntactic categories. The issue of the availability of modal meanings across different structures, and of the modal "flavours" associated with different structures, has thus become a live empirical question. The chapters in the current volume support a view that considers that modality may infuse a much more extensive number of syntactic domains than traditionally thought. The twelve chapters have as unifying theme a cross-categorial perspective where modal meanings are related to varied syntactic categories and levels of syntactic structure. The book has been organized in terms of three main cartographic configurations: (i) LOW modality refers to modality as it appears embedded in the verbal and nominal domains (i.e. roughly in structures dominated by VP or NP). Modality at this level has remained relatively understudied in the traditional literature, but constitutes a lively current area of research and the most extensive area of research under investigation in this volume. (ii) MIDDLE modality refers to modality structurally linked to tense and aspect (i.e. roughly in the central areas of the structure of the sentence commonly known as the inflectional layers). (iii) HIGH modality refers to modality as it appears above the domain of tense and aspect taking widest interpretive scope (i.e. roughly in the highest portions of the clause associated with complementizers and related syntactic categories).

The following twelve chapters are concerned with the interpretation of modal items in the verbal and nominal cartographies, in the cartography internal to the clause, and in the cartography that has come to be known as the left periphery. They offer enticing combinations of cross-linguistic discussions on traditional sources together with novel or unexpected sources of modality, presenting specific case studies that show how meanings associated with low, middle, and high modality crystallize in a variety of languages.

1.2 The case of "low" modality

As stated, traditional studies of modality have mostly focused on languages such as English or German, in which modal meanings are often conveyed by means of operators that appear in the inflectional domain of the clause. This section shifts the focus to modal meanings that are constructed "lower" in the clause, namely in the domain both of nouns and of verbs across a range of languages from both synchronic and diachronic perspectives. For the purpose of this introduction, we have separated this group into two parts: modality in the nominal domain and modality in the verbal domain.

1.2.1 Modality in the nominal domain

The authors grouped together under the above heading address challenges posed by modality in the nominal domain. How are modal meanings generated in structures that do not have the complexity of full clauses or even verbal projections? The chapters explore the construction of epistemic effects in the absence of traditional epistemic modals, parameters of cross-linguistic variation in such interpretations, as well as the introduction of conditional meanings within the noun phrase.

In Chapter 2, "Epistemic indefinites: On the content and distribution of the epistemic component," Alonso-Ovalle and Menéndez-Benito investigate the nature of the ignorance effects triggered by so-called epistemic indefinites, as well as their distribution. They compare two approaches to epistemic effects in indefinites: those in terms of "conceptual covers" and those in terms of implicatures. Alonso-Ovalle and Menéndez-Benito note that the content and distribution of epistemic effects actually pose challenges to both types of account. They propose a reconciliation of the two views by maintaining an implicature-style account of epistemic effects generated on the basis of competition between the maxims of quantity and quality, while at the same time enriching the original implicature-based proposal. This allows constraints on the properties that identify domains of quantification to play a role, reconstructing insights from approaches in terms of conceptual covers.

Alonso-Ovalle and Shimoyama's Chapter 3, "Modal indefinites: Where do Japanese *wh-kas* fit in?", explores modality in Japanese indeterminates that are constructed with a *wh*-word and the *-ka* particle. In other languages, so-called "epistemic indefinites" have been shown to convey a range of effects, including different types of speaker ignorance such as type vs. token, "free choice" readings under the scope of deontic modals, and implicature-style behavior in downward entailing contexts. Alonso-Ovalle and Shimoyama provide a comparative overview of Japanese *wh-ka* indeterminates, contrasting them with expressions found in other languages, and contribute towards a general theory of nominal modality by tracking their behavior with respect to relevant parameters of variation.

In Chapter 4, "Modality in the nominal domain: The case of adnominal conditionals," Frana investigates the interpretation of *if*-clauses associated with NPs known as "Adnominal Conditionals" (ACs), which include *The price if you pay now is predictable* and *No possible explanation to Telepathy if you believe in the laws of Physics exists*. ACs provide an interesting window into the parallelism between modality in the nominal and sentential domains. Frana pursues an analysis that highlights this parallelism by proposing a compositional analysis that builds on restrictor-style proposals for sentence-level *if*-clauses commonly accepted in the literature. She provides a unified account that can address both ACs with overt modal adjectives such as *possibly*, and cases which are implicitly modalized with a covert operator similar to *necessary*, solving problems for earlier proposals.

1.2.2 Modality in the verbal domain

The authors contributing to this section focus on the interpretation of lexical verbs that carry modal interpretations, in particular those signaling desires, hopes, the speaker's beliefs, or planned events. The chapters show that the boundary between true "modals" and other types of verb can become rather blurred, while at the same time there appear to be distinctions that differentiate between modality at the level of lexical verbs vs. more traditional modals.

In Chapter 5, "The non-modality of opinion verbs," Bouchard establishes a comparison between opinion verbs such as *find (that)* and epistemic verbs such as *think*, arguing that in spite of similarities in their meanings, their underlying semantics is fundamentally different. Bouchard's chapter offers insights into the diverse mechanisms that construct modally flavored interpretations, making a distinction between the systems that manipulate a judge parameter, for example, in predicates of personal taste and opinion verbs, and semantic mechanisms that construct modal interpretations by quantifying over possible worlds, as with epistemic modals and epistemic verbs. By arguing for the separation of the two systems and studying their interaction, Bouchard's chapter furthers our understanding of the multiplicity of parameters that contribute towards the construction of subjectivity in language.

In Chapter 6, "Sublexical modality in defeasible causative verbs," Martin and Schäfer investigate a class of verbs they dub "defeasible causatives" (which includes *offer*-type verbs), offering a typological study with empirical focus on French and German. They note that with agentive subjects, defeasible causative verbs give rise to the intuition that there was an intention to bring about a change of state, but it is not given that such a change was in fact brought about. With causative subjects, however, the change of state is implicated much more strongly (maybe entailed). Martin and Schäfer contribute towards our understanding of modality at the sublexical level by providing an analysis of these verbs according to which, in addition to a situational core component (pertaining to arguments and event structure), there is a sublexical modal component that identifies the world evaluation indices in terms of "causally successful worlds." By enriching lexical representations with a modal dimension, Martin and Schäfer argue for a more complex view of verb meanings that incorporates a richer range of modal interpretations.

In Chapter 7, "Straddling the line between attitude verbs and necessity modals," Rubinstein examines the expression of desires and goals in attitude verbs and modals, thus probing into the semantic and syntactic characterization of modality across these categories. Challenging previous accounts based on sets of alternatives, she develops a characterization of *want*-type verbs in terms of comparisons based on desires that simply take into account the prejacent and its negation. Rubinstein then goes on to propose that *necessary* as prototypical means to express necessity is a teleological modal, differing from *want* in lacking an individual ("subject") argument. Requiring a teleological ordering source to determine its quantification domain, *necessary* is also argued to differ from general-purpose necessity modals such as *have to*. The claim is that there is a continuum between *want*-type attitude verbs and general-purpose necessity modals, with modals like *necessary* occupying a middle ground. The chapter thus makes a contribution towards our understanding of the relation between structural configurations and the construction of modal meanings. Namely, while *want*-type attitude verbs and *necessary*-type modals differ with respect to the relativization of modality to an individual, they share common semantic features that can be grouped under a "teleological" interpretation, and differ from modals like *have to*, which display greater interpretive flexibility.

In Chapter 8, "*May* under verbs of hoping: Evolution of the modal system in the complements of hoping verbs in Early Modern English," Yanovich investigates the historical development of modals in the scope of verbs of hoping. He notes that the usual meaning of possibility associated with modal verbs such as *may* appears to be absent in this context, and argues that the role of *may* was to take over the functions from the disappearing subjunctive. Yanovich makes this point tracing the development of modals in the scope of *hoping*-verbs, from Old English, in which such modals were completely absent, up to Modern English, in which the construction became more common and acquired its unexpected interpretation. By examining the development of the interpretation of *may* in this particular context, he makes a contribution to our understanding of how modal interpretations may be affected by the modal values of other elements in the structure. In this case, the compositional interpretation disappears as other functions are taken on.

1.3 Middle modality

This section investigates the construction of modal meanings in relation to tense and aspect. Even though traditional classifications have separated tense and aspect from modality, a growing body of evidence suggests that "temporal" categories also have modal components. Research in this area has often focused on a specific language, obscuring the range of variation that can lead to the construction of modal interpretations. This section of the volume includes considerable cross-linguistic data arguing to the effect there is no one-to-one correspondence between flavors of modality and tense/aspect configurations.

Bjorkman and Halpert's Chapter 9, "In an imperfect world: Deriving the typology of counterfactual marking," examines the interpretation of counterfactual conditionals from a cross-linguistic perspective, making a contribution towards lively current debates regarding the interpretation of temporal morphology in this environment. Examining in detail a wide range of languages not widely discussed in the previous literature, Bjorkman and Halpert argue for a novel typology for marking counterfactuality. Some languages appeal to past tense as a marker of counterfactuality, giving rise to "fake tense" interpretations, while other languages require imperfective aspect as a marker of counterfactuality, giving rise to "fake aspect" interpretations. Crucially, argue Bjorkman and Halpert, no language requires both. The authors suggest that this may indicate that there is a single dedicated syntactic position associated specifically with the semantic composition of counterfactual conditionals, and explore its relation with the interpretation of temporal morphology.

In Chapter 10, "Dimensions of variation in Old English modals," Gergel examines the morphosyntax and semantics of modal verbs in Old English in relation to their categorical status, modal flavor, and force, as well as their ability to give rise to actuality entailments. Gergel departs from standard assumptions in arguing that Old English modals were already functional elements at the height of Aspect, thus locating them within the inflectional domain. By examining differences in modal flavor and quantificational force, he shows that the system of modals in Old English displayed a broad range of variation, arguing against a strict link between a specific type of interpretation and a specific type of complementation structure. The chapter thus makes a contribution not only to the diachronic study of semantics but also to our understanding of the interaction between syntactic structure and modal interpretation.

1.4 High modality

This section investigates modal meanings that have traditionally been associated with elements located high in the left periphery of the clause. Such syntactic positions are often associated with epistemic and evidential types of meanings, and have been said to host "pragmatic" operators (e.g. encoding illocutionary force). The chapters in this section explore how epistemic/evidential/non-declarative meanings may be constructed, arguing for more flexible approaches than those often found in the existing literature. The consensus seems to be that nothing very special needs to be said about the construction of "high" modal meanings: we observe the expected interaction with other operators in the clause and we are able to account for observed interpretations without ad hoc operators.

In Chapter 11, "Aspect and tense in evidentials", Arregui, Rivero, and Salanova investigate the interaction between evidential and temporal categories, establishing a comparison between Bulgarian, a South Slavic language, Mẽbengokre, a Jê language in Central Brazil, and Matses, a Panoan language in the Amazon region in Brazil and Peru. The chapter addresses current concerns in research on evidentiality, which has been associated with operators taking wide sentential scope. It has been noted in the literature that evidentials at times appear to interact with temporal categories, giving rise to the proposal that there is a special dedicated system of "evidential tense." Arregui, Rivero, and Salanova present arguments against this view by showing that a standard interpretation of tense can be maintained in evidential contexts across a set of unrelated languages with a broad range of morphosyntactic mechanisms. Complex data that appears to point to a temporal shift in evidential contexts is explained once the contribution of aspect is taken into account.

In Chapter 12, "Past possibility cross-linguistically: Evidence from twelve languages," Chen, Hohaus, Laturnus, Louie, Matthewson, Rullmann, Simchen, Turner, and Vander Klok investigate the interaction between modality and temporal operators across languages from seven language families. The authors provide support for the view that temporal operators scoping above modals are responsible for the modal's temporal perspective, while temporal operators scoping below the modal give it its temporal orientation. In many cases, the temporal operator scoping above the modal is tense, and the one below is aspect, but the authors show that there is cross-linguistic variation arising from differences in temporal systems found across languages. Importantly, the authors point to robust cross-linguistic evidence showing that the temporal perspective of epistemic modals may be shifted towards the past, thus contributing to ongoing debates regarding the temporal anchoring of epistemic markers.

Von Fintel and Iatridou's Chapter 13, "A modest proposal for the meaning of imperatives," provides a novel perspective on the compositional interpretation of imperatives, evaluating the roles played by semantics and pragmatics. Contrary to views that analyze illocutionary force in terms of operators scoping high on the inflectional domain, von Fintel and Iatridou account for the interpretation of imperatives on the basis of a minimal semantics together with a sophisticated account of pragmatic force. Their chapter brings a wide range of data to bear on the discussion, contemplating the puzzles arising from "non-canonical" uses of imperatives, such as conditional conjunctions and imperatives that signal acquiescence and indifference, across a large set of languages.

1.5 Conclusion

The range of case studies presented in this volume offers exciting insights into the construction of modal meanings. Novel data, some from well-studied languages and other from very understudied languages, helps flesh out a new picture of the landscape of modality. While modal interpretations constructed at the various levels of structure in syntactic representations share a family resemblance and appeal to similar mechanisms, the distinct environments within the clause also lead to specialization in the construction of modal meanings.

The theoretical proposals in this volume take steps towards a novel charting of modal domains, bringing together the study of "expected" and "unexpected" modality. Perhaps more importantly, the chapters in this volume highlight the relevance of a perspective that combines the careful study of language-specific details in morphology and syntax with a broad view that can identify the building blocks of modal meanings across languages.

Acknowledgments

This volume presents a collection of work originating at the conference "Modality @OttawaU," held at the University of Ottawa on April 20–21, 2012. We would like to thank all participants who helped to make the meeting a success, and gratefully acknowledge the support of the Linguistics Department at the University of Ottawa. The conference received partial support from the Social Sciences and Humanities Research Council of Canada (Research Grant 410-2010-2040 to A. Arregui (PI), M. L. Rivero and A. Salanova (co-investigators)). We would also like to thank profusely Lyra Magloughlin, who provided invaluable editorial assistance with this volume.

Part I

Low modality

2

Epistemic indefinites: On the content and distribution of the epistemic component

LUIS ALONSO-OVALLE AND PAULA
MENÉNDEZ-BENITO

2.1 Epistemic indefinites

Epistemic indefinites make an existential claim and signal that the speaker cannot identify the individual that satisfies that claim. Consider the contrast between the two Spanish sentences in (1).

(1) a. María sale   con un estudiante, y   yo sé   quién es.
María goes out with UN student   and I   know who   is
'María is dating a student and I know who.'
b. María sale   con algún estudiante, # y   yo sé   quién es.
María goes out with ALGÚN student   and I   know who   is
'María is dating some student and I know who.'

Both of these sentences convey that there is a student that María is dating. However, while (1a), with the plain indefinite *un*, is consistent with the speaker knowing who the student is, (1b), with the epistemic indefinite *algún*, is not. As a result, the continuation 'and I know who' is odd in (1b).[1]

Epistemic indefinites may vary with respect to what counts as knowing who. This can be seen by contrasting Spanish *algún* with English *some*. Examples like (2a) (attributed to Michael Israel in Farkas 2002a) show that English singular *some* is an

---

[1] We will translate *algún* as *some*, although, as shown below, the two indefinites differ in their interpretation.

Modality Across Syntactic Categories. First edition. Ana Arregui, María Luisa Rivero, and Andrés Salanova (eds.).
This chapter © Luis Alonso-Ovalle and Paula Menéndez-Benito 2017. First published 2017 by Oxford University Press.

epistemic indefinite.[2] It is not possible to follow (2a) with (2b), which names the movie that verifies the existential claim made by (2a).

(2) a. Susan rented some movie for us to watch yesterday.
    b. # It was *The Maltese Falcon*. (Farkas 2002a, 70)

Alonso-Ovalle and Menéndez-Benito (2003) noted that *some* and *algún* impose different restrictions on what the speaker can know. In the scenario in (3), P can felicitously utter (4a) but not (4b). The type of knowledge that P has about the professor in this context rules out the use of *algún*, but not of *some*.

(3) L and P are visiting the Math department. They don't know anything about the people working there, and they haven't seen any of them before. They suddenly see an individual, who can be inferred to be a professor, frantically dancing on his desk.

(4) a. Look! Some professor is dancing on the table!
    b. # ¡Mira! ¡Algún profesor está bailando encima de la mesa!
       Look! ALGÚN professor is dancing on of the table
       'Look! Some professor is dancing on the table!'

Contrasts like the one in (4) raise the question of what counts as (not) knowing who for different epistemic indefinites, and how this requirement should be encoded. To our knowledge, the only account of epistemic indefinites that explicitly addresses this question is the one put forward in Aloni and Port 2013 (circulated since 2010), which we will label the Conceptual Cover Approach in what follows.[3]

Another issue that theories of epistemic indefinites need to address is the fact that the ignorance effect is absent in some environments. One such environment is the scope of downward entailing operators. For instance, the sentence in (5), where *algún* is in the restrictor of a universal quantifier, can be uttered by a speaker who is able to identify the students that the different professors are talking to. The behaviour of the epistemic effect in examples like (5) parallels that of quantity implicatures. This has given rise to a family of accounts that derive the epistemic effect as a quantity implicature (see e.g. Kratzer and Shimoyama 2002, Alonso-Ovalle and Menéndez-Benito 2008, 2010, Fălăuş 2009, Fălăuş 2014, Chierchia 2013). We will refer to this family of approaches as the Implicature Approach.

---

[2] Farkas attributes the example to Israel (n.d.). Israel (2000) does not include this example to illustrate the epistemic component of *some*. On the epistemic effect of *some*, see e.g. Becker (1999), Farkas (2002a), Weir (2012), and Maher (2013). Israel (2000) quotes Warfel (1972) and Mazodier (1998) as describing the epistemic effect of *some*.

[3] See also Aloni and Port (2015).

(5) Todos los profesores que están hablando con algún estudiante
    All   the professors who are   talking   with ALGÚN student
    llevan sombrero.
    wear   hat
    'Every professor who is talking to a student wears a hat.'

The epistemic effect also disappears in some upward entailing contexts. Consider, for instance, the sentence in (6).

(6) Todos los profesores están hablando con algún   estudiante.
    All   the professors are   talking with ALGÚN student
    'Every professor is talking to some student.'

When *algún* is interpreted with scope over the universal quantifier, it conveys an ignorance effect. In a situation where all the professors are talking to the same student, (6) is only felicitous if the speaker cannot identify the student. However, when *algún* is interpreted in the nuclear scope of the universal quantifier, there is no ignorance effect. If different professors are dancing with different students, a speaker could felicitously utter (6) even if she knew exactly which professors are dancing with which students. In what follows, we will call these contexts 'co-variation contexts.'[4]

Building on previous work (Alonso-Ovalle and Menéndez-Benito 2013a, Alonso-Ovalle and Shimoyama 2014), this chapter assesses the extent to which the Conceptual Cover Approach and the Implicature Approach can account for the content and the distribution of the epistemic effect of *algún*.[5] Sections 2.2 and 2.3 focus on the Conceptual Cover Approach. Sections 2.4 and 2.5 deal with the Implicature Approach. The discussion in these sections leads us to conclude that neither approach can capture the whole range of data. Section 2.6 sketches a preliminary proposal that incorporates insights from the two theories. While this preliminary proposal gives us a way of handling the challenges for the theories we are discussing, it would need to be developed further in order to be considered a full-fledged account. We conclude by briefly discussing in Section 2.7 one of the developments that is needed.

2.2 The Conceptual Cover Approach

Aloni and Port (2013) develop a theory of epistemic indefinites at whose core is the contextual dependency of *knowing who*. This work builds on Aloni (2001), who observes that the interpretation of *know who* depends on what method of identification is salient in the context. Aloni (2001) illustrates this with the context in (7).

---

[4] Fox (2007) discusses the same behavior for disjunction. For *algún*, see Alonso-Ovalle and Shimoyama (2014).

[5] For a comparison between the two approaches that focuses on aspects other than the ones discussed here, see Alonso-Ovalle and Menéndez-Benito (2013b).

(7) In front of you lie two face-down cards. One is the ace of spades, the other is the ace of hearts. You know that the winning card is the ace of hearts, but you don't know whether the ace of hearts is the card on the left or the card on the right. (Aloni 2001, 16)

Aloni (2001) notes that whether (8) is judged as true in the context in (7) or not depends on the method of identification chosen: (8) is true if cards are identified by their suit (identification by description) but false if they are identified by their position (identification by ostension).

(8) You know which card is the winning card. (Aloni 2001, 16)

Building on this observation, Aloni and Port assume that the context provides a relevant way of knowing who (a relevant identification method), and claim that epistemic indefinites signal that the speaker cannot identify the witness of the existential claim using that method.

Following Aloni (2001), Aloni and Port model methods of identification as conceptual covers. A conceptual cover CC is a set of individual concepts (functions from worlds to individuals) $\{i_1, i_2, \ldots\}$ that jointly 'cover' the domain of quantification (in any w, each individual concept is true of one individual, and in any w each individual is picked out by one of these individual concepts). The use of an epistemic indefinite depends on conceptual covers in the following way.[6] Suppose that there are two professors, Professor Smith and Professor Jones. A sentence like (9) could in principle be interpreted with respect to the three covers in (10). The use of an epistemic indefinite in (9) signals (i) that the speaker can identify the professor with respect to some cover CC (in the sense that the condition in (11) holds), and (ii) that the CC made salient by the context is not available to the speaker.

(9) Mary is dating some professor.

(10) a. $\left\{ \begin{array}{l} \lambda w.\iota x.\text{TO-THE-LEFT}_w(x), \\ \lambda w.\iota x.\text{TO-THE-RIGHT}_w(x) \end{array} \right\}$ (Ostension)

b. $\left\{ \begin{array}{l} \lambda w.\iota x.\text{PHONOLOGIST}_w(x), \\ \lambda w.\iota x.\text{SEMANTICIST}_w(x) \end{array} \right\}$ (Description)

c. $\left\{ \begin{array}{l} \lambda w.\text{Smith}, \\ \lambda w.\text{Jones} \end{array} \right\}$ (Naming)

(11) There is at least one c in CC such that for all w compatible with what the speaker believes, Mary is dating $c(w)$ and $c(w)$ is a professor.

---

[6] This is a simplification. Aloni and Port's theory is cast in a dynamic semantics with conceptual covers (Aloni 2001). What we present here is an informal rendition of (part of) their proposal. The reader is referred to Aloni and Port (2013) for the details of the technical setup.

To see how this proposal works, consider the sentence in (12) against the context in (13) (inspired by similar contexts presented in Aloni 2001).

(12) I have to meet with some professor.

(13) We are looking for a professor in the Linguistics department. All we see are closed office doors with nameplates.

Presumably, the relevant cover in this context is Naming (since knowing the name of the professor would be the most efficient way of finding her). Aloni and Port's proposal predicts that the sentence in (12) should be fine in the context in (13) as long as the speaker does not know the name of the professor, even if she knows, for instance, that the professor is the head of the department (i.e., even if she can identify the professor by description).

To account for the contrast between *algún* and *some* in (4), and for a parallel contrast between Italian *un qualche* and German *irgendein*, Aloni and Port assume the existence of the hierarchy of methods of identification in (14) and the principle in (15).

(14) Ostension $>_{higher\ than}$ Naming $>_{higher\ than}$ Description

(15) In Romance, but not in Germanic, the identification method required by knowledge must be higher in order [in (14)] than the identification method required for epistemic indefinites.

Together, (14) and (15) predict that epistemic indefinites in Romance are incompatible with pointing (as ostension is the highest method in (14)). Thus, (4b), repeated below as (16b), is ruled out, but (4a), repeated as (16a), will be acceptable if ostension is not the relevant identification method.

(16) a. Look! Some professor is dancing on the table!
    b. # ¡Mira! ¡Algún profesor está bailando encima de la mesa!
       Look! ALGÚN professor is dancing on of the table
       'Look! Some professor is dancing on the table!'

2.3 The challenge of *algún*

In this section we will discuss several challenges that *algún* poses for the Conceptual Cover Approach. The first challenge (section 2.3.1) builds on Giannakidou and Quer (2013), who contend that *algún* is incompatible with *all* the identification methods considered by Aloni and Port. We agree that *algún* is indeed incompatible with naming and description, and extend Giannakidou and Quer's discussion by showing that this is so regardless of what method of identification is salient in the context. This argues against the claim that epistemic indefinites involve a conceptual cover shift.

The second challenge (section 2.3.2) comes from the fact that, despite examples like (16b), *algún* is not always incompatible with ostension.[7] The third challenge (section 2.3.3), already noted by Alonso-Ovalle and Shimoyama (2014), has to do with the distribution of the epistemic effect: the Conceptual Cover Approach does not predict the lack of epistemic effect in co-variation contexts.

2.3.1 Challenge 1: No context shift

Giannakidou and Quer (2013) argue that *algún* is incompatible with all the methods of identification in Aloni and Port's hierarchy. As evidence for their claim, they provide the examples in (17–19).[8] They use the example in (17) to illustrate incompatibility with ostension (as in Alonso-Ovalle and Menéndez-Benito's 2003 examples), the one in (18) to illustrate incompatibility with naming, and the one in (19) to illustrate incompatibility with description. Giannakidou and Quer (2013) conclude from this that Aloni and Port's account is not tenable.

(17) Tengo que leer un artículo de algún profesor. # Es aquel señor
 have:1s read an article of ALGÚN professor is that guy
 de allí.
 of there
 'I have to read an article by some professor or other. ??It's this guy over there.'
 (Giannakidou and Quer 2013, 140)

(18) Tengo que quedar con algún profesor. # Se llama Bob Smith.
 have:1s meet with ALGÚN professor SE is-named Bob Smith
 'I have to meet with some professor or other. # His name is Bob Smith.'
 (Giannakidou and Quer 2013, 140)

(19) Tengo que quedar con algún profesor. # Es el director del
 have:1s meet with ALGÚN professor is the director of-the
 departamento de filosofía.
 department of philosophy
 'I have to meet some professor or other. # He is the Head of the Philosophy Department.'
 (Giannakidou and Quer 2013, 140)

Note, however, that for this argument to be complete, we would need to provide relevant scenarios for the examples above. This is so because, under the Conceptual Cover Approach, epistemic indefinites signal that the speaker cannot identify the witness of the existential claim by the contextually relevant method of identification. Examples like (18) and (19) will only challenge the Conceptual Cover Approach to

---

[7] A previous version of the discussion in sections 2.3.1 and 2.3.2 appears in Alonso-Ovalle and Menéndez-Benito (2013a).
[8] They also discuss parallel facts for Greek *kapjios*.

the extent that they cannot be uttered in contexts where the salient identification method is not the one available to the speaker.[9] This is indeed the case. According to our intuitions, (18) is deviant in the context in (20), where ostention is salient, but not available to the speaker. Similarly, (19) is ruled out in the context in (21), where naming is relevant but the speaker does not know the name of the professor.[10]

(20) We are looking for a professor in a crowded room. Pointing at him would be the most effective way of singling him out. We know that the professor's name is Bob Smith, but we cannot locate him in the room.

(21) We are looking for a professor in the Philosophy department. All we see are closed office doors with nameplates. We know that the professor is the director of the department, but we don't know her name.

We conclude that the data presented above argues against the claim that *algún* imposes a conceptual cover shift.

2.3.2 Challenge 2: Ostension is sometimes possible

Surprisingly, however, *algún* is not *always* incompatible with ostension. To illustrate this point, consider the contrast in (22–24). Suppose that P looks out of the window and sees María kissing a boy. If the circumstances are as in (22), P cannot felicitously utter the sentence in (23).

(22) *Clear vision.* P hasn't seen the boy before, but she can see him very clearly now.

(23) ¡Mira! ¡María está besando a algún chico!
Look! María is kissing A ALGÚN boy!
'Look! María is kissing some boy!'

In the scenario in (24), however, P can felicitously utter (23) even when pointing at the boy.

(24) *Blurry vision.* María and the boy are far away. P can see that María is kissing a boy, but she cannot make out the boy's features.

Interestingly, Slade (2015) has independently noted that the same pattern obtains for the Sinhala epistemic indefinite *wh-hari*. He reports that the sentence in (25) is infelicitous when the person dancing is in full view of the speaker (as in (22)) but can be used in the context in (26), where the speaker cannot make out the person's features.

---

[9] Example (17) is actually not problematic for Aloni and Port, as they predict that ostension rules out epistemic indefinites in Romance. But see below.
[10] These scenarios are based on similar contexts presented in Aloni (2001).

(25) Kauru hari mese uda natanava.
 who HARI table on dance-pres
 'Someone is dancing on the table.' (Slade 2015, 83)

(26) The speaker is walking down a long hallway with his friend Chitra. At the far end of the hallway there is an open door. Through the open door the speaker can make out the shape of a humanoid figure dancing on a table, but cannot see the figure clearly—the speaker cannot, for instance, even determine whether the person is a male or female, or make out any distinguishing features.
 (Slade 2015, 87)

Like the examples in (18) and (19) above, the contrast between (22) and (24) strongly suggests that *algún* is not sensitive to what method of identification is relevant in the context. It is not clear what method of identification would be required in (22) and (24), but whatever it might be, there is no reason to assume a difference between the two contexts. Additionally, the acceptability of (23) in (24) shows that identification by ostension does not necessarily rule out epistemic indefinites in Romance.

Note that the compatibility of *algún* and pointing is not limited to cases where the speaker has only limited visual access to the individual that satisfies the existential claim. Given the context in (27), P can felicitously utter the sentence in (28)—even though she would be able to point at the individual that satisfies the existential claim whom, furthermore, she sees very well. The crucial factor that distinguishes (22) and (27) is that in (27), the speaker will not take the physical properties of the boy as identifying.

(27) *The triplets.* The Pérez triplets are completely identical. P knows them well. She sees María kissing one of them. P can see the guy very clearly, but of course cannot figure out which triplet María is kissing.

(28) ¡Mira! ¡María está besando a alguno de los trillizos!
 Look! María is kissing A ALGUNO of the triplets
 'Look! Maria is kissing one of the triplets!'

The upshot of the discussion so far is that (i) *algún* does not seem to be sensitive to what method of identification is salient in the context (cf. Giannakidou and Quer 2013) and (ii) ostension does not necessarily rule out the use of *algún*.

2.3.3 Challenge 3: Co-variation

In the clear vision context in (22), the speaker has access to a set of properties that (she believes) uniquely identifies the witness (i.e., a description). In the blurry vision context in (24), the speaker can only identify by ostension. Given this, one possibility that comes to mind is to maintain one of the core insights in Aloni and Port (2013)—that knowing who is relative to methods of identification, modeled by means of contextual covers—but to specify that *algún* rejects identification by naming and description (section 2.3.1) and allows identification by ostension (section 2.3.2). On this view, the sentence in (29a) would be (roughly) interpreted as in (29b).

(29) a. María está besando a algún   estudiante.
      María is   kissing A ALGÚN student
      'María is kissing some student.'
   b. There is at least one c in CC such that for all w compatible with what the speaker believes, Mary is dating $c(w)$ and $c(w)$ is a student (where CC cannot be Naming or Description).

This, however, is not enough. If the only available types of covers are Naming, Description, and Ostension, (29b) predicts that the speaker of (29a) should always be able to identify the student by ostension. But this is contrary to fact, as it is possible to use *algún* in cases where we do not have visual access of any sort to the relevant individual.

Moving beyond this problem, the Conceptual Cover Approach (modified or not) cannot capture the distribution of the epistemic effect. In section 2.1, we noted that the ignorance effect triggered by *algún* disappears in downward entailing contexts, and in what we have called co-variation contexts. Aloni and Port (2013) have a way of predicting the absence of the epistemic effect under downward entailing operators, but their approach (modified or not) makes wrong predictions for co-variation cases.[11] Given (29b), the sentence in (30), on the narrow-scope reading of the indefinite, would be interpreted as in (31).

(30) Todos los profesores están bailando con algún   estudiante.
     all   the professors are dancing with ALGÚN student
     'Every professor is dancing with some student'.

(31) a. For every professor x, there is a c in CC such that in all worlds w compatible with what the speaker believes in w_0, $c(w)$ is a student and x is dancing with $c(w)$.
   b. CC is not Naming.

This predicts that (30) should be ruled out if the speaker can identify the students by name or description. But this sentence can be felicitously used in the scenarios in (32) and (33).

---

[11] Explaining Aloni and Port's account of the disappearance of the epistemic effect in downward entailing contexts would require us to present a non-simplified version of their proposal, something that we will not be able to do here for space reasons. The reader is referred to Aloni and Port (2013) for details and Alonso-Ovalle and Menéndez-Benito (2013b) for discussion. The claim that the co-variation cases pose a challenge to the Conceptual Cover Approach was made by Alonso-Ovalle and Shimoyama (2014), based on observations by Fox (2007) about the free-choice component of disjunction.

(32) The professors in the department are Smith, Jones, and Peters. Each student in the department comes from a different country. The speaker knows that Smith is dancing with the student from Italy, Jones is dancing with the student from France, and Peters is dancing with the student from Spain.

(33) The professors in the department are Smith, Jones, and Peters. The speaker knows that Smith is dancing with Anna, Jones is dancing with John, and Peters is dancing with Lester.

2.4 The Implicature Approach

As noted in section 2.1, there is a family of approaches that—building on Kratzer and Shimoyama (2002)—derive the epistemic effect as a quantity implicature (Alonso-Ovalle and Menéndez-Benito 2003, 2008, 2010, 2011a; Fălăuş 2009, 2014; Chierchia 2013). These approaches are designed to capture the distribution of the epistemic effect, but are not sensitive to the issue of methods of identification. In this section we illustrate this approach with Alonso-Ovalle and Menéndez-Benito's 2008, 2009 proposal, and show that their analysis, unlike the Conceptual Cover Account, accounts for the behavior of *algún* in co-variation contexts. However, section 2.5 argues that this account falls short of characterizing the content of the epistemic effect.

The core idea in Alonso-Ovalle and Menéndez-Benito (2008, 2010) is that *algún* imposes a constraint on its domain of quantification, which triggers a pragmatic competition with other domains. We proposed that *algún* is an anti-singleton indefinite: it requires its domain to contain more than one individual. Motivation for this constraint comes from contrasts like the one in (34). The restriction *book that turned out to be the most expensive one in the bookstore* picks out a singleton domain. While this restriction is acceptable with the plain indefinite *un*, it is ruled out with *algún*.

(34) Juan compró { un / # algún } libro que resultó ser el más
 Juan bought { UN / # ALGÚN } book that turned-out be the most
 caro de la librería.
 expensive of the bookstore
 'Juan bought a book that happened to be the most expensive one in the bookstore.'

Following e.g. von Fintel (2000) and Kratzer (2005), we modeled domain restrictions by means of subset selection functions (which take a set and return one of its subsets). Our proposed denotation for *algún* is in (35): *algún* takes as arguments a subset selection function f and two functions of type $\langle e, t \rangle$, P and Q, and is defined only if $f(P)$ is not (the characterizing function of) a singleton set.

(35) $[\![algún]\!] = \lambda f. \lambda P_{\langle e,t \rangle} : |f(P)| > 1. \lambda Q_{\langle e,t \rangle}. \exists x [f(P)(x) \& Q(x)]$

The anti-singleton constraint triggers a pragmatic competition with alternative assertions that range over singleton domains. Let us illustrate this with the example in (36). Asume the domain of rooms selected by f is the set containing the bedroom, the living room, and the study. Example (36a) will then make the assertion in (36b).

(36) a. Juan está en alguna   habitación de la   casa
       Juan is   in ALGUNA room   of the house.
       'Juan is in a room of the house.'
    b. Juan is in a room in {bedroom, living room, study}

The pragmatic competitors would be those in (37), all of which are more informative than the assertion. By the Maxim of Quantity, the speaker should choose the most informative assertion relevant for the purposes of the conversation. Given this, any of the competitors in (37) would have been a better choice. Why didn't the speaker choose any of them? It must be because she is not able to commit to them. From this, we can conclude that the speaker does not know what room Juan is in.[12]

(37) a. Juan is in a room in {bedroom}
    b. Juan is in a room in {living room}
    c. Juan is in a room in {study}

As the reader can easily verify, in downward entailing contexts the competitors are weaker than the assertion, and so the reasoning above does not apply. Thus, the epistemic effect is correctly predicted to disappear in those contexts. Furthermore, the Implicature Account derives the absence of the epistemic effect in co-variation contexts.[13] Consider again the sentence in (30). Suppose that the domain of students selected by f is the set containing Juan, Lola, and Sara. When *algún* has narrow scope, the sentence will make the assertion in (38). The pragmatic competitors will be those in (39).

(38) Every professor is dancing with a student in {Juan, Lola, Sara}

(39) a. Every professor is dancing with a student in {Juan}
    b. Every professor is dancing with a student in {Lola}
    c. Every professor is dancing with a student in {Sara}

As before, the implicature will be that the speaker cannot commit to any of the competitors. This rules out situations where all the professors are dancing with the

---

[12] For the sake of illustration, we are assuming that the hearer knows what domain the speaker intends to use. However, often the hearer does not know which subset selection function the speaker has in mind, and hence does not know which proposition the speaker is asserting. The idea is that whatever the value of f is, the speaker is signaling that she is not in a position to assert the propositions that result from using a function that picks up a singleton subset of the set selected by f.

[13] This was noted in Fox (2007) for disjunction.

same student and the speaker knows who the student is, but is compatible with situations where different professors are dancing with different students and the speaker can identify the pairs.[14]

We have seen that the Implicature Approach can account for the disappearance of the epistemic effect in downward entailing and co-variation contexts. However, in the next section we show that this approach is not fine-grained enough to account for the content of the epistemic effect.

2.5 A challenge: the content of the epistemic effect

To see the problem that the Implicature Approach faces when characterizing the content of the epistemic effect, it is useful to consider contexts like the ones in (40).

(40) P knows that all the first-year students wear a particular uniform, which she is familiar with. She knows all the first-year students. She looks out the window and sees María kissing a boy wearing the first-year uniform.
 a. *Blurry vision.* P cannot make out the boy's features.
 b. *Clear vision.* P can see the boy very clearly.

P can felicitously utter the sentence in (41) in the context in (40a), but not in the context in (40b).

(41) ¡Mira! ¡María está besando a algún estudiante!
 Look! María is kissing A ALGÚN student
 'Look! María is kissing some student.'

In the Implicature Account that we presented in section 2.4, the domain is a set of individuals. Ignorance amounts to not being able to restrict the domain to just one of those individuals. This condition is met in (40a) but not in (40b), and therefore the judgments reported above are predicted. But consider now the slightly modified scenario in (42).

(42) P knows that all the first-year students wear a particular uniform. She is familiar with the uniform but she has never met the students. She looks out of the window and sees María kissing a boy wearing the first-year uniform.
 a. *Blurry vision.* P cannot make out the boy's features.
 b. *Clear vision.* P can see the boy very clearly.

---

[14] The correct prediction only holds if f is not parametrized (i.e. if it does not take an extra individual argument that could be bound by the higher quantifier). For suppose f were parametrized, as in (i).
(i) a. Every professor x is dancing with a student in $f_x(\{y : y \text{ is a student}\})$.
 b. For any $x, f_x(\{y : y \text{ is a student}\})$ is not a singleton.
This would yield pragmatic competitors like (ii), and therefore wrongly predict (36) to be ruled out if the speaker knows which professor is dancing with which student.
(ii) Prof. A is dancing with Sara and Prof. B is dancing with Juan and Prof. C is dancing with Marta.

As before, P can felicitously utter the sentence in (41) in the context in (42a), but not in the context in (42b). Does the Implicature Approach predict this contrast? Is the speaker unable to restrict the domain of quantification to one individual in (42a)? In a sense, yes. The speaker is not able to tell us, for example, whether María is kissing Juan, Marcos, or Pedro. In a sense, no. The speaker is able to tell us that María is kissing that guy over there, in front of her. And what about (42b), where *algún* does not work? Is the speaker able to restrict the domain to a singleton? Again, yes and no. The speaker is still not able to tell us whether the individual is Juan, Marcos, or Pedro, but she can tell us that the individual is that one over there and, furthermore, has access to the individual's physical description.

In view of the discussion above, we conclude that the Implicature Account is not fine-grained enough to capture the content of the epistemic effect. However, we will show in the next section that the basic architecture of the Implicature Account can meet the challenge posed by the previous examples once we import a central insight from the Conceptual Cover Approach: that epistemic indefinites are sensitive to the ways in which the speaker can identify the individual that satisfies the existential claim.

2.6 Reconciling the two approaches

2.6.1 The starting point

Our starting point is the discussion of *some* in Weir (2012). Weir shows that *some* behaves differently depending on whether it combines with NPs denoting things (*some NP_{thing}*) or people (*some NP_{people}*), contends that *some NP_{thing}* patterns with *algún*, and characterizes this use as in (43).[15]

(43) A speaker uses *some NP_{thing}* to signal that she could not, if presented with the extension of *NP*, 'pick out' the witness of the existential claim.

We think that this intuitively reflects what we see in the contrasts presented in section 2.3.2, and discussed further in section 2.5. In the clear vision context, the speaker of (44) believes that she would be able to pick out the student that María is kissing if she was presented with the set of all students later (say, in a line-up). In the blurry vision context, she believes that she would not. Accordingly, (44) is felicitous only in the blurry vision context.

(44) ¡Mira! ¡María está besando a algún estudiante!
 Look! María is kissing A ALGÚN student
 'Look! María is kissing some student.'

---

[15] Contrary to what we are arguing here, Weir (2012) assumes that the account of *algún* put forward by Alonso-Ovalle and Menéndez-Benito (2008, 2010) captures the effect described in (43).

Note, however, that in both contexts, the speaker can ascribe to the student a property that she believes only holds of one individual. In the blurry vision context, she knows that the student is in front of her at the time of utterance, and that there is only one individual in the world that has this property. In the clear vision context, she additionally has access to the physical appearance of the witness. This, unlike the location of the individual, is a stable property. As stable properties hold across times, having access to a stable "singleton property" would allow the speaker to pick out the witness if presented with the set of students at a different time.

Given this, we would like to suggest that by using *algún*, the speaker signals that she is not using a restriction that (i) she believes picks out exactly one individual, and (ii) is a stable property.[16] Let's call properties that meet (i) and (ii) "identificational properties." Upon hearing *algún*, the hearer will infer that the speaker is not restricting the domain with an identificational property because she is not able to. This is true in the blurry vision context but not in the clear vision one.

Note that this way of characterizing the epistemic effect makes an additional prediction: if the location of the witness can be considered a permanent property, ostension will be ruled out. This prediction is borne out. Suppose that we are looking out of the window in a hotel room. We arrived at the hotel at night, and we haven't yet seen any of the surroundings. The window overlooks a square with a statue in the center. From our vantage point, we can see the statue, but we cannot see its features clearly. All we can make out is that it is a statue, and that it represents a human figure. Suddenly, we see our friend María approach the statue and hug it. In this new blurry vision context, we could not felicitously utter the sentence in (45).

(45) # María está abrazando (a) alguna estatua.
    María is hugging   A   ALGUNA statue
    'María is hugging some statue.'

2.6.2 A possible implementation

In what follows, we will spell out a modification of the implicature account presented in section 2.4 that captures the intuitions discussed in section 2.6.1. We start by minimally revising our denotation for *algún* as in (46). Now the arguments of *algún* are what we will call a "property selection function," defined as in (47), and two functions of type $\langle s, et \rangle$, P and Q.[17]

---

[16] This raises the question of how to determine what properties count as stable. We will not be able to address this question here. But see Lewis and Langton (1999) for a discussion of the definition of the intrinsic properties of an individual as those that are preserved under duplication of the individual.

[17] We are assuming the standard definition of cross-categorial entailment in (i). If a property P entails a property Q we will call P a "sub-property" of Q.

(i) a. For p, q of type t: $p \Rightarrow q$ iff p = False or q = True.
    b. For f, g of type $\langle \sigma, t \rangle$, $f \Rightarrow g$ iff for all x of type σ : $f(x) \Rightarrow g(x)$.

(46) $[\![algún]\!]^{w,c} = \lambda f_{\langle\langle s,et\rangle,\langle s,et\rangle\rangle}.\lambda P_{\langle s,et\rangle} : f(P)$ is not identificational for the speaker of c in w. $\lambda Q_{\langle s,et\rangle}.\exists x[f(P)(w)(x)\ \&\ Q(w)(x)]$

(47) A property selection function takes a function P of type $\langle s, et\rangle$ (a property) and yields a property Q that entails P.

The definedness condition in (46) requires $f(P)$ not to be an identificational property for the speaker. Following our discussion in section 2.6.1, we will take identificational properties (for an individual, in a world) to be characterized as in (48). (This will eventually have to be refined by saying more about what counts as a stable property.)

(48) A property P is identificational for an individual d in w *iff*
 a. In all the worlds w' compatible with d's beliefs in w, $|\{x : f(w')(x)\}| = 1$, and
 b. d believes in w that f is a stable property.

Given our assumptions, the sentence in (49) will express a proposition that is defined for w_0 only if (50a) is true. When this condition obtains, (49) is true just in case the truth conditions in (50b) are satisfied.

(49) María está besando a algún estudiante.
 María is kissing A ALGÚN student
 'María is kissing some student.'

(50) a. $f(\text{STUDENT})$ is not identificational for the speaker of c in w_0.
 b. $\exists x[f(\text{STUDENT})(w_0)(x)\ \&\ \text{KISS}_{w_0}(x)(\text{MARIA})]$

In both the clear and blurry vision scenarios, a plausible value for f, made salient by pointing, would be the function that combines with a property P and returns the property in (51a). Given this value for f, the restriction of *algún* in (49) would be (51b), and the sentence would express the proposition in (52). Note that, given the scenario, the extension of (51b) in the world of evaluation is a singleton, something that would have been blocked by the original account in section 2.4.

(51) a. $\lambda w.\lambda x.\ P(x)$ and x is in front of the speaker in w.
 b. $\lambda w.\lambda x\ .x$ is a student that is in front of the speaker in w.

(52) $\lambda w.\exists x[\text{STUDENT}_w(x)\ \&\ \text{IN-FRONT-OF-SP}_w(x)\ \&\ \text{KISS}_w(x)(\text{M})]$

To account for the lack of epistemic effect in downward entailing contexts and in the co-variation scenarios, we will assume, as in the Implicature Approach already presented, that an assertion with *algún* invokes a set of pragmatic competitors. But what are those competitors now?

In the implicature account in section 2.4, the competitors were generated by restricting the domain to a singleton set. This was motivated by assuming that the hearer reasons as follows: the speaker signaled that she is not restricting the domain to a singleton. Using a singleton restriction would have given rise to a stronger statement, and would thus have been more informative. The speaker is, thus, not obeying Quantity. What could be the reason? Assuming that she is being cooperative, it must be because of Quality. That is, it must be because she is not able to commit to an assertion with a singleton domain.

This way of generating alternatives cannot be directly imported into the new setup. Suppose that, in parallel with the reasoning above, we say that an assertion with *algún*, which flags that the restriction is not an identificational property, evokes alternative assertions where the restriction *is* identificational. On this view, (52) would compete, for instance, with (53a), where APPEARANCE stands for the property in (53b), which is identificational for the speaker.

(53) a. $\lambda w.\exists x[\text{STUDENT}_w(x) \,\&\, \text{APPEARANCE}_w(x) \,\&\, \text{KISS}_w(x)(M)]$
  b. $\lambda w.\lambda x.$ x has in w the exact same physical appearance as the individual in front of the speaker in w_0

As will be obvious to the reader, assuming this type of alternative would not allow us to derive the epistemic effect as a quantity-based implicature. The alternative in (53a) does not entail the assertion in (52).

To get the epistemic effect from a clash between Quantity and Quality, we need the restriction in the competitors to be a sub-property of the property that restricts *algún* in the assertion. This will give rise to alternatives that are stronger than the assertion, as needed. To make sure that we derive the epistemic effect that we characterized in section 2.6.1, these sub-properties should result from conjoining the property that restricts the assertion with an identificational property. If we assume this type of alternative, the example in (52) will compete with the alternatives in (54).

(54) $\left\{ \lambda w.\exists x[f'(\text{ST})(w)(x) \,\&\, \text{K}_w(x)(M)] \,\middle|\, \begin{array}{l} \exists Q \,[Q \text{ is identificational for the sp \&} \\ f' = \lambda P.\lambda w.\lambda x.\,f(P)(w)(x) \,\&\, Q_w(x)] \end{array} \right\}$

Now, we can run the pragmatic reasoning that yields quantity implicatures, predicting that the speaker cannot commit to any of the pragmatic competitors. This will give us the attested contrast between our clear and blurry vision contexts. Let us see how.

One of the alternatives in (54) is (55). In the clear vision context, the speaker *can* commit to the proposition in (55). In the blurry vision context, she cannot. Accordingly, *algún* is ruled out in the clear vision context, but acceptable in the blurry vision one.

(55) $\lambda w.\exists x[\text{STU}(w)(x) \,\&\, \text{IN-FRONT-SP}(w)(x) \,\&\, \text{APPEAR}(w)(x) \,\&\, \text{KISS}(w)(x)(M)]$

One important issue now is that the motivation of the pragmatic competitors is not as transparent as in the original version of the implicature account. In that proposal, the competition was between non-singleton and singleton domains. (The fact that the speaker chose a non-singleton domain triggered a competition with the singleton ones.) But the competition that we need to assume here is not a competition between identificational and non-identificational properties: being in front of the speaker and having a particular appearance, for instance, would not count as an identificational property given (48) (as being in front of the speaker is not a stable property). Given this, we need to stipulate that *algún* evokes these particular alternatives as part of its semantic contribution.

While having to stipulate the competitors makes the implicature account less appealing, we think that there is a reasonable trade-off. As we have seen, the proposal outlined above overcomes the challenge in section 2.5, and correctly captures the content of the epistemic effect. Furthermore, like the original account, this proposal predicts the distribution of the epistemic effect. Consider again the example in (30), repeated below as (56):

(56) Todos los profesores están bailando con algún estudiante.
     all   the professors   are dancing with ALGÚN student
     'Every professor is dancing with some student.'

When (56) is defined, it denotes the proposition in (57), where $f(\text{STUDENT})$ is not an identificational property. Restricting $f(\text{STUDENT})$ with an identificational property, in the way described above, results in a stronger claim that conveys that all professors are dancing with one student. In the co-variation scenarios, all these claims are false.

(57) $\lambda w. \forall x [\text{PROFESSOR}_w(x) \rightarrow \exists y [f(\text{STUDENT})(w)(y) \, \& \, \text{DANCE}_w(y)(x)]]$

Finally, given the way that the competitors are determined, they will be entailed by the assertion in downward entailing environments, so the lack of epistemic effect in those contexts is predicted, just as in the original setup of the implicature account.

2.7 Conclusion

We will sum up and point out one issue for further research. We have discussed the relative merits of two theories of epistemic indefinites. The Conceptual Cover Approach contributes the important insight that in order to characterize what counts as *(not) knowing who*, we need to talk about ways of identifying individuals. But it cannot account for the disappearance of the epistemic effect in co-variation contexts, and it assumes identificational constraints that do not capture the type of ignorance conveyed by *algún*. The Implicature Approach gives us a straightforward way to derive the lack of ignorance in co-variation contexts, but it is not fine-grained enough to capture the content of the epistemic effect. We have also aimed to combine the insights of both approaches in a proposal that keeps the basic architecture of the Implicature Approach—a pragmatic competition between the assertion and more informative alternatives—but where identification methods play a crucial role.

The reconciling proposal that we have presented opens up a number of issues for further research. We will conclude by pointing out one. The discussion has focused on unembedded sentences. For the proposal presented in Section 2.6.2 to be considered a full-fledged account, it would have to be extended to embedded cases. But this extension might not be straightforward. Consider the example in (58) in the scenario in (59).

(58) Pedro cree   que María está besando a alguno   de los
     Pedro believes that María is   kissing A ALGUNO of the
     trillizos Pérez.
     triplets Pérez
     'Pedro believes that María is kissing one of the Pérez triplets.'

(59) Pedro knows the Pérez triplets and sees María kissing one of them. He concludes from this that María and the triplet are dating. He sees the triplet very clearly. He can even see that he has a mole on his right hand. Pedro mistakenly believes that only one of the triplets has a mole on his right hand. I know everything that Pedro knows but I also know that all the Pérez triplets have a mole on their right hand.

According to our intuitions, (58) is deviant in the scenario in (59). To predict this judgment, we could assume that (60) (the proposition that Pedro believes that María is kissing a Pérez triplet who has a mole on his hand) is one of the pragmatic competitors of the assertion made by (58). This could be the case if one of the competing selection functions returned the property in (61). If (60) were one of the pragmatic competitors, the implicature would convey that the speaker is not committed to the proposition that Pedro believes that María is kissing one of the triplets with a mole on his hand. But, in our scenario, the speaker *is* committed to that proposition.

(60) $\text{BEL}_{w_0}(\text{PEDRO})(\lambda w.\exists x[\text{PÉREZ-TRIPLET}_w(x) \& \text{MOLE}_w(x) \& \text{KISS}_w(x)(\text{M})])$

(61) $\lambda w.\lambda x.\, x$ is one of the Pérez triplets in w and x has a mole on x's right hand in w

However, this does not fall out from the proposal in section 2.6.2, where the properties that determine the competitors are those that are identificational *for the speaker*. The property of being a Pérez triplet having the appearance that the individual that María is kissing actually has is not identificational for the speaker (in any world compatible with what the speaker believes, the property is not a singleton), but it *is* identificational for Pedro.

To account for examples like this, we would presumably need to allow for the option that the identificational properties that determine the pragmatic competitors be identificational for the attitude holder, rather than the speaker. We leave this issue for further research.

Acknowledgments

We are grateful to an anonymous reviewer as well as to the editors of the volume, Ana Arregui, María Luisa Rivero, and Andrés Salanova, for their extremely helpful comments and advice. This research was supported by the following grants: a Marie Curie Intra European Fellowship ("Modal determiners", PIEF-GA-2013-622311) within the 7th European Community Framework Program (Paula Menéndez-Benito); Social Sciences and Humanities Research Council of Canada (Insight Grant), "Modality in the nominal domain" (435-2013-0103) (Principal Investigator: Luis Alonso-Ovalle), and FQRSC "Variations entre langues dans la sémantique des groupes nominaux indéfinis: l'expression de l'ignorance et de l'indifférence" (2013-NP-164823) (Principal Investigator: Luis Alonso-Ovalle). The financial support to GLiF (Formal Linguistics Group, Universitat Pompeu Fabra) by the Government of Catalonia (AGAUR, 2014 SGR 698) is also gratefully acknowledged. The authors are listed in alphabetical order.

3

Modal indefinites: Where do Japanese *wh-ka*s fit in?

LUIS ALONSO-OVALLE AND JUNKO SHIMOYAMA

3.1 Introduction

The study of the expression of modal notions in natural language has been at the forefront of formal semantics for several decades now (see Portner 2009 and Hacquard 2011 for a recent overview). However, even when it is well known that modal expressions span syntactic categories (Kratzer 1981), most of the classic work on modality has focused on the study of modal auxiliary verbs. As a result, we still do not have a clear understanding of the extent to which the expression of modal notions is comparable or varies across categories.

Moving beyond modal auxiliaries, a considerable amount of semantic literature has been devoted in recent years to the study of modal indefinites. These are existential determiners or determiner phrases that convey a modal component (see Alonso-Ovalle and Menéndez-Benito 2013b for a recent overview). Consider the sentence in (1), which features the Spanish modal indefinite *algún* (Alonso-Ovalle and Menéndez-Benito 2003, 2008, 2010).

(1) A: María está saliendo con algún estudiante del departamento.
    María is dating with ALGÚN student from.the department
    'María is dating a student from the department.'

    (Alonso-Ovalle and Menéndez-Benito 2010)

Like other items in this class, *algún* conveys ignorance on the part of the speaker in unembedded contexts. By uttering (1), A signals that she does not know which student María is dating. Because of this, it would be deviant for A to follow (1) with a *namely* continuation (2a) or for her interlocutor B to ask who María is dating (2b). In contrast, the counterpart of (1) with the non-modal indefinite *un*, would naturally allow for the continuations in (2).

Modality Across Syntactic Categories. First edition. Ana Arregui, María Luisa Rivero, and Andrés Salanova (eds.).
This chapter © Luis Alonso-Ovalle and Junko Shimoyama 2017. First published 2017 by Oxford University Press.

(2) a. A: ... # en concreto con Juan.
       namely   with Juan
       '... namely Juan.'
  b. B: # ¿Con quién?
        with whom
        'With whom?'

If the semantic literature on modality has focused on verbs, the semantic literature on modal indefinites has in turn focused on a small sample of languages, and therefore has only provided a limited picture of what the cross-linguistic empirical landscape looks like in this domain. Although much progress has been made in trying to determine the properties with respect to which modal indefinites can vary, the development of a semantically based typology of modal indefinites (and of modal expressions more generally) can benefit from the consideration of data from a broader sample of languages (see Alonso-Ovalle and Menéndez-Benito 2013b).

This chapter aims to contribute to fulfilling this need, at least partially. Our goal is primarily descriptive. We focus on situating the properties of an existential construction in Japanese (the so-called *wh-ka* indeterminates) in the broader typology of modal indefinites by taking into consideration some of the parameters of variation that have been discussed in the literature. We will refrain here from discussing the challenges that *wh*-ka indeterminates pose for current theories of epistemic indefinites, a discussion that we have embarked upon in Alonso-Ovalle and Shimoyama (2014), to which the curious reader is referred.

The chapter is organized as follows. Section 3.2 surveys the form of *wh-ka* indeterminates, sections 3.3 and 3.4 describe the ignorance component that these indeterminates convey in unembedded contexts, section 3.5 describes the interaction of *wh-ka* indeterminates with overt modals, section 3.6 focuses on their behavior in downward entailing contexts, and sections 3.7 and 3.8 contrast *wh-ka* indeterminates and other modal indefinites with respect to the presence or absence of agent indifference and ignorance of quantity implications.

3.2 Form: what do Japanese *wh-ka* indeterminates look like?

So-called indeterminate pronouns (Kuroda 1965) are Japanese *wh*-words that appear in construction with external particles. Different particles correlate with different grammatical functions. For instance, as illustrated in (3–5), when *wh*-words appear with the clause-final interrogative particle *ka*, they behave like interrogative *wh*-words (3); when they associate with *mo*, they behave like universal quantifiers (4), and when they associate with *ka*, they behave like existential quantifiers (5).[1]

---

[1] See Szabolcsi et al. (2014), Szabolcsi (2014), and references there for discussions of particles that seem to have multiple functions.

(3) Yuki-wa dare-o hihanshimashita ka?
    Yuki-TOP who-ACC criticized Q
    'Who did Yuki criticize?'

(4) Yuki-wa dare-mo-o hihanshimashita.
    Yuki-TOP who-MO-ACC criticized
    'Yuki criticized everyone.'

(5) Yuki-wa dare-ka-o hihanshimashita.
    Yuki-TOP who-KA-ACC criticized
    'Yuki criticized someone.'

The table in (6) illustrates the form of some *wh*-indeterminates. The columns list the different forms that the *wh*-word can take, while the rows list the different grammatical functions that they can have, depending on which particle they associate with. *Wh-ka* indeterminates occupy the last row of the table.

(6)
	who	what	which N	which one$_{\text{NONHUMAN}}$	which$_{\text{DUAL}}$
Q	dare...ka	nani...ka	dono N...ka	dore...ka	docchi...ka
∀	dare-mo	<gap>	dono N-mo	dore-mo	docchi-mo
∃	dare-ka	nani-ka	dono N-ka	dore-ka	docchi-ka

Wh-ka indeterminates come in different types, depending on how the restriction of their domain of quantification is syntactically realized. In examples (7) and (8), the restriction of the domain of quantification seems to be conveyed lexically by the *wh*-word. While *nani* 'what' restricts the domain to non-humans in (7), *dare* 'who' restricts the domain to humans in (8). As we see in (6), different *wh*-words can quantify over different types of entities. In contrast with the examples in (7) and (8), in the examples in (9–11) a noun contributes the (additional) restriction. In this case, the association of the *wh*-word with its restriction can take different forms. In (9), *dono* 'which' combines with the noun, the resulting constituent associates with the particle -*ka* and is case-marked. In (10) and (11) we see a split between the *wh*-element and the expression providing the semantic restriction: the *wh*-element combines with the particle -*ka* and not with the expression providing the semantic restriction. Instead, the restriction part occurs "externally" to *wh-ka* and bears the case marking.

(7) nani-ka-ga soto-de hoe-tei-ru. [*what-KA*]-CASE
    what-KA-NOM outside-LOC bark-PROG-NONPAST
    'Something is barking outside.'

(8) dare-ka-ga soto-de hoe-tei-ru. [*who-KA*]-CASE
    who-KA-NOM outside-LOC bark-PROG-NONPAST
    'Someone is barking outside.'

(9) dono inu-ka-ga soto-de hoe-tei-ru. *[[which dog]-KA]-CASE*
which dog-KA-NOM outside-LOC bark-PROG-NONPAST
'Some dog is barking outside.'

(10) nani-ka inu-ga soto-de hoe-tei-ru. *[what-KA][dog]-CASE*
what-KA dog-NOM outside-LOC bark-PROG-NONPAST
'*what-ka* dog is barking outside.'

(11) dore-ka inu-ga soto-de
which.one-KA dog-NOM outside-LOC
hoe-tei-ru. *[[which one]-KA][dog]-CASE*
bark-PROG-NONPAST
'*which one-ka* dog is barking outside.'

At first sight, the 'internal' construction in (9) is reminiscent of the form of indefinite modal determiner phrases in Romance, illustrated with a Spanish example in (1) and again in (12). In cases like (12), we find an indefinite determiner phrase formed by combining a determiner with a noun phrase (semantically an argument of the determiner), which contributes the semantic restriction.

(12) Algún perro está ladrando fuera.
ALGÚN dog is barking outside
'Some dog or other is barking outside.'

The division of labor in the "external" cases in (10) and (11) might not be as familiar. It is not clear whether the relation between the *wh*-word and the nominal providing its restriction is of the same nature as the one usually assumed for (12). Notice, with respect to this, that, as is well-known, bare nominals can be arguments in Japanese. Thus, removing *nani-ka* 'what-*ka*' or *dore-ka* 'which one-*ka*' from (10) and (11) preserves their grammaticality, as shown in (13).

(13) inu-ga soto-de hoe-tei-ru.
dog-NOM outside-LOC sing-PROG-NONPAST
'A/The dog(s) is/are barking outside.'

Note also that the bare nominals that seem to contribute the semantic restrictions in (10) and (11) do not need to be local to *wh-ka*, as (14) illustrates (see Kaneko 2011 for further examples).

(14) nani-ka/dore-ka soto-de inu-ga
what-KA/which.one-KA outside-LOC dog-NOM
hoe-tei-ru. *[wh-KA] ... [dog]-CASE*
bark-PROG-NONPAST
'*What-ka/which one-ka* dog is barking outside.'

Furthermore, the two examples below illustrate that when the bare nominals contributing semantic restrictions occur externally to *wh-ka*, *wh-ka* can be postnominal. In this case, *wh-ka* can still associate with the bare nominal at a distance.

(15) inu-ga nani-ka/dore-ka soto-de
 dog-NOM what-KA/which.one-KA outside-LOC
 hoe-tei-ru. *[dog]-CASE [wh-KA]*
 bark-PROG-NONPAST
 'What-ka/which one-ka dog is barking outside.'

(16) inu-ga soto-de nani-ka/dore-ka
 dog-NOM outside-LOC what-KA/which.one-KA
 hoe-tei-ru. *[dog]-CASE ... [wh-KA]*
 bark-PROG-NONPAST)
 'What-ka/which one-ka dog is barking outside.'

The examples in (10), (11), and (13–16) suggest that, unlike what we see in (12), the nominal expression that contributes the semantic restriction may be independent of the *wh-ka* part.

Moving beyond the cases above, where *wh-ka* indeterminates seem to range over individuals, we note that we also find *wh-ka* indeterminates in sentences that make claims about quantities, as in (17).

(17) Sota-wa nan-satsu-ka(-no) hon-o katta.
 Sota-TOP what-CL-KA-GEN book-ACC bought
 'Sota bought several books.'

In degree *wh-ka* indeterminates like this, *ka* combines with the result of combining *what* with a classifier (*satsu*) that we find in construction with numerals, as in (18).

(18) Sota-wa san-satsu(-no) hon-o katta.
 Sota-TOP three-CL-GEN book-ACC bought
 'Sota bought three books.'

When, in combination with the classifier *satsu*, *what* associates with interrogative *ka*, it results in a *how many* question, as illustrated in (19):

(19) Sota-wa nan-satsu(-no) hon-o kai-mashi-ta ka?
 Sota-TOP what-CL-GEN book-ACC buy-POL-PAST KA
 'How many books did Sota buy?'

As in the case of the *wh-kas* that range over individuals, the degree *wh-kas* can also appear postnominally. This is illustrated in (20). The examples in (21) and (22) show that the degree *wh-ka* can also associate with the nominal non-locally.

(20) Sota-wa hon-o nan-satsu-ka katta.
Sota-TOP book-ACC what-CL-KA bought
'Sota bought several books.'

(21) Sota-wa hon-o kinoo nan-satsu-ka katta.
Sota-TOP book-ACC yesterday what-CL-KA bought
'Sota bought several books yesterday.'

(22) Sota-wa nan-satsu-ka kinoo hon-o katta.
Sota-TOP what-CL-KA yesterday book-ACC bought
'Sota bought several books yesterday.'

Having reviewed the form that *wh-ka* constructions can take, we move next to their content, in particular to the epistemic effect that they convey in unembedded contexts. We will describe the content of the constructions without getting into compositional details.

3.3 Content: the epistemic component

With the sentence in (1) we illustrated the behavior of Spanish *algún* in unembedded contexts. Sudo (2010) and Kaneko (2011) noticed that in the same environments *wh-ka* indeterminates also convey ignorance on the part of the speaker as to which individual satisfies the existential claim (see also previous references cited in these works). This is illustrated in (23) for a stand-alone *wh-ka* indeterminate (like (7) and (8)) and for the *wh-ka* plus restriction construction (like (10) and (11)) in (24). As we saw in the case of the sentence in (1), an utterance of the sentence in (23) would indicate that the speaker does not know who John met yesterday, and therefore a question asking who John met would feel inappropriate. Likewise, an utterance of (24) would signal that the speaker does not know who Mariko married, which makes the continuation infelicitous.

(23) A: John-wa kinoo dare-ka-ni atteta yo
John-TOP yesterday who-KA-DAT was.meeting PRT
'John was meeting somebody yesterday.'

B: # honto? aitsu dare-ni atteta?
really he who-DAT was.meeting
'Really? Who was he meeting?' (Sudo 2010: 4)

(24) Mariko-wa dare-ka gengogaku-no gakusei-to kekkonshita.
Mariko-TOP who-KA linguistics-GEN student-with married
'Mariko married a linguistics student.'

Sunawachi, Taro-to da.
namely Taro-with COP
'Namely, Taro.'

We have also mentioned before that the Spanish epistemic determiner *algún* contrasts with its non-epistemic counterpart *un*. *Wh-ka* indeterminates contrast with bare noun phrases in a similar way: the dialogues in (25) and (26) illustrate that bare noun phrases allow for hearers to ask about the identity of the witness of the existential claim and tolerate *namely* continuations.

(25) A: John-wa kinoo hito-ni atteta yo
John-TOP yesterday person-DAT was.meeting PRT
'John was meeting somebody yesterday.'

B: honto? aitsu dare-ni atteta?
really he who-DAT was.meeting
'Really? Who was he meeting?' (Sudo 2010: 4)

(26) Mariko-wa gengogaku-no gakusei-to kekkonshita.
Mariko-TOP linguistics-GEN student-with married
'Mariko married a linguistics student.'

Sunawachi, Taro-to da.
namely Taro-with COP
'Namely, Taro.'

Having seen that *wh-ka* indeterminates behave like other modal indefinites in that they convey an ignorance component in unembedded contexts, we will illustrate in the next sections where *wh-ka*s fit in the larger typology of modal indefinites by looking at a number of parameters of variation that have been identified in the literature.

3.4 *Wh-ka* indeterminates in unembedded contexts: types of ignorance

We will start by reviewing in this section the type of ignorance expressed by *wh-ka*s. Section 3.4.1 shows that *what-ka* indeterminates can contrast with *which-ka* indeterminates with respect to whether they express ignorance in relation to types or tokens. Section 3.4.2 shows that the type of ignorance in relation to tokens that *wh-ka* indeterminates express in unembedded contexts is similar to that of *algún*. Section 3.4.3 concludes by showing that, unlike other modal indefinites like *algún*, *wh-ka* indeterminates do not seem to be sensitive to the type of evidence available to the speaker.

3.4.1 *Types vs. tokens: what-ka vs. which-ka*

In Alonso-Ovalle and Shimoyama (2014) we point out that *what-ka* indeterminates and *which-ka* indeterminates can contrast with respect to the type of ignorance that they express in unembedded contexts. The discussion turns around the following scenario:

(27) *The troop of mushrooms*
J and L are hiking in the woods. As they go down a steep hill, they see a troop of mushrooms. J's hand inadvertently touches one. She clearly sees the mushroom that she touched.

We note that, in this situation, J cannot utter the sentence in (28), which contains *dore-ka* 'which.one-ka'. The deviance of (28) in this scenario contrasts with the appropriateness of its counterpart in (29), which contains *nani-ka* 'what-ka', instead of *dore-ka* 'which.one-ka'.

(28) J: # Dore-ka kinoko-ni sawat-ta!
 which.one-KA mushroom-DAT touch-past
 '(I) touched *which one-ka* mushroom!'

(29) J: Nani-ka kinoko-ni sawat-ta!
 what-KA mushroom-DAT touch-PAST
 '(I) touched *what-ka* mushroom!'

The sentences in (28) and (29) are truth-conditionally equivalent: they both convey that the speaker touched a mushroom. If the ignorance component of *wh-ka* indeterminates were uniform across types of *wh*-words, the contrast between (28) and (29) would be unexpected. In Alonso-Ovalle and Shimoyama (2014) we note that, in this case, the *which-ka* indeterminate seems to convey that the speaker cannot determine which individual satisfies the existential claim. This implication is false in the context at stake, since J can clearly see which particular mushroom she touched. In contrast, *what-ka* seems to convey that the speaker cannot describe the mushroom that she touched in a more precise way. This implication can be true in the context in (27) if J is not an expert on mushrooms. The contrast between (28) and (29) can then be reduced to a contrast in their modal implications.

Note, in this connection, that sentences containing a *what-ka* + NP indeterminate are degraded in case it is unlikely that the speaker can identify different subtypes of NPs. The contrast between (30) and (31) can be seen as stemming from the fact that it is unlikely for a speaker to be able to identify different types of flies, but not different types of bugs. We can see that this way of characterizing the contrast in (30) and (31) is on the right track from the appropriateness of example (32), uttered by an entomologist in a lab, as she can in principle identify different types of flies.

(30) # Suupu-no naka-ni nani-ka hae-ga iru.
 soup-GEN inside-LOC what-KA fly-NOM exist
 'There's some fly in the soup.'
  (Sudo 2010, based on an example in Strawson 1974)

(31) Suupu-no naka-ni nani-ka mushi-ga iru.
 soup-GEN inside-LOC what-KA bug-NOM exist
 'There's some bug in the soup.'

(32) Shaare-no   ue-ni   nani-ka hae-ga   iru.
     petri.dish-GEN top-LOC what-KA fly-NOM exist
     'There's some fly on the Petri dish.'

The contrast between *what-ka* and *which-ka* indeterminates presented above singles out *wh-ka* indeterminates. Other types of modal indefinites can also convey both types of ignorance, but the contrast is not marked overtly. For instance, Weir (2012) points out that English *some* can also convey both types of ignorance. When it combines with singular NPs, *some* can express ignorance about tokens, as in (33), or ignorance about types, as in (34), which, in parallel to (29), can be uttered by a speaker pointing to the plant that is growing through the wall.

(33) Some file on this computer is infected, {but I don't know which one/ # namely, this one here}   (Weir 2012)

(34) Some plant is growing through the wall of my room.   (Weir 2012)

The contrast between (28) and (29) leads to the question of how the form of *wh-kas* is mapped to the meanings that can be expressed, an issue that has not been tackled yet and will not be commented upon any further here.

We will leave aside for now the contrast between token-level vs. type-level ignorance to comment on the issue of the *force* of the ignorance component by looking at cases that express token-level ignorance.

3.4.2 Wh-ka indeterminates convey partial ignorance

Alonso-Ovalle and Menéndez-Benito (2008, 2010) show that the ignorance component that *algún* conveys is partial, both in unembedded contexts and under epistemic modals such as *tener que* 'have to.' In other words, as far as the speaker knows, it does not have to be the case that *any* of the entities in the domain of quantification could be the entity that satisfies the existential claim. This is illustrated by noting that the sentence in (35) can be felicitously uttered in a context where both the speaker and hearer know which are the rooms of the house even if the speaker knows that Juan cannot be in some of the rooms.

(35) Juan está / tiene que estar en alguna   habitación de la casa.
     Juan is   has to be   in ALGUNA room   of the house
     'Juan is /has to be in a room of the house.'
                                    (Alonso-Ovalle and Menéndez-Benito 2008, 2010)

This contrasts with the English sentence in (36) with free-choice *any*, which clearly conveys that *all* of the rooms of the house are possibilities for the speaker. The same is true for the counterpart of (36) with other universal free choice items, like Spanish *cualquiera* (Alonso-Ovalle and Menéndez-Benito 2008, 2010).

(36) Juan can be in any of the rooms of the house.

Sudo (2010) notes that Japanese *wh-ka* indeterminates also convey partial ignorance in unembedded contexts. Much like (35), the sentence in (37) is compatible with the speaker being able to exclude some rooms.

(37) John-wa dore-ka/doko-ka ie-no naka-no heya-ni
John-TOP which.one-KA/where-KA house-GEN inside-GEN room-LOC
iru hazuda.
be must
'John must be in {which one-ka/where-ka} room of the house.'

We will get back to the issue of the *force* of the modal component in section 3.5, when we talk about the behavior of *wh-ka* indeterminates when they are embedded under non-epistemic modals.

We will conclude the overview of the properties of the ignorance component of *wh-ka* indeterminates by pointing out a difference between these items and other modal indefinites in the next subsection.

3.4.3 *Sources of evidence*

Some modal indefinites seem to be sensitive to the source of the evidence that the speaker has to make the existential claim. Alonso-Ovalle and Menéndez-Benito (2003) point out that the sentence in (39), with Spanish *algún*, is deviant in the context in (38), where the evidence that the speaker has allows her to clearly identify visually the person dancing the lambada. In contrast, the counterpart of (39), with English *some*, in (40) is not deviant (see Aloni and Port 2011, 2013).

(38) *The dancing professor*
Speaker does not know anything about a person dancing on a table, only that he is a professor. Speaker can clearly see the person dancing on the table.

(39) # ¡Mira! Algún profesor está bailando la lambada encima de
look ALGÚN professor is dancing the lambada on of
la mesa.
the table (Alonso-Ovalle and Menéndez-Benito 2003)

(40) Look! Some professor is dancing lambada on the table.
(Alonso-Ovalle and Menéndez-Benito 2003)

The following contrast, presented in Alonso-Ovalle and Menéndez-Benito (2013a), illustrates this point clearly: while the sentence in (41) is perfectly fine in the context in (42), where the perceptual evidence available to the speaker does not allow her to single out the individual satisfying the existential claim, it is deviant in the context in (43), which does.

(41) P: ¡Mira! ¡María está besando a algún chico!
　　　look María is kissing A ALGÚN chico
　　　'Look! María is kissing some boy!'
　　　　　　　　　　　　　　　(Alonso-Ovalle and Menéndez-Benito 2013a)

(42) *Blurry vision*
　　　The speaker looks out of the window and sees María kissing a boy. The speaker hasn't seen the boy before, but she can see him very clearly now. (Alonso-Ovalle and Menéndez-Benito 2013a)

(43) *Clear vision*
　　　The speaker looks out of the window and sees María kissing a boy. María and the boy are far away, and P cannot make out the boy's features. (Alonso-Ovalle and Menéndez-Benito 2013a)

The type of evidential restriction imposed by *algún* seems to be found in other languages that, just like Japanese, use *wh* morphology in the expression of existential claims with a modal component. Slade (2015) analyzes two indeterminate constructions (*wh-hari* and *wh-də*) from Sinhala (Indo-Aryan). He shows that the sentence in (44), with *wh-hari*, is ruled out whenever the speaker can identify the dancer visually.

(44) Kauru hari mese uda natanava
　　　who HARI table on dance.pres
　　　'Someone is dancing on the table.'　　　　　　　　　　　(Slade 2015)

Wh-kas contrast with *algún* and with *wh-hari*. Sudo (2010) shows that the sentence in (45) is perfectly fine in the dancing professor context in (38).

(45) Mite! dare-ka kyooju-ga tsukue-no ue-de odotteru yo!
　　　look who-KA professor-NOM desk-GEN up-LOC is.dancing PRT
　　　'Look! Some professor is dancing on the desk!'　　　(Sudo 2010: 12)

Notice also that the sentence in (46), the Japanese counterpart of the Spanish sentence in (41), is fine in both of the contexts provided in (42) and (43): blurry vision vs. clear vision. This contrasts with *algún* in Spanish in (41), which was only fine with the blurry vision context in (42).

(46) Mite! Maria-ga dare-ka otokonoko-ni kisushiteru yo!
　　　look Maria-NOM who-KA boy-DAT is.kissing PRT
　　　'Look! Maria is kissing some boy!'

We finish here the presentation of the behavior of *wh-ka* indeterminates in unembedded contexts. We turn next to surveying the behavior of *wh-ka* indeterminates when embedded under overt modals.

3.5 Interaction with overt modals

Just like a standard indefinite, the German modal indefinite *irgendein* can be interpreted both under and over a deontic modal. Kratzer and Shimoyama (2002) point out that the example in (47) is ambiguous: it can convey that Mary had to marry a man (and that she was allowed to marry any man) or that there was some man that Mary had to marry (and the speaker does not know or care about who it was.)

(47) Mary musste irgendeinen Mann heiraten.
Mary had-to IRGENDEINEN man marry
(Kratzer and Shimoyama 2002: 10)

Not all modal indefinites behave like *irgendein*. For instance, Italian *un qualche* conveys an ignorance component akin to that of *wh-ka*s in unembedded contexts, but Aloni and Port (2013) report that this item cannot be interpreted under the scope of an overt deontic modal. According to them, the sentence in (48) cannot convey that Maria has the obligation to marry some doctor or other; it can only convey that there is some particular doctor that Maria must marry.

(48) Maria deve sposare un qualche dottore.
Maria must marry UN QUALCHE doctor
'There is a doctor that Maria must marry I don't know which.'
(Aloni and Port 2013: 4)

Likewise, Farkas (2002b) and Fălăuş (2009, 2011a, 2011b, 2014) analyze the behavior of the Romanian modal indefinite *vreun*, and show that this item is licensed under the scope of some epistemic operators or in downward entailing contexts, but not under overt deontic modals.

Sudo (2010) reports that *wh-ka* indeterminates behave like *irgendein*. He points out that the sentence in (49) would be true and appropriate in both of the situations in (50).

(49) John-wa dare-ka onnanoko-ni kisushi nakutewaikenai
John-TOP who-KA girl-DAT kiss must
'John must kiss a girl.' (Sudo 2010: 6)

(50) a. There is a particular girl that John is required to kiss, the speaker does not know which girl.
b. John is required to kiss a girl and he can kiss any girl.

Although *wh-ka*s can be interpreted under the scope of a deontic modal, they still differ from German *irgendein*. As the paraphrases of (47) indicate, when interpreted under the scope of a deontic modal, *irgendein* triggers a so-called "free choice" effect: it conveys that *any* individual in the domain of quantification is a permitted option (Kratzer and Shimoyama 2002; Aloni and Port 2013). In contrast, despite the paraphrases in (50), when interpreted under a deontic modal, *wh-ka*s do not convey a free choice effect, but instead are merely *compatible* with it. Note, for instance, that the sentence in (51) can be true (and can be appropriately uttered) in the context in (52), where it is not true that there is a particular applicant that the department is required to hire but it is not true that the department is allowed to hire any of the applicants either.

(51) Gakka-wa   dare-ka   sono posuto-ni   ooboshita koohosha-o
     department-WA who-KA the position-DAT applied   candidate-ACC
     saiyoosi-nakereba ike-nai.
     hire-not.if   good-not
     'The department must hire *who-ka* candidate who applied for the position.'

(52) *Ph.D.s required*
     The pool of applicants includes people with and without a Ph.D. The department cannot hire applicants without a Ph.D.

The lack of a free choice effect can also be seen by contrasting (53) with its counterpart in (54) with the universal free-choice item *dare-de-mo*. In contrast with (53), the sentence in (54) is clearly false in the scenario in (52).

(53) Gakka-wa   dare-ka   sono posuto-ni   ooboshita koohosha-o
     department-WA who-KA the position-DAT applied   candidate-ACC
     saiyoosi-te ii.
     hire-TE   good
     'The department can hire *who-ka* candidate who applied for the position.'

(54) Gakka-wa   dare-de-mo sono posuto-ni   ooboshita koohosha-o
     department-WA who-DE-MO the position-DAT applied   candidate-ACC
     saiyoosi-te ii.
     hire-TE   good
     'The department can hire any candidate who applied for the position.'

With respect to their interpretation under deontic modals, *wh-ka*s behave like Spanish *algún*. As illustrated in Alonso-Ovalle and Menéndez-Benito (2010), the counterpart of (53) with *algún*, in (55), is also compatible with the department not being allowed to hire some applicants, and is therefore true in the scenario in (52).

(55) El departamento puede contratar a alguno   de los candidatos que
     the department   can   hire   ALGUNO of the candidates who
     han solicitado el puesto.
     have applied for the position
     'The department can hire some of the candidates that have applied to the position.'   (Alonso-Ovalle and Menéndez-Benito 2010)

Moving beyond deontic modals, we note that *wh-ka*s can also be interpreted under the scope of epistemic modals, as in (56), repeated from (37), and under the scope of epistemic propositional attitude verbs as in (57). The sentence in (56) is compatible with John not being in a room of the house and the one in (57) with Mariko not having married a linguistics student.

(56) John-wa dore-ka/doko-ka ie-no naka-no heya-ni
John-TOP which.one-KA/where-KA house-GEN inside-GEN room-LOC
iru hazuda.
be must
'John must be in {which one-ka/where-ka} room of the house.'

(57) Hanako-wa Mariko-ga dare-ka gengogaku-no gakusei-to
Hanako-TOP Mariko-NOM who-KA linguistics-GEN student-with
kekkonshita-to omotteiru.
married-that think
'Hanako thinks that Mariko married some linguistics student.'

We conclude here the description of how *wh-ka* indeterminates interact with overt modals. In the next subsection, we examine the behavior of *wh-ka* indeterminates in downward entailing contexts.

3.6 Downward entailing environments

We have just seen that the behavior of modal indefinites in modal contexts is not uniform. Their behavior in downward entailing environments is not uniform, either. Kratzer and Shimoyama (2002) note that German *irgendein* cannot be interpreted under sentential negation, unless it bears stress. *Algún* and French *quelque* seem to behave just the same (Alonso-Ovalle and Menéndez-Benito 2010; Jayez and Tovena 2008, 2011, 2013). Romanian *vreun* is generally ungrammatical under the scope of clausemate sentential negation, but can be rescued in this environment if preceded by a negative concord item (Fălăuş 2009).

In line with this, we note that *wh-ka* indeterminates cannot be interpreted under regular sentential negation in the same clause: the sentence in (58) only allows the wide scope interpretation of 'who-*ka* girl'. Note that this restriction disappears in the scopally ambiguous sentence in (59), where a bare nominal *gengogakka-no onnanoko* 'girl in the linguistics department' is used.

(58) Juan-wa dare-ka gengogakka-no onnanoko-ni denwashi-nakat-ta.
Juan-TOP who-KA linguistics.dept-GEN girl-with call-NEG-PAST
'Juan didn't call *who-ka* girl in the linguistics department.'

(59) Juan-wa gengogakka-no onnanoko-ni denwashi-nakat-ta.
Juan-TOP linguistics.dept-GEN girl-with call-NEG-PAST
'Juan didn't call a girl in the linguistics department.'

In contrast to (58), *wh-ka* indeterminates are perfectly fine under the scope of negation if a bi-clausal structure is used, as in the sentence in (60). In the narrow-scope interpretation of *gengogakka-no onnanoko* 'girl in the linguistics department', sentence (60) is more or less interchangeable with sentence (61), in which a bare nominal is used without *dare-ka* 'who-*ka*'.

(60) Juan-wa dare-ka gengogakka-no onnanoko-ni
 Juan-TOP who-KA linguistics.dept-GEN girl-DAT
 denwashi-ta-no-de-wa nai.
 call-PAST-NO-DE-WA NEG
 'It's not that Juan called *who-ka* girl in the linguistics department.'

(61) Juan-wa gengogakka-no onnanoko-ni denwashi-ta-no-de-wa nai.
 Juan-TOP linguistics.dept-GEN girl-DAT call-PAST-NO-DE-WA NEG
 'It's not that Juan called a girl in the linguistics department.'

Similarly, *wh-ka* indeterminates can be interpreted under '*if*' or in the restriction of '*every*', as shown in (62) and (64), and in these readings *wh-ka* indeterminates are more or less interchangeable with their bare nominal counterparts, as in (63) and (65).

(62) dare-ka gakusei-ga kita-ra oshiete kudasai.
 who-KA student-NOM came-if tell please
 'If *who-ka* student comes, please let me know.'

(63) gakusei-ga kita-ra oshiete kudasai.
 student-NOM came-if tell please
 'If a student comes, please let me know.'

(64) dare-ka kyooju-o shootaishita dono gakusei-mo kookaishita.
 who-KA professor-ACC invited which student-MO regretted
 'Every student *who* had invited *who-ka* professor regretted it.'

(65) kyooju-o shootaishita dono gakusei-mo kookaishita.
 professor-ACC invited which student-MO regretted
 'Every student who had invited a professor regretted it.'

It has been reported for a number of modal indefinites that the epistemic effect that they convey in unembedded contexts disappears in downward entailing contexts (see Kratzer and Shimoyama 2002 for *irgendein*; Alonso-Ovalle and Menéndez-Benito 2008, 2010 for *algún*; Fălăuş 2009, 2011a, 2011b, and 2014 for Romanian *vreun*; and Jayez and Tovena 2006 for French *un quelconque*). The epistemic effect of *wh-ka* indeterminates also disappears in these contexts: the sentence in (60) simply conveys that Juan is not dating *any* girl in the linguistics department, not that it is not the case that Juan is dating a girl in the linguistics department and the speaker does not know who.

The disappearance of the modal effect of these indefinites in downward entailing environments was taken to support the claim that this meaning component is an implicature (see Kratzer and Shimoyama 2002; Alonso-Ovalle and Menendez-Benito 2013b for an overview.) As is the case with some other modal indefinites, there are indeed reasons to believe that the ignorance component of *wh-ka*s is an implicature. As we note in Alonso-Ovalle and Shimoyama (2014), the sentence in (66) shows that this implication can be cancelled, and the sentence in (67) that it can be reinforced without redundancy, as expected if this component is an implicature. For further evidence supporting the implicature status of the ignorance component of *wh-ka*, see Alonso-Ovalle and Shimoyama (2014).

(66) Mariko-wa dare-ka gengogaku-no gakusei-to kekkonshita. jitsuwa
Mariko-TOP who-KA linguistics-GEN student-with married. in.fact
dare-ka know
who-Q shitteru.
'Mariko married a linguistics student. In fact, (I) know who it is.'

(67) Mariko-wa dare-ka gengogakka-no gakusei-to tsukiatteiru kedo,
Mariko-TOP who-KA linguistics.dept-GEN student-with dating but
dare-ka shira-nai.
who-Q know-not
'Mariko is dating a student in the linguistics department, but (I) don't know who.'

To sum up: we have seen that, just like other modal indefinites, the ignorance component that *wh-ka* indeterminates convey in unembedded contexts disappears in downward entailing environments. To conclude our overview of the behavior of *wh-ka* indeterminates, we will briefly discuss two ways in which the behavior of *wh-ka* indeterminates differs from that of other modal indefinites.

3.7 Lack of agent-oriented readings

In section 3.6, we noted that *wh-ka* indeterminates trigger an ignorance effect in unembedded contexts. Some modal indefinites can convey other types of modal effects in the absence of an overt modal. For instance, Spanish *uno cualquiera*, Italian *uno qualsiasi*, or the Korean *-na* indeterminates can convey indifference on the part of an agent (Kratzer and Shimoyama 2002; Choi 2007; Choi and Romero 2008; Rivero 2011a, 2011b; Alonso-Ovalle and Menéndez-Benito 2011b; Chierchia 2013). To illustrate, the sentence in (68), with *uno cualquiera*, claims (i) that Juan grabbed a book, and (roughly speaking) (ii) that he was indifferent as to which book to grab.[2]

---

[2] The exact nature of this agent indifference component is under debate. See Alonso-Ovalle and Menéndez-Benito (2013c).

(68) Juan cogió un libro cualquiera.
 Juan grabbed UN book CUALQUIERA
 'Juan grabbed a random book.'

While some indefinites, like the ones above, are specialized in conveying this agent indifference implication, others, like German *irgendein*, can also convey an ignorance effect. The sentence in (69) can convey either that Hans bought a book and that the speaker does not know which one or, roughly speaking, that he bought a random book.

(69) Hans hat irgendeinen Buch gefaukt.
 Hans has IRGENDEIN book bought
 'Hans bought some book or other / a random book.'

Finally, we also find modal indefinites that can only convey an ignorance effect in the absence of an overt modal. In Spanish, *algún* always conveys ignorance and *uno cualquiera* always conveys agent indifference.

Where do *wh-ka* indeterminates fit into this picture? The situation in Japanese seems to be similar to the one that we find in Spanish. *Wh-ka* indeterminates unambiguously convey ignorance in unembedded contexts. The sentence in (70), for instance, will be deviant in a context where Mika grabbed a book randomly and the speaker knows which one.

(70) Mika-wa nani-ka hon-o totta.
 Mika-TOP what-KA book-ACC took
 'Mika took *what-ka* book.'

Much as in Spanish, agent indifference is conveyed in Japanese by a different item: a combination of a *wh*-word plus the particle *demo*, occurring inside what has the appearance of an adverbial clause.[3] The sentence in (71) conveys that Mika took a random book.

(71) Mika-wa [nan-demo ii-kara] hon-o totta.
 Mika-TOP what-DEMO good-as book-ACC took
 'Mika took a book randomly.'

The modal component of this construction has interesting properties. When embedded under a deontic modal, the indifference component seems to be speaker-oriented. The sentence in (72) conveys that the choice of book is indifferent to the speaker, much

---

[3] The particle *-demo* here is used in typical free-choice examples like (i), and is arguably decomposed into a copula *-de* and universal *-mo*.

(i) Kono mondai-wa dare-demo tokeru.
 this problem-TOP who-DEMO solve-can'
 'Anyone can solve this problem.'

like the sentence in (73), with the free choice item *which.one-demo*, does. The situation is different with epistemic modals. The sentence in (74) does not convey that Mika might take any book, but that it might be the case that she takes a book randomly. We will leave the discussion of this pattern for further research.

(72) dore-demo   ii-kara   hon-o   totte-ii-yo.
      which-DEMO   good-as   book-ACC take-good-PRT
      'You can take any book.'

(73) dore-demo   hon-o   totte-ii-yo.
      which.one-DEMO   book-ACC take-good-PRT
      'You can take any book.'

(74) Mika-wa nan-demo   ii-kara   hon-o   toru-kamo shirenai.
      Mika-WA what-DEMO   good-as   book-ACC take-might
      'Mika might take a book randomly.'

So far, we have found a number of similarities between *wh-ka* indeterminates and Spanish *algún*: they both express partial ignorance in unembedded contexts and in both cases their modal component evaporates in downward entailing contexts. We have also shown one area where *wh-ka* indeterminates and *algún* differ from each other: *algún*, but not *wh-ka*, is sensitive to the source of the evidence that the speaker has to make the existential claim. We will conclude by pointing out another difference between the two items.

3.8 Ignorance about quantity

We have seen that in cases like (1), repeated below as (75), *algún* conveys that the speaker does not know *which* individual satisfies the existential claim.

(75) A: María   está saliendo   con   algún estudiante del   departamento.
         María   is   dating   with   algún student   from.the department
         'María is dating a student from the department.'
                                    (Alonso-Ovalle and Menéndez-Benito 2010)

Usually, (75) is interpreted in a context where it is taken for granted that María is dating at most one student. Alonso-Ovalle and Menéndez Benito (2010) show that the situation is different if we consider cases that are compatible with the possibility of there being more than one individual satisfying the existential claim. Consider the sentence in (76).

(76) Hay   alguna mosca en la   sopa.
      there is   alguna fly   in the   soup
                                    (Alonso-Ovalle and Menéndez-Benito 2010: 24)

In cases like this, *algún* conveys that the speaker does not know the total number of individuals satisfying the existential claim. The sentence in (76) conveys that there is at least one individual satisfying the existential claim, but the speaker does not know how many.

We find a similar effect in the sentences in (77). The sentence in (77a) may signal that the speaker does not know how many dents his car has and the one in (77b) may indicate that the speaker does not know how many baby teeth Juanito has.

(77) a. Mi coche tiene algún abollón.
My car has algún dent

b. Juanito todavía tiene algún diente de leche.
Juanito still has algún tooth of milk
(Alonso-Ovalle and Menéndez-Benito 2010: 24)

Getting back to *wh-ka* indeterminates, we observe that, as we indicated in section 3.2, unlike what happens with *algún*, the "ignorance of the identity of the witness" and "ignorance of the quantity" interpretations are associated with different morphology, as the examples in (78) and (79) illustrate.

(78) Sota-wa nani-ka hon-o katta.
Sota-TOP what-KA book-ACC bought
'Sota bought some book(s).'

(79) Sota-wa nan-satsu-ka(-no) hon-o katta.
Sota-TOP what-CL-KA-GEN book-ACC bought
'Sota bought several books.'

3.9 To conclude

We have provided in this chapter a description of some properties of *wh-ka* indeterminates that either parallel or depart from those of other modal indefinites.

Our aim was to bring into the arena some data that can fuel further research in the topic and eventually help to shape a semantic typology of modal indefinites, modal determiners, and, more generally, modal expressions in natural language that can advance our understanding of how the expression of modal notions behaves across syntactic categories.

4

Modality in the nominal domain: The case of adnominal conditionals

ILARIA FRANA

4.1 Introduction

In 1996, Peter Lasersohn discovered a construction in which an *if*-clause appears as an NP-modifier, rather than a sentential adjunct. He dubbed this type of *if*-clause "adnominal conditionals" (henceforth, ACs); some examples are provided in (1).

(1) a. The price *if you pay now* is predictable. The price *if you wait a year* is not.
    b. The fine *if you park in a handicapped spot* is higher than the fine *if your meter expires*. (Lasersohn 1996: (3a,b))

Lasersohn (1996) convincingly argues that ACs are not matrix conditionals occurring in an unusual position. Rather, they are nominal modifiers, akin to relative clauses. He proposes that the denotation of a complex NP containing an AC is derived in the way shown in (2), which is modeled after the possible-worlds semantic analysis of counterfactual conditionals developed by Stalnaker (1968) and Lewis (1973).

(2) $[\![N \textit{ if } S]\!]^w = \{x \in U: \forall w' \text{ closest to } w \text{ such that } S(w') = 1, x \in [\![N]\!]^{w'}\}$

For instance, the NP *price if you pay now* will denote in a given world w the set of entities that are prices in all the (closest to the actual world) worlds w' in which you pay now. Assuming that we are pragmatically concerned with the price of a single object whose price value is the same in all the closest worlds w', this set is a singleton, hence the use of the definite determiner is allowed.

Lasersohn's analysis correctly captures the intuitive meaning of examples like (1a,b). However, as I will show later, the interpretation rule in (2) produces wrong truth-conditions for examples that already contain a modal operator within the NP, as in the examples in (3a–c).

Modality Across Syntactic Categories. First edition. Ana Arregui, María Luisa Rivero, and Andrés Salanova (eds.).
This chapter © Ilaria Frana 2017. First published 2017 by Oxford University Press.

(3) a. No **possible** explanation to telepathy *if you believe in the laws of physics* exists.
b. An **unlikely** outcome *if John gets to vote* is Peter's election as president of the company.
c. The **necessary** precautionary measures *when tropical cyclone warning signals are in force* are listed on the web.

Building on Lasersohn's proposal that ACs are nominal modifiers, I take examples such as (3a–c) to be the basic cases and propose a compositional analysis of ACs within a restrictor-based analysis of conditionals (Lewis 1975; Heim 1982; Kratzer 1986). According to my proposal: (i) ACs always restrict the domain of an operator within the NP they modify (a modal adjective) and (ii) when there is no overt operator within the NP, as in (1a,b), ACs restrict the domain of a covert necessity modal adjective (cf. Kratzer 1986's analysis of matrix indicative conditionals). Case (ii) comes closest to Lasersohn's original proposal: in the absence of an overt modal adjective, the default force of the covert modal operator is universal.

The rest of the chapter is structured in the following way. In section 4.2, I review Lasersohn's (1996) arguments against a displacement-based analysis of ACs and introduce novel data distinguishing matrix conditionals from ACs. In section 4.3, I discuss Lasersohn's proposal and its shortcomings. In sections 4.4 and 4.5, I introduce background assumptions and spell out my analysis.

4.2 Adnominal conditionals are not displaced matrix conditionals

Before starting to think about possible analyses of ACs, it is crucial to first discard the hypothesis that sentences like (1a,b) are derived via movement of a matrix *if*-clause. If that was the case, semantic interpretation could apply to the structure before movement takes place, hence reducing adnominal *if*-clauses to matrix *if*-clauses. This hypothesis has some initial plausibility. In fact, examples with ACs often feel semantically equivalent to their corresponding matrix conditionals variants, as shown by the pairs of sentences in (4a,b) and (5a,b).

(4) a. The location of the party *if it rains* must be Villa Ada.
b. *If it rains*, (then) the location of the party must be Villa Ada.

(5) a. An unlikely outcome *if John gets to vote* is Peter's election.
b. *If John gets to vote*, (then) an unlikely outcome is Peter's election.

The goal of the section is to convince the reader that, despite the equivalences above, ACs are not displaced matrix conditionals. I will use two types of evidence: (i) tests showing that ACs must syntactically occur within NPs and (ii) semantic environments (concealed questions and extensional contexts) where adnominal and matrix conditionals are not truth-conditionally equivalent.

4.2.1 Preliminary evidence

4.2.1.1 No parenthetical intonation necessary
As Lasersohn points out, ordinary *if*-clauses may also appear between the subject DP of a sentence and the VP. However, in such cases, the *if*-clause must be set off by parenthetical intonation. Without this parenthetical (or comma) intonation, an ordinary *if*-clause in this position sounds marked. This is shown by the contrast in (6a,b), parenthetical intonation rendered by the comma (Lasersohn 1996: (8a)).

(6) a. John, if you bother him long enough, will give you five dollars.
    b. *John if you bother him long enough will give you five dollars.

According to Lasersohn, the contrast above shows that examples with mandatory parenthetical intonation (6a) are structurally different from true ACs (1a,b). Adnominal *if*-clauses do not require parenthetical intonation, and this can be taken as evidence that they do not in fact appear between the subject DP and the VP. Rather, they are generated as part of the DP, hence the rule according to which an *if*-clause that appears between the subject and the main predicate must be set off by parenthetical intonation does not apply. The question that remains open is why some nouns—i.e. proper names—cannot be modified by an adnominal *if*-clause. I will return to this in section 4.3.

4.2.1.2 Constituency structure
The examples in (7) and (8) (Lasersohn 1996: (7,8)), involving conjunction and relative clause modification, show that the *if*-clause and the noun it modifies must form a syntactic constituent, as the bracketing suggests.

(7) [The location if it rains] and [the location if it doesn't rain] are within five miles of each other.[1]

(8) The [[consequences if we fail] that he mentioned] are not nearly as bad as the [[consequences if we fail] that he didn't mention].

4.2.1.3 Contexts where extraction is not allowed
The examples in (9) and (10) show that *if*-clauses in *given*-phrases and unconditional adjuncts headed by *regardless* or *no matter* must be interpreted in situ.[2]

(9) Given the fine *if you park in a handicapped spot*, you shouldn't park over here.

(10) Regardless of the fine *if you park in a handicapped spot*, you shouldn't do it.

---

[1] A matrix conditional paraphrase for this sentence is not even possible, unless we replace conjunction with disjunction (*If it rains #and/or if it doesn't rain the locations are within five miles of each other*).

[2] Thanks to Kyle Rawlins for bringing these examples to my attention.

4.2.2 More meaningful evidence

The data above provides convincing evidence in support of the claim that ACs should not be reduced to matrix conditionals. However, setting aside a few exceptions, most of the AC examples considered so far admit a matrix conditional paraphrase. There are two environments, though, in which the adnominal and the matrix variant clearly come apart: embedding contexts and extensional contexts.

4.2.2.1 Embedding contexts (concealed questions)

Although attitude verbs canonically select for clausal complements (e.g. *that*-clauses and *wh*-questions), they can also, in some cases, select for DP complements, as in (11). A DP complement of an attitude verb such as *find out* can be intuitively paraphrased with an embedded identity question; hence the name "concealed questions" (e.g. Heim 1979; Romero 2005; Frana 2010).

(11) John found out Mary's phone number. CQ
(= John found out what Mary's phone number is)

Lasersohn points out that the CQ+AC example in (12) and the matrix conditional example in (13) are not truth-conditionally equivalent: while (12) makes a claim about our actual knowledge, (13) makes a claim about our knowledge in the hypothetical worlds in which we fail.

(12) We all know the consequences *if we fail*.
(= We all know what the consequences are *if we fail*)

(13) *If we fail*, we all know the consequences.
(= *If we fail*, (then) we all know what the consequences (of our failure) are)

[(12)] does not condition our knowledge of the consequences of our failure. Rather it asserts that we do actually know the consequences. Which consequences? The ones that would result, if we were to fail. (Lasersohn 1996: 1)

The truth-conditional difference between (12) and (13) may appear rather subtle, and there is a potential confounding factor due to the fact that the relational noun *consequences* is interpreted as elliptical for *consequences of our failure*, with the *if*-clause seemingly providing the content for the internal argument of the noun. However, the contrast can be reproduced with other CQ sentences that do not include potential confounding factors, such as the examples in (14a,b) and (15a,b).

(14) a. We all know the outcome of the meeting *if John gets to vote*.
b. *If John gets to vote*, (then) we all know the outcome of the meeting.

(15) a. Guess the price of the iPhone *if one doesn't sign up for a contract*.
b. *If one doesn't sign up for a contract*, (then) guess the price of the iPhone.

Under its most natural interpretation, (14a) says that we now know the answer to the question *what is the outcome of the meeting in case John gets to vote?* This is different from saying that if John gets to vote, then we would know what the outcome of the meeting would be, which clearly implies that John's voting conditions our knowledge of the outcome.[3] Similarly, under its most salient reading, (15a) expresses an invitation to guess the answer to the question *what is the price of the iPhone in case one doesn't sign up for a contract?* Under this reading, the *if*-clause is not interpreted as conditioning your guessing, rather as part of the CQ.

Note that not all *if*-clauses occurring in this position must be interpreted adnominally. The example in (16) is a clear case of a sentence-final matrix conditional.

(16) You would know the answer *if you had studied harder*.
       (= *If you had studied harder*, you would know what the answer is)

It is really hard, if not impossible, for this example to interpret the *if*-clause within the CQ (*what is the answer if you had studied harder?*). Aside from a strong pragmatic bias against the adnominal interpretation (the correct answer to a question does not depend on how much you study), it seems plausible that the adnominal interpretation is ruled out because *would* requires a matrix conditional in order to be licensed.

4.2.2.2 *Extensional contexts* In most of the AC examples considered the matrix predicate was intensional: an attitude verb (17a), a modal auxiliary verb (17b), or an intensional adjective (17c).

(17) a. We all *know* the consequences if we fail.
       b. The outcome if John gets to vote *must* be unpleasant.
       c. The price if you pay now is *predictable*.

Lasersohn wonders whether ACs might be some kind of "modal polarity item," which is licensed only in intensional contexts. He also notes that examples that do not contain an overt modal could be analyzed as being implicitly modal. For instance, (18) has a generic interpretation.

(18) (Generally,) the fine if you park in a handicapped spot is higher than the fine if your meter expires. (Lasersohn 1996: (16))

Apart from standard intensional contexts, like those in (17), ACs occur very naturally in specificational identity statements (cf. Higgins 1979), as in (19a,b).

(19) a. The location of the party *if it rains* is Villa Ada.
       b. The price of the car *if you pay in cash* is $2,000.

Following a tradition starting with Montague's (1974) discussion of the "temperature paradox," I will assume that copular identity statements create intensional contexts.

---

[3] As in Lasersohn's example (13), this sentence has a future-oriented noun (*outcome*). However, in my example, the internal argument of the relational noun has been saturated (by the PP *of the meeting*) and does not bear a relation to the *if*-clause.

For instance, according to Romero (2005), the copula of "specification" is an intensional predicate with respect to its second argument (the subject of the clause). Under this view, specificational *be* denotes a 2-place relation between an individual and an individual concept (a function from worlds to individuals). When evaluated at the actual world, the specificational sentence in (20a) is analyzed as saying that the value of the individual concept *the location of the party* at the actual world is Villa Ada. In an analogous fashion, (19a) could be paraphrased along these lines: the value of the concept *the location of the party* in all the worlds in which it rains (at some salient location) is Villa Ada.

(20) a. The location of the party is Villa Ada.
b. $\lambda w.\ \iota x_e$ [x is the location of the party at w] (w_0) = Villa Ada

Are there examples in which ACs occur in truly extensional contexts? Lasersohn (1996) provides the following as an example.

(21) *The biased elections scenario* (Lasersohn 1996: 158)
Suppose that John holds the deciding vote for the chairman of the committee. Bill and Mary are discussing the probable outcome of the election. Mary has some idea of John's intentions and says: "The chairman if John gets to vote is sure to be a man." Bill happens to know that John is not only planning to vote for a man, but specifically, planning to vote for him and utters (22):

(22) The chairman of the committee *if John gets to vote* is sitting right here in front of you!

The main predicate—*is sitting right here in front of you*—in the example above is not an intensional predicate; in fact Bill might have also truthfully uttered (23) instead of (22) (substitution of equivalents is allowed):

(23) I am sitting right here in front of you!

Thus, Lasersohn concludes, the distribution of ACs is not limited to intensional contexts, though any analysis of this construction should make clear why intensional contexts provide the most natural environments for ACs.

When looking at extensional contexts, more differences between matrix and adnominal conditionals can be appreciated. Consider the contrast between examples in (24a,b).

(24) a. The chairman of the committee *if John were to vote tomorrow* **is sitting** next to you.
b. **If John were to vote tomorrow*, the chairman of the committee **is sitting** next to you.

The sentence in (24b) is marked—the subjunctive conditional requires its consequent to bear subjunctive morphology (*would*). The same requirement does not hold for the adnominal variant in (24a). Note, moreover, that the grammatical sentence in (25) is not equivalent in meaning to the adnominal variant in (24a). One can easily imagine scenarios that would verify one but not the other. For instance, suppose that, as in Lasersohn's scenario, Bill is aware that John would enforce Bill's election if he gets to vote. Suppose further that Bill and Mary regularly sit next to each other during those committee meetings. However, their conversation is taking place over the phone, while they are sitting in their respective homes. In this scenario, (25) can be true (under the reading, *If John were to vote tomorrow, the chairman of the committee would be sitting next to you tomorrow/at the next meeting*), while (24a) is clearly false.

(25) *If John were to vote tomorrow*, the chairman of the committee **would be sitting** next to you.

More examples displaying analogous contrasts are given below. In these examples, the (a)-sentences are perfectly acceptable in the given scenarios and can be used to make a contingent claim about the extension of the complex DP at the actual world. The matrix conditional sentences, on the other hand, cannot be used this way.

(26) Context: Campbell is the current head of accounts. We heard that if Campbell gets fired Cosgrove will be hired to replace him. After some investigation, I find out that Cosgrove works for a competing agency in London.

(27) a. The new head of account *if Campbell gets fired* **works** for a competing agency in London.
  b. *If Campbell gets fired*, (then) the new head of accounts #**would work**/ ***works** for a competing agency in London.

(28) Context: Walker is the current leader of the party. Suppose we heard that if Walker resigns, Underwood will become the new leader. I just read in the news that Underwood was prosecuted five years ago.

(29) a. The new leader of the party *if Walker resigns* **was** prosecuted 5 years ago.
  b. *If Walker resigns*, (then) the new leader of the party #**would have been**/***was** prosecuted 5 years ago.

4.2.3 Summary

The data presented in this section show that ACs should be analyzed as NP modifiers both for syntactic (conjunction; modification; extraction) and semantic reasons (CQs; extensional contexts). According to the restrictor-analysis, matrix *if*-clauses are syntactic adjuncts whose semantic contribution is to restrict the domain of various types of operators (Lewis 1975; Heim 1982; Kratzer 1986). If we pursue a unified semantic analysis of sentential and adnominal *if*-clauses, we need to answer the following question: which operator is the *if*-clause restricting in AC constructions? In the remainder of this chapter, I pursue an analysis according to which ACs restrict the domain of a (possibly covert) modal adjective within the NP they modify. Before presenting my analysis I will first introduce Lasersohn's (1996) analysis, which constitutes my starting point.

4.3 Discussion of Lasersohn (1996)

Lasersohn (1996) proposes that in AC constructions, the *if*-clause combines with the noun it modifies in the way described by the rule in (30), which is an adaptation to the nominal domain of the semantic analysis of counterfactual conditionals developed by Stalnaker (1968) and Lewis (1973). For instance, the NP *chairman of the committee if John gets to vote* in (22) will denote in a world *w* the set of individuals in (31). Assuming that John would vote for the same person in all the closest worlds w' and that we are pragmatically concerned with a particular election, the set in (31) is a singleton, hence the use of the definite article is allowed.

(30) $[\![N \textit{ if } S]\!]^w = \{x \in U : \forall w' \text{ closest to } w \text{ such that } S(w') = 1, x \in [\![N]\!]^{w'} \}$

(31) $\{x : \forall w' \text{ closest to } w \text{ such that } J. \text{ votes in } w', x \in [\![\text{chairman-of-the-c.}]\!]^{w'} \}$

Lasersohn points out that the analysis above can capture two of the facts observed in the previous section, namely, the tendency of using ACs in intensional contexts and the fact that adnominal *if*-clauses cannot modify proper names (see example (6)).

> I suspect this is the reason why adnominal *if*-clauses so often appear in intensional contexts; they have a semantics which makes it very easy for them to denote non-existent objects, and extensional predicates can never be true of non-existent objects, by definition. Second, because adnominal *if*-clauses exploit variation in denotation from world to world, it would make little sense to combine one with a rigid designator. [...] *John* denotes the same individual in all possible worlds, and certainly not a different individual in worlds where you bother him and worlds where you don't. (Lasersohn 1996: 161)

Lasersohn further points out that if we reanalyze sentences as involving reference to (or quantification over) sets of events (Davidson 1967; Parson 1990), we can give a unified analysis of adnominal and matrix conditional. If sentences denote, at some level, predicates of eventualities and an utterance of a sentence is true in a given world *w iff* its extension in *w* is not empty, we could have a unified rule for adnominal and matrix conditional, such as (32), where *x* ranges over individuals or events and *X* ranges over predicates of individuals or predicates of events (Lasersohn 1996: 162).

(32) $[\![X \textit{ if } S]\!]^w = \{x \in U : \forall w' \text{ closest to } w \text{ such that } \exists y \in [\![S]\!]^{w'}, x \in [\![X]\!]^{w'} \}$

Following Stalnaker (1968) and Lewis (1973), Lasersohn's analysis is a similarity-based version of the strict implication analysis of conditionals, which assumes that conditional constructions involve universal quantification over a restricted set of

Modality in the nominal domain 57

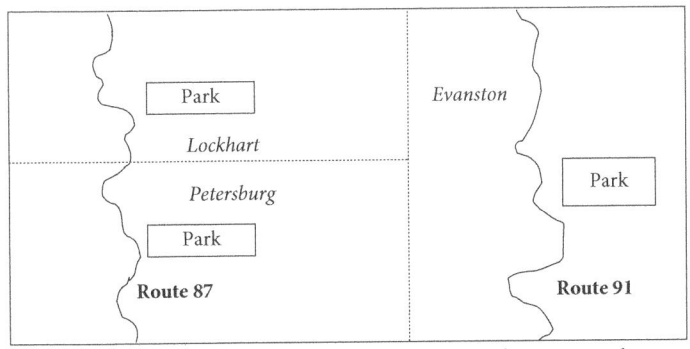

○ Route 87 passes by two parks, one in Lockhart and one in Petersburg.
○ Route 91 passes by one park, in Evanston.

FIG. 4.1

Source: These handy pictures are from Seth Cable's lecture notes "Formal Semantics," Spring 2011. Used with permission (Seth Cable p.c.).

possible worlds (those that are most similar to the evaluation world).[4] However, starting with Lewis (1975) and Kratzer (1986), the assumption that *if*-clauses introduce a conditional (or modal) operator has been abandoned in favor of the view that *if*-clauses have no modal meanings of their own and they are simply used to restrict the domain of a (possibly covert) modal operator.

The strongest argument against the strict-implication analysis comes from conditional sentences that contain an overt modal. Consider the following scenario:[5]

(33) *The lost highway scenario* (variation from von Fintel and Heim 2011)
Mary and Susan are in the car, Susan driving. They don't know for sure where they are. However, they do know the following:
a. They are either on Route 87 or Route 91.
b. They have just passed a park.
Mary checks the map and sees the pictures in Fig. 4.1.

In this scenario, an utterance of (34) by Mary would be judged false.

(34) If we are on Route 91, we might be in Lockhart now. (False)

Following standard assumptions, the modal *might* existentially quantifies over a contextually restricted set of possible worlds. Assuming that the epistemic accessibility relation $\lambda w.\lambda w'$. *w' is compatible with Mary's evidence in w* restricts the domain of

---

[4] It should be stressed though that Lasersohn's rules are also compatible with a restrictor-based analysis of conditionals. Since Lasersohn is not considering examples that involve other modal operators, his rules could be interpreted as saying that, in the absence of an overt modal operator, the *if*-clause is interpreted as restricting the domain of a covert universal modal operator. This will be the approach that I will adopt and spell out here.
[5] This problem is discussed in von Fintel and Heim (2011: ch. 4) (see also references therein).

might as well as the domain of the universal modal introduced by the interpretation rule in (30) (or (32)), we obtain the truth conditions in (35), which reads as (36) (abstracting away from events).

(35) $[\![(34)]\!]^w = \{x \in U : \forall w'$ compatible with Mary's evidence in w such that $\exists y \in [\![$we are on R 91$]\!]^{w'}, \exists w''$ compatible with Mary's evidence in w', such that $x \in [\![$we are in Lockhart$]\!]^{w''}\}$

(36) True *iff* all the (closest) worlds w' compatible with Mary's evidence in w where they are on R. 91 are such that there is some w'' compatible with Mary's evidence in w' where they are in Lockhart in w''.

However, in the given scenario, Mary doesn't know where she is for sure: even if they happened to be on Route 91, this will not affect her epistemic state. Thus, the truth-conditions just derived would predict (34) to be true as long as it is compatible with the evidence available to Mary that they are in Lockhart; and since Mary does entertain this possibility, the sentence is incorrectly predicted to be true.[6]

When looking at adnominal conditionals in combination with modal adjectives, an analogous problem arises. Consider the example in (37).

(37) *The lost highway scenario* (adnominal variant)
Mary and Susan are in the car. Susan is driving Mary to a surprise destination. Mary doesn't know where she is exactly and doesn't know what their final destination is. However, she knows the following:
a. Their final destination is after a park.
b. They are either on Route 87 or on Route 91.
c. They have just passed a park.

Suppose Susan asks Mary: "So, where do you think we are going?" Mary checks the map and sees the same pictures as in (33, Fig. 4.1).

(38) a. A possible destination if we are on Route 91 is Lockhart. (False)
b. A possible destination if we are on Route 87 is Lockhart. (True)
c. A possible destination if we are on Route 91 is Evanston. (True)

Assuming Lasersohn's interpretation rule(s), we would again derive truth-conditions that contain two layers of modality: there will be the universal modal introduced by the conditional construction and the existential modal introduced by the adjective

---

[6] Note that even if we assign the modal higher scope over the *if*-clause, we would still not arrive at the right truth-conditions, as shown in (i) below. What we need, instead, is one layer only of modality.

(i) If we are on Route 87, we must be in Lockhart now. (False)

Predicted T-conditions: For every (closest) w' compatible with M's evidence in w such that in all w'' compatible with M's evidence in w' and where they are on 87 in w'', they are in Lockhart in w''.

possible.⁷ Assuming both modals are restricted by the contextually determined (epistemic) accessibility relation $\lambda w.\lambda w'$. *w' is compatible with Mary's evidence in w*, the complex DP *a possible destination if we are on Route 91* would denote the following set of entities:

(39) $\{x: \forall w'$ closest to w such that they are on R. 91 in w', $\exists w''$ compatible with Mary's evidence in w', such that $x \in$ [[**destination (of their trip)**]]$^{w''}\}$

This set consists of entities that qualify as destinations of their trip in (at least) some of the worlds compatible with Mary's evidence in all the closest worlds in which they happen to be on Route 91. However, as before, the evidence available to Mary in all the closest worlds in which they happen to be on Route 91 is unlikely to change in any significant way from the evidence she has available in the actual world. Thus, this set will contain all destinations compatible with her current evidence, namely both Lockhart and Evanston. As a result, we would incorrectly predict (38a) to be true in the given scenario.

Taking examples like (40) as the basic cases, I propose that AC constructions do not introduce universal quantification over possible worlds; rather, the adnominal *if*-clause semantically restricts the domain of the existing operator, i.e. the modal adjective.⁸

(40) a. A **possible** location for the party *if it rains* is 20 miles away.
   b. No **possible** explanation to telepathy *if you believe in the laws of physics* exists.
   c. An **unlikely** outcome *if John gets to vote* is Peter's election as president of the company.
   d. The **necessary** precautionary measures *when tropical cyclone warning signals are in force* are listed on the web.

More specifically, I propose a unified account of ACs with and without overt modal modifiers, according to which (i) ACs always restrict the domain of a modal operator within the NP they modify (often a modal adjective) and (ii) when there is no overt operator within the NP, ACs restrict the domain of a covert epistemic necessity modal adjective, analogue to *necessary*. My account can thus be seen as a way of combining Lasersohn's proposal, according to which adnominal *if*-clauses are nominal modifiers and AC constructions involve quantification over possible worlds, with independently

---

[7] I will later address the specific semantics of modal adjectives; for now I am just assuming that modal adjectives, like modal auxiliaries, introduce modal quantifiers over possible worlds.

[8] Lasersohn (1996: 161) briefly notes that the universal force may be just a default and presents the examples in (i) with frequency adjectives. However, he leaves this issue open and suggests that the examples in (i) might be better dealt in the manner of Stump (1981).

(i) a. the *usual* consequences if John gets to vote
   b. the *occasional* fine if you park in the wrong place
   c. a *rare* problem if it rains

motivated accounts of conditionals, in particular Kratzer's (1986) analysis of matrix indicative conditionals.

4.4 Background for the analysis

4.4.1 Matrix *if-clauses and modals*

There are many dimensions to the interpretation of conditionals that I will not be able to address. Here I spell out some simplifying assumptions about the syntactic structure and the semantics of modal and conditional sentences in order to provide a concrete setting for the discussion of my proposal. In particular, I will follow the restrictor approach (Lewis 1975; Kratzer 1979; Heim 1982), according to which matrix conditionals are syntactic adjuncts, whose semantic contribution is to restrict the domain of various types of operators, usually modal auxiliaries (*If it rains, we **might** stay home*) and (temporal or modal) adverbs (*If it rains, we **usually** stay home*). Under this view, a conditional sentence forms a tripartite structure where the antecedent of the conditional is in the restrictor of the modal operator, and the consequent is in its nuclear scope. As for the semantics of modals, I will follow (with some significant simplifications) Kratzer (1977, 1981, 1991, 2012) and assume that modals are relativized to two contextual parameters, or conversational backgrounds: a modal base, which provides the relevant set of worlds the modal quantifies over, and an ordering source, which induces a strict partial order of the worlds in the modal base, as shown in (41) (cf. Lewis 1981; Kratzer 1991: 644).

(41) Given a set of worlds X and a set of propositions A, define the strict partial order $<_A$ as follows:
$\forall w, w' \in X: w <_A w'$ iff $\{p: p \in A$ and $w' \in p\} \subset \{p: p \in A$ and $w \in p\}$
(= For any pair of worlds w and w', w is closer to the ideal set by A than w' iff the set of propositions of A true in w is a superset of the set of propositions of A true in w'.)

For sake of simplicity I will also make the limit assumption, i.e. I will assume that the set of propositions in a given conversational background A is finite and that there are worlds that are, so to speak, most ideal.[9] The operator Max, defined in (42), selects the worlds from the modal base that come closest to the ideal set by the conversational background A.[10]

(42) Let X be any set of worlds, and let $<_A$ be an ordering on X:
$\text{Max}_{<_A}(X) = \{w \in X: \neg \exists w' \in X: w' <_A w\}$
= those worlds from X that satisfy the most proposition from A
= those worlds from X that come closest to the ideal set by A

---

[9] Kratzer (1981, 1991, 2012), following Lewis (1973), does not make the limit assumption.
[10] See also Portner's (2009) operator *Best*.

Modality in the nominal domain 61

As for the syntax of modal sentences, I will assume that modals are raising predicates (e.g. Wurmbrand 1999) and that the subject undergoes reconstruction, so that the LF of a modal sentence consists of a modal operator and an unmodalized prejacent, as shown in (43). The denotations I am adopting for a universal and an existential modal are given in (44). Following standard assumptions (e.g. von Fintel and Heim 2011), the modal base is represented as a free variable over functions of type $<s,t>$, whose value is determined via the contextual parameter f (e.g. $f_{EPIS} = \lambda w.\lambda w'$. w' *is compatible with the available evidence in* w), in the way shown in (45). The ordering source, on the other hand, is provided via the contextual parameter g (e.g. $g_{STEREOTYPICAL} = \lambda w.\ \lambda p.\ p$ *is a reasonable expectation in* w). The final truth-conditions of a modal sentence are given in (46).[11]

(43) a. (Given the available evidence,) John must be home.
b. Schematic LF: Must [John be home]

(44) Denotations of modal auxiliaries
a. $[\![\text{must}]\!]^{w,f,g} = \lambda B_{<s,t>}.\ \lambda p_{<s,t>}.\ \forall w' \in \text{Max}_{<g(w)}(B): p(w') = 1)$
b. $[\![\text{may}]\!]^{w,f,g} = \lambda B_{<s,t>}.\ \lambda p_{<s,t>}.\ \exists w' \in \text{Max}_{<g(w)}(B): p(w') = 1)$

(45) $[\![\text{Base}_i]\!]^{w,f,g} = f(i)(w)$ \hfill (e.g. $f(i)(w) = f_{EPIS}(w)$)

(46) $[\![(42)]\!]^{w,f,g} = \forall w' \in \text{Max}_{<gSTER(w)}(\{w'': w''$ is compatible with the evidence in $w\})$: John is home in w'
= John is at home in all the closest (given a stereotypical metric) worlds w' compatible with the evidence available in w.

Conditional sentences receive a tripartite structure, with the *if*-clause functioning as the restrictor of the modal quantifier and the consequent as its nuclear scope. Following an assumption often made in the literature, I take *if* to not have any semantic function. Consequently, the *if*-clause simply denotes a proposition, which can combine with the first argument of the modal via generalized predicate modification:[12] the set of worlds selected by the modal base conjoins with the set of worlds denoted by the *if*-clause, with the resulting set serving as the restrictor of the modal operator.[13] The ordering source then ranks the worlds in the modal base where the antecedent is true according to how close they are to some "ideal" in a world.

---

[11] I am assuming, for convenience, that modal bases are represented as free variables in the syntax (at LF), whereas ordering sources are purely contextual parameters. However, nothing hinges on this particular technical choice: both parameters could be represented at LF, or they could be both left unrepresented.

[12] Predicate Modification (world version, after Heim and Kratzer 1998: 95):
If X is a branching node, Y and Z its daughters, and $[\![Y]\!]$ and $[\![Z]\!]$ are both functions of type $<s,t>$, then $[\![X]\!] = \lambda w \in W.[\![Y]\!](w) = [\![Z]\!](w) = 1$.

[13] In the semantic system I am adopting, sentences denote truth-values, not propositions. I will follow a standard practice and assume that an argument of type $<s,t>$ can be derived by Intensional Functional Application (as defined in Heim and Kratzer 1998: 308).

(47) a. If it rains, we might stay home.
b. [[might B [if it rains]] [we stay home]]
c.

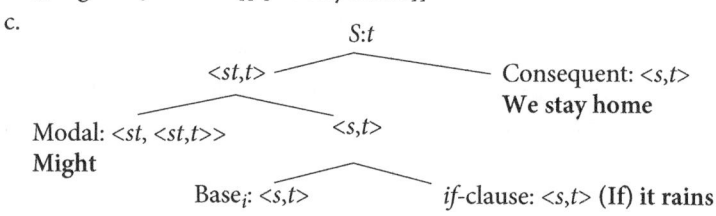

```
                            S:t
          <st,t>                      Consequent: <s,t>
                                      We stay home
  Modal: <st,<st,t>>      <s,t>
  Might
                Base_i: <s,t>      if-clause: <s,t> (If) it rains
```

Assuming an epistemic modal base and a stereotypical ordering source, we arrive at the truth-conditions in (48).

(48) $[\![(47a)]\!]^{w,f,g} = \exists w' \in \text{Max}_{<\text{STER}(w)}(\{w'': w''$ is compatible with the evidence in w & it rains (at some salient location) in $w''\})$: We stay home in w'
= Among the closest worlds compatible with the evidence available in the actual world and in which it rains, there are some in which we stay home.

Under the restrictor analysis, the *if*-clause is interpreted at a position different from its position at surface structure. Alternatively, one could assume the syntax in (49) (cf. Bhatt and Pancheva 2006), which better reflects the word order of conditional sentences and allows us to derive equivalent truth-conditions.[14]

(49)

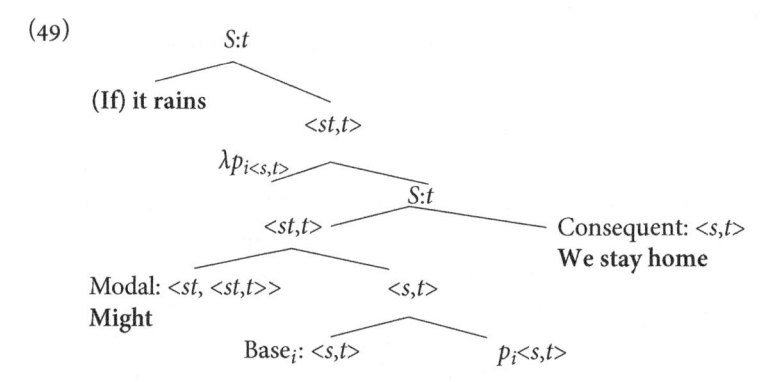

```
         S:t
  (If) it rains
                <st,t>
        λp_{i<s,t>}
                    S:t
           <st,t>              Consequent: <s,t>
                               We stay home
  Modal: <st,<st,t>>    <s,t>
  Might
              Base_i: <s,t>    p_i<s,t>
```

Under this line of approach, conditional sentences without overt modals are analyzed as being implicitly modalized by either a covert habitual/generic operator ((*Generally*), *if he leaves work on time, he has dinner with his family*)—whose existence is independently known (cf. Krifka et al. 1995)—or a covert "epistemic necessity modal" (Kratzer 1986), whose (simplified) denotation is provided in (51).

---

[14] Fully understanding the interpretation of conditional structures requires a more complex syntax (see e.g. Iatridou 1991; von Fintel 1994; Bhatt and Pancheva 2006).

(50) a. If the lights in his study are on, Roger is home.
b. If the lights in his study are on, Roger MUST$_{EPIST}$ be home.

(51) $[\![MUST_{EPIST}]\!]^{w,f,g} = \lambda B_{<s,t>}. \lambda p_{<s,t>}. \forall w' \in Max_{<g(w)}(B_{EPI}: p(w') = 1)$

(52) $[\![(50a)]\!]^{w,f,g} = \forall w' \in Max_{<g(w)}(\{w'':$ everything known in w is true in w'' & the lights in R.'s study are on in $w''\})$: Roger is home in w'

4.4.2 A textbook analysis of modal adjectives

Modal adjectives are traditionally analyzed along with sentential modals—mostly relying on data such as (53a), which in a possible-worlds semantics is analyzed along the lines of (53b).

(53) a. It is *possible* that it's raining.
b. *It is possible that S* is true in a world *w iff S* is true in some world accessible from *w*.

This type of analysis, however, is not viable for modal adjectives in attributive positions. Consider the examples in (54a,b):

(54) a. Mary interviewed a *possible* candidate.
b. Luisa is a *potential* prima ballerina.

Obviously, the adjectives in (54a,b) cannot be analyzed as sentential modal operators. Example (54a) does not have the same meaning as *It is possible that Mary interviewed a candidate*. As for (54b), a sentential paraphrase would deliver an ill-formed sentence (*It is potential that Luisa is a prima ballerina*). In (54a,b), it is not the information conveyed by the whole sentence that is modally displaced; rather, modal displacement affects the sub-sentential information conveyed by the noun phrase. In what follows, I will adopt a conservative extension of the analysis of modal auxiliaries to modal adjectives. This analysis will work for our purposes, though it is unlikely to be the last word on the semantics of modal adjectives.

Consider an utterance of (56) in the context described in (55).

(55) Context: The police gathered some facts (e.g. John made a suspicious call yesterday, the recording says ...) and now suspect that John might be a terrorist and proceed to arrest him. A police officer utters (56a,b).

(56) a. John is a possible terrorist (given the available evidence).
b. We arrested a possible terrorist.

The lexical entry I am going to assume for an existential attributive modal adjective, like *possible*, is given in (57).

(57) $[\![possible]\!]^{w,f,g} = \lambda B_{<s,t>}. \lambda P_{<s,<e,t>>}. \lambda x. \exists w' \in Max_{<g(w)}(B): P(w')(x)$

(58) $[\![B_i]\!]^{w,f,g} = f(i)(w)$ (e.g. $f(i)(w) = f_{\text{EPIS}}(w)$)

The internal structure and composition of the NP *possible terrorist* is given in (59). As in the discussion of modal auxiliaries, I will appeal to Intensional Functional Application (Heim and Kratzer 1998) to combine a function and the intension of its argument. Assuming an epistemic modal base (the set of worlds w' compatible with the evidence available in the world of evaluation) and a stereotypical ordering source ($\lambda w. \lambda p. p$ *is a reasonable expectation in* w), semantic composition proceeds in the way outlined in (60) and (61).

(59) LF of the NP: *possible terrorist*.

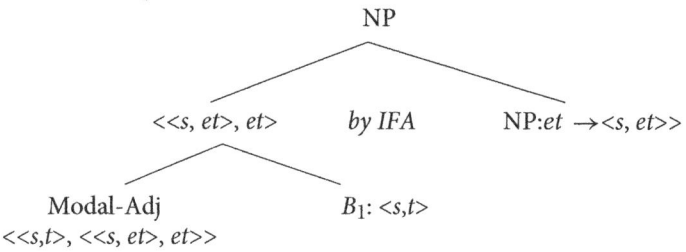

```
                    NP
                   /  \
          <<s,et>,et>   by IFA   NP:et → <s,et>>
           /       \
       Modal-Adj   B₁: <s,t>
    <<s,t>, <<s,et>,et>>
```

(60) $[\![\text{possible terrorist}]\!]^{w,f,g}$ = (by IFA)
$= [\![\text{possible}]\!]^{w,f,g}(\lambda w^*. [\![\text{terrorist}]\!]^{w^*,g}) =$
$= \lambda x. \exists w' \in \text{Max}_{<\text{STER}(w)}(B_{\text{EPIST}}): (\lambda w^*. [\![\text{terrorist}]\!]^{w^*,f,g})(w')(x) =$
$= \lambda x. \exists w' \in \text{Max}_{<\text{STER}(w)}(B_{\text{EPIST}}): [\![\text{terrorist}]\!]^{w',f,g}(x) =$
$= \lambda x. \exists w' \in \text{Max}_{<\text{STER}(w)}(B_{\text{EPIST}}): x$ is a terrorist in w'

(61) $[\![\text{The police arrested a possible terrorist}]\!]^{w,f,g} = 1$ *iff*
$\exists x$ [the-pol. arrested x in w & $\exists w' \in \text{Max}_{<\text{STER}(w)}(B_{\text{EPIST}}): x$ is a terrorist in w']
= There is some x that the police arrested in the actual world w and (the counterpart of) x is a terrorist in some of the worlds compatible with the evidence in w.

4.5 The proposal for ACs: a parsimonious extension to the nominal domain

4.5.1 ACs with overt modals

We are now in a position to introduce the restrictor-based analysis of ACs. The main advantage of the present analysis is that examples with overt modal adjectives fall out automatically. Consider again the lost highway scenario, repeated in (62).

(62) *The lost highway scenario* (adnominal variant)
Mary and Susan are in the car. Susan is driving Mary to a surprise destination.

Mary doesn't know where she is exactly and doesn't know what their final destination is. However, she knows the following:
a. Their final destination is after a park.
b. They are either on Route 87 or on Route 91.
c. They have just passed a park.

Suppose Susan asks Mary: "So, where do you think we are going?" Mary checks the map and sees the same pictures as in (33, Fig. 4.1).

(63) A possible destination if we are on Route 91 is Lockhart.   (False)

The internal structure of the complex NP is shown in (64), semantic composition proceeds in the way outlined in (66). As in the case of matrix conditionals, the modal base, identified as a contextually determined set of worlds, intersects with the proposition expressed by the *if*-clause, with the resulting set of worlds serving as the restrictor of the modal adjective.

(64) Internal structure of the NP *possible destination if we are on 91* (simplified)

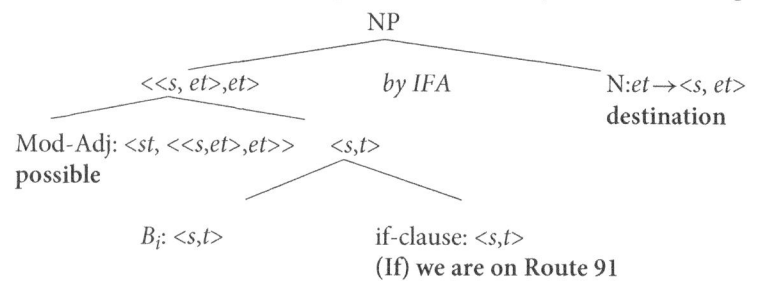

```
                        NP
         ┌──────────────┼──────────────┐
      <<s,et>,et>      by IFA        N:et → <s, et>
    ┌──────┴──────┐                   destination
Mod-Adj: <st,<<s,et>,et>>  <s,t>
possible         ┌──────┴──────┐
              B_i: <s,t>    if-clause: <s,t>
                            (If) we are on Route 91
```

(65) $[\![B_i]\!]^{w,f,g} = f(i)(w)$ (e.g. $= f_{\text{EPIS}}(w)$)

(66) $[\![\text{NP}]\!]^{w,f,g} = \lambda x_e. [\exists w' \in \text{Max}_{<g(w)} (\{w'' \text{ is compatible with the evidence in } w$ & they are on R. 91 in $w''\}) x$ is a destination in $w']$

(67) a. A possible destination if we are on Route 91 is Lockhart.
b. [a possible [B [if we are on R 91]] destination] λx. x is Lockhart
c. Lockhart ∈ {x: ∃w' ∈ Max$_{<g(w)}$ ({w'' is compatible with the evidence in w & they are on R. 91 in w''}) x is a destination in w']}

Note that the truth-conditions in (67c) come out pretty close to those of the matrix conditional sentence in (68a). This is a welcome prediction, given that the two sentences are very close in meaning.

(68) a. If we are on Route 91, our final destination might be Lockhart.
b. Might [B [if we are on 91]] [our final destination (be) Lockhart]
c. ∃w' ∈ Max$_{<g(w)}$ ({w'' is compatible with the evidence in w & they are on R. 91 in w''}): our-final-destination (w') = Lockhart

The analysis provides an explanation for why there is no significant difference in meaning between matrix and adnominal conditionals in this type of examples. Note that what falls outside the scope of the modal operator in the adnominal variant is the copula (which, under this treatment, is either semantically null, as in (67), or the copula of specification, as in (68) and the proper name *Lockhart*. In the matrix variant, on the other hand, both elements are under the scope of the modal. However, given that proper names are rigid designators and that the copula is null (or denotes an identity function), whether they are within the scope of a modal operator or not is not going to make a difference.

As in the case of matrix conditionals, one could assume a slightly different syntax to better reflect the position of the *if*-clause at surface structure. Something along the lines of (69) would do. However, in what follows, I will stick to the simpler structure in (64).

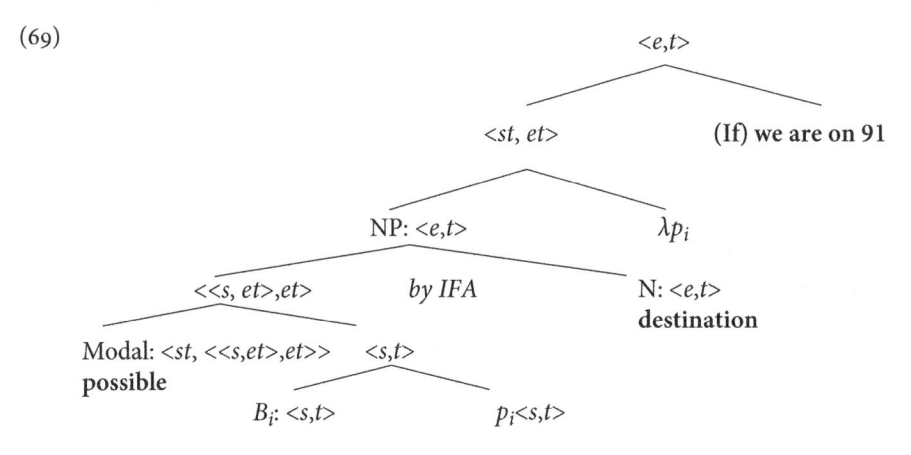

(69)

```
                                    <e,t>
                          ┌──────────┴──────────┐
                      <st, et>              (If) we are on 91
                  ┌──────┴──────┐
              NP: <e,t>         λp_i
          ┌──────┴──────┐        │
     <<s, et>,et>     by IFA   N: <e,t>
     ┌──────┴──────┐           destination
Modal: <st,<<s,et>,et>>  <s,t>
possible         ┌──────┴──────┐
              B_i: <s,t>    p_i<s,t>
```

4.5.2 ACs without overt modals

A natural extension of Kratzer's (1986) analysis of bare indicative conditionals to the nominal domain would be to assume that AC sentences without overt modal operators are also implicitly modalized. However, in this case, the implicit modal operator is located within the NP and takes the form of a covert necessity modal adjective, analogue to *necessary*. The denotation of the covert modal adjective is given in (70).[15]

(70) $[\![\text{NECESSARY}]\!]^{w,f,g} = \lambda B_{<s,t>}.\, \lambda P_{<s,et>}.\, \lambda x.\, \forall w' \in \text{Max}_{<g(w)}(B): P(w')(x)$

---

[15] Since Kratzer (1986) it has been assumed that the modal flavor of the covert modal operator in matrix conditionals is epistemic. Here, I leave the modal flavor of the covert modal adjective unspecified.

Modality in the nominal domain 67

Next, consider a sentence with an extensional verb, such as (71a). Semantic composition proceeds in the way outlined in (72).

(71) Context: Campbell is the current head of accounts. We heard that, if Campbell gets fired, Cosgrove will be hired to replace him. After some investigation, I find out that Cosgrove works for a competing agency in London.
   a. The head of accounts if Campbell gets fired works for a competing agency in London.
   b. [The [NECESSARY B [if C. gets fired] [head-of-acc.] works in London

(72) Internal structure of the NP *head of accounts if Campbell gets fired*

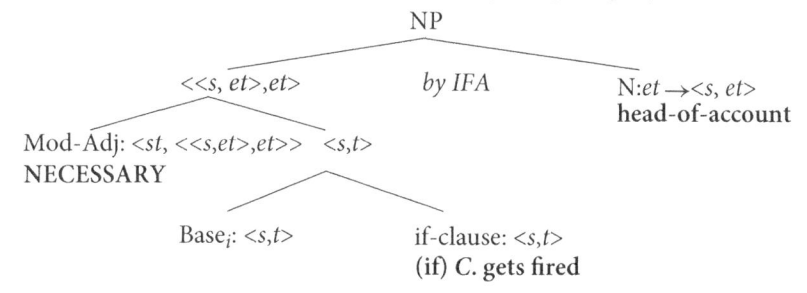

```
                                    NP
           <<s, et>,et>          by IFA        N:et →<s, et>
                                                head-of-account
   Mod-Adj: <st, <<s,et>,et>>  <s,t>
   NECESSARY
                Base_i: <s,t>      if-clause: <s,t>
                                   (if) C. gets fired
```

$[\![NP]\!]^{w,f,g} = \lambda x_e. \forall w' \in \text{Max}_{<g(w)} (\{w'' \text{ is } f\text{-accessible from } w \ \& \ \text{Campbell gets fired in } w''\}): \text{head-of-accounts } (w')(x)$

Assuming that we are pragmatically concerned with a particular hiring replacement and that the new head of accounts is the same in all the (closest) accessible worlds w', the function above picks out a singleton set, hence the use of the definite determiner is allowed. The final truth-conditions are given in (73).

(73) $[\![(71b)]\!]^{w,f,g} = \iota x_e \ [\forall w' \in \text{Max}_{<g(w)} (\{w'' \text{ is } f\text{-accessible from } w \ \& \ \text{C. gets fired in } w''\}): \text{head-of-accounts } (w')(x)]$ works for a competing agency in London at w
= There is a unique x that is the head of account in all the closest accessible worlds in which Campbell gets fired and (the counterpart of) x works in London in the actual world (at the time of speaking).

Recall that the corresponding matrix conditional sentence with *would* feels quite different in meaning (and present tense on the matrix predicate is just ungrammatical).

(74) a. If Campbell gets fired, (then) the new head of accounts would work for a competing agency in London.
   b. Would [B [if C. gets fired]] [new HoA work in London]
   c. Predicted truth-conditions (informally): in all the best worlds (given a body of rules/desires) in in which C. gets fired, there exists a unique x such that x is head of accounts and x works in London in w'.

4.5.3 Iterated modality

Next, consider sentences with an AC as well as a modal auxiliary. Under the given analysis, the adnominal *if*-clause does not restrict the domain of the overt modal predicate—unlike its matrix counterpart. Rather, it restricts the domain of a (possibly covert) modal adjective. The two pairs of sentences below are then expected to have different truth-conditions, and this prediction partially matches our intuitions. Take (75a), for instance. Suppose that you are informing me that the woman I just talked to will become the new president of the committee if John resigns. Suppose I take you to be a reliable source and suppose, further, that during my chat with this woman I noted that she had an accent, which I take to be Italian. In this scenario, I could then utter (75a) to you to tell you that I have enough evidence to believe that the referent of the complex DP is Italian. This interpretation is hard to get for (75b) (if not impossible). The most natural reading of (75b) is one in which the modal receives a root interpretation (deontic or teleological) and the property of being Italian is ascribed to a not-yet-existing individual: in all the best worlds (given a body of rules/desires) in which John resigns, the new president in those worlds (whoever that will be) is Italian.

(75)   a. The president of the committee if John resigns must be Italian.
       b. If John resigns, (then) the (new) president of the committee must be Italian.

Similarly, (76a) can be used to make a claim about a particular actual villa where the party is going to happen in case of rain. The sentence would then claim that, given my body of evidence, this location happens to be one of the few Italian villas in the area. As in the previous case, this interpretation does not seem to be available to (76b), whose most natural reading can be paraphrased as: in all the best worlds (given a body of rules/desires) in which it rains, the location of the party in those worlds (whatever that will be) is one of the few Italian villas in the area.

(76)   a. The location of the party if it rains must be one of the few Italian villas in the area.
       b. If it rains, (then) the location of the party must be one of the few Italian villas in the area.

However, what is unexpected is that the (a)-sentences above are ambiguous and they also have a reading in which the *if*-clause does not seem to be interpreted adnominally. Angelika Kratzer (p.c.) suggested to me that in these examples the *if*-clause may be playing a double role by pragmatically restricting a distant operator (the modal auxiliary) in addition to grammatically restricting a local operator (the modal adjective).[16] Under this view, (75a) would be analyzed along the lines of (77).

---

[16] See Kratzer (2014) on conditional *if*-clauses pragmatically restricting the domain of quantificational determiners.

In (77), the conditional *if*-clause is interpreted DP-internally, but this contribution is rendered vacuous by it also restricting the overt matrix modal pragmatically.

(77) The best worlds where John resigns are worlds where the unique individual that is president if John resigns is Italian.

Investigating these data would require more time and space than what I have left here, hence an account is left for further research.

4.5.4 One further prediction: ACs and relative clauses

If ACs are devices for restricting the domain of modal operators within the NP they modify, they should interact with any modal operator within the NP, not just modal adjectives. This expectation is met: ACs can restrict the domain of overt modals within relative clauses (78) and they also restrict (covert) modals within infinitival relative clauses (79), cf. Bhatt (1999), Hackl and Nissenbaum (1999, 2012).

(78) a. The fee that you **must** pay *if you park in a handicapped spot* is higher than the fee that you **must** pay *if your meter expires*.

   b. The paper that you **can** write *if you follow the TA's suggestions* is going to be easier than the problem you **must** solve *if you take the exam*.

(79) a. The thing **to do** *if you are visiting a small town in Germany* is eating cakes at the local pastry shop.
   (= The thing you **should** do if you are visiting ...)

   b. This book talks about the strategy *to pursue* if you find yourself with a writing block.
   (= the strategy that you **could/should** pursue *if you find yourself with a writing block* ...)

Note though that these uses are adnominal in the sense that the *if*-clause does not escape the DP, but they are also sentential, given that the *if*-clause is restricting a clausal modal operator.

5
The non-modality of opinion verbs

DAVID-ÉTIENNE BOUCHARD

5.1 Introduction

The purpose of this chapter is to clearly distinguish the semantic contribution of opinion verbs and epistemic verbs, two classes of verbs that often produce nearly identical truth-conditions and correspondingly have sometimes been given nearly identical semantic analyses. I will show that while some similarities do exist between the two, they are largely accidental, and the two classes of verbs differ in systematic ways that warrant providing them with quite different semantic treatments.

Opinion verbs like *find* and *consider* are a little-known class of verbs whose importance in semantics has recently come to light in the investigation of the properties of so-called predicates of personal taste, or PPTs (e.g. Stephenson 2007a,b; Nouwen 2007; Sæbø 2009; Lasersohn 2009). Such predicates are essentially defined by their ability to give rise to judgments of faultless disagreement (Kölbel 2004), i.e. the intuition that two apparently contradictory assertions made by two different speakers can both be true at the same time, presumably because the truth of each assertion is in some way relativized to someone, most often the speaker.

(1) A: This chili is delicious!
     B: No, it's not!

A and B's statements are clearly contradictory, and yet we have the intuition that both speakers are speaking truthfully (assuming that they are honest about their opinion), since whether or not something is delicious is a matter of personal taste. How exactly the PPT *delicious* is relativized to the speaker is the subject of considerable debate. According to Lasersohn (2005), the interpretation function ⟦ ⟧ is relativized not only to a possible world,[1] but also to a judge, whose reference is fixed by the context of utterance. Some lexical items have as part of their denotation a reference to the contribution of the judge index and can have different extensions at different judge

---

[1] Lasersohn also makes use of a time index, which to keep things simple I will not discuss, since tense is not relevant to the issues discussed here.

Modality Across Syntactic Categories. First edition. Ana Arregui, María Luisa Rivero, and Andrés Salanova (eds.).
This chapter © David-Étienne Bouchard 2017. First published 2017 by Oxford University Press.

indices in a given world, while others do not. Predicates of personal taste like *fun* and ordinary predicates like *alive* thus differ in that only the former actually contains a reference to the judge index.

(2) ⟦ fun ⟧$^{w, j}$ = λ*x*. *x* is fun according to *j* in *w*

(3) ⟦ alive ⟧$^{w, j}$ = λ*x*. *x* is alive in *w*

As observed by Sæbø (2009) (and also Ducrot 1975, for the French verb *trouver*), this lexical difference is reflected in the acceptability of predicates inside the complement of opinion verbs, in that these verbs can only take complements that contain a predicate whose value can vary across judges—a restriction that I call the Subjectivity Requirement. The contrast between the two following sentences is a consequence of the fact that whether dinosaurs are extinct or not is a matter of ordinary, objective fact, while whether or not they are terrifying is a matter of opinion.

(4) Billy finds dinosaurs terrifying.

(5) #Billy finds dinosaurs extinct.

A relatively straightforward way of interpreting the semantic contribution of *find* and to understand the contrast between (4) and (5) is to say that the role of the opinion verb is to shift the judge index of its complement and set it to the matrix subject. The following denotation from Sæbø (2009) makes *find* into nothing more than a judge-shifter:

(6) ⟦ find ⟧$^{w, j}$ = λϕ.λ*x*. ϕ$^{w, x}$

If the complement does not contain any sort of judge-dependent predicate, as in (5), then the result is infelicitous because shifting the judge can have no truth-conditional effect, a state of affairs that could presumably be ruled out on pragmatic grounds. We will discuss this kind of infelicitous example in more detail in section 5.2.

But *find* is not the only verb that can be used to express someone else's opinions. A more common way of expressing this is with the ordinary epistemic verb *think*. Examples (4) and (7) appear to make equivalent contributions to any discourse.

(7) Billy thinks dinosaurs are terrifying.

Typically, epistemic verbs are treated as simple propositional attitudes that involve an epistemic accessibility relation. The following fairly standard denotation states that *x thinks that p* is true *iff* p is true in all of *x*'s epistemically accessible worlds.

(8) ⟦ think ⟧$^{w, j}$ = λϕ.λ*x*.∀*w*′∈Acc$_{\text{Epistemic}}$(*w*)(*x*), ϕ$^{w′, j}$ = 1

Note that this denotation leaves the judge index untouched, while the denotation of *find* contains no reference to an epistemic accessibility relation, so what can be done to account for the similarity between (4) and (7)? There are several ways to do this. We could conclude with Stephenson (2007a) that both *find* and *think* have as part of their lexical semantics a special relation with judge indices, namely that they replace the contextually specified value with the matrix subject. Another option would be to take the view expressed in Lyons (1977) and Wolf (2012) (and also discussed in Nouwen, 2007, who rejects it), that *think* is ambiguous between a subjective and objective use, in which case the similarity between (4) and (7) would reflect the similar meanings attributed to *find* and the subjective variant of *think*. Yet another view is that *find* is actually a sort of epistemic propositional attitude, but one that is only concerned with a special subset of epistemically accessible worlds, namely those that are made available by direct personal evidence (Nouwen 2007). I will not adopt any of these views, but will instead claim that the similarity between (4) and (7) is accidental. Epistemic verbs are ordinary attitude ascriptions whose interpretation concerns quantification over a set of possible worlds accessible by some epistemic accessibility relation as in (8), while opinion verbs involve shifting of a judge index. I thus argue for a strict separation of the two classes of verbs. The only reason that *think* appears to shift the judge index is that it often makes the attitude holder's mental state salient in the discourse.

An important reason to clear up the relation between various classes of verbs and their embedded subjective predicates is the fact that these verbs have been used to test the alleged judge-dependency of other lexical items, in particular epistemic modals like *might* and *must* (Stephenson, 2007a; von Fintel and Gillies, 2007, 2008, 2010). I will show that these modals have a special relation with epistemic verbs, but not with opinion verbs. From this I will conclude that epistemic modals are not judge-dependent in the sense intended in Stephenson (2007a).

This chapter is organized as follows. In section 5.2, I describe the semantic properties of *find* and show that this verb has a special relation with predicates of personal taste. I will also show that it has a special relation with the evaluation world, since it involves a kind of factivity akin to that of *know*. Both of these facts will receive a common explanation in terms of a partially factive presupposition introduced by *find*. In section 5.3, I turn to epistemic modals and the relation that they have with both *think* and *find*, from which I will conclude that *think* has nothing to do with the judge index. Section 5.4 is concerned with the view that *find* has some epistemic properties, a view that I will reject on the grounds that it does not correctly account for the interpretation of this verb, and its apparent evidentiality can be reduced to that of predicates of personal taste themselves, not opinion verbs that embed them. Section 5.5 concludes the chapter.

5.2 *Finding* judges

Predicates of personal taste that appear in matrix clauses are usually interpreted relative to the tastes of the speaker. If John says (9), then it is usually understood that what is claimed is that roller-coasters are awesome for John.

(9) Roller-coasters are awesome!

That is, the contextually provided judge index is typically the same individual as the speaker. This is not always the case, however, even in unembedded cases. Lasersohn (2005) shows that interpreting the speaker as the judge for PPTs, yielding what he calls an endocentric reading, is merely the more frequent option, and taking an exocentric reading, where another individual sufficiently salient in the discourse is used as the judge, is also perfectly possible, albeit less common. This is exemplified in (10), where it is clear that the speaker's opinion on the merry-go-round or the water slide is irrelevant, since it is Billy's opinion that is the subject of the conversation.

(10) Mary: How did Billy like the rides?
John: Well, the merry-go-round was fun, but the water slide was a little too scary.

Nothing in John's utterance explicitly shifts the identity of the judge, but the previous discourse makes it sufficiently clear that we are only interested in Billy's assessment of the rides. What this example shows is that we are free to interpret the judge for PPTs as just about any relevant individual in the discourse. There is no special relation between the judge and the speaker.

A more explicit way to make a claim about the tastes and opinions of other people is to embed a small clause or a full clause[2] under the verb *find*. Once a PPT is embedded in this environment, the judge is no longer determined by the context of utterance, but rather is strictly fixed as the matrix subject. If we alter John's response in (10) as in (11), then his response is no longer a felicitous contribution to the conversation since the judge for *fun* and *scary* can no longer be Billy and can only be John himself.

(11) Mary: How did Billy like the rides?
John: #Well, I found the merry-go-round fun, but I found the water slide a little too scary.

So contextual variation in the identity of the judge is a feature of unembedded PPTs, but not of PPTs that appear inside the complement of *find*. This is expected, given the denotation that we have given to *find* in (6) according to which it alters the judge index.

---

[2] There is some individual variation as to the acceptability of full clauses under *find*. While some speakers find them perfectly fine and others merely stilted, a certain number of speakers I have consulted have reported that they only accept small clauses in this environment. Speakers are particularly resistant to full-clause complements to *find* that are simply made up of a subject, a copula, and a predicate, possibly because the same meaning may be expressed with a small-clause complement.

(i) ??John finds that Mary is pretty.
(ii) John finds Mary pretty.

This can plausibly be explained in terms of a blocking effect, say because of a Gricean reasoning making use of the subclause of the maxim of Manner "Be brief." In any event, I will concentrate on the more tolerant dialect here and leave the issue of individual variation for further work.

A little-known fact about sentences in *find* is that this verb involves what I call a partially factive presupposition (cf. Bouchard 2013). In informal terms for the moment, what this means is that sentences with *find* as the main verb presuppose the non-subjective part of their complement. Although this is imperceptible when this verb takes small-clause complements, it becomes quite clear when larger constituents are embedded. For example, in (12), it is presupposed that Bill has an office, while the asserted content is simply that this office is nice according to John's opinion.

(12) John finds that Bill has a nice office.

We can use ordinary presupposition projection tests to show that this is indeed a presupposition. All the following examples entail that Bill has an office, despite the fact that (12) has been embedded under sentential negation (13), a question (14), or the antecedent of a conditional (15):

(13) John doesn't find that Bill has a nice office.

(14) Does John find that Bill has a nice office?

(15) If John finds that Bill has a nice office, you should show him mine!

How can we characterize this presupposition more precisely? In simple cases like (12), where the PPT is a modifier, we may construct the presupposition simply by taking the full complement of *find* and removing the subjective predicate. In this case, this yields the correct presupposition *Bill has an office*. However this cannot be the right algorithm more generally. It would obviously be a strange rule for the grammar to make use of, but it also has the deeper problem of yielding incorrect presuppositions in some cases, and entirely ungrammatical sentences in others:

(16) John finds that Bill behaved strangely yesterday evening.
      Presupposition ≠ Bill behaved yesterday evening.

(17) John finds that Billy became nervous around 5 pm.
      Presupposition ≠ *Billy became around 5 pm.

It is actually possible to formulate the partially factive presupposition of sentences in *find* in a way that will have the welcome side effect of enforcing the Subjectivity Requirement. I propose to do this by stating that sentences in *find* require that it be possible to judge their complement true or false in the actual world. If the complement clause can only be judged true or can only be judged false, the sentence will be considered infelicitous.[3] I call this the Subjective Contingency Presupposition.

---

[3] In principle, such a situation should produce a presupposition failure, which is a qualitatively different intuition compared with mere infelicity. However, since the boundary between subjective and non-subjective predicates is not so well defined, I believe that speakers faced with an infelicitous use of *find* like (5) cooperatively attempt to coerce the non-subjective predicate (*extinct*, in this case) into something subjective, but fail to do so in any plausible manner. This is a similar situation to when a particularly

(18) *Subjective Contingency Presupposition*
Any sentence of the form "*x* finds (that) *p*," interpreted at world *w*, is only defined if *p* can be judged either true or false in *w*.

Now I must specify what it means to say that "*p* can be judged either true or false in *w*." Clearly, it cannot mean that there is an individual in *w* that would judge *p* true and another that would judge it false. This is because this can be overtly contradicted without resulting in an infelicitous sentence:

(19) Nobody finds Billy smart.

This sentence is felicitous despite the fact that it claims that there is no individual (or at least none relevant in the discourse) who would judge the embedded small clause as true. But this does not mean that it is not possible to judge *Billy smart* true, just that no one actually does. So the Subjective Contingency Presupposition is concerned with possible judgments, not with actual judgments.

In Lasersohn (2005)'s fragment grammar, PPTs can have different extensions at different judge indices for a given world, but also different extensions at different world indices for a given judge. That is, the extension of *tasty* relative to John as the judge can change across worlds, as is shown in (20) with a conditional.

(20) If John found liver tasty, I would make it every day.

We can make use of this feature of the formal system to define what a possible judgment is. In order to do this, I propose to make use of an accessibility relation $Acc_{OPINION}$ which, for any given world–judge pair $<w, j>$, gives a set of world–judge pairs $<w', j>$ in which the extension of every non-subjective predicate is kept constant, while the extensions of subjective predicates are allowed to vary. This corresponds to what I will call the opinion space on *w*. Every world–judge pair in the opinion space is a possible judgment.

I further stipulate that the world–judge indices in the opinion space exhaust every possible way of assigning an extension to a subjective predicate that conforms to its domain restrictions. That is, given a subjective predicate like *tasty* with a domain restriction that says that only edible things can be part of its extension, for every set *S* in the power set of its domain, there is a world–judge pair in the opinion space where the extension of *tasty* is equal to *S*. So there is an index in $Acc_{OPINION}(w, j)$ where the judge finds every kind of food tasty, and there is a world where the judge finds nothing tasty, and everything in between.

---

non-gradable predicate combines with the comparative or degree modifiers. It is very hard to find any way to make the adjective *even* gradable, which explains why #*very even* sounds so odd, in contrast e.g. with *very pregnant*, which finds a natural interpretation by coercing *pregnant* into a gradable predicate relating individuals to how far ahead they are in their pregnancy. It is the failure to make any such coercion that explains the infelicitous nature of examples that are in violation of the Subjective Contingency Presupposition.

We will now see in turn how this accounts for both the Subjectivity Requirement and the fact that some material is presupposed by sentences in *find*.

It is fairly straightforward how the Subjectivity Requirement follows from the Subjective Contingency Presupposition. Let us examine an example that is in violation of this requirement again:

(21) #Billy finds dinosaurs extinct.

The world–judge pairs that are part of any set $\text{Acc}_{\text{OPINION}}(w,j)$ are only distinguished in the extension that they assign to subjective predicates. That is, for any pairs $<w,j>$ and $<w',j>$ in the opinion space, the extension of ordinary predicates like *extinct* is identical, so ⟦ extinct ⟧^{w,j} = ⟦ extinct ⟧$^{w',j}$. In this example, the Subjective Contingency Presupposition imposes that the small clause *dinosaurs extinct* be true in some world–judge pair in the opinion space and false in some other. But this cannot be the case, since in all these world–judge pairs, the extension of *extinct* (and that of *dinosaur*) is exactly the same. Since dinosaurs are indeed extinct in the real world, the small clause is true at all the indices in the opinion space, and the sentence is judged infelicitous.

Of course, the result is no better if the complement of *find* is false at all indices in the opinion space, rather than true at all of them. Replacing *dinosaurs* with *horses* makes the small clause *horses extinct* false at all indices in the opinion space accessible from the real world, but (22) is just as bad as (21):

(22) #Billy finds horses extinct.

Let us now turn to the partially factive presupposition, which was illustrated above with (12), repeated here as (23):

(23) John finds that Bill has a nice office.

Again, the Subjective Contingency Presupposition states that the embedded clause must be true at some index in the opinion space, and false at some other. There are many ways in which *Bill has a nice office* could be false. It would be false, for example, if Bill had a tiny office with no windows and flickering lights, at least according to most judges, and it would also be false if he had no office at all. In order for it to be true, however, it must be the case that Bill has an office, and that it be nice according to the judge.

The only element in this clause whose value varies across these indices is the adjective *nice*. The extension of *office* and *has*, on the other hand, are constant in all these indices, and they have the same value that they have in the actual world, so either Bill has an office at all these world–judge indices, or at none. But as discussed above, it is only if he has an office that *Bill has a nice office* can be either true or false. If he doesn't have one, then the embedded clause is necessarily false and the Subjective Contingency Presupposition is not respected.

This setup correctly predicts that the partially factive presupposition should be exactly the same if the embedded clause is negated:

(24) John finds that Bill doesn't have a nice office.

In order for this complement to be possibly judged true or false, it must be the case that Bill has an office, otherwise *Bill doesn't have a nice office* would simply be true at all the world–judge pairs in the opinion space.

What we have seen so far is that *find* has two major semantic properties. First it removes the contextual dependence of subjective predicates by fixing the judge relative to whom they are interpreted, and second, it presupposes that all the non-subjective material present in the complement clause is true in the evaluation world.

We now turn to Stephenson's attempt at extending the analysis of subjective predicates to epistemic modals and verbs.

5.3 *Thinking* epistemic modals

Stephenson (2007a) observes a certain number of similarities between the interpretation of predicates of personal taste and epistemic modals. Intuitively, they both implicitly refer to the mental state of some individual(s), a "knower" or a judge, which in unembedded contexts usually defaults to the speaker. A sentence like (25) is often given a meaning of the sort shown in (26), where *might* introduces existential quantification over a set of worlds defined loosely as "what is known." The modal takes scope over the full clause *John is in his office*, which we call the prejacent, and the full sentence is true *iff* the prejacent is true in at least one epistemically accessible world.

(25) John might be in his office.

(26) In some world compatible with what is known in the actual world, John is in his office.

Whose knowledge precisely must be used to define those worlds is the subject of considerable debate, but it at least often defaults to the speaker. As discussed in the previous section, PPTs are also often interpreted relative to the speaker, but not necessarily so.

Stephenson proposes to account for the behaviour of *might* and PPTs in a similar way, namely by making epistemic modals judge-dependent in a similar way to how PPTs are. That is, (25) would be interpreted as (27):

(27) In some world compatible with what is known **by the judge** in the actual world, John is in his office.

If we utter (25) out of the blue, the most easily available interpretation, if not the only one, is that it is the speaker's knowledge that should be used to evaluate the sentence.

We have seen that this is not a necessary feature of PPTs, and it is not a necessary feature of epistemic modals either, as shown by Egan et al. (2005). Although it is not quite as easy to find examples with this property, it is still possible for unembedded epistemic modals to be interpreted relative to a body of knowledge that is not the speaker's. They give the following scenario.

(28) Context: Ann is planning a surprise party for Bill. Unfortunately, Chris has discovered the surprise and told Bill all about it. Now Bill and Chris are having fun watching Ann try to set up the party without being discovered. Currently Ann is walking past Chris's apartment carrying a large supply of party hats. She sees a bus on which Bill frequently rides home, so she jumps into some nearby bushes to avoid being spotted. Bill, watching from Chris's window, is quite amused, but Chris is puzzled and asks Bill why Ann is hiding in the bushes. Bill says:

(29) I might be on that bus.

Clearly, Bill is aware that he is not on that bus, and so according to his own body of knowledge, the sentence he uttered would be false. Yet this sentence is fine in this context. Bill is taking an exocentric perspective, to borrow Lasersohn's terminology, using the epistemic modal to refer to the body of knowledge of some other salient individual in the discourse, namely Ann. Bill's claim can be paraphrased as (30):

(30) In some world compatible with what is known **by Ann** in the actual world, Bill is on that bus.

Evidently, the speaker's knowledge does not necessarily come into play in evaluating the contribution of the epistemic modal. What this shows is that as long as the context makes this sufficiently clear, it is possible for a speaker to use *might* to say things about other people's epistemic states even in unembedded contexts, just as a speaker may use a PPT to refer to someone else's opinion. If both types of elements are interpreted relative to a judge index whose value is supplied by the context, then we expect them to both be able to vary in this way.

The individual relative to whom an epistemic modal or a PPT is interpreted can be altered in a variety of manners. First, when embedded under *think*, both the knower that is relevant for *might* and the judge for the PPT are naturally understood as being shifted to the matrix subject.

(31) John thinks that Bill might be in his office.

(32) John thinks that Mary is pretty.

Stephenson takes this to show that *think* has in its semantic contribution the role of shifting the judge index exactly as *find* does, in addition to its better-known epistemic contribution.

It is also possible to use a variety of prepositions to obtain a similar effect. PPTs can have their judge parameter shifted by the prepositions *to* and *for*, while epistemic modals require *according to*:

(33)　This ride was fun for/to Bill.

(34)　According to Bill, John might be in his office.

In fact, *according to* is just like *think* in that it can be used to shift either the judge or the knower.

(35)　According to Bill, Mary is pretty.

These similarities (as well as others that I do not mention here) are the basis for Stephenson's project of constructing a unified analysis of PPTs and epistemic modals. The main obstacle to such a unified analysis of the individual-relative character of these two types of predicates is the fact that while the shifting of the knower by *think* and *according to* is obligatory, shifting of the judge by these same items is optional. In the following examples, the judge for *tasty* is naturally understood to be cats in general, and not my veterinarian.

(36)　My veterinarian thinks that this brand of cat food is tasty.

(37)　According to my veterinarian, this brand of cat food is tasty.

Both of these sentences can be used to state that my veterinarian thinks that this brand of cat food tastes good to cats. These would be felicitous, for example, in a context where I am talking about the fact that my cats are picky eaters and won't eat what I feed them, and my veterinarian proposed to fix this problem by switching to this other brand of food that they will surely find tasty. My veterinarian does not need to find this food tasty himself. In fact, he does not need to have ever tasted it.

Epistemic modals do not have this freedom. Whenever *might* appears inside the complement of *think*, the relevant body of knowledge that is used is necessarily that of the attitude holder. Assume again the scenario in (28). The following sentence is infelicitous in that context.

(38)　Bill thinks he might be on that bus.

If the embedded *might* were allowed to be interpreted relative to a body of knowledge corresponding to a contextually provided knower (Ann, in particular), then this sentence should be perfectly fine here, since it would say that Bill thinks that it is compatible with Ann's body of knowledge that he is on that bus. But this is not an available interpretation for this sentence.

Even more striking is the fact that if both an epistemic modal and a PPT are present under *think*, it is possible to understand the knower and the judge to be distinct individuals. Stephenson provides the following example to show this:

(39) John thinks that this brand of cat food might be tasty.

This sentence is felicitous if John has some reason to believe that the cat food is tasty for cats. The individual whose body of knowledge is relevant is necessarily John, while the understood judge is preferably cats, but could also be John, if we had reason to think that John sometimes eats cat food. Again, the semantic calculus does not impose a judge for *tasty*, despite the fact that it appears in the complement of *think*, and it is only our world knowledge that allows us to pick cats as the judge instead of John, in the absence of any disambiguating context.

In order to account for both the similarities and the differences between *might* and *tasty*, Stephenson proposes that while epistemic modals are inherently judge-dependent, PPTs are not. Rather, a PPT like *tasty* is a two-place predicate relating foodstuffs to individuals who find them tasty. Its denotation contains no reference to the judge index, thus making it technically non-judge-dependent.

(40) ⟦ tasty ⟧$^{w, j}$ = $\lambda x.\lambda y.y$ is tasty to x

The judge argument can be expressed overtly by a *for* or *to* PP, such as in (33), or covertly by a null pronominal. This null pronoun may be an ordinary *pro* that gets its interpretation from the variable assignment function just as pronouns usually do, thus allowing for exocentric readings, or it may be a special null PRO^j whose value is provided by the judge index, defined as follows:

(41) ⟦ PRO ⟧$^{w, j}$ = j

This means that the truly subjective predicates, in the technical sense that their extensions may vary across judge indices for a fixed world, are epistemic modals and PRO^j, but not *tasty* and other PPTs. PPTs only appear to be judge-dependent themselves because they often combine with PRO^j.

The optional character of the judge-shifting with PPTs under *think* and *according to* is thus analysed as following from the fact that they can take these two kinds of null pronouns. If a PPT appearing in a judge-shifted environment is accompanied by silent PRO^j, then its judge argument will be shifted, but if it is accompanied by ordinary *pro*, it will not. In contrast, since Stephenson builds the judge-dependency directly in the denotation of *might*, it cannot take a judge argument, and it thus does not have the option of combining with *pro* to avoid being interpreted relative to the shifted judge index. So the difference in behaviour between *tasty* and *might* is a consequence of their relative ability to take a judge argument in the syntax.

We can summarize Stephenson's proposals as follows. First, epistemic modals are judge-dependent and are interpreted relative to a contextually specified judge index. Second, *think* not only quantifies over epistemically accessible worlds, but also shifts the judge index of its complement to the matrix subject. Third, predicates of personal taste are not judge-dependent, but sometimes combine with PRO^j, which is. I will argue below that the two first claims must be given up, while I remain agnostic about the third (although, see Bouchard 2012 for arguments against this view of PPTs). Epistemic verbs have a relation with epistemic modals and opinion verbs have a relation with PPTs, but there is no interaction between the two.

The distinction that Stephenson makes between inherently judge-dependent predicates and predicates that are judge-dependent indirectly through their combination with PRO^j only becomes necessary if we accept that *might* is judge-dependent at all. However, this is not a very well motivated position. Initial evidence against the view that *might* is judge-dependent is the observation that the following dialog does not consistently give rise to the intuition of faultless disagreement, which is generally taken to be the defining property of subjective predicates:

(42) A: John might be in his office.
B: No, you're wrong. (I know this because I just saw him outside.)

Although judgments are notoriously difficult on such examples (see, in particular, MacFarlane, 2004; von Fintel and Gillies, 2008), it is not clear that this disagreement is faultless. As MacFarlane argues, it should be possible for speaker A to defend his position by saying something along the lines of (43), which is quite strange in this context:

(43) A: OK, then, he can't be in his office, but when I said that he might be in his office, it was still true at the time.

Stephenson focuses on the observation that disagreement is at least possible in response to an utterance with *might*, which she claims is not predicted if the sentence were interpreted relative to the speaker's epistemic state. That is, answering "no" to a claim modulated by *might* should only be allowed to deny that the prejacent is compatible with the speaker's epistemic state. But this is not what the denial contributes. Rather, she claims, it is used to convey that the prejacent is incompatible with the second speaker's own epistemic state. Disagreement is possible despite the fact that the two utterances are relativized to different speakers. This is similar to the intuition that a faultless disagreement dialog involving PPTs is possible despite the fact that the two PPTs are relativized to different individuals, as shown in the dialog in (1), repeated here as (44).

(44) A: This chili is delicious! (=to speaker A)
B: No, it's not! (=to speaker B)

A much simpler explanation of what the denial of a *might*-claim contributes would be to say that it only targets the unmodalized prejacent itself (cf. von Fintel and Gillies, 2008). That is, answering "no" to A's statement in (42) serves to deny the truth of *John is in his office*. There is nothing inherently strange in using direct denial to target an embedded proposition, as the felicitous nature of the following dialog illustrates:

(45) A: John thinks/said you'll be coming to work tomorrow.
    B: No, I won't come in until Wednesday.

B's denial does not concern whether John thinks or said that B would come to work, but just serves to deny that B will come to work. It is perfectly fine for an utterance of *no* to deny an embedded constituent. So there is nothing mysterious about the fact that we can answer "no" to a *might*-claim, since this denial can target the prejacent itself. There is no need to appeal to Lasersohn (2005)'s mechanism for judge-dependent disagreements here. In addition to this, the fact that the disagreement does not appear to be faultless as it would be with PPTs argues straightforwardly against a subjective treatment of epistemic modals.

Next, a fairly obvious point given the discussion in section 5.2 concerning opinion verbs is that *might* is not an adequate licenser for *find*. As discussed extensively already, opinion verbs require a subjective predicate in their complement clause, which is why (46) sounds degraded. If *might* were judge-dependent in the way proposed by Stephenson, however, the sentence should be made better by adding this modal to the complement clause. However, as (47) shows, this is not the case.

(46) #John finds that Bill is in his office.

(47) #John finds that Bill might be in his office.

We are faced with the options of either giving up the Subjectivity Requirement of *find*, which seems to hold very well for ordinary PPTs, or giving up the claim that *might* is judge-dependent. Note in passing that it is not the case that modals are not appropriate licensers for *find* for independent, say syntactic, reasons. As Sæbø (2009) shows, *should* is a perfectly acceptable licenser for *find*:

(48) #I find that smoking in a car is illegal.

(49) I find that smoking in a car should be illegal.

Since I see no reason to give up the Subjectivity Requirement of *find* and there is little to no positive evidence in favour of the claim that *might* is judge-dependent, I conclude that the fact that (47) is infelicitous is direct evidence against Stephenson's analysis.

The judge-dependency of a predicate (or lack thereof) is not a property for which there are well-defined tests; but the two main such tests that are used in the literature, namely the intuition of faultless disagreement and the licensing of *find*, both point in the same direction, namely that *might* is not judge-dependent. If *might* is not judge-dependent, we lose the main motivation for claiming that *think* shifts the judge index of its complement clause. This only leaves the examples where a PPT appears inside the complement of *think*. Recall that in such cases, the judge for the PPT is only optionally interpreted as the matrix subject, as shown in (36) above. That is, the identity of the relevant judge is context-dependent when the PPT appears inside the complement of *think*, just as it is in unembedded contexts, although interpreting the subject of *think* as the judge is favoured. This is in contrast to PPTs appearing inside the complement of *find*, where the identity of the judge is not context-dependent, but rather fixed unambiguously to the matrix subject. Given this situation, we may wonder whether there is any reason to postulate a great difference between the way that PPTs are interpreted in matrix contexts and below *think*. I propose that there is none, and that cases of apparent judge-shifting by *think* are merely cases of exocentric readings. The judge index of the embedded proposition is not altered by *think* in any way, and so any PPT that appears in this environment is free to be interpreted relative to any contextually provided judge, in principle. This is not to say that any individual will be equally likely to be interpreted as the judge, however. The verb *think* is used to make statements about the mental state of its subject, and so it will always have the effect of making this subject's thoughts and opinions a part of the object of discussion. Because of this, it will often but not always be the case that the most salient individual to use as the judge is the attitude holder. In many cases, this seems inevitable, such as in (50).

(50) John thinks that Mary is beautiful.

Clearly in this example it is next to impossible to understand *beautiful* as being interpreted relative to any other judge than *John*. But this should not be encoded in the semantics in terms of judge-shifting by *think*, since other examples like (36) that do not differ from (50) in any relevant way other than the plausibility of using the matrix subject as the judge do not share this property.

To summarize, I have shown that epistemic modals like *might* differ from PPTs in major ways that cast serious doubts on the validity of analysing them as judge-dependent in the way proposed by Lasersohn (2005) for predicates of personal taste, namely because they do not yield judgements of faultless disagreement, they do not license the use of genuine judge-shifting verbs like *find*, and denials of utterances with *might* can be reanalyzed as denials of the prejacent itself, an option that is generally possible for embedded propositions. Since all of Stephenson (2007a)'s stronger arguments in favor of treating *think* as a judge-shifter involve the alleged judge-dependency of *might*, these arguments must be given up. Finally, the remaining cases of apparent judge-shifting of a PPT below *think* can be viewed as ordinary exocentric interpretations, which are made salient simply because this verb highlights the attitude holder's mental state.

It remains true that the context-dependency of unembedded PPTs and epistemic modals is quite similar, defaulting to the speaker in most cases but nevertheless allowing for exocentric interpretations when the context requires it. It is also the case that the knower that is relevant for *might* can be obligatorily shifted by a higher epistemic verb and the phrase *according to*, just as the judge for PPTs can be obligatorily shifted by *find* and PPs headed by *to* or *for*. However, the lack of interactions between the domains of epistemicity and subjectivity argues against the view that the judge and the knower are provided in the same manner. At best, the similarities between the two sets of facts could be accounted for in a parallel fashion, rather than a common one, say by further enriching the index on the interpretation function to include both a judge and a knower. This would make it possible to account for the similarities in the interpretation of PPTs and epistemic modals while at the same time accounting for their relative independence, although I do not fully explore the consequences of such a proposal here since it would take us too far afield.

5.4 Radical reductionism

Concerning the comparison between *think* and *find*, so far I have shown that *think* has nothing to do with judge indices, while *find* does. In this section I show that *find* is not an epistemic verb in any sense of the term. Indeed, I will go further and argue that this verb is not an attitude ascription at all, and its entire semantic contribution is to shift the judge index of its complement, as shown in the denotation in (6). In this I take Sæbø (2009)'s "radically reductionist" view of the semantics of opinion verbs.

This is in direct contradiction with the claim by Stephenson (2007b) and Pearson (2012) that *find* is distinguished from *think* in that the former requires that the subject have direct evidence for supposing that the complement clause holds—a feature of interpretation that both authors integrate as a presupposition directly into the verb's denotation. Nouwen (2007) goes further and makes this proposed evidential component a part of the truth-conditions of *find*. He claims that this verb involves a distinct accessibility relation from epistemic verbs, and is only concerned with a subset of the subject's belief worlds, namely those that are "based on his subjective experience of the world."

This appeal to evidentiality is justified by the following contrast:

(51) John thinks that the cat food is tasty.

(52) John finds the cat food tasty.

Example (52) triggers the inference that John has tasted the cat food, while (51) does not. As Stephenson remarks, (51) can be understood as claiming that the cat food is tasty for the cat, or for John himself. Even in the second case, this can be based on indirect evidence, say looking at the list of ingredients and concluding that he would probably like it.

However, the source of the evidence in (52) should not be treated as part of the lexical entry of *find*, since it can be shown to follow purely from the fact that John is interpreted as the judge of the embedded clause. Indeed, this inference even holds if the claim that cat food is tasty is made in an unembedded context:

(53) This brand of cat food is tasty.

This sentence can be interpreted relative to various judges, but it is clear that whoever is the understood judge, it must be the case that this individual has tasted the cat food. It seems to be simply the case that we cannot imagine any other way to be a competent judge of something's tastiness, rather than some special property of *find*. Indeed, it is unclear to me that this inference is even linguistically based at all. Since this inference that the judge has direct evidence of the relevant sort is an integral part of any attribution of an opinion to a judge, then the fact that this presupposition is found in *find* sentences follows naturally from the fact that these sentences always involve attributing an opinion to a judge. Nothing further needs to be said to obtain this result.

What I conclude from this discussion is that the necessity for direct evidence in *find* sentences does not constitute an argument in favor of adding an evidential component to the denotation of opinion verbs, since it can be traced back to the way we understand any judge-dependent sentence.

The radically reductionist view of *find* makes it into a rather unusual embedding verb, since the truth-conditions of the sentences containing it are only calculated relative to the evaluation world, rather than to some set of worlds accessible from it. A final reason to think that this may be on the right track is the fact that it seems to be impossible to find any plausible *de dicto* reading with this verb. For example, observe the following sentence:

(54) John finds that you married someone with a strange name.

In (54), the PPT is inside the indefinite noun phrase headed by *someone*. On the assumption that *de dicto* readings correspond to an LF where the indefinite has not raised out of the scope of the intensional predicate, then if the complement of *find* is an opaque context, this sentence should only be allowed to receive a *de dicto* interpretation, since moving the DP would have the effect of removing the PPT *strange* from the complement of *find*, triggering a violation of the Subjectivity Requirement. Thus, what this example does is force the DP to be interpreted low. Despite this, it is perfectly possible for *someone* to get a *de re* interpretation here, and no *de dicto* reading seems to be available.

Although this does not show with certainty that *de dicto* interpretations are always impossible under *find*, the fact that we cannot find conclusive evidence that any such reading is in fact available is suspicious. I tentatively conclude that there is simply no positive evidence that *find* is intensional in any way.

5.5 Conclusion

In this chapter, I have argued against the view that a unified analysis of subjective predicates and epistemic attitudes is desirable. Rather, the data seem to suggest that opinions are treated by the semantic component in a manner entirely separate from other mental states. There is clearly a relation between *think* and *might*, since whenever the latter is in the scope of the former, the understood knower for *might* is shifted to the subject of *think*. Similarly, there is clearly a relation between *find* and PPTs, since whenever the latter are found in the scope of the former, the judge is the subject of *find*. However, the fact that *think* does not actually shift the judge for PPTs and *find* is not licensed by *might* argues strongly against the view that there is any interaction between these two domains. Furthermore, the absence of any detectable *de dicto* readings under *find* makes it difficult to maintain the notion that this verb is fundamentally intensional. Thus, I believe that the data examined here offers support for the view that opinion verbs are best modeled in a special way that only concerns the judge index, rather than the world index.

6

Sublexical modality in defeasible causative verbs

FABIENNE MARTIN AND FLORIAN SCHÄFER

6.1 Verbs under consideration

As Oehrle (1976: 25) observes, with an agentive subject, *offer* necessitates only that the possessor is willing to give the internal argument's referent up to somebody: no uptake is required on the latter's part. However, the uptake seems more strongly taken for granted with causer subjects; see the contrast in (1). Similarly, Oehrle observes that while no change of state is required by the agentive use of *teach*, some learning has to take place with a causer subject; see the contrast in (2). The contrasts in (3) and (4) illustrate the same phenomenon in French and German.[1]

(1) a. Peter offered us a bed. But we didn't want to lie there.
 b. Leaves, mingled with grass, offered us a bed.[2] #But we didn't want to lie there.

(2) a. Ivan taught me Russian, but I did not learn anything.
 b. Lipson's textbook taught me Russian, # but I did not learn anything.

(3) a. *Pierre m'a   offert   une nouvelle vie, mais je n'en   voulais pas.*
 Pierre me has offered a   new   life but I NEG-of it wanted NEG
 'Pierre offered me a new life, but I didn't want it.'

---

[1] Kamp (2013) observes that English *offer* differs from French *offrir* in that the contrast between the agentive vs. non-agentive use seems to be much less prominent. He also more generally suggests that for the English counterparts of verbs listed in (1)–(7) below, the inference that the result takes place seems to be cancellable with causer subjects, too, although it is much stronger than the inference with agentive subjects. He suggests that this may have to do with the fact that English is much more tolerant than French on the point of using primarily agentive verbs with non-agentive subjects. We have to leave these cross-linguistic variations aside here, but we hope to come back to them in future research.

[2] Ovid, *Heroides*, V. Oenone to Paris.

Modality Across Syntactic Categories. First edition. Ana Arregui, María Luisa Rivero, and Andrés Salanova (eds.).
This chapter © Fabienne Martin and Florian Schäfer 2017. First published 2017 by Oxford University Press.

b. *Ce livre m'a   offert   une nouvelle vie, #mais je n'en   voulais*
   this book me has offered a   new   life, but I   NEG-of it wanted
   pas.
   NEG
   'This book offered me a new life, but I didn't want it.'

(4) a. *Hans schmeichelte Maria, aber sie fühlte sich   überhaupt nicht*
       Hans flattered   Marie but she felt   REFL absolutely NEG
       geschmeichelt.
       flattered
       'John flattered Mary, but she felt absolutely not flattered.'

   b. *Dieses Detail schmeichelte Maria, #aber sie fühlte sich   überhaupt*
      this   detail flattered   Marie but   she felt   REFL absolutely
      nicht geschmeichelt.
      NEG   flattered
      'This detail flattered Mary, but she felt absolutely not flattered.'

This chapter is dedicated to verbs displaying the same ambiguity as *teach* in French and German. With agentive subjects, these verbs are by default used to denote an act performed with the intention of triggering a certain change of state (CoS). But this CoS does not have to occur for the sentence to be true, as shown by the non-contradictory continuation in (3a, 4a). This is why we call these verbs "defeasible causatives." With causer subjects, the same verbs implicate much more strongly (and even often seem to entail) the occurrence of the CoS; cf. the contradictory continuations in (3b, 4b). The question raised is how one should handle this ambiguity in the semantics of these verbs.

Following Gropen et al. (1989) and Beavers (2010), we call "prospective component" the subevent that does not need to obtain for the predicate to be satisfied, and "non-prospective component" the subevent that must obtain for the predicate to be satisfied. Adopting the typology of non-culminating construals proposed in Demirdache and Martin (2015), the reading which strongly implicates the CoS will be called the "culminating" reading, and the reading under which the CoS is entirely denied the "zero-CoS non-culminating reading" ("zero-CoS NC reading" for short).[3]

---

[3] Note that what we call the "zero-CoS non-culminating reading" roughly corresponds to the "failed attempt" non-culminating reading of Tatevosov and Ivanov (2009). Under this reading, the expected CoS does not take place at all, even partially. This reading has also been described for some speech act verbs by Austin (1962), who labels it the 'proleptic' reading (from Greek *prolepsis* 'anticipation'). Under what Tatevosov and Ivanov call the "partial success" non-culminating reading (labelled "partial-CoS non-culminating reading" by Demirdache and Martin), the expected CoS takes place, although only partially.

It has been claimed that for English verbs of transfer, the "double-object variant" triggers the culminating reading, while the *to* variant does not (see e.g. Green 1974: 157). However, Oehrle (1976: 129f.) shows that many *give* verbs have the culminating reading on either variant, while with agentive subjects, verbs of future having like *offer* fail to entail caused possession in either variant. That the meaning of the specific verb plays

Defeasible causatives are found in different semantic classes listed in (1)–(7). For some of them, the ambiguity has already been observed in the literature (e.g. Oehrle 1976 for verbs of caused possession/perception; Hacquard 2006 for *permettre* 'allow/enable,' Ruwet 1994, 1995; Martin 2006: 397–8, and Mari and Martin 2009 for psych-verbs). In order to arrive at a (more) complete list of verbs, we automatically extracted from the searchable version of the *Lexique des verbes français* (Bédaride 2012) all verbs which allow animate and inanimate subjects (around 5,000) and identified manually those which alternate between a culminating and zero-CoS NC reading (around 60 verbs). Examples are given in French and German, as it turns out that the German counterparts of most French verbs identified show the same behavior. These can be further divided into six semantic verb classes. We list some French and German verbs for each subclass. Roughly the same set of verbs give rise to the same ambiguity in many other languages, like Greek (A. Alexiadou, p.c.), Bulgarian (R. Pancheva, p.c.), Spanish, Rumanian (G. Iordăchioaia, p.c.) or Hebrew (N. Boneh, p.c.).

1. Agentive object experiencer psych-verbs and verbs of social interaction: *encourager/ermutigen* 'encourage,' *décourager* 'discourage,' *flatter/schmeicheln* 'flatter,' *provoquer/provozieren* 'provoke,' *offenser/beleidigen* 'offense,' *pousser à/ermuntern* 'push to,' *rassurer/beruhigen* 'reassure,' *embêter/belästigen* 'tease,' *insulter/beleidigen* 'insult,' *humilier* 'humiliate' (cf. Martin 2006: 397–8; Mari and Martin 2009).

(5) a. *Pierre l'a   provoquée, mais cela ne   l'a   pas touchée*
       Pierre her has provoked   but   this NEG her has NEG touched
       du tout.
       at all
       'Pierre provoked her, but this didn't touch her at all.'

   b. *Cette remarque l'a   provoquée, #mais cela ne   l'a   pas*
      this remark   her has provoked   but   this NEG her has NEG
      touchée du tout.
      touched at all
      'This remark provoked her, but this didn't touch her at all.'

2. Verbs of communication: *annoncer/vorhersagen* 'predict,' *attester/bestätigen* 'attest,' *contredire/widersprechen* 'contradict,' *expliquer/erklären* 'explain,' *prédire/vorraussagen* 'predict,' *prévenir/warnen* 'warn,' *questionner* 'question,' *rappeler/erinnern* 'remind,' *avertir* 'inform,' *suggérer/suggerieren* 'suggest.'[4]

---

a critical role in the availability of the inference is also argued for in Rappaport Hovav and Levin (2008: sect. 5).

[4] The CoS denoted by these verbs is *not* the event described in the internal argument, but a psychological CoS in the addressee of the speech act. For instance, *annoncer la fin du monde à y* 'predict the end of the world to y' can roughly be analysed as *cause y to know the end of the world in advance*.

(6) a. *Hans suggerierte ihnen,   dass er ein Genie ist, aber sie   haben es*
Hans suggested   to them that he a   genius is but they have it
keinen   Moment lang geglaubt.
NEG-INDEF.SG moment long believed
'Pierre suggested to them that he is a genius, but they didn't believe it for a moment.'

b. *Sein Verhalten suggerierte ihnen,   dass er ein Genie ist, #aber sie*
his behavior suggested to them that he a genius is but they
haben es keinen   Moment lang geglaubt.
have it NEG-INDEF.SG moment long believed
'His behavior suggested to them that he is a genius, but they didn't believe it for a moment.'

3. **Influence verbs:** Under their agentive reading, these verbs describe an action to induce or to allow someone to perform an action, (cf. Sag and Pollard 1991); these verbs are analysed as causative verbs (meaning 'causing an other to act') by e.g. Koenig and Davis (2001) and Rau (2010): *appeler à/appellieren* 'call for,' *demander/verlangen* 'ask,' *exiger/fordern* 'demand,' *inciter/anstacheln* 'incite,' *inviter* 'invite,' *pousser/drängen* 'push,' *permettre/erlauben* 'allow' (cf. Hacquard 2006: 41, 202), *presser/antreiben* 'urge,' *réclamer/verlangen* 'urge,' *solliciter* 'to urge, call upon,' *exhorter* 'exhort, urge.'

(7) a. *Pierre leur a   demandé beaucoup d'argent, mais personne ne   lui*
Pierre them has asked a lot of money but nobody NEG him
en   a   donné.
some has given
'Pierre asked them for a lot of money, but nobody gave him any.'

b. *Ce projet leur a   demandé beaucoup d'argent, #mais personne*
this project them has asked a lot of money but nobody
n'y   a   consacré un centime.
NEG to it has devoted a penny
'This project asked them for a lot of money, but nobody devoted a penny to it.'

4. **Verbs of caused perception:** *interpeller* 'to shout at, to question,' *montrer/zeigen* 'to show' (cf. Oehrle 1976: 68–113), *manifester* 'to indicate,' *dévoiler* 'reveal,' *révéler* 'reveal,' *témoigner* 'show.'

(8) a. *Marie zeigte   ihm die Schwächen der   Analyse, aber er hat*
Marie showed him the weaknesses of the analysis but he has
sie   nicht gesehen.
them NEG seen
'Marie showed him the weaknesses of the analysis, but he didn't see them.'

b. *Diese Tatsache zeigte   ihm die Schwächen der   Analyse, #aber er*
   this fact   showed him the weaknesses of the analysis, but he
   hat sie   nicht gesehen.
   has them   NEG   seen
   'This fact showed him the weaknesses of the analysis, but he didn't see them.'

5. **Verbs of caused possession**: *attribuer/zuweisen* 'allocate, grant,' *destiner* 'designate, to destine,' *léguer* 'bequeath,' *enseigner/lehren* 'teach' (cf. Oehrle 1976: 76), *envoyer* 'send,' *offrir/bieten* 'offer.'

(9) a. *Der Professor lehrte   sie   Russisch, aber sie   haben kein Wort*
        the professor taught them Russian, but they have no   word
        gelernt.
        learned
        'The professor taught them Russian, but they didn't learn a word.'
    b. *Der Aufenthalt lehrte   sie   Russisch, #aber sie   haben kein Wort*
        the stay   taught them Russian   but they have no   word
        gelernt.
        learned
        'The stay taught them Russian, but they didn't learn a word.'

6. **Epistemic verbs**: *vérifier/verifizieren* 'verify,' *assurer/zusichern, versichern* 'assure/ensure,' *authentifier/bestätigen* 'authenticate,' *garantir/garantieren* 'guarantee,' *certifier/bestätigen* 'certify,' *justifier* 'justify,' *excuser* 'justify', *attester* 'attest,' *démentir* 'contradict.'

(10) a. *L'expert   a   vérifié le   résultat, et   il était incorrect.*
         the expert has verified the result   and it was   incorrect
         'The expert verified the result, and it was incorrect.'
     b. *Ce fait a   vérifié le   résultat, #et   il était incorrect.*
         this fact has verified the result   and it was   incorrect
         'This fact verified the result, and it was incorrect.'

7. **Others**: *soigner* 'cure, treat,' *imperméabiliser* 'waterproof,' *chasser* 'chase away,' *réparer* 'repair/mend' (cf. Ryle 1949),[5] *nettoyer* 'clean' (cf. Levin and Rappaport Hovav 2014), *anesthésier* 'anaesthetize,' *aromatiser* 'flavour,' *cacher* 'hide,' *aider* 'help.'

(11) a. *Ils ont   réparé   mais cela ne   fonctionne toujours pas.*
         they have repaired but   this NEG works   still   NEG
         'They repaired [it] but it still doesn't work.'[6]

---

[5] "'mend' [. . .] is sometimes used as a synonym of 'try to mend'" (Ryle 1949: 132).
[6] fr.board.bigpoint.com/drasaonline/showthread.php?t=660463

b. *Le choc l' a réparé #mais cela ne fonctionne toujours pas.*
   the shock it has repaired but this NEG works still NEG
   'The shock repaired it but it still doesn't work.'

It is important to underline that the non-culminating (NC) reading which appears to require agentivity on the part of the subject is the one where the occurrence of the whole CoS is denied, which, following Demirdache and Martin (2015), we call the "zero-CoS" NC construal. As Demirdache and Martin observe, the "partial-CoS" NC reading, where the occurrence of a final proper part of the CoS only is denied, or where the CoS obtained does not satisfy the maximal value on the relevant scale, is available with verbs associated with a multi-point scale (those whose past participle can be successfully modified by a completion adverbial),[7] and this even in the context of a causer subject. For instance, the sentence in (12) is unproblematic.[8]

(12) *Sa réaction m'a découragée, quoique pas complètement.*
     His reaction me has discouraged, although not completely
     'This reaction discouraged me, although not completely.'

The difference in the continuations in (3a, 11a) vs. (3b, 11b) might suggest that these sentence pairs differ in terms of event structure. The a-examples seem mono-eventive, while the b-examples seem bi-eventive since they describe a CoS besides the causing event. In section 6.3, we show however that for most of the listed verbs, this solution is not tenable: many arguments, including standard event structure tests, show that defeasible causative verbs are bi-eventive under both their culminating and zero-CoS NC readings.[9] The ambiguity should therefore be handled without assuming different event structures. Before this, we show in the next section that, contrary to what happens with modal verbs (see e.g. Hacquard 2006), perfectivity is not required for the culminating reading to be triggered.

The rest of the chapter is structured as follows. In section 6.4, we sketch our analysis of defeasible causatives, which assumes a sublexical modal component in their semantics both with agent and causer subjects. In section 6.5, we show that the zero-CoS NC reading of these verbs is available either with "intentional" or with "non-intentional" agents. In section 6.6, we investigate the conditions under which the zero-CoS NC reading becomes acceptable even with inanimate subjects. Section 6.7 concludes.

---

[7] See e.g. Beavers (2006) and Rappaport Hovav (2008) on verbs that lexicalize a multi-point scale vs. those that lexicalize a two-point scale. Two-point scales have only two values to attribute: to have or not to have the attribute (see e.g. *die*). In contrast, multi-point scales have more than two values for the attribute lexicalized.

[8] See Kearns (2007) and Kennedy and Levin (2008) for related observations about degree achievement verbs derived from an adjective using a scale with a maximal degree, e.g. *darken*.

[9] We come back to mono-eventive verbs showing the same contrast as defeasible causatives in the conclusion. Potential candidates are *demander/verlangern* 'ask,' *exiger/fordern* 'demand.'

6.2 The role of outer aspect

It has been claimed that perfective morphology is required for the so-called implicative reading to be triggered with modal verbs like *pouvoir* 'can' or *permettre* 'allow' (see e.g. Bhatt 1999, Hacquard 2006 on the "actuality entailment" of modal verbs). For instance, *permettre* is said to be implicative under what Hacquard calls the "goal-oriented reading" with a perfective (cf. (13)), but not with an imperfective (cf. (14)).[10]

(13) La carte m'a permis d'entrer dans la bibliothèque, #mais je
 the card me allow.PERF to enter in the library but I
 ne suis pas entrée.
 NEG be NEG entered.
 'The card enabled me to enter the library, but I didn't enter.'

(14) La carte me permettait d'entrer dans la bibliothèque, OK mais je
 the card me allow.IMPERF to enter in the library but I
 ne suis pas entrée.
 NEG be NEG entered.
 'The card enabled me to enter the library, but I didn't enter.'

The so-called "actuality entailment" does not arise in perfective sentences under the deontic reading; cf. (15):

(15) Le professeur m'a permis d'entrer dans la bibliothèque, OK
 the professor me allow.PERF to enter in the library
 mais je ne suis pas entrée.
 but I NEG am NEG entered
 'The professor allowed me to enter the library, but I didn't enter.'

This contrast is similar to ours, since the "non implicative" reading always has an agent subject, and a causer subject always triggers an implicative reading (in perfective sentences at least).

Despite this similarity, we claim that the perfective is not necessary for the contrast with defeasible causatives to arise. We have three arguments in favour of this claim. First, the correlation between the culminating reading and the presence of the causer is also found with the German simple past, which does not entail completion or perfectivity (cf. Reyle et al. 2007). In fact, the result inference arises with a causer no

---

[10] French has two perfective forms, the *passé simple*, which is almost only used in written texts and cannot appear in a range of contexts (e.g. epistemic modals, past subjunctive conditionals), and the *passé composé*, which is the unmarked perfective form. The *passé composé* can be used either as a perfective or as a present perfect. Throughout the examples, we only consider its perfective use, since we do not know yet if the *passé composé* licenses exactly the same range of non-culminating readings for the same predicate when used as a present perfect or a perfective.

matter what reading the German simple past has, including the progressive reading induced by the particle *gerade*; cf. (16):

(16) a. *Sie zeigte ihm gerade die Schwächen der Analyse, aber er*
she show.SP him PROG the weaknesses of the analysis but he
erfasste sie nicht.
understood them NEG
'She was showing him the weaknesses of the analysis, but he didn't understand them.'

b. *Diese Tatsache zeigte ihm gerade die Schwächen der Analyse,*
this fact show.SP him PROG the weaknesses of the analysis
#*aber er erfasste sie nicht.*
but he understood them NEG
'This fact was showing him the weaknesses of the analysis, but he didn't understand them.'

Secondly, with multi-point scale verbs (e.g. *enseigner* 'teach,' *soigner* 'cure'), the causer blocks the zero-CoS NC reading in imperfective sentences too (in this case, of course, only a proper subpart of the CoS is entailed). This is the case when the progressive reading of the imperfective is selected, so that the generic and counterfactual readings of the imperfective are discarded. The progressive construal *en train de V* 'V-ing' univocally selects the progressive reading.[11]

(17) a. *Ce voyage était en train de lui enseigner le russe.* #*Et pourtant,*
this trip was PROG him teach the russian and yet
il n'apprenait rien du tout.
he NEG learn.IMPERF. nothing at all
'This trip was teaching him Russian. And yet, he wasn't learning anything.'

b. *Ce séjour dans la nature était en train de la soigner.* #*Et*
this stay in the nature was PROG her treat and
pourtant, elle ne guérissait pas du tout.
yet she NEG cure.IMPERF. NEG at all
'This stay in nature was treating her but she wasn't recovering at all.'

Thirdly, with some of our French verbs, causers tend to trigger the result inference, unlike agents with the *futur simple*, which does not encode perfectivity:

(18) a. *Pierre lui enseignera le russe, mais elle ne l'apprendra pas.*
Pierre her teach.FUT the russian but she NEG it learn.FUT NEG
'Pierre will teach her Russian, but she won't learn it.'

[11] For obvious reasons, with two-point scale verbs like *offrir* 'offer,' however, no partial event is entailed with the progressive reading of imperfective tenses, since these verbs cannot be used to denote a partial change of state.

b. *Ce voyage lui enseignera le russe, #mais elle ne l'apprendra*
   this trip her teach.FUT the russian but she NEG it learn.FUT
   pas.
   NEG
   'This trip will teach her Russian, but she won't learn it.'

In conclusion, we assume that perfective outer aspect is not necessary for the contrast between the culminating and zero-CoS NC reading to appear with defeasible causatives.

6.3 A first analysis in terms of event complexity

6.3.1 Introduction

Let us return to the question of whether the two readings differ in event complexity. This would mean that the verbs under discussion productively have two event construals. Two ways of implementing this are imaginable. Either these verbs have two different lexical entries—a solution which does not look attractive to us, given that verbs show the same ambiguity language after language. Alternatively, these verbs could basically be result verbs, which however can be coerced into mono-eventive (manner) verbs. Such an ambiguity between a mono-eventive (manner) and a bi-eventive (result) reading has already been proposed for potential counter examples of what has been called "manner/result complementarity" (see Rappaport Hovav and Levin 2010, Levin and Rappaport Hovav 2013, 2014). In Martin and Schäfer (2012), we spelled out in detail how this second hypothesis could be implemented using the framework of Levin and Rappaport Hovav (1995). However, several arguments repeated below show that an analysis along these lines cannot explain the behavior of defeasible causative verbs. The conclusion will be that the verbs at hand do not differ in event structure under their culminating and zero-CoS NC readings. We will begin with a first battery of tests suggesting that with most of our verbs, causers and agents *can* occur in a resultative structure. We will then present arguments showing that agents *have* to occur in a resultative structure even under the zero-CoS NC reading.

6.3.2 Event structure tests

The tests presented below show that not only causers but also agents can trigger a result implication with defeasible causative verbs and, therefore, can occur in a bi-eventive structure. First, not only causers but also agents can license the restitutive reading of *again* (if the result state is reversible and can hold without previous causation). Observe that in (20), the *with*-clause ensures that the animate subject is an agent rather than a causer.

(19) *Dieses Gespräch hat mich endlich wieder ermutigt.*
this conversation has me finally again encouraged
'Finally, this conversation encouraged me again.'

(20) *Hans hat mich mit seiner Rede endlich wieder ermutigt.*
Hans has me with his discourse finally again encouraged
'Finally, Hans encouraged me again with his talk.'

Secondly, verbs like *rassurer* 'calm/reassure' allow time-frame adverbials to measure the change of state. Both causers and agents are compatible with this interpretation of frame adverbials. For instance, (21) can be true if it is the psychological change of state that took five minutes; Pierre's action might have taken more time to be completed.

(21) *Pierre l'a rassurée avec ses mots doux en cinq minutes.*
Pierre her-has reassured with his sweet words in five minutes
'Pierre reassured her with his sweet words in five minutes.'

Observe that again, the *avec* adjunct ensures that Pierre is an agent rather than a causer in (21). Thirdly, with some of our verbs, durative adverbials can measure how long a reversible result state holds. This is possible with causers and agents.

(22) *Hans ermutigte ihn einige Minuten entlang, aber dann verlor er*
Hans encouraged him some minutes long but then lost he
seinen Mut wieder.
his courage again
'Hans encouraged him for some minutes, but then he lost his courage again.'

Fourthly, most of the German defeasible causative verbs form *-ung* nominalizations with both agents and causers as external arguments (cf. (23)). But Roßdeutscher and Kamp (2010) extensively argue that *-ung* nominalizations can only be formed from bi-eventive, i.e. resultative verbs (cf. (24a) vs. (24b)).

(23) *die Ermutigung der Kinder durch den Lehrer/ durch das*
the encouragement of-the children by the teacher/ by the
Ereignis
event
'the encouragement of the children by the teacher/by the event'

(24) a. *Sperr-ung* (clos-ing); *Warn-ung* (warn-ing)
b. **Tanz-ung* (danc-ing); **Ess-ung* (eat-ing)

We conclude that not only causers but also agents *can* occur in a bi-eventive structure. But there are also arguments which point to the stronger conclusion that, in the context of defeasible causatives, agents *must* occur in a bi-eventive structure just as causers.

First, German *-ung* nominalizations do not necessarily have a culminating interpretation, cf. (25). If they do indeed depend on a bi-eventive event structure, the lack of a result implication cannot be explained by the absence of a CoS in the event structure.

(25)   *Er schickte ihnen eine Warn-ung, aber sie haben sie nicht verstanden.*
      he sent   them a   warn-ing but they have it not understood
      'He sent them a warning, but they did not understand it.'

Secondly, many of the defeasible causatives are polymorphemic and involve a result-noun, an adjective, or a resultative preposition in their morphology:

(26) a. en-courage$_N$-er [$_{VoiceP}$ subj.DP Voice [$_{vP}$ v$_{cause}$ [$_{PP}$ DP en$_P$ [$_{DP}$ courage]]]]
     b. er-mutig$_A$-en [$_{VoiceP}$ DP Voice [$_{vP}$ v$_{cause}$ [$_{AdjP}$ DP mutig$_A$]]]
     c. an-regen [$_{VoiceP}$ DP Voice [$_{vP}$ v$_{cause}$ [$_{PP}$ DP. an$_P$]]]

The zero-CoS NC uses of these verbs show, of course, the same morphological complexity (and observe that in languages like Hebrew, overt causative morphology shows up with the zero-CoS NC reading of defeasible causative verbs too; Nora Boneh, p.c.). If there is a strict mapping from form to interpretation and a meaningful composition of the meaning of the complex word from the meanings of its subparts, then even the zero-CoS NC uses must build on a bi-eventive composition. Otherwise, we would have to assume morphologically complex roots acting as manner modifiers. But it is not clear where these complex roots should come from.

Thirdly, many of the verbs studied are ditransitives. Given the proposal that indirect objects are not lexical arguments of verbal constants but are introduced by (low) applicative heads or stative/possessive event predicates (e.g. Pylkkänen 2008), it is not clear how an indirect object could be licensed in a mono-eventive structure (recall that the presence of an indirect object does not necessarily make the sentence culminating).

Fourthly, defeasible causatives with agent subjects also do not show other properties of non-core transitive verbs such as resultative formation (27) (cf. Levin 1999).

(27) **Er ermunterte die Kinder zuversichtlich.*
     he encouraged the children confident
     'He caused the children to be confident by encouraging them.'

The hypothesis that the zero-CoS NC use of defeasible causatives involves a mono-eventive event structure is thus hardly tenable: defeasible causatives are bi-eventive with causers *and* agents.

In the next section, we briefly summarize our analysis of defeasible causatives. It makes use of the sublexical modal component of Koenig and Davis (2001).

6.4 Defeasible causatives as sublexical modal verbs

6.4.1 Sublexical modality

Some defeasible causatives like *offer*, *urge*, and *require* are addressed by Koenig and Davis (2001), who introduce modality in their semantics. They propose to divide the semantics of verbs into two components.[12] The "situational core component" categorizes types of relations between participants in situations and the roles the participants play in them (i.e. argument and event structures). The "sublexical modal" component (a modal base) evaluates these relations at various world indices. Koenig and Davis (2001) assume that, while in the case of plain modal verbs like *must*, the selection of the modal base is contextually determined, for verbs like *offer* or *require*, the modal base is lexically specified.[13]

Most of our defeasible causative verbs are what Koenig and Davis call "energetic modals": the modal base contains all worlds in which the action of the agent achieves her/his goal (see the paraphrase (28b) of (28a)).

(28) a. Susan offered Brenda 10 euros.
 b. Susan caused Brenda to have 10 euros in all worlds where the goal of her offer is achieved.

Introducing modality in the semantics of these verbs nicely allows us to keep a bi-eventive decomposition for these verbs (as (28b) shows, the event structure of *offer* involves a cause relation; cf. also (33)), without having to assume that they entail a CoS in all their uses. Given the conclusion adopted here that verbs at hand are bi-eventive in both uses, this is what we need. Note in passing that in adopting Koenig and Davis' sublexical modal component, we depart from the often-adopted implicit premise (cf. e.g. Rappaport Hovav and Levin 2010) that the event with which the root is associated has to be entailed by the verb in the actual world w_0. For us, a verb's root can be associated to the CoS even if a CoS is not entailed in w_0.

Koenig and Davis (2001) focus on the agentive use of defeasible causatives, and therefore do not address the ambiguity between the culminating and zero-CoS NC readings. The same is true of Rappaport Hovav and Levin (2008) and Beavers (2010), who also adopt their sublexical modality component. In order to capture the difference

---

[12] Under the assumption that linking constraints (for direct arguments) only depend on the situational core component and are insensitive to the sublexical modality, this allows them to explain that verbs like *give* and *offer* have the same linking pattern, although only the former entails a result in the actual world.

[13] As e.g. the circumfix *ka...-a* lexically encodes circumstantial modality in Salish languages, (cf. Davis et al. 2009). See Vander Klok (2012) for a cross-linguistic semantic typology of modals with respect to the lexicalization of the modal force and/or the modal base.

in interpretation of verbs at hand with causer and agent subjects, one could at first sight assume a lexical ambiguity with a sublexical modal component present with agents but not with causers. However, this is not the right way to go, because, as will be shown in section 6.6, in some contexts it is possible to cancel the inference that the CoS takes place even with causer subjects. This can only be accounted for if the modal base can operate with both types of subjects.

6.4.2 Proposal

In Martin and Schäfer (2012), we argue that defeasible causatives are bi-eventive and involve a modal base on any use, and lexically encode the modal force of necessity. An argument in favor of positing a sublexical modal component for these verbs relates to scopal ambiguities. If defeasible causative verbs have a modal operator in their lexical representation, we indeed predict ambiguities to occur in the presence of other quantifiers. Scopal interactions between pure modal verbs and quantifiers have been observed, for example, by von Fintel and Iatridou (2003: 175) for deontic modals and by Huitink (2008) and Wolf (2014) for epistemic modals. In Martin and Schäfer (2012), we could not report any ambiguity of this type with defeasible causative verbs, conjecturing that this might be related to the type of modality involved. But Kratzer (2013) observes that existential quantifiers do indeed trigger an ambiguity with verbs like *offer*. As she notices, if I offer you a bench, either there is no bench that I offer you (the indefinite direct object is in the scope of modality) or there is such a bench in the base world (the existential quantifier outscopes the modal component).[14]

In Martin and Schäfer (2012), we captured the differences between the culminating and zero-CoS NC readings through the choice of the modal base:

- With agent subjects, the modal base is typically energetic (or goal-oriented): it contains those worlds where the goal of the agent is achieved. Since the world of evaluation is not necessarily included in the modal base, the CoS does not have to take place in the actual world. The verb therefore triggers a "CoS implicature" rather than a "CoS implication."
- With causer subjects, the modal base is typically circumstantial. The world of evaluation is therefore not filtered out and, thus, necessarily quantified over. However, in some contexts, defeasible causatives with causer subjects are evaluated with respect to a stereotypical modal base. In that case, the verb does not have its culminating reading.

---

[14] In fact, Kratzer (2013) observes that existential transportation even fails with a subset of non-defeasible causative verbs, e.g. *give* (vs. *hand*), that she consequently treats as involving sublexical modality too. Her argument runs as follows. Let us assume that Ede sells 75 balls to Mats, gives him 25 balls for free, and puts 100 balls in a box. In that case, it is not true that there are 25 balls such that Ede gave them to Mats. However, existential transportation is ensured with English *hand* or French *passer* 'pass,' as the reader may check.

We cast this proposal in the way illustrated in (29), through the lexical representation associated to the VP *offrir y à z* in (33). In (33), ρ is a free variable for the modal base, where a modal base is viewed as a function from worlds to sets of worlds. So, for example, $\rho(w)$ is the set of worlds that are ρ-compatible with w.

(29) [$_{VP}$ offrir y à z] ⤳ (to be revised)
$\lambda y \lambda z \lambda e [\text{offer}(e) \wedge \text{theme}(e, y) \wedge \text{recipient}(e, z) \wedge$
$\Box_\rho \exists e'(\text{cause}(e, e') \wedge \text{have}(e') \wedge \text{possessee}(e', y) \wedge \text{possessor}(e', z))]$
$=_{\text{def}} \lambda y \lambda z \lambda e [\text{OFFER}(\rho, e, z, y)]$
Conditions:
(i) $\forall e \forall z \forall y (\text{OFFER}(\rho, e, z, y) \wedge \exists x(\text{agent}(e, x))) \rightarrow$
$\rho = \text{energetic})$
(the existence of an agent implies an energetic modal base)
(ii) $\forall e \forall z \forall y (\text{OFFER}(\rho, e, z, y) \wedge \exists x(\text{causer}(e, x))) \rightarrow$
$\rho = \text{circumstantial} \vee \rho = \text{stereotypical})$
(the existence of a causer implies a circumstantial or a stereotypical modal base)

The representation ensures that in all uses, *offrir y à z* entails the occurrence of an event which is an offer, has y as its theme, and z as its recipient. But since the caused possession is within the scope of the modal operator, it takes place only in those worlds which are contained in the modal base. The verb is furthermore associated with two conditions. The first ensures that the existence of an agent implies an energetic modal base, while the second ensures that the existence of a causer implies a circumstantial or a stereotypical modal base. The truth conditions for $\Box_\rho$ are standard, with respect to a model M, an assignment function g, and a world w:

(30) $[\![\Box_\rho \phi]\!]^{M,g,w} = 1$ *iff* for all $w' \in \rho(w)$, $[\![\phi]\!]^{M,g,w'} = 1$.

Piñón (2014) points out that this analysis raises a problem. In Martin and Schäfer (2012), we suggested that the analysis sketched above does not oblige us to postulate that defeasible causative verbs are lexically ambiguous. However, Piñón argues that it actually does, because the choice of agent or causer is mutually exclusive (and the choice of modal base depends on this choice). Moreover, since it is not clear how to relate agents and causers, it is also not clear how to relate the two senses of defeasible causative verbs.

Additionally, Martin (2015) shows that standard (i.e. non-defeasible) causatives like *ouvrir* 'open' also confirm the link between agentivity and CoS deniability in progressive sentences. For instance, the inference that the door started to open is much more strongly conveyed by (32) (with a causer subject) than (31) (with an agentive subject).

(31) Ana is opening the door. But it is so well stuck in the frame that there is a good chance that it will take a long time before it starts moving even a little bit.

(32) The wind is opening the door. #But it is so well stuck in the frame that there is a good chance that it will take a long time before it starts moving even a little bit.

We therefore looked for a unified account for the two phenomena, which made us give up our original hypothesis that the contrast between the culminating and zero-CoS NC construal of defeasible causatives has to be captured through the choice of the modal base.

A third problem of the account sketched in Martin and Schäfer (2012) is that it redescribes the facts rather than explaining them, since the question of why the modal base is typically energetic with agents and typically circumstantial with causers is left unanswered.

In the new analysis adopted here, the sublexical modal causative structure encodes a modal base that contains what we call "causally successful" worlds in both their agentive and nonagentive uses. We therefore assume a single lexical entry for defeasible causatives, both with agent and with causer subjects, see (33).

(33) [$_{VP}$ offrir y à z] ⇝
$\lambda y \lambda z \lambda e [\textbf{offer}(e) \wedge \textbf{theme}(e, y) \wedge \textbf{recipient}(e, z) \wedge$
$\Box_{\text{causal\_success}} \exists e'(\textbf{cause}(e, e') \wedge \textbf{have}(e') \wedge \textbf{possessee}(e', y) \wedge \textbf{possessor}(e', z))]$
$=_{\text{def}} \lambda y \lambda z \lambda e [\textbf{OFFER}(e, z, y)]$

We define causally successful worlds as those worlds that have duplicates of the event described by the verb, where the encoded CoS is obtained, and where the "conditions of success" that are possibly associated with the event described by the verb are fullfilled. This is very much in the spirit of Kratzer's (2013) definition of the modal domain of transfer of possession verbs like *offer* or *bequeath*, which she defines as containing those worlds "that have duplicates of the event described by the verb, where whatever obligations were established by that event are honored, where whatever rights were conferred by that event are exercised."

For *offer*, the encoded CoS is a change of possession, and the conditions of success are that the offer is accepted by the beneficiary and honored by the offerer. Conditions of success are very prominent for those defeasible causatives that are performative verbs, like *offer*.[15] For other verbs like *soigner* 'treat' or *enseigner* 'teach', conditions of success are much less salient, and perhaps even inexistent. Therefore, for these purely descriptive (i.e. non-normative) verbs, causally successful worlds trivially amount to those worlds in which the CoS takes place.

This analysis has not yet accounted for the difference in interpretation of these verbs with agent vs. causer subjects. We refer the reader to Martin (2015), which offers an

---

[15] Those verbs can be used in explicit performative sentences, e.g. *I hereby offer you to come*. On these verbs, see e.g. Searle (1989) and Condoravdi and Lauer (2011). There is a huge literature on the conditions of success of performative verbs in the tradition initiated by Austin and Searle, which could help to define more precisely, for each verb, what exactly are the conditions that make the speech act successful.

analysis that explains the variation in the interpretation of these verbs through an extralexical pragmatic principle that has to do with the conceptualization of agentive vs. non-agentive causation events. This principle accounts for why the base world is typically within the modal base with causers, and under which particular conditions it can be filtered out even with such inanimate subjects.[16]

In the next sections we investigate the relation between agentivity and intentionality, in order to clarify under which conditions the result implication can be cancelled with an agent (section 6.5), and look at cases where the inference that a result takes place can be cancelled with inanimate subjects (section 6.6). The data presented in section 6.6 are crucial in that they justify our proposal, illustrated in (33), according to which defeasible causative verbs have a modal component with both agent and causer subjects.

6.5 Defeasible causatives with animate subjects

The observation reported in this section is that the CoS inference can be cancelled as soon as the subject's referent performs an action which satisfies the description of the VP. This is true even when there is a discrepancy between this event description and the content of the intention of which this action is the direct execution.

Prima facie, in the context of an animate subject, we would expect the CoS inference not to be cancellable as soon as the VP is modified by an adverbial like *sans le faire exprès* 'without doing it on purpose,' *sans le vouloir* 'without wanting it,' or *non-intentionnellement* 'unintentionally.' Indeed, "non-intentional" agents seem at first sight to be identifiable with causers. However, examples (34a,b) show that this is a wrong move.[17] They illustrate that it is sometimes possible to cancel the inference that a CoS takes place with animate subjects even in the presence of these adverbials.

(34) a. *Marie lui a montré sans le vouloir les problèmes de son*
Marie him has showed without it want the problems of his
analyse, mais il ne les a pas du tout perçus.
analysis but he NEG them NEG has at all perceived

---

[16] Martin's (2015) account builds on the recent analysis of the progressive by Varasdi (2014). Very briefly, her idea is that the zero-CoS NC construal is possible in progressive and perfective sentences *iff* the "CoS-less causation event" has properties that "indicate" and "sustain" (in Varasdi's sense) the CoS type encoded by the verb. The advantage of the account proposed is that it provides a unified explanation for zero-CoS NC interpretations of causative verbs in perfective *and* progressive sentences, even if the modality does not have the same source in both cases: in progressive sentences, the CoS is shifted to possible worlds by outer aspect (PROG), while in perfective sentences, this job is done by the sublexical component (which explains why in perfectives sentences, the zero-CoS NC reading is lexically restricted).

[17] Control morphology in Salish languages also suggests that agentive readings are not systematically intentional (see e.g. Demirdache 1997, Jacobs 2011, and references therein). Furthermore, Martin (2016) shows that zero-CoS NC readings are available with some of the interpretations of adverbials like *inadvertently* or *by mistake* in Mandarin Chinese and Korean. See also Martin and Schäfer (2014) on a typology of external arguments distinguishing agentivity, intentionality, and control.

'Marie showed him without wanting to the problems of his analysis, but he didn't perceive them.'

b. *Il   les   a   prévenus   sans   le faire   exprès   de sa   visite*
   he them has told   without it make intentionally of his visit
   qu'il   voulait   garder   secrète, mais heureusement   ils   ne   l'ont
   that he wanted keep   secret   but   fortunately   they NEG it have
   pas   réalisé.
   NEG realized
   'He told them unintentionally about his visit that he wanted to keep secret, but fortunately they didn't take notice of it.'

The CoS inference can thus be cancelled, although these adverbials indicate a discrepancy between the content of the agent's intention and the description of the VP (Kamp 1999–2007).

This does not mean that any animate subject licenses the zero-CoS NC reading. In order to cancel the inference that the CoS takes place, we need a context which makes clear that the subject's referent performs an action which coincides with the description of the VP (although the intention motivating this action might not coincide with this description). If, on the contrary, the context indicates that the subject's referent, although animate, does not perform any action, the CoS inference acts like an entailment. For instance, the CoS inference seems systematically entailed in presence of the adverbial *without doing a thing* (on a related point, see Oehrle 1976: 84):

(35) a. *Sans   rien   faire, Pierre lui   a   montré les   problèmes de*
        without nothing do   Pierre her has showed the problems   of
        l'analyse,   # mais elle ne   les   a   pas vus.
        the analysis but   she NEG them has NEG seen
        'Without doing a thing, Pierre showed her the problems of the analysis, but she didn't see them.'

   b. *Sans   rien   faire, il   les   a   prévenus de sa   visite qu'il*
      without nothing do   he them has told   of his visit that he
      voulait garder secrète, # mais heureusement ils   ne   l'ont   pas
      wanted keep   secret   but   fortunately   they NEG it have NEG
      réalisé.
      realized
      'Without doing a thing, he told them about his visit that he wanted to keep secret, but fortunately they didn't take notice of it.'

In conclusion, in the context of an animate subject, the CoS inference cannot be cancelled if the subject's referent does not perform an action; and it can be cancelled as soon as the action performed coincides with the description of the VP, no matter whether or not the content of the intention executed by this action coincides with this description. In the typology of Dowty (1972: ch. 5) and Kamp (1999–2007), the sentences in (34) are examples of the "non-intentional agentive reading" (the act performed verifies the description provided by the VP, but not the content of the agent's intention), while (35) gives examples of the "non-agentive reading" (the causing event is not an act, under any description).

6.6 Defeasible causatives with inanimate subjects

With an inanimate subject, there are at least two types of contexts where defeasible causatives allow us to cancel the inference that the result takes place, which we review in the next subsections.

6.6.1 Causers vs. instruments

With some defeasible causative verbs at least, the result implicature is more easily cancellable if the subject's referent can be conceived as the instrument of an implicit agent; compare the a- and b-examples below.

(36) a. *Le discours du recteur l'a vraiment flatté à plusieurs*
 the discourse of the dean him has really flattered on several
 reprises, mais cela l'a laissé complètement indifférent.
 occasions but this him has left completely indifferent
 'The speech of the dean really flattered him on several occasions, but it left him totally unmoved.'

 b. *Ce détail l'a vraiment flatté, #mais cela l'a laissé*
 this detail him has really flattered but this him has left
 complètement indifférent.
 completely indifferent
 'This detail really flattered him, but it left him totally unmoved.'

(37) a. *Ce traitement médical l'a soigné, et pourtant ça n'a*
 this therapy medical him has treated and yet this NEG has
 rien changé à son état.
 nothing changed on his state
 'This medical therapy treated him, and yet it didn't change his state at all.'

 b. *Ce séjour chez ma soeur l'a soigné, #et pourtant ça*
 This stay at my sister him has treated and yet this
 n'a rien changé à son état.
 NEG has nothing changed on his state
 'This stay at my sister's place treated him, and yet it didn't change his state at all.'

As the reader may check, the inanimate subject of the a-sentences can easily be expressed with an overtly instrumental *avec/with*-PP (see e.g. *The doctor treated him with this medical therapy* in (37a)). This paraphrase is less natural for the subject of b-sentences. Why instruments enable us to cancel the CoS inference is accounted for in Martin (2015).

6.6.2 Abnormal reactions

With an inanimate subject, it is also possible to cancel the CoS inference in a context making clear that the reaction of the internal argument's referent to the eventuality involving the causer is abnormal and/or unexpected. For example, in the a-examples in (38, 39), the context indicates that the object's referent reacts in an unexpected, absent-minded, crazy, or stupid way to the event involving the subject's referent.

(38) a. *Objectivement, la chute de pierres les a bel et bien prévenus*
objectively the fall of stones them has well and truly warned
du danger! Il faut vraiment qu'ils aient été bien
of the danger it must be really that they have-SUBJ been well
étourdis pour ne pas s'en rendre compte.
absent-minded for NEG NEG REFL of it render account
'Objectively, the stone fall well and truly warned them of the danger! They must have been really absent-minded not to realize it.'

b. *La chute de pierre les a prévenus du danger. #Mais ils*
the fall of stone them has warned of the danger but they
ne s'en sont pas rendu compte.
NEG REFL of it be NEG rendered account
'The stone fall warned them of the danger. But they didn't realize it.'

(39) a. *Clairement, cette situation leur a bel et bien montré le*
clearly this situation them has well and truly showed the
problème! C'est fou qu'ils ne l'aient pas vu!
problem it is crazy that they NEG it have-SUBJ NEG seen
'Clearly, this situation well and truly showed them the problem! It is crazy that they didn't see it!'

b. *Cette situation leur a montré le problème, #mais il ne*
this situation them has showed the problem but they NEG
l'ont pas vu.
it have NEG seen
'This situation showed them the problem, but they didn't see it.'

Interestingly, this inference is much easier to cancel in presence of the evidential adverb *objectivement* 'objectively' and *clairement* 'clearly.' Often, the suspension of the inference is even easier in the presence of the discourse marker *bel et bien* 'well and truly' or *tout de même* 'nevertheless'. In a similar way, in German the CoS inference becomes cancellable in such abnormal contexts and in presence of evidential adverbials like *objektiv betrachtet* and *klar und deutlich* and discourse markers like *zwar...aber* or *doch*:

(40) a. *Diese Situation hat ihnen doch klar und deutlich das Problem*
the situation has them after all well and clearly the problem
gezeigt. Es ist verrückt, dass sie es trotzdem nicht gesehen
showed it is crazy that they it nevertheless not seen
haben!
have
'This situation after all well and truly showed them the problem. It is crazy that they didn't see it nevertheless!'

b. *Diese Situation hat ihnen das Problem gezeigt, #aber sie haben es*
the situation has them the problem showed but they have it
nicht gesehen.
not seen
'This situation showed them the problem, but they didn't see it.'

We refer the reader to Martin and Schäfer (2012) and Martin (2015) for an account of the reason why evidential adverbials *objectivement/clairement* 'objectively/clearly' and adverbials of contrast like *bel et bien* 'well and truly' help to cancel the CoS inference.

6.7 Conclusions

We started from the observation that the interpretation of defeasible causative verbs like *offer* varies with the nature of the external theta-role. We adopted the hypothesis argued for in Martin and Schäfer (2013) that the two uses do not differ in event complexity—even the zero-CoS NC reading involves a bi-eventive structure. We argued that these verbs involve a sublexical modal base with both agent and causer subjects, but abandoned Martin and Schäfer's (2012) proposal to capture the difference between the culminating and zero-CoS NC readings through the choice of the modal base. Nevertheless, we do not account for the role of the external argument on the interpretation of these verbs, and do not explain why the zero-CoS NC construal is systematically available with an agent subject and sometimes available only in the context of a causer subject.

The analysis sketched throughout this chapter leaves open several questions. First, we have not investigated in detail the aspectual shifts that seem to be involved in the switch from an agent subject to a causer subject (also noted for some of our verbs by Piñón 2014). Often, what looks like an accomplishment with an agent suddenly exhibits some characteristic properties of an achievement verb with a causer: adverbials tend to scope lower in the event structure, and so on. In other cases, what looks eventive with an agent seems stative with a causer. We deliberately left these aspectual differences aside because the aspectual switch is not consistent through the whole class of defeasible causatives. But we will have to investigate these differences to check whether they undermine our proposal that we only need one lexical entry for these verbs.[18] A second question concerns verbs of desire like *vouloir* 'want,' *demander* 'ask,' or *exiger* 'demand,' which raise two problems. For reasons that we do not understand, they invariably trigger a CoS implication with causer subjects, even in presence of evidential adverbials like *objectivement, clairement* 'objectively, clearly,' which normally help to license a zero-CoS NC reading.

(41) Objectivement, ce projet a bel et bien demandé beaucoup d'argent! # Mais contre toute attente, personne n'y a accordé un centime!
'Objectively, this project well and truly asked for a lot of money! But against all expectations, nobody devoted a single cent to it!'

Furthermore, contrary to defeasible causative verbs, these verbs seem mono-eventive: they do not form *-ung* nominalizations in German and look monomorphemic (cf. Martin and Schäfer 2013).[19] If they are indeed mono-eventive, how should we handle the difference between their culminating and zero-CoS NC readings? Martin and Schäfer (2014) show that *laver* 'wash,' a mono-eventive verb conventionally associated with a CoS (i.e. *get clean*), also sees its interpretation varying with the theta-role of the external argument: while "agent" *laver* easily allows the denial of the conventionally associated CoS (cf. Talmy 2000 for *wash*), "causer" *laver* does not. So it seems that the contrast under consideration extends to a subset of mono-eventive verbs that can take either an agent or a causer subject.

Finally, it remains to be seen whether the connection explored here between agentivity and zero-CoS non-culmination can be extended to similar predicates in other languages. Demirdache and Martin (2015) showed that in many languages with productive non-culminating construals, like Mandarin (Demirdache and Sun 2014) and Salish languages (Bar-el et al. 2005; Jacobs 2011), whenever an accomplishment (and particularly a causative accomplishment) admits a non-culminating construal, this is the case only when some agentive properties are ascribed to the subject (crucially, they leave open the possibility that the relevant agentive properties are instantiated by inanimates in particular contexts). Demirdache and Martin refer to this correlation as the AGENT CONTROL HYPOTHESIS (ACH). Importantly, they show that languages differ

---

[18] Note that we can capture both the eventive and stative readings of a causative verb through one semantic representation if we assume that its Davidsonian argument can have dynamic events *or* states in its range (see e.g. Kratzer 2000 for such an approach applied to verbs like *obstruct*).
[19] This problem arises also for verbs like *enseigner/lehren* 'teach'; for instance, *lehren* does not have *-ung* nominalization.

with respect to the type of non-culminating reading requiring agenthood. On one hand, Mandarin resembles French and German in that only "zero-CoS" NC construals require an agentive subject. On the other hand, in Salish languages, even "partial-CoS" NC seem to require agenthood properties (through control morphology). The question, then, is to see how these cross-linguistic differences can be accounted for.

Acknowledgments

We are very grateful to Christopher Piñón for his valuable comments and suggestions on previous versions of this chapter, as well as to David-Étienne Bouchard and the editors for their constructive reviews. We would also like to thank Artemis Alexiadou, Nora Boneh, Hamida Demirdache, Hans Kamp, Jean-Pierre Koenig, Antje Roßdeutscher, and Peter Svenonius as well as the audiences and reviewers of WCCFL 30, the Semantics and Pragmatics Workshop of Stanford University (especially Cleo Condoravdi and Sven Lauer), the "Modality in Ottawa" workshop (especially Angelika Kratzer and Robert Truswell), and the workshop "Agent control over non-culminating events" in Chronos 11, Pisa, for their feedback. This work is part of the projects B5 "Polysemy in a conceptual system" and B6 "Underspecification in voice systems and the syntax–morphology interface" of the Collaborative Research Center 732 hosted by the University of Stuttgart and financed by the Deutsche Forschung Gemeinschaft.

7

Straddling the line between attitude verbs and necessity modals

AYNAT RUBINSTEIN

7.1 Introduction

What is the relationship between attitude verbs and modals? Although the analysis of attitude verbs as modal operators has been the standard approach in semantics since Hintikka's (1969) seminal work, direct comparison of the range of meanings expressed by modals and attitude verbs has not been systematically undertaken. Understanding the differences and similarities between these predicates is important for several reasons. Theoretically, this understanding is a prerequisite for a theory of modality that aspires to predict the range of modal meanings that languages can express. It also has applications in the acquisition of modality, in typology, and in language change.

In this chapter, I approach the question of the relationship between attitude verbs and modals by looking at representative lexical items from these two categories, which seem to express meanings that are closely related and have to do with what follows from one's desires or goals: the verb *want* as a prototypical attitude of desire (1a), and the adjective *necessary* as a prototypical modal expressing goal-oriented necessity (1b).

(1)   a. Sue **wants** to teach Tuesdays-Thursdays.
      b. It is **necessary** that Sue teach Tuesdays-Thursdays.

I begin with an evaluation of recent developments in the semantics of desire predicates, focusing on comparative and modal accounts stemming from Heim (1992). I show that Heim's original approach, which compares the desirability of a proposition to the desirability of its negation, is capable of dealing with a type of supposed counterexample that has motivated the introduction of sets of alternatives to recent semantic analyses of desire predicates. This paves the way for a more unified analysis of desire verbs and goal-oriented modals, updating the Heimian analysis with insights from the recent literature.

Modality Across Syntactic Categories. First edition. Ana Arregui, María Luisa Rivero, and Andrés Salanova (eds.).
This chapter © Aynat Rubinstein 2017. First published 2017 by Oxford University Press.

The second part of the chapter concerns *necessary*. Contrary to widespread assumptions, I argue that this modal receives only goal-oriented interpretations in the configuration in (1b); other types (or "flavors") of modality are ruled out, even in supporting contexts.

I propose a modal analysis of *want* and *necessary* and end with a comparison of these predicates with prototypical modal verbs that express necessity, in particular *have to* and *ought to*. The subtle differences between members of this family of predicates paint an intricate picture of how expressions of modal necessity may vary.

7.2 Attitude verbs of desire

Attitude verbs of desire intuitively have a preference-based meaning: what we want, long for, desire, wish, or hope to do reflects the preferences we have regarding different states of affairs. Wanting to go on vacation, for example, reflects a preference for going on vacation, which in turn can be modeled in a number of ways: (i) comparing the options of going on vacation to not doing so and preferring the former (a comparative analysis), (ii) singling out vacation as the best possible outcome (a modal analysis), or (iii) evaluating the expected gain of going on vacation as the highest among the available options (a utilitarian analysis). All three analytical options have been explored in the literature.[1] In this section, I review the well-known comparative analysis of *want* developed by Heim (1992) as well as its modal implementation (due to von Fintel 1999) in order to evaluate a range of amendments to this analysis that have been proposed by Villalta (2000, 2006, 2008).

Villalta's work addresses two key aspects of the Heimian analysis: the idea that desires are related to (and restricted by) beliefs, and the idea that wanting is a comparative attitude. Villalta (2008) argues convincingly that the relationship between desire and belief is rather loose, since even if one believes that two propositions are equivalent, one may still desire one of them more than the other. Second, she argues that a two-way comparison between the prejacent proposition and its negation is insufficient to capture the meaning of desire predicates. Instead, the prejacent is said to be compared in the general case not just to its negation, but to a set of contextually determined alternatives.

In this section, I evaluate the evidence that has been brought to bear on the mechanics of comparison in desire statements, contending that in fact there is no theoretical motivation for complicating the original Heimian analysis by introducing sets of alternatives to the semantics. I then propose a comparative-modal analysis of *want* that incorporates Villalta's (2006, 2008) insight about a relaxed reliance of belief in desire statements.

---

[1] The utilitarian approach to the semantics of desire predicates will not be discussed in detail here, but see van Rooij (1999), Levinson (2003), Lassiter (2011).

One important issue I set aside here concerns the monotonicity properties of desire predicates. The question of whether or not, or under what conditions, verbs of desire give rise to monotonic inferences has played a central role in motivating the different analyses of *want* that will be discussed here. See Crnič (2011) for an overview and the most recent word in this debate.

7.2.1 Comparison of alternatives

The comparative approach to desire predicates originates in Stalnaker's (1984) diagnosis of wanting as an attitude that involves comparison of alternatives.

[...] wanting something is preferring it to certain relevant alternatives, the relevant alternatives being those possibilities that the agent believes will be realized if he does not get what he wants. (Stalnaker 1984: 89)

Heim (1992) uses this characterization as motivation for a conditional comparative semantics for desire verbs. According to her proposal, every desire statement is implicitly conditional. In her words:

An important feature of this analysis is that it sees a hidden conditional in every desire report. A little more explicitly, the leading intuition is that *John wants you to leave* means that John thinks that if you leave he will be in a more desirable world than if you don't leave. (Heim 1992: 193)

Both the comparative and the belief-related aspects of Heim's analysis are present in this informal description. Within the realm of what the subject (John) believes is the case, the prejacent (that you leave) is required to represent a better possibility for the subject than its negation (that you don't leave). The idea that desires are evaluated in light of one's beliefs, not in light of what is actually the case, is motivated by examples like (2). Patrick may have a desire to sell a cello which is not in fact in his possession, but which he thinks is.

(2) Patrick is under the misconception that he owns a cello, and he **wants** to sell his cello. (Heim 1992: 183(2))

More formally, the conditional paraphrase is used to implement a semantics for desire verbs using a version of the semantics proposed for conditionals (indicative and counterfactual) by Stalnaker (1968) and Lewis (1973). In this tradition, a conditional sentence of the form *If ϕ, then ψ* is true in a world w if and only if the consequent ψ is true, not necessarily in w, but in the worlds most similar to w in which the antecedent ϕ is true. For any proposition p and world w, the p-worlds most similar to w are abbreviated as $Sim_w(p)$.

(3) $Sim_w(p) = \{w' \in W : w' \in p$ and w' resembles w no less than any other world in $p\}$. (Heim 1992: 195, 197)

According to the conditional paraphrase, *a wants p* means, roughly, that *a* considers the *p*-worlds she can think of to be better than the ¬*p*-worlds she can think of. Thus, in addition to the above comparison of possibilities based on similarity, there is a second comparison of possibilities (von Fintel 1999: 119). This comparison, defined in (4a) for worlds and in (4b) for propositions, is based on the desires or preferences of the subject.[2]

(4) a. For any $w, w', w'' \in W$,
$w' <_{a,w} w''$ iff w' is more desirable to *a* in *w* than w''.
b. For any $w \in W, X \subseteq W, Y \subseteq W$,
$X <_{a,w} Y$ iff $w' <_{a,w} w''$ for all $w' \in X, w'' \in Y$. (Heim 1992: 197)

Putting the pieces together, an informal version of Heim's (1992) analysis of *want* is given in (5). Motivation for the two additional ingredients of the analysis is discussed immediately below. The formal version is given in (7).

(5) *Basic idea for want*:
Compare the desirability of the *q*-worlds most similar to *w* to the desirability of the ¬*q*-worlds most similar to *w*, for every world *w* in the subject's belief worlds.
Additional ingredients:
(i) Only compare the desirability of worlds that agree with the subject's beliefs.
(ii) Presuppose that the subject believes neither *q* nor ¬*q*.

Motivation for restricting the desirability comparison to the subject's belief worlds (as in (i)) comes from examples like (6).

(6) I **want** to teach Tuesdays and Thursdays next semester. (Heim 1992: 195(35))

Let's assume a situation in which the possibility that I don't teach at all next semester is more desirable to me than the possibility that I get a good teaching assignment. Suppose moreover that teaching next semester is a given, and that I believe that it is impossible for me not to teach. That is, in all the worlds that represent my beliefs in the evaluation world (these worlds are called my "doxastic alternatives" in the evaluation world, or the worlds "doxastically accessible" to me in the evaluation world, or simply my "belief worlds"), I teach next semester. Even though worlds in which I don't teach at all are more desirable to me, (6) is typically judged true if it is taken for granted that I will teach. Thus, it seems that the desirability comparison cannot reach out to worlds that are not doxastically accessible to the subject in a given situation.

---

[2] Note that Heim uses a non-standard definition for comparing the desirability of propositions here. Villalta (2008) suggests to follow Kratzer's (1991) definition of *better possibility* instead:
(i) a. For any $w, w', w'' \in W, w' <_{a,w} w''$ iff w' is more desirable to *a* in *w* than w''.
b. For any $p \subseteq W, q \subseteq W, p <_{\text{DES}(a,w)} q$ iff $\forall w'' \in q\, \exists w' \in p$ such that $w' <_{a,w} w''$, and it is not the case that $\forall w' \in p\, \exists w'' \in q$ such that $w'' <_{a,w} w'$. (Villalta 2008: 479(35), notation adapted)

The second additional ingredient, (ii), guards against the invalid inference that if an individual believes a certain proposition p, then they also want p. Clearly, even if I believe I will teach next semester, it does not follow that I want to teach next semester. According to Heim's proposal, the sentence *want p* suffers under these circumstances from presupposition failure and hence is infelicitous.[3]

Assuming that comparisons of desirability are restricted by the subject's doxastic alternatives, Heim (1992) defines the semantics of *want* as in (7). (This is a static rendering of her dynamic proposal, 1992: 197(39), following Villalta 2008: 474(22).)

(7) $\| want \|(q)(a)(w)$ is defined *iff* $\text{DOX}(a, w) \cap q, \text{DOX}(a, w) \cap \neg q \neq \emptyset$.
If defined, $\| want \|(q)(a)(w) = 1$ *iff*
$\forall w' \in \text{DOX}(a, w).Sim_{w'}(\text{DOX}(a, w) \cap q) <_{\text{DES}(a,w)} Sim_{w'}(\text{DOX}(a, w) \cap \neg q)$,
where:
$\text{DOX}(a, w)$ are the worlds that match the subject a's beliefs in the evaluation world (their *doxastic alternatives*);
$Sim_w(q)$ is the set of q-worlds most similar to w;
$<_{\text{DES}(a,w)}$ defines the comparative desirability of propositions for a in w.

Heim's motivation for crafting an analysis of desire predicates is to account for Karttunen's (1974) observations about presupposition projection from complements of attitude verbs. Although the original observations have not gone uncontested,[4] Heim's (1992) analysis of *want* has become the benchmark for much subsequent work on the semantics of attitude predicates.

7.2.2 Less reliance on belief and multiple alternatives: Villalta's contribution

In more recent work, Villalta (2006, 2008) has argued for two amendments to the Heimian analysis. She proposed, first, that the desirability comparison for *want* should not be restricted to the subject's doxastic alternatives, and second, that it should be carried out between q and a set of contextually determined alternatives, not just between q and $\neg q$.

The first issue, which I will call the "Doxastic Problem", concerns conflicting desires about propositions that are believed to be equivalent. The example in (8) shows that one may desire such propositions to different degrees.

(8) a. I want to teach Tuesdays and Thursdays next semester.
 b. I believe that I will teach Tuesdays and Thursdays next semester if and only if I work hard now.
 c. Invalid inference:
  ∴ I want to work hard now.   (Villalta 2008: 478)

---

[3] See Heim (1992: 198), von Fintel (1999: 117).   [4] See Geurts (1998), Moltmann (2006).

Intuitively, the sentence in (8c) is false if there is a possibility to get the desirable Tuesday–Thursday schedule without working hard. The inference fails in this case due to worlds that are outside the realm of what the subject believes to be the case. In other words, worlds that are not part of the subject's doxastic alternatives seem nevertheless to affect the desirability comparison. Villalta (2008) proposes to amend the Heimian analysis in (7) accordingly, to avoid the incorrect prediction in cases like this ((8c) is predicted to be true if the desirability comparison is restricted to worlds in the subject's doxastic alternatives).

A second issue Villalta raises for Heim's (1992) analysis concerns the "granularity" of the alternatives that determine the truth of desire statements. What happens, she asks, when multiple contextual alternatives seem to be compared, and those that are most similar to each other happen to be less desirable? Example (9) is a scenario of this kind.

(9) Sofía has promised to bring a dessert to the picnic. Victoria believes that there are three possibilities for what she may actually do. She could prepare a chocolate cake, even though Victoria considers that extremely unlikely because it represents far too much work. She might bring an apple pie, which Victoria considers very likely since she can just buy it at the bakery nearby. Or Sofía might bring ice cream, which seems most likely to Victoria, since she usually has some in her freezer. Victoria prefers the chocolate cake over the apple pie and the apple pie over the ice cream. (Villalta 2008: 476)

The picnic scenario introduces three alternatives that have different likelihoods of materializing and different degrees of desirability for the subject:

  i. Most likely, least desirable: the guest brings ice cream.
  ii. Very likely, somewhat desirable: the guest brings apple pie.
  iii. Extremely unlikely, highly desirable: the guest brings chocolate cake.

It is clear that (10) is false in this scenario.[5]

(10) ^{False}Victoria **wants** Sofía to bring an apple pie.

The claim is that a similarity-based analysis following Heim incorrectly predicts the sentence to be true in the given context (Villalta 2008: 477), if the option of the guest bringing apple pie is only compared to its negation. The crux of the argument, which I will challenge shortly, is that apple-pie worlds are compared in terms of desirability only to ice-cream worlds (since it is highly unlikely that the guest will bring chocolate cake). Of the two alternatives, worlds in which the guest brings apple pie are more desirable.

---

[5] Villalta (2008) uses a version of this sentence with *wish* instead of *want* (her example: 477(30)), but it is clear that she is making an argument about *want*.

In response to the Doxastic Problem and the problem of multiple alternatives, Villalta (2008) proposes the lexical entry for *want* in (11). The desirability comparison invoked by this lexical entry is carried out between the prejacent p and a set of contextually available alternatives. In addition, the dependency of desire on belief is relaxed. The subject's beliefs are relegated to a definedness condition and no longer restrict the desirability comparison. Wanting p requires that p and its alternatives be represented in the subject's doxastic alternatives, but the desirability comparison is not restricted to worlds in this set.[6,7]

(11) $[\![want_C]\!]^g (p)(a)(w)$ is defined *iff* $\forall q \in g(C) . \text{DOX}(a,w) \cap q \neq \emptyset$.
If defined, $[\![want_C]\!]^g (p)(a)(w) = 1$ *iff* $\forall q . q \neq p \ \& \ q \in g(C): p <_{\text{DES}(a,w)} q$.
where:
C is a variable that is anaphoric to a contextually determined set of propositions (and receives its value from the variable assignment g).

(Villalta 2008: 480(37))

Assuming that the three alternatives in the picnic scenario are directly compared to each other (i.e. $g(C) = \{ [\![\textit{S. brings chocolate cake}]\!], [\![\textit{S. brings apple pie}]\!], [\![\textit{S. brings ice cream}]\!] \}$), this proposal predicts the falsity of (10). It also accounts for the invalidity of the reasoning in (8); that is, it avoids the Doxastic Problem.

7.2.3 Evaluation

The picnic scenario is presented as a central piece of evidence for introducing sets of alternatives into the semantics of desire predicates. Upon reviewing the argument more closely, however, it is clear that the crucial judgment in the scenario can be explained equally well by the simpler version of Heim's (1992) comparative semantics.

The argument, recall, is that Heim (1992) predicts the sentence in (10) to be true because apple-pie worlds (q worlds) are compared to ice-cream worlds (*not q* worlds), and the former are more desirable than the latter for Victoria, the subject. The important point to note is that there are also certain worlds, compatible with the subject's beliefs, in which the most desirable thing happens—as if against all odds. In these worlds, the guest brings chocolate cake to the picnic. Crucially, if this is a viable option, the universal quantification over doxastic alternatives in (7) ensures that the sentence is (correctly) predicted to be false. This chain of reasoning is presented in more detail below.

---

[6] For present purposes I limit myself to discussion of the pre-final version of Villalta's proposal, ignoring the compositional degree-based refinement she introduces (see Villalta 2006, 2008: §8.3).

[7] A further virtue of this analysis is that it avoids the universal quantification over belief worlds in Heim's proposal. Concerns about this aspect of the original comparative desire semantics have been voiced in the literature. E.g. Levinson (2003: 230) argues that according to an analysis like (7), "a person wants something only if he/she believes that it will necessarily improve the situation in any possible case.... this excludes many actual cases of wanting."

(12) According to (7), *Victoria wants Sofía to bring an apple pie* is true *iff*:
$\forall w' \in \text{DOX}(a, w).Sim_{w'}(\text{DOX}(a, w) \cap q) <_{\text{DES}(a,w)} Sim_{w'}(\text{DOX}(a, w) \cap \neg q)$,
where q is the proposition that Sofía brings apple pie, and a is Victoria.
- Consider some world w'' in $\text{DOX}(V, w)$ such that
  $w'' \in [\![\textit{Sofía brings chocolate cake}]\!]$.
- $Sim_{w''}(\text{DOX}(V, w) \cap \neg[\![\textit{Sofía brings apple pie}]\!])$ equals $\{w''\}$, since a world is always most similar to itself.
- w'' is more desirable than any minimally different world w''' in $\text{DOX}(V, w) \cap [\![\textit{Sofía brings apple pie}]\!]$.

(10) is false in the picnic scenario.

In conclusion, scenarios of this type do not support introducing more complicated machinery into the semantics of desire predicates.

Villalta's approach nevertheless provides a solution to the Doxastic Problem, raising the question of whether the dependency of desire on belief can be relaxed while prejacents of desire predicates, as on a Heimian analysis, are compared simply to their negations.

7.2.4 Simple contextually restricted comparison, based on desires

At this juncture, it is useful to introduce a modal implementation of Heim's (1992) semantics for desire predicates. Originally developed by von Fintel (1999) in an effort to endow *want* with a monotonic semantics, the lexical entry in (13) utilizes standard modal parameters to interpret desire statements, namely a "modal base" and an "ordering source" (Kratzer 1981, 1991, 2012). The modal base, f, is a function from individual–world pairs to sets of worlds. It is lexically restricted by the verb to be doxastic, thereby mapping a pair (a, w) to the worlds doxastically accessible for a in w. The ordering source, h, is a function from individual–world pairs to sets of propositions representing relevant ideals. It is restricted by the verb to be bouletic, hence maps a pair (a, w) to the set of propositions representing a's preferences or desires in w.[8]

(13) $[\![\textit{want}]\!]^{f,h}(q)(a)(w)$ is defined *iff* $f(a, w) = \text{DOX}(a, w)$, $h(a, w) = \text{DES}(a, w)$, and $f(a, w) \cap q, f(a, w) \cap \neg q \neq \emptyset$.
If defined, $[\![\textit{want}]\!]^{f,h}(q)(a)(w) = 1$ *iff* $\forall w' \in max_{h(a,w)}(f(a, w)) . w' \in q$,
where $max_A(X)$ selects the set of $<_A$-best worlds in X.

An important lesson learned from Villalta's (2008) proposals concerns the nature of the possibilities compared in desire statements. These possibilities are contextually

---

[8] This is an adapted version of the modal analysis developed by von Fintel (1999: 115–118). The function *max* is defined as follows: for any $X \subseteq W$ and strict partial order $<_A$ on worlds (induced by a set of propositions A in the method proposed by Kratzer 1981), $max_A(X) = \{w \in X : \neg \exists w' \in X : w' <_A w\}$.

determined and they stand in a particular relationship to the subject's doxastic alternatives. Context-dependency, which is captured by $g(C)$ in Villalta's (2008) analysis above, can also be modeled by a modal base function in a standard modal analysis.[9] However, following Villalta, this modal base should not be identified with the subject's belief worlds (contra (13)),[10] but it should overlap with a subset of the subject's belief worlds that is diverse with respect to the prejacent.

A comparative-modal semantics for *want* that incorporates Villalta's (2008) solution for the Doxastic Problem is given in (14). The semantics is Heimian in the sense that it only compares the prejacent to one alternative—its negation—and not to a set of alternatives (following the discussion in the previous section). Crucially, the comparison of desirability is not semantically confined to the subject's doxastic alternatives.

(14) $[\![want]\!]^{f,h}(q)(a)(w)$ is defined *iff* $h(a,w) = \text{DES}(a,w)$, $\bigcap f(w) \cap \text{DOX}(a,w) \cap q \neq \emptyset$, and $\bigcap f(w) \cap \text{DOX}(a,w) \cap \neg q \neq \emptyset$.
If defined, $[\![want]\!]^{f,h}(q)(a)(w) = 1$ *iff* $\bigcap f(w) \cap q <_{h(a,w)} \bigcap f(w) \cap \neg q$.

According to (14), context circumscribes the possibilities invoked for comparison through the modal base f (here, the modal base is a function from worlds to sets of propositions).[11] Among these possibilities, q is required to be more desirable for the subject than its single alternative, $\neg q$. In addition, the prejacent and its negation are both presupposed to be represented among the subject's doxastic alternatives, specifically in those worlds that are both doxastically and contextually accessible.[12]

The crucial cases discussed by Villalta (2008) are accounted for by this analysis. If $f(w)$ includes the proposition that I teach next semester, worlds in which I do not teach at all cannot influence the desirability comparison; hence, *I want to teach Tuesdays and Thursdays next semester* ((6) above) is correctly predicted to be true, even if not teaching at at all is what I would like the most. Second, concerning the Doxastic Problem of (8), if the worlds determined by the modal base include ones in which my desires are realized without working hard, *I want to work hard now* is correctly predicted to be false, even if I believe that hard work is the only way for me

---

[9] Villalta (2008: 491) comments explicitly on this connection with the modal analysis: "One of my main goals has exactly been to show this last point, namely, that for different examples, different contextual alternatives are relevant. At the core of my proposal is the idea that contextual alternatives are an important ingredient of the semantics of these predicates."

[10] Or the superset of the doxastic alternatives arrived at by ignoring beliefs the subject has about their own future actions, which is what Heim (1992) ends up proposing.

[11] This is a true Kratzerian modal base, which in contrast to f in (13) is not directly dependent on the subject. Anchoring the modality to the subject can nevertheless be achieved with an event-relative approach to modality, along the lines proposed by Hacquard (2006, 2010).

[12] The explicitly comparative semantics of (14) is only superficially distinct from the quantificational one in the modal analysis above; under certain theoretical assumptions such comparison of a proposition and its negation is indistinguishable from universal quantification along the lines of (13). See von Fintel and Iatridou (2008) for details.

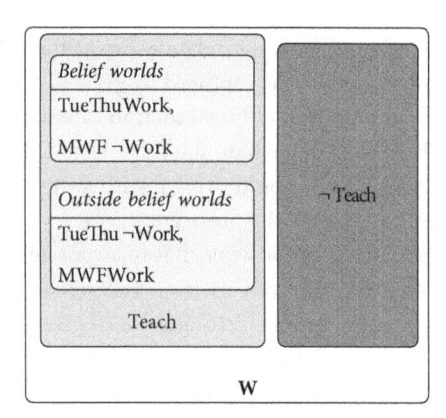

FIG. 7.1 Accessible worlds for *want* in the teaching scenario

to get the teaching schedule I want. Figure 7.1 depicts the relation between modal base and doxastic alternatives that is relevant in this scenario.

The idea behind the proposed (14) is that an individual's belief worlds may be a subset of the worlds determined by the modal base. In the teaching scenario, for example, the modal-base worlds are circumstantially accessible worlds in which I teach next semester (left-hand panel, "Teach," comprising "Belief Worlds" and "Outside belief worlds"). Only a proper subset of these are the belief worlds of the subject. The larger set is relevant for evaluating *I want to (not) work hard*. This captures the intuition that the sentence *I want to work hard now* is false in the teaching scenario of (8c) if there is a conceivable possibility of getting the desirable Tuesday–Thursday schedule without working hard.

Note that the larger set of contextually accessible worlds may also be relevant for evaluating the basic desire statement in the scenario *I want to teach Tuesdays and Thursdays next semester*, although focusing just on the doxastic alternatives would also predict the truth of the sentence since the MWF schedule is less desirable than the TueThu schedule in general. The analysis proposed does not force us to assume that the value of the contextual parameters changes from the premises to the conclusion in (8).

What can be said about the relation between the subject's doxastic alternatives and the contextually accessible worlds (i.e., $\text{DOX}(a, w)$ and $\bigcap f(w)$) in the general case? The teaching scenario suggests that the relation may be one of inclusion, such that the accessible worlds are a superset of the doxastic alternatives, arrived at by potentially suspending some of the subject's beliefs. The doxastic alternatives also play a role in the picnic scenario, as discussed above: it is true that Victoria wants Sofía to bring chocolate cake to the picnic partly because she considers this to be a viable, if somewhat unlikely, option. The context is set up in such a way that it makes relevant Victoria's beliefs about what Sofía might bring, and these possibilities cannot be ignored.

Given a modal analysis like (14), in which the domain of relevant possibilities for any given *want* statement is determined by context, one might go a step further and challenge the very assumption that beliefs semantically restrict desire statements at some level. This possibility is raised by examples like (15), which are a lingering loose end for the Heimian analysis and its descendants (see Heim 1992: 199(42)). The analysis proposed in (14), in particular, predicts the sentence to be infelicitous due to presupposition failure (since, presumably, my beliefs rule out the possibility of an endless weekend).

(15) I **want** this weekend to last forever. (But I know, of course, that it will be over in a few hours.) (Heim 1992)

It seems worthwhile to explore an alternative explanation of those examples that originally motivated Karttunen and Heim to posit a link between desire and belief (e.g. (2)). Heim (1992) herself suggests two paths of exploration: anaphoric accommodation of the modal base as in modal subordination, and revision of the modal base as in a counterfactual conditional. I leave a detailed investigation of these options for another occasion.

7.3 Extending the analysis to modals

Not only do certain attitude verbs and modals contribute similar meanings, e.g. a desire- or goal-oriented necessity in (16), there are also more tangible grammatical properties that single them out as a natural class.

(16) a. I **want** you to see the pyramids.
b. You **have** to see the pyramids.
c. It's **necessary** for you to see the pyramids.

In Spanish, for example, both *es necesario* 'it is necessary' and *querer* 'want' select subjunctive-marked verbs in their embedded clauses. This shared morphosyntactic property leads Villalta (2008) to extend a comparison-based semantics like that of 'want' to the modal adjective 'necessary'.

The goal of this section is to examine the type of modality expressed by *necessary* and to characterize the comparison it invokes. I argue contra existing claims in the literature that *necessary*, at least in English, does not contribute likelihood-based comparison, and neither is it a general purpose necessity operator. Instead, I expose the inherently teleological nature of this modal as a clausal operator and describe how it differs from a modal like *have to*, which is more the polyfunctional necessity modal *necessary* is often assumed to be. The semantic profile of *necessary* is supported with a small corpus study in section 7.3.2.

7.3.1 Necessary that there be a goal

The first contender for a comparative analysis of *necessary* is the one proposed by Villalta (2008) in (17), following Krasikova (2008). According to this analysis, the main difference between *necessary* and *want* is that the former compares propositions according to likelihood—implemented as closeness to the actual world—while the latter compares propositions according to how desirable they are for an attitude holder. Two ancillary differences are that the modal, unlike the verb, does not have an individual argument, and that the alternatives it compares are not required to overlap with any particular set of beliefs.

(17) $[\![\textit{be necessary}_c]\!]^g(p)(w) = 1$ iff $\forall q : q \neq p \ \& \ q \in g(C) \ . \ p <_{\text{LIKELY}_w} q$,
where:

For any $p \subseteq W, q \subseteq W, p <_{\text{LIKELY}_w} q$ iff $\forall w'' \in q \ \exists w' \in p$ such that $w' <_w w''$, and it is not the case that $\forall w' \in p \ \exists w'' \in q$ such that $w'' <_w w'$;
For any $w, w', w'' \in W, w' <_w w''$ iff w' is closer to w than w''.

(Villalta 2008: 482(42))

A likelihood-based analysis of *necessary* is problematic for at least two reasons. It predicts an entailment relation between *necessary* and *likely* that does not exist in ordinary uses of the adjective. More importantly, it misses a generalization about the modality type that the adjective expresses.

First, consider the pair *necessary* and *likely*. Assuming, as Villalta does, that the scale of likelihood associated with both predicates is the same,[13] an analysis like (17) predicts an entailment relation between *necessary q* and *likely q*. Consider the proposal that for a proposition to be likely, it must be at least as likely as its negation, or exceed a contextual standard for likelihood (see e.g. Yalcin 2010, Lassiter 2011). If *necessary q* is true, it follows from (17) that q is more likely than any of its contextual alternatives, hence that q is likely. In certain logical jargon, *necessary q* does seem to entail *likely q*. For example, one might conclude from a set of premises that *It is necessary that x is prime*, from which it follows that *It is likely that x is prime*. However, in everyday English this entailment does not exist. What is necessary may be unlikely, as in (18a), and what is likely may not be necessary (18b).

(18) a. Marijuana reform **necessary**, but **unlikely**.[14]
b. [In the picnic scenario of (9)]
It is **necessary** that Sofía bring ice cream.
It is **necessary** for Sofía to bring ice cream.

---

[13] "Other predicates from this class such as *es probable* ('it is likely'), *es posible* ('it is possible') and *dudar* ('doubt') can also be analyzed as contributing the scale of likelihood" (Villalta 2008: 483).

[14] Opinion, http://www.thecorsaironline.com/opinion/marijuana-reform-necessary-but-unlikely-1.1374244

Independently of the meaning of *necessary*, the definition of likelihood in (17) is problematic because it equates likelihood with greater similarity to the evaluation world. This is problematic because, as we know from good detective stories, the real world can be host to highly unlikely events (Kratzer 1981). Since a world is most similar to itself, (17) predicts that if *q* is actually the case, then it is necessary.

Turning to modality types, there is a connection between *necessary* and teleological (goal-oriented) modality that is not acknowledged by a likelihood-based analysis. Likelihood is an epistemic or circumstantial type of modality that pertains to what is projected to be the case based on certain facts or circumstances, potentially taking into account additional considerations such as the normal course of events. It contrasts with what may be called "priority" modalities (a term from Portner 2009), in which ideals such as desires, goals, or rules are relevant for reasoning about possible states of affairs. Priority modalities include teleological (goal-oriented) modalities, bouletic (desire-based) modalities, and deontic (rule-based) modalities. In addition to epistemic and priority modalities, a third category of modality will be relevant in this discussion: the alethic modality of what is necessarily or possibly true.

The main claims of this section are that *necessary* is a priority-type necessity modal and that it is primarily teleological as a clausal operator. My focus will therefore be on sentences such as (18b), in which *necessary* is complemented by an untensed *that*-clause or a *(for) to* infinitive. Note that the necessity of the embedded event in this example, Sofía bringing ice cream, can only be determined with respect to a contextually provided goal or priority. Was it necessary that Sofía bring ice cream in the picnic scenario? Without further information about the context, we simply don't know. This intuitive judgment will be supported with corpus data in section 7.3.2. Additional support for the modal's specialized interpretation comes from contrasts in felicity between *necessary* and other necessity modals in non-teleological contexts, and from the semantic nature of the modal's synonyms.

A rough guide to the semantics of *necessary* are its synonyms, a cohort that includes the modal adjectives *essential* and *crucial*. Tracing the diachronic development of *essential* and *crucial* in English, Van linden et al. (2008) describe how over time these adjectives have developed what we would call teleological or goal-oriented interpretations.[15] The fact that *necessary* is often provided in definitions of these two modals and is offered as their synonym (especially *essential*—see the *Oxford English Dictionary*) suggests that it too is a teleological modal at least in some of its uses.

Necessary with an untensed complement is odd in alethic contexts. Alethic contexts are by nature uncommon in non-philosophical everyday discourse, but even within the genre, whether or not *necessary* can be felicitously used to describe an alethic necessity depends on the type of complement it takes. In the trio of sentences below,

---

[15] They also conclude that the adjectives have undergone a further semantic change and are able to express deontic modality as well. This conclusion is not warranted, as will be shown.

inspired by an example in a scholarly philosophical paper,[16] the variant with an untensed embedded CP (19a) is notably degraded in comparison to variants with a tensed complement, regardless of whether the embedding modal is an adjective (19b) or an adverb (19c).

(19) If this particle is Helium, then...
    a. ...?it is **necessary** that it have atomic number 2.
    b. ...it is **necessary** that it has atomic number 2.
    c. ...**necessarily** it has atomic number 2.

Similarly, Brennan (1993: 88, n. 19) notes that epistemic interpretations of *necessary that* are found only when the modal's complement is tensed. It is tempting to relate this finding to observations about the epistemic/root distinction, especially the claim that modals take scope over tense when they are interpreted epistemically (Groenendijk and Stokhof 1975; Cinque 1999; Hacquard 2006, 2010, 2011). (Alethic modals would be treated as members of the same semantic category as epistemics; see Portner 2009: 135.) From this perspective, what is surprising is that *necessary* has a limited interpretation when complemented by a smaller phrase—in other words, that it does not exhibit the full range of non-epistemic, root interpretations when its complement is untensed.

Necessary is goal-oriented where a more polyfunctional necessity modal like *have to* can be purely circumstantial. *Have to* can be used to express the circumstantial necessity that non-parallel lines intersect (20a), or that I can't help sneezing when I'm out in the sun (21a).

(20) a. If these lines are not parallel, they **have** to intersect at some point.
    b. If these lines are not parallel, it is **necessary** that they intersect at some point.

(21) a. I **have** to sneeze.
    b. It is **necessary** for me to sneeze.

The corresponding sentences with *necessary* express a type of modality that is goal-oriented; they invite a *What for?* follow-up. Example (21b), for example, cannot be used to express an uncontrollable urge to sneeze. Rather, it suggests that sneezing is a necessity in light of achieving some goal or priority—for example, making it difficult to hear what someone next to me is about to say.

Not only is *necessary* incapable of expressing pure circumstantial modality, the range of priority modalities it can express is also limited. A surprising finding is that deontic interpretations of the modal are ruled out in the relevant complementation configuration. This is surprising on the traditional view, where all non-epistemic

---

[16] See Halbach and Welch (2009: 72). These authors argue that from a formal logical perspective, there are reasons to treat phrases in which the adjective *necessary* is interpreted in an alethic sense as standing in for (perhaps as a shorthand for) phrases including the adverb *necessarily* and a predicate of truth.

modalities are grouped together in one natural class, generating the expectation that a polyfunctional modal will allow different interpretations of this class in different contexts of utterance.

Consider (22). Rationing food is a teleological necessity if one's priority is to survive a famine. It can also be a deontic necessity if there are rules mandating the rationing. Both (22b) and (22a) would be true in a famine scenario of this kind, but they would be true for different reasons. Example (22a) describes the content of a law, whereas (22b) describes survival during difficult times.

(22) During the famine, ...
    a. ... it was **mandated by law** that food be rationed.
    b. ... it was **necessary** that food be rationed (and retired laboratory animals eaten).

Next, consider the necessities that characterize the post-famine era, a time in which a famine ended but the rationing law was still in place. This context supports food rationing as a deontic necessity, and therefore (23a) is clearly true. However, since an abundance of food means that there are multiple ways for people to survive without rationing, a teleological claim oriented toward the priority of survival is false. *Necessary that q* in (23b) does not receive the same interpretation as *mandated by law that q* does; there is a sense in which it does not accurately describe the scenario.

(23) [After the famine ended there was plenty of food again for everybody, but the law hadn't changed for a while.]
During that interim period, ...
    a. ... it was **mandated by law** that food be rationed.
    b. ... it was **necessary** that food be rationed.

Why are we still hesitant to say that (23b) is false—full stop—in this context? The reason is that *necessary* depends on a priority, and a different priority could make the sentence true. In particular, since the prejacent to the modal matches what is deontically necessary in the scenario, the preference for abiding by the law would do the trick. Imagine that (23b) is uttered by a lawmaker who is an adamant believer in upholding and enforcing the law. Example (23b) is true in the context of (23) if *necessary* means 'necessary in order to behave in accordance with the law.' To the extent that we are willing to judge (22b)/(23b) as deontic, it is not because the modal describes the content of the law in these examples (arguably, this *necessary* cannot do), but rather because it is restricted by a priority that exists *because* the law exists.

7.3.2 Corpus study

The judgments presented in the section 7.3.1 are subtle. To test their validity and to answer the more general question of whether syntactic configuration might influence the meaning of *necessary*, a corpus study was carried out on the interpretation of the modal in naturally occurring texts. The study addressed two questions:

i. What is the range of modality types expressed by *necessary*?
ii. Is the modal's interpretation constrained by the syntactic structures it appears in?

To answer these questions, examples of *necessary* in different syntactic configurations were extracted from a large corpus (COCA, the Corpus of Contemporary American English 1990–2012; Davies 2008). The search was limited to the years 2000–2012 in order to yield a manageable dataset for annotation. It consisted of three search queries (a substitute for a structural search, since the corpus is not syntactically parsed): *necessary* immediately preceding the complementizer *that* (24a), *necessary for* separated by up to five words from a following *to* (24b), and *necessary to* followed by a verb and separated by up to three words from a preceding *it* (24c). Examples of relevant sentences that matched these queries are given in (24). There were 109 relevant sentences that matched the pattern in (24a) in the section of the corpus from 2000-2012; the same number of examples were sampled randomly from matches to each of the other two patterns.

(24) a. *necessary that*:
　　　　The rapid change of society has outdated some of the statutes in the law and it is **necessary that** it be revised.

　　b. *necessary for . . . to*:
　　　　I know many of you have been farming for many years but it will be **necessary for** all farmers **to** become certified.

　　c. *It . . . necessary to V*:
　　　　"Yes, that would have certainly been more convenient," he said, "but I felt **it** was **necessary to** talk to you in person."

Among the 109 sentences with *that*-clause complements, the vast majority had untensed complements (100/109 = 91.7%). The connection between finiteness and modal interpretation in the data is discussed in more detail below.

The overall picture that emerges from the annotation of modality types (Table 7.1) is that *necessary* is primarily used as a teleological or bouletic modal. This is true regardless of the syntactic configuration that the adjective appears in (98/109 = 89.9%, 96/109 = 88.1%, 94/109 = 86.2% of occurrences in the three configurations that were examined). Only a small fraction of these sentences were determined to have a bouletic flavor (7/98, 0/96, 7/94), but all of them could be interpreted teleologically as well.[17] Since conceptually an individual's desire can always be construed

---

[17] Example (24c) is an example of a sentence in the *necessary to V* configuration annotated as having both flavors. An example in the configuration *necessary that* is given in (ii).

(ii)　With Sugarloaf and The River Club only six miles apart, it was **necessary that** each luxury community have different atmospheres and architecture.

TABLE 7.1 The interpretation of *necessary* in the corpus (COCA, 2000–2012; Davies 2008).

	Epistemic	Deontic	Teleological/bouletic	Other	Total
necessary that	3	0	98	8 (T/E?)	109
necessary for . . . to	0	13 (T/D)	96	0	109
it . . . necessary to V	0	14 (T/D?)	94	1 (T/E?)	109

as their goal, teleological and bouletic modalities are treated as one category in the summary.

The first configuration, *necessary that*, stands out in two ways from the other configurations that were examined: it was the only one to allow non-ambiguous epistemic uses of the modal, and it showed no trace of deontic interpretations.

Evidence of the epistemic (alethic) interpretation of *necessary* was found in the corpus, but only when the modal was complemented with a *that* clause. In addition to three examples that were annotated as exclusively epistemic (one is given in (25)), eight were annotated as being ambiguous (26) or potentially ambiguous (27) between teleological and epistemic interpretations.

(25) [Following Saddam Hussein's capture, the speaker lists a number of groups that pose a threat to coalition forces in Iraq.] And it's not **necessary$_E$ that** each of these groups is connected or will be impacted by this man's capture.

(26) 'I don't think that's a be-all and end-all. I don't think it's **necessary$_{T/E}$ that** that happens because ultimately I'm going to make the call on it with a lot of input from my staff,' he said.

(27) . . . because it was **necessary$_{T/E?}$ that** Christ suffer only once.

This is the only complement type in the study that can potentially be tensed, and based on the discussion in the previous section one would expect to find a correlation between tense and non-priority interpretations in precisely this configuration. I argued above that epistemic interpretations require a tensed *that* complement. The actual findings are not so categorical. Of the three epistemic examples of *necessary that*, one ((25) above) had a tensed complement and one had an untensed predicate of truth (*But it is not necessary that these hypotheses should be true, nor even probable*, from a translation of Copernicus; see n. 16). Of the five examples annotated as ambiguous between teleological and epistemic interpretations, only one had a tensed complement ((26) above). Two of the remaining four examples, with untensed complements, were from articles in an academic journal on theology. The three potentially ambiguous examples in which the epistemic overtone was unclear were also all found in this journal and arguably do not represent everyday English.

Zooming in on the nine examples with tensed *that* clauses in the annotated corpus, many of them (7/9 = 77.7%) express priority modality and only two are epistemic or partly epistemic. This may also seem to challenge a theory that predicts a modal to be interpreted epistemically if it takes scope over tense. However, some of these examples occur in texts that appear to have been written by non-native speakers (e.g. (28)). In others (e.g. (29)), tense marking in the embedded clause may be affected by the tense of a parallel sentence in the surrounding context.

(28) . . . it is **necessary that** internet is used to get information and make project on studies about school . . .

(29) Yes, some motorcycles are too loud, but from a rider's standpoint, it is **necessary that** motorcycles are not too quiet.

Due to these considerations and the small number of examples, I will not attempt to draw conclusions about the connection between tense and epistemic interpretation based on this data.

Turning to the question of deontic interpretation, the corpus gives us some evidence that complements with infinitives are able to express this type of modality. Thirteen examples of *necessary* complemented by a *for to* infinitive were ambiguous between a teleological and a deontic interpretation (13/109 = 11.9%; for example, (30)). In the infinitival complement construction, nine examples were ambiguous between a teleological and a deontic interpretation (as in (31)), and in five cases the deontic interpretation was not clearly intended, but also not ruled out by the context (see (32)).

(30) The goal is to engage clients, not coerce. It is not **necessary**$_{T/D}$ **for** every client **to** present a story.

(31) A Serenitatis newslogger asked why some deputies weren't working on the case, and she explained that the department had other normal duties it was **necessary**$_{T/D}$ **to** fulfill.

(32) In Strauss's view, it was **necessary**$_{T/D?}$ **to** reaffirm the dignity of the political by returning to a natural, or prescientific, understanding of the political.

The evidence for deontic interpretations of *necessary* is weak, however, because the deontic examples were all annotated as ambiguous or potentially ambiguous between deontic and teleological meaning. None were in the type of context that is capable of distinguishing the two modality types, a context like the post-famine scenario in (23), where the relevant rules are in conflict with the goals. A larger sample of examples may have helped in this respect, although the finiteness of any corpus places a limitation on the conclusions one can draw using this methodology.

Summing up, an examination of all the examples of *necessary that* in COCA between 2000 and 2012 suggests that the modal is interpreted primarily as a teleological modal when complemented by a *that*-clause. Epistemic/alethic interpretations are rare, and a larger body of examples would be needed to investigate whether, as suggested in the literature, the modality expressed is correlated with the tense in the complement (or other features of interest). Although the results show no difference in the interpretation of *necessary* with *for to* infinitives and with simple infinitival complements, they suggest that there is no simple correlation between the (syntactic) size of *necessary*'s complement and the range of modality types it can express. Given that corpus research is inherently limited by the finiteness of corpora, an experimental study might be necessary in order to probe the subtle contrast in judgments reported in the previous section between *(for) to* and *that*-CP configurations of the modal.[18]

Finally, the uneven distribution of interpretations found in the corpus for *necessary*—all essentially clustered around teleological modality— is different from the profile of interpretations one would expect a general-purpose modal to have. A comprehensive corpus study would confirm this conclusion by comparing *necessary* to more flexible modals of necessity, such as *need to* or *have to* (see (20), (21)). Evidence that *need*, in particular, has a wider range of meanings is found in recent corpus studies of English modals (e.g., Leech et al. 2009: 109ff.). Crowdsourcing experiments with non-expert annotators show that bouletic, deontic, circumstantial, and epistemic uses of the modal are attested alongside a majority of teleological examples (Rubinstein et al. 2012).

I conclude on the basis of the results of this initial corpus study that in its most natural uses, *necessary* depends on a goal or priority to get its domain of quantification. In certain syntactic configurations (in particular, with *that*-clause complements that tend to be untensed), it primarily expresses shades of goal-oriented necessity. This claim is new and surprising. It contradicts what seems to be a common, if mostly silent, assumption that *necessary* is a general-purpose necessity modal that can be used deontically and even non-circumstantially in appropriate contexts.

7.3.3 *Proposal: a requirement for a contextually provided goal*

A lexical entry for *necessary* should capture the observation that the modal is teleological, and thereby different from a general purpose-necessity modal like *have to* or *must*. The proposal I pursue in this section is that the modal requires the application of a (teleological) ordering source, and that this ordering source operates on top of other contextually determined modal backgrounds to determine the modal's quantification domain. I couch the proposal within Kratzer's doubly relative semantics of modality, the framework adopted for the meaning of desire predicates in section 7.2.4. This will enable a direct comparison of the two types of displacement operators in what follows.

To explain the inability of *necessary* to receive pure circumstantial interpretations (as observed in (20), (21) and suggested in the corpus study), I propose that the modal

---

[18] See Rubinstein (2012: 142ff.) for a relevant experimental setup.

places a condition on the context, requiring it to supply a quantification domain that is a subset of the worlds determined by the modal base alone. This boils down, roughly, to a requirement that the context provide the modal with a non-empty ordering source. If *have to* contrasts with *necessary* in placing no restrictions on the contextual parameters it draws on, we can explain why the former is able to express necessities that characterize the set of modal base worlds in its entirety, as in the case of pure circumstantial modalities.

It is clear, however, that the condition placed by *necessary* cannot be as simple as requiring a domain of quantification that is a proper subset of the accessible (modal base) worlds. This is so because deontic modals as well as epistemics are typically analyzed as having access to ordering sources, hence they too quantify over a select subset of the accessible worlds. For epistemics, the ordering source describes the stereotypical or normal course of events in the world of evaluation; for deontics, the ordering source describes relevant laws and regulations (Kratzer 1981, 2012). But even when such considerations are salient, we have seen that *necessary* is interpreted in relation to a goal, not the rules, and that it goes beyond what the stereotypical ordering source provides. Example (18a), repeated here, shows this last point.

(18a)   Marijuana reform **necessary**, but unlikely.

The author of this sentence, who claims that marijuana reform is necessary yet unlikely, is clearly attuned not just to the possibilities opened up by the relevant circumstances, but also to what is likely and unlikely to take place. His necessity claim is thus sensitive to a modal base, a stereotypical ordering source, and some additional priorities that further restrict the possibilities that count as "best." (In all of these, there is marijuana reform.) *Necessary* requires these additional priorities, in addition to the norms represented by the stereotypical ordering source. It also requires that the priorities be of the teleological type, as shown by the interpretation of the modal in the sentence describing the post-famine situation:

(23b)   During the interim period, it was **necessary** that food be rationed.

The salient deontic norms in this scenario are not able to satisfy the needs of the modal, which cannot receive a simple deontic interpretation in the context. A different kind of priority is responsible for the teleological interpretation it receives.

Both of the above considerations are incorporated into the lexical entry in (33): the modal selects for a contextually provided teleological ordering source, h', which applies on top of any (stereotypical or other) ordering source h to determine the modal's domain of quantification.[19]

---

[19] A sequence of ordering sources can be thought of as a hierarchy of ranked priorities, where ordering sources toward the end of the sequence cannot change the ordering determined by ones higher up, only add to it. The formalization in the text follows the proposal for weak necessity in von Fintel and Iatridou (2008).

(33) ⟦*necessary*⟧ $^{f,h,h'}(q)(w)$ is defined *iff* h' is teleological.
If defined, ⟦*necessary*⟧ $^{f,h,h'}(q)(w) = 1$ *iff* $\forall w' \in max_{h'(w)}(max_{h(w)}(\bigcap f(w)))$. $w' \in q$, where $max_A(X)$ selects the set of $<_A$-best worlds in X.

Goal orientation has been hard-wired into this lexical entry of the clausal operator *necessary*—a move that might seem suspect in light of the prevalent view that modality type is a feature that can be derived to some extent from the syntactic configuration a modal appears in (e.g. Cinque 1999; Hacquard 2006, 2011). While this move might be appropriate for *necessary*—perhaps this modal adjective is lexically restricted to a particular type of modality, just like we assume the verb *want* is—it is also possible that there is a more principled explanation for the emergence of teleological modality in some of the syntactic configurations that have been surveyed here.

As I have shown elsewhere, a restriction to teleological modality is characteristic of a variety of general purpose necessity modals when they take CP complements, in English and in other languages (Rubinstein 2012). Pointing in this direction is also the observation that *necessary* is somewhat more open to deontic interpretations in corpora when its prejacent includes an infinitive (recall Table 7.1). Moreover, in scenarios that are able to distinguish deontic from teleological modality, the range of interpretations that the modal receives seems to be correlated with the type of complement it takes. Thus, of the two sentences in (34), the first is somewhat more felicitous than the second if the context supports the prejacent as a deontic but not a teleological necessity (I gloss over the active/passive contrast in the sentences).

(34) [In the post-famine scenario of (23).]
  a. It was **necessary** to ration food.
  b. It was **necessary** that food be rationed.

It may be that these fine fluctuations in the adjective's interpretation (as well as the rare epistemic uses it has) are not idiosyncratic and should receive a grammatical explanation. Such an explanation has not yet been provided, however.

Settling on a teleological semantics for *necessary* and denying its polyfunctionality underscores the affinity between the modal adjective and a bouletic attitude verb like *want*. The net difference between the denotation proposed for the adjective in (33) and that arrived at for the verb in (14) is minimal and concerns (i) the modality type lexically encoded for each item, and (ii) the involvement of an attitude holder in the latter. These two differences are presumably not unrelated. As noted in the previous section in the context of annotation, it is difficult to deny that modal claims that are based on an attitude holder's desires can also be construed teleologically (with the desires functioning as goals). What seems to characterize prototypical bouletic

---

See Katz et al. (2012) for an alternative implementation, which ranks all accessible worlds, not only the "best of the best."

examples is the identifiability of an individual who is the source of the priorities that are relevant for evaluating the modal claim; when the source of a priority is unknown, it cannot be classified as a desire (or a law), merely a goal.

In the next and final section, the semantics of *necessary* and *want* is situated in the context of a larger group of necessity modals.

7.4 Concluding remarks: attitude verbs and modals compared

In this chapter, I offered detailed discussion of the interpretation of bouletic attitudes and priority modals, concluding that such predicates share a quantificational modal semantics and are principally distinguished by whether (*want*) or not (*necessary*) their modality is lexically relativized to an individual. In passing, I compared *necessary* to other necessity modals, arguing that not all such modals are created equal. *Necessary* was shown to allow only a subset of the interpretations that necessity modals like *have to* and *need to* can accommodate. On the one hand, the lexical specification of modality type proposed for *necessary* makes it similar to an attitude verb; on the other hand, not being lexically anchored to an individual is a property it shares with typical necessity operators.

In terms of the range of modality types they allow, attitude verbs and polyfunctional necessity modals seem to occupy extremes of a continuum, with *necessary* somewhere in the middle. However, considerations of modal strength group *necessary* squarely with verbs like *have to*, exposing another parameter of variation within the class of necessity modals. To appreciate this similarity, it is necessary to include "weak-necessity" modals like *ought* or *should* in the discussion. Weak-necessity modals are characterized by the scalar inferences they exhibit in relation to so-called "strong-necessity" modals. Such patterns are used to classify *have to* and *must* as both being strong (hence giving rise to a contradiction in (35a), keeping the teleological interpretation fixed throughout), in contrast to *ought to* and *should*, which are weaker and do not give rise to a contradiction in (35b) (von Fintel and Iatridou 2008). The examples with *necessary* in (35) suggest that this modal is strong rather than weak.[20]

(35) a. #You must take the train, but you don't have to (/but it's not necessary).
　　b. You ought to take the train, but you don't have to (/but it's not necessary).
　　c. #It's necessary that you take the train, but you don't have to.

---

[20] It is not the lack of overt specification of a goal for *necessary* that is responsible for the infelicity of (35c), as no goal is specified in (35b) and this sentence is perfectly coherent. Not surprisingly, if different goals are specified for the two modals, the two necessity statements are no longer contradictory:

(iii) It's necessary that you take the train if you want to reduce your carbon footprint, but you don't have to in order just to get to where you need to go.

Exploring the roots of the weak-strong distinction would take us too far afield,[21] so I will conclude by merely mentioning a few open issues that these data raise for a comprehensive theory of modal and attitudinal necessity. If strength is a reflection of a difference in modality type (as argued by Bybee et al. 1994 and reflected in von Fintel and Iatridou's 2008 domain-restriction approach), how is the largely priority-type interpretation of weak *ought/should* different from the priority-type interpretation of the strong modal *necessary*? Second, how can an inherently teleological modal like *necessary* be as strong as a general-purpose modal like *have to* in light of this approach? Indeed, in terms of the range of modality types it can express, *necessary* is more similar to *ought* (and to *want*) than to *have to* or *must* (and in Spanish, 'necessary' and weak necessity 'likely' both belong to the set of subjunctive-selecting predicates; Villalta 2008). It is an open question whether a more refined classification of modality types will provide answers to these questions, or whether the data are better explained by an independent property (e.g. the discourse status of the priorities that are relevant for the different modals; Rubinstein 2012).

Acknowledgments

I thank Angelika Kratzer, Rajesh Bhatt, Kai von Fintel, and Paul Portner for fruitful discussions. The material in the first part of the chapter was presented in 2011 in the seminar "Modals, attitudes, and evidentials" at the University of Maryland. I thank Valentine Hacquard and the seminar participants for their interest and feedback. The final version of the chapter benefited from comments by an anonymous reviewer and the participants of the modality workshop in Ottawa. These are gratefully acknowledged.

---

[21] For a taste of the approaches available, see von Fintel and Iatridou (2008), Finlay (2009), Lassiter (2011), Rubinstein (2012, 2014), Silk (2012).

8

May under verbs of hoping: Evolution of the modal system in the complements of hoping verbs in Early Modern English

IGOR YANOVICH

8.1 Introduction

Consider (1), an example from a private letter from year 1891 taken from the CLMEP corpus (Denison et al. 1994). In (1), *may* does not contribute existential quantificational force: speakers find it incompatible with the statement in (2). Example (1) on the existential meaning of *may* would have conveyed *hope(◊such.terms)*, which does not contradict *hope(◊¬such.terms)*, the schematic meaning for (2). The fact that (1) and (2) are not compatible with each other shows that *may* does not contribute a ◊ meaning in (1). Indeed, it seems to make little direct contribution to the assertion: the hope expressed in (1) seems to be for simply being on such terms, not for the possibility of being on them.[1]

(1) (1891) Dearest, I hope we may be on such terms twenty years hence.
(from CLMEP, Denison et al. 1994)

(2) *Compatible with (1) under the existential meaning of may*
I also hope that it will be possible for us not to be on such terms twenty years from now.

---

[1] The chapter significantly benefited from the comments of the audiences at MIT and at Ottawa, from discussions with Kai von Fintel, Irene Heim, and Sabine Iatridou, from reviews by Marisa Rivero and Remus Gergel, and also from Lyra Magloughlin's editorial help. The chapter is closely related to Chapter 3 of Yanovich (2013). I have drawn on the data from the following corpora: BNC (2007); CLMEP (Denison et al. 1994); COCA (Davies 2008); CASO (Davies 2012); and PCEEC (2006). Searches in PCEEC were performed with *CorpusSearch 2*, written by Beth Randall at UPenn. Statistical tests were computed using R, a free software.

Modality Across Syntactic Categories. First edition. Ana Arregui, María Luisa Rivero, and Andrés Salanova (eds.).
This chapter © Igor Yanovich 2017. First published 2017 by Oxford University Press.

The plan of the chapter is as follows. In section 8.2, I provide the background on the modern *may*-under-*hope* construction, highlighting the fact that it features a lexical variant of the modal that is confined to a very particular syntactic context. A brief review of the formal semantics of hoping attitudes is given in section 8.3. Section 8.4 describes modals in the complements of attitude verbs of hoping in the earliest section of the Parsed Corpus of Early English Correspondence PCEEC (2006), covering the years 1425–1520. Among other things, the section shows that *may* was still marginal under verbs of hoping well into the 16th century. Section 8.5 argues, based on a comparison between the 1425–1520 subcorpus of PCEEC and corpus data from Present-Day English, that the marginal status of *may* under verbs of hoping in Early Modern English cannot be explained by semantic factors alone. Some further constraint, not belonging to the compositional semantics, must have been in place. In section 8.6, I discuss modals under verbs of hoping in the latest section of the PCEEC corpus, covering the years 1630–81. By that time, the special non-possibility variant of *may* under *hope* was already in place. In section 8.7, I put forward a hypothesis about how the rise of *may*-under-*hope* could have happened. The hypothesis says that the driving force of the change was a preference for preserving the special elevated category of hopes about good health, expressed earlier with the inflectional subjunctive.

8.2 *May* under *hope*: a syntactically restricted semantic variant of a lexeme

A word usually has the same range of meanings across different syntactic contexts. But sometimes a word in a particular construction can have a special meaning, not attested elsewhere in the language. One example of this in modern English is *may* in the *may*-under-*hope* construction, exemplified in (1) above and here in (3):

(3) While investigators hope for a break in technology, they also **hope** there **may** be a crack in the kidnapper's conscience. (from COCA)

If *may* had its usual possibility meaning in (3), the sentence would have meant roughly (4). This is not the case: what the investigators in (3) hope for is clearly not just the possibility of there being a crack in the kidnapper's conscience. We can show this by observing that (3) is incompatible with a sentence in (6). This is expected if (3) means something like (5). (We have already made a similar argument for (1) above.)

(4) Absent meaning of (3)
    hope($\Diamond$ *there.is.a.crack*)(*the.investigators*)

(5) Rough paraphrase of the actual meaning of (3)
    hope(*there.is.a.crack*)(*the.investigators*)

(6) The following sentence contradicts (3), showing that the meaning in (4) is truly absent
The investigators also hope that it will be possible that there is no crack in the kidnapper's conscience.

Thus no possibility is conveyed by *may* in (3), and the relevant part of the sentence is roughly synonymous with one with a non-modal complement in (7):

(7) The investigators hope there will be a crack in the kidnapper's conscience.

Speakers do report subtle differences between (3), with *may*, and the non-modal (7): the former sounds more solemn, and perhaps more hedging, than the latter.

Not every *may* under *hope* lacks its usual semantic contribution. Example (8) features regular deontic *may* that occurs in other matrix and embedded contexts, and (9) arguably features something close to a regular epistemic *might* (it may be a bit too much for the police to hope that the owners would indeed recognize their belongings, but hoping that at least it's not *impossible* for them to do so is perfectly rational).

(8) I do hope I may remain a member? (from BNC 2007)

(9) Serial numbers are missing from much of the electrical equipment but police properties officers hope people might recognise their belongings.
(from BNC 2007)

Portner (1997) argues that *may* in examples like (1) and (3) is "mood-indicating." To account for its special semantics, he introduces a separate lexical entry restricted to a small range of syntactic contexts. He proposes that *may* as in (1) and (3) conveys the presupposition that its propositional argument is doxastically possible for the hoper (i.e. that the hoper believes the described situation to be possible), and contributes nothing to the assertion. I do not endorse the presupposition that Portner assigns to *may*,[2] but I accept his claim that the modal in the construction does not contribute anything directly to the assertion. I assume that the elevated flavor of *may* under *hope* is not encoded in the narrow compositional semantics, but rather results from the construction expressively signaling that a particular register of the language is being used. I conjecture that the hedging effect arises pragmatically: the speaker of (3) could have used non-register-marked (7), yet hasn't, so perhaps she is trying to

---

[2] Which does not change the overall semantics for the relevant sentences. Given the lexical semantics of *hope*, Portner's presupposition would have no effect: non-modal complement of *hope* is presupposed to be doxastically possible for the subject of hoping as well. E.g. if the speaker knows that Gillian believes she cannot win, she cannot utter (i) truly, and (ii) is a contradiction. The presupposition that Portner ascribes to *may* as in (1) and (3) simply doubles the presupposition triggered by *hope*, so the semantic predictions are the same with Portner's presupposition for *may* and without it.

(i) Gillian hopes she will win.
(ii) # Gillian knows she won't win, but she hopes she will.

signal something special with her choice of *may*. Given this pragmatic story, it is expected that sometimes speakers will find only register effects by *may*, other times only hedging effects, and yet other times, both register and hedging effects.

How could a construction with a special variant of *may* be created by language users in the first place? Below, I propose a particular hypothesis addressing the rise of *may* under *hope* and the elevated flavor it can convey.

8.3 Semantics of hoping

Before we turn to historical data, it is useful to formally analyze the semantics of hoping. What makes the attitude of hoping special is the way it relates beliefs and desires (see Anand and Hacquard 2013 for both an overview of the literature and an approach to the semantics of hoping close to the one described below). A number of tests suggest that a hope report conveys information both regarding the agent's beliefs and the agent's desires. Namely, one can only hope that p if A considers p possible; B does not consider p necessary; and C prefers p to its alternatives. A and B form the belief part, and C forms the desire part of the attitude.

That a hope report conveys some measure of doxastic uncertainty about p (i.e. a combination of A and B) is shown by examples modeled after Scheffler (2008):

(10)   Mark: Is Peter coming today?
    a. Bill: ^{OK}I hope he is.
    b. Bill: * I want him to.

(11)   It is raining. That's exactly what I {*hope/^{OK}want}.

In (10b), the report of a desire for Peter to be coming today cannot serve as a direct answer: simply expressing a preference for his coming does not help with resolving the question of whether he is.[3] The fact that *hope* is felicitous in (10a) shows, according to Scheffler and to Anand and Hacquard, that a hope report may convey a belief about its complement along with a preference for it.

The contrast in (11) shows that in the situation of epistemic certainty about p, hoping for p is inappropriate. That *want* is OK in (11) demonstrates that there is nothing wrong with mere preference for what is known to be true. Therefore *hope*'s inappropriateness in (11) must have something to do with the attitude's doxastic component. If a hope report conveys that the agent considers p possible and at the same time not-necessary, we expect exactly the pattern we see in (10) and (11).

What examples (10) and (11) show is that in addition to the preference component similar to that of *want*, *hope* also has a belief component in its semantics. The status

---

[3] Example (10b) in this context would often *implicate* an answer to the question: a cooperative speaker who knows whether Peter is coming would not use (10b), which can trigger an inference on the part of the hearer.

of both meaning components seems to be that of assertion. Consider B's utterance in (12). Being a felicitous answer to A's question, it must assert something about Mary's beliefs. At the same time, C's reply targets the preference component: C argues that B's assertion cannot be true appealing to Mary's preferences regarding the weather. This is as expected if B asserted both a statement about Mary's beliefs and Mary's desires.

(12)   A: Does Mary think it is raining?
            B: Well, she certainly hopes so.
            C: That cannot be true. Mary prefers sunny weather to rain.

Another source of evidence for the parity status of the belief and desire components of the semantics of *hope* is the behavior of adverbial modifiers: they may target either part of the meaning.

In (13) the degree modifier *very much* signals the strength of Ann's preference, and has nothing to do with her beliefs:

(13)   Ann hopes very much that Mary will be elected.

In (14) as well, the continuation favors interpreting the temporal adverbial *still* as modifying the desire component. We do not know if Ann's opinion on Mary's electoral chances changed, but the structure of her preferences has been adjusted recently, as we learn from the second clause. This favors interpreting *still* as belonging to the desire component.

(14)   Ann still hopes that Mary will be elected, though she was really disappointed by her position on the nuclear power plant.

However, in (15) both the degree modifier *a little bit* and the temporal modifier *still* attach to the belief component, not the desire component: *a little bit* conveys that the likelihood of Mary's win is not that great according to Ann, and *still* signals that Ann continues to consider Mary's win a live option.

(15)   Ann still hopes a little bit that Mary will be elected, though she considers it quite unlikely.

I adopt the following lexical entry for *hope*, in line with Anand and Hacquard (2013).[4] If one wishes to have a preference semantics along the lines of Villalta (2008) for *hope*, modifying (16) accordingly is straightforward.

(16) $[\![hope]\!]^w = \lambda p.\lambda x. (Dox_x(w) \cap p \neq \emptyset) \wedge (Dox_x(w) \cap \neg p \neq \emptyset) \wedge$
          $\wedge \forall w' \in Dox_x(w)$: p-worlds most similar to w' are more desirable for x in w than $\neg p$-worlds most similar to w'

---

[4] More accurately, in line with Anand and Hacquard's informal analysis, but not with their technical implementation within event semantics.

The only other class of attitudes that relates beliefs and desires in a similar way is the class of attitudes of fearing. The difference between hoping that *p* and fearing that *p* is that in the latter case, one prefers *p*'s alternatives to *p*, not the other way round. But both for hoping and for fearing one has to consider argument *p* possible and not-necessary. Anand and Hacquard (2013) call the natural class of attitudes of hoping and fearing "emotive doxastics."

In this chapter, I will only discuss verbs of hoping, leaving verbs of fearing aside. The reason for that is more practical than theoretical: in the Early Modern English data I used, verbs of hoping with finite complements outnumber verbs of fearing more than four times in each historical section. There are too few examples with verbs of fearing for meaningful analysis. If there were significant differences between the modal system under hoping and fearing attitudes, the scarcity of data in my sample would not have allowed me to distinguish that from random fluctuations.

8.4 Modals under verbs of hoping in the 15th century

In Old English, *may* did not appear under verbs of hoping, at least in the sample of Ogawa (1989) (which covers a large part of the whole surviving corpus of Old English texts). This is contrary to Visser's (1963–73) claim that "the use of *may* and *might* in clauses depending on such verbs as ... hope ... is common in all periods" (§1678). As we will see in this section, the sought *may*-under-*hope* construction was still absent in the 15th century.

A 411,000-word dataset covering the years 1425–1520 was drawn from the Parsed Corpus of Early English Correspondence (PCEEC 2006).[5] The dataset forms the earliest section of this corpus of historical letters. PCEEC was chosen for this study for three reasons: first, it exists in the parsed form which allows for rapid and accurate searching, with the help of the *CorpusSearch 2* utility written by Beth Randall at UPenn; second, consisting of letters, PCEEC is relatively uniform in terms of genre and register; and third, early letters to a large extent represent functional writing, and are often closer to the contemporary vernacular than texts of many other genres (see Nevalainen and Raumolin-Brunberg 2003 for discussion).

---

[5] My 1425–1520 subcorpus consisted of the following PCEEC collections: CELY (51,000 words), FOX (11,000), MARCHALL (5,000), PASTON (234,000), PLUMPTO (37,000), RERUM (6,000), RUTLAND (1,000), SHILLIN (14,000), SIGNET (15,000), and STONOR (38,000).

There are several letters written before 1425 in some of the collections, but none of them contains a hope report. At the other end of the period, the Plumpton Correspondence contains several letters written after 1520, but as their usage does not seem to be different from that of the earlier letters, and they belong to the same circle of authors and recipients as the earlier letters in the collection, I chose to include them in the analysis. In those later Plumpton letters, there were 2 examples with *shall*, 2 with *will*, 1 with *would*, and 5 non-modal examples, of which 3 feature a non-ambiguous subjunctive (two instances of the subjunctive are in formulaic wishes of good health, and one is in a sentence conveying a non-performative hope regarding a certain future situation).

It turned out that in the 15th century *may* was still practically absent from the complements of hope attitudes. Moreover, so was *can*, which frequently occurs under *hope* in Present-Day English. Modal *must*, which was relatively common under hoping verbs *hopian* and *hyhtan* in Old English (see Ogawa 1989), was also absent. The 15th-century distribution was thus markedly different both from the Old English one and from the modern one.

Further in this section, I describe the distribution of modals, of the unambiguous subjunctive of lexical verbs, and of other non-modal forms in the complements of verbs of hoping in the 1425–1520 subcorpus of PCEEC. In the next section I show that the absence of *may* in that sample is in fact surprising given the compositional semantics of the modal at the time. Together, the facts described in these two sections will form the basis for comparison with the mid-17th-century situation discussed in the next section.

In a pilot study using a 177,000-word part of the 1425–1520 subcorpus (all letter collections from the actual sample except the Paston letters), I examined all examples with verbs with a *that*-clause complement in order to determine the precise membership in the class of verbs of hoping at the time. I concluded that two verbs were used predominantly for expressing hopes in that period: *hope* and *trust*. According to lexicographers (cf. *hōpen* and *trusten* in MED 2002), both of them could express several meanings other than that of hoping (e.g. that of confidence). But in my data sample, wherever the context provides enough support for disambiguation, both verbs denote a hoping attitude. For example, in (17) the wife of the recipient asks the author to recommend her to her husband in the letter, and can hardly be *confident* that he received a lock she sent in her previous letter: there was no communication between her and him from the moment she sent the lock. However, a *hope* that he received it makes sense in the context.

(17) Syr, my masterys youre wyffe recomaund har harteley vnto you, sche enformyng you that sche sent a lettere vnto you the last weke be on Rechard Cartar of Darbey, in the wyche lettere sche sent vnto you a lytell locke of gould y-closed in the sayd lettere, **the wyche sche trust to God ye haue ressayved.**

CELY,223.142.3134

'Sir, my mistress your wife recommends her heartily to you, she informing you that she sent a letter to you last week with Richard Carter of Darby, in which letter she sent you a little golden lock enclosed in the said letter, which she hopes to God you have received.'

Thus I included into the analysis all instances of *hope* and *trust* taking finite-complement clauses, with the understanding that in a few cases they might in principle have been used to express a different attitude. But given the semantic uniformity of the unambiguous examples, such cases must have been quite rare.[6]

---

[6] Analyzing all instances of a given verb together rather than trying to divide them by their semantics is common in the historical research on modals; see e.g. Visser (1963–73) and Ogawa (1989).

In (17) and other examples from PCEEC, the orthography is as in the corpus. For examples from the 1425–1520 subcorpus, I provide "translations." Their purpose is not to be perfect sentences of Present-Day English, but rather to help the reader unfamiliar with Late Middle/Early Modern English to understand the structure and meaning of the original examples. Tags such as CELY,223.142.3134 are from PCEEC, and uniquely identify the passage within the corpus.

8.4.1 Modals under verbs of hoping in the 15th century: an overview

The overall distribution of modals and finite forms under *hope* and *trust* in the 1425–1520 subcorpus is given in Table 8.1. Non-modal complements are counted in the columns "nm subj" and "nm other." The "nm subj" column counts the examples where the embedded lexical (=non-modal) verb is unambiguously in the inflectional subjunctive. The "nm other" column counts both the examples of the unambiguous indicative and those with ambiguous forms.

The main features of this distribution are: (1) virtual absence of *may*, *might*, *can*, and *mote/must*; (2) predominance of *shall* (and *should*); and (3) a relatively high proportion of unambiguous subjunctives. At least the first two features are not trivial, as we can see from a comparison with the distribution of modals under verbs of asking; cf. Table 8.2, cited from Castle et al. (2012).[7]

Consider the absence of *may* and *mote* first. In Old English, the complements of both verbs of hoping and verbs of asking frequently contained *motan* > modern *must*, Ogawa (1989). In particular, for verbs of asking, *motan* was very common when the matrix subject had the same reference with the embedded subject. In the 1425–1520 segment of PCEEC, in such contexts with verbs of asking we largely find *may* and *might*, which must have replaced *motan* at some point. But in contrast to

TABLE 8.1 Complements of verbs of hoping, 1425–1520, PCEEC (Percentages)

may	might	can	must	shall	should	will	would	nm subj	nm other	ALL
1.2	0.4	0.4	0	43.8	9.8	20.0	4.7	8.6	11.3	100 (N=256)

TABLE 8.2 Complements of verbs of asking, 1425–1520, PCEEC (Percentages)

may	might	can	must	shall	should	will	would	nm all	ALL
17.4	3.7	0	0.4	0.3	7.0	27.2	7.0	37.0	100 (N=702)

(Castle et al. 2012)

---

[7] Castle et al. (2012) report the results of an investigation into the modal system under verbs of asking, namely *beseech*, *desire*, *labor*, *pray*, and *request*, in the same 411,000-word 1425–1520 subcorpus of PCEEC. The data on verbs of hoping reported here and the data on verbs of asking from Castle et al. (2012) are thus directly comparable.

that, under verbs of hoping *motan* disappeared without being replaced by *may* in our 15th-century subcorpus. The absence of *may* is thus a significant fact about the particular context of hoping attitudes.

For the second feature of the distribution, while *shall* is the most frequent modal under verbs of hoping in our sample, it is almost absent from the complements of verbs of asking. Both the complements of verbs of hoping and of verbs of asking usually denote desirable states of affairs in the texts, so there is no immediately obvious semantic reason for such a discrepancy.

To understand the actual distribution of modals under verbs of hoping, we need to look more closely at individual examples rather than at the broad distributional profile. The rest of this section is devoted to that.[8]

8.4.2 *Will and would*

When verbs of hoping have *will* in their complement, the embedded clause predominantly (48 out of 51 instances) has 2nd and 3rd person animate subjects. In most cases (44 out of 51), whether the desired situation described in the complement will actually happen is under the control of the subject of *will*, see (18) and (19).

(18) but I trvst ʒe wyl be pacient.   PASTON,I,150.041.1045
'but I hope you will be patient.'

(19) and be the tyme my lord hathe herde me **I trust to good he wylle be my good lorde,** ho have yow, my good modyr, and alle yowrs yn hys one fyfull kepeyng,
STONOR,I,121.022.340
'and by the time my lord has heard me, I hope to God that he will be my good lord; who [=God] may have you, my good mother, and all yours, in his one faithful keeping.'

Some examples deviate from this pattern; e.g. in (20) the embedded subject is not animate, and in (21) the control over whether the desired outcome will obtain is definitely not in human hands.

(20) I trust, thou I be fer fro yow, that **þis lytyll byll this cold whedere, and my erand wull make me and shew me present.**   STONOR,II,117.098.1718
'I hope that even though I am far from you, this little letter and my errand, in this cold weather, will make me present [by your side] and show me so.'

---

[8] I will not systematically compare what we find in this type of context with the distribution of those forms elsewhere in the language, in the absence of available fine-grained data on the latter. Such a comparison would have required a novel primary study of the modal system in PCEEC as a whole, which is beyond the scope of this chapter.

(21) I pray you se a fayre weder or ye take youre passage for onny haste, for the weche I tryste to God **Wyll Maryon and ȝe wyll se that weder and wynde be fayre.**
CELY,33.029.567
'I pray you see fair weather before you take your passage in any haste, for which I trust to God Will Marion and you will see that the weather and wind are fair.'

Would appears to mostly function as the regular past tense of *will*, occurring under a past-tense matrix clause. In some examples it also seems to convey additional politeness, as in (22), where an expression of hope is in fact an indirect form of request.

(22) And this considered in your wise discrecion, I trost, my lord, thow here prisonyng were of oderes labore **ye wuld help here;**
PASTON,I,81.025.481
'And this having being considered at your wise discretion, I hope, my lord, that though her prisoning was done by another, you would help her.'

Overall, *will* and *would* function in the sample as significantly restricted forms. When those modals appear with an animate subject and concern a situation that can be controllable by humans, that control lies with their subject. Note, however, that the overall distribution of *will* and *would* is not easily amenable to a narrowly semantic analysis: a meaning for *will* that includes a desire component would explain the cases where the subject of *will* is in control of the situation, which is the majority of cases, but it will not explain *will*'s presence in e.g. (20). If we say that there is only one meaning of *will*, including a desire component, we cannot explain the rare examples where that component cannot be present. On the other hand, if we say that *will* is ambiguous between a desire and non-desire variant (which *is* the correct thing to say given the distribution), this by itself does not explain (i) why we do not see such non-desire *will* with animate subjects, and (ii) why non-desire *will* is rare compared to desire *will*.

The puzzle, of course, disappears once we allow for constraints that are fully usage-based, not semantics-based. If the non-desire meaning of *will* is a recent innovation, then we expect it to be rare. That rarity would have nothing to do with the meaning of the innovation. It is caused by the forces of inertia of use, which only allow the new meaning to enter the usage slowly.

8.4.3 Shall and should

The most frequent modal in the complements of verbs of hoping, *shall*, is close to an unmarked option in this context. It appears with the 2nd and 3rd person animate subjects (where *will* also appears), with 1st person and inanimate subjects, and with expletive *it* and *there*.

(23) and yf it lyke yowe to com on Thursday at nyght, < ... > I trusty to God **þat ȝe schall so speke to myn husbonde,**
PASTON,II,436.467.11971
'and if you would like to come on Thursday at night, ... I hope to God that you would be able to speak that way with my husband.'

Sometimes in examples with *shall* it is clear that the embedded subject has little control over the matter. Example (23) is one such case: the larger context shows that it is the embedded subject who really needs the author's husband to speak to him, not the other way round. However, it is hard to say with certainty whether there are any examples requiring that the embedded subject be in control of the situation. For example, in (24) the addressee should most probably have control over whether he does anything to satisfy his correspondent; but it is also possible that the author is concerned not so much with the addressee's willingness to do the work, but rather with whether it would be objectively possible to obtain the desired outcome given the circumstances.

(24) < . . . > Walsyngham, whych y trust to God **by your help shall be corryged**.
PASTON,II,191.352.9514
'Walsingham, which I hope to God will be corrected with your help.'

Without definitive examples of the embedded subject's control, we cannot decide whether *shall* was in semantically complementary distribution with *will* in such contexts, or was an unmarked, more general form.

The form *should*, as was the case with *would*, mostly functions as the past tense form of *shall*. In addition to its sequence-of-tense uses, *should* is also used in irrealis consequents of conditionals as in (25).

(25) And if ye comaund me so for to do, I trist **I shuld sey nothyng to my ladys displesure, but to youre profyt**;   PASTON,I,666.229.6881
'And if you command me to do so, I hope I would say nothing to my lady's displeasure, but [at the same time] [only] to your profit.'

Interestingly, while deontic interpretations could be sensible in some of the examples, I did not find any instance of *should* under verbs of hoping where the deontic reading would be the only one possible.

8.4.4 Non-modal forms except the unambiguous subjunctive

Complements with *will* and *shall* describe future situations. But hopes targeted at the present or the past are also possible, and when such hopes are reported, we see non-modal complements in the segment of PCEEC under consideration. The finite verb in such cases is either in the unambiguous indicative form, (26), or a form ambiguous between the indicative and the subjunctive, (27).

(26) but I hope and trust verrayly þe **matier of his informacion is vntrewe**.
PASTON,I,5.003.37
'But I hope very much that the content of his news is untrue.'

(27) < . . . > like as I have writon to you in a letter sent ouer at Shorfftyde, the whech I truste **ye have receyued** /   CELY,229.143.3150
'< . . . > like as I have written to you in a letter sent over at Shorfftyde, which I hope you have received'

8.4.5 Unambiguous inflectional subjunctive

Twenty-two out of the 51 non-modal complements in the subcorpus feature a verb in an unambiguously subjunctive form. Twenty-one of those 22 contain the same form *be*, and the remaining one contains *have*.[9] The lexical composition here is not too different from other non-modal complements: out of the 17 cases where we have the unambiguous indicative, 14 feature verb *be*. Overall, there are only 4 non-modal complements, out of 51, that feature a finite verb other than *be*, *have* or *do*. But while "lexical poverty" is not a special feature of the unambiguous subjunctive examples, another feature is: many of such examples (namely, 15 out of 22) express, in a relatively formulaic way, hopes pertaining to good health and recovery from illness, (28).

(28) And yf it lyke you ser to her of my helthe, at the makyng of thys sympyll letter I was in good helthe of bode, blessyd be Jhesu as I troste **þat ye be**, or I wold be ryght sorye. CELY,222.141.3108
'And if you'd like, sir, to hear about my health, at the making of this simple letter I was of good health of body, blessed by Jesus, just as I hope you ___, or I would be very sorry.'[10]

Though formulaic, such expressions of hopes about good health are not a necessary component of any letter template. For example, in the letters of William Maryon, of which we have 12, such a hope is expressed only once. In other words, though such examples approach formulas, their appearance in letters is not fully automatic.

Not all examples with the unambiguous subjunctive belong to this good-health group. But the subjunctive in other examples seems to have had little semantic import, as in (29).

(29) Syr, I wndyrstonde be yowr letter that aull the whowlschypys ar cwm to Calles sauyng vij, qwherof ij be spent. I trwste to God **that the Crystowyr of Rayname be cwm to Calleys be thys**. CELY,126.099.2220
'Sir, I learned from your letter that all the wool-ships have come to Calais except for seven, whereof two are wrecked. I hope to God that the Christopher of Rayname has come to Calais by [the time you receive] this.'

Given the overall role of the subjunctive in the language of the time, its concentration in hopes about good health calls for attention. Its presence as such is not surprising, but its concentration in sentences serving a single narrow communicative function is unusual. Such restriction of a grammatical form to a narrow set of semi-fossilized contexts is generally a sign that the form is fading away.

---

[9] The corresponding indicative forms would have been *are* or *is* (or forms corresponding to those in the relevant dialect), and *hap/has* for *have*. For a concise introduction to the Middle English morphology, see Fulk (2012).

[10] I intentionally omit the exact translation of the subjunctive form in these examples, in order to not smuggle in my analysis.

It is worth stressing just how narrow the subjunctive's special niche was in the considered data: not all hopes which may be taken to be ceremonial or formulaic are expressed with the subjunctive. For instance, hopes about the recipient's "good speed" (i.e. success) are not less formulaic than hopes regarding good health, but nevertheless they are not expressed with the subjunctive (cf. (30)).

(30) And I praye God sende yow as goode speede in þat mater as I wolde ye hadde, and as I hope **ye shall have er thys letter come to yow**; PASTON,I,501.161.4937
'And I pray that God sends you such success in that matter as I would like you to have, and as I hope that you will have [success] before this letter comes to you;'

If the subjunctive was already on its way out of the system of hope reports in the language of our 1425–1520 sample, such entrenchment in one narrow type of context is to be expected. When a form ceases to be used in a particular class of contexts, it may be retained longer in narrowly defined subclasses. For instance, Modern English still retains the morphological subjunctive in *Long live the Queen*, even though it is no longer normal to use the subjunctive in matrix wishes in general.

8.4.6 May, might, and can

Turning finally to *may* and *can*, there are only four examples with *may/might*, and 1 example with *can* in our 1425–1520 subcorpus. Though it is hard to recover the exact modal flavor for each example, as we do not have a large sample for cross-checking, the overall range of possible meanings encompasses internal ability, circumstantial possibility (cf. (31)), and perhaps permission.

(31) And as I conceiue to my grete comfort and gladnesse, my saide brothre is wele recouered and amended, thanked be God, and soo I truste **he may nowe spare you.**
'And as I understand to my great comfort and gladness, my brother mentioned above is well recovered and cured, God be thanked, and so I hope he can now do without you.'

This range is not surprising, as it coincides with the regular meanings for those modals in the language as a whole at the time. We can extrapolate that latter distribution using the study of Gotti et al. (2002). Gotti et al. analyze 19 per cent of the 677 instances of *may* in their 1350–1420 subcorpus as conveying internal ability, and 53 per cent as conveying circumstantial possibility. For the 1640–1710 subcorpus, they give the shares of 6 per cent for internal ability, 35 per cent for circumstantial possibility, and 6 per cent for the innovative meaning of permission for *may*. The distribution of meanings for *may* for our sample may be taken to be in between those two distributions, thus definitely featuring internal ability and circumstantial possibility, and perhaps featuring the innovative meaning of permission. For *can*, a similar extrapolation suggests the range of internal ability and circumstantial possibility.

Given those ranges of meanings, is it expected that *may* and *can* are absent from the complements of verbs of hoping? The answer is no, and we show that in the next section.

8.5 Why the absence of *may* and *can* in the complements of hoping verbs in the 15th century is conspicuous

Based on the above extrapolation from Gotti et al. (2002), we can note that *may*'s distributional profile in terms of percentages of particular modal flavors in the 15th century must have been close to that of *can* in Present-Day English (for the latter, see Coates 1983: 86). But despite that, there is a vast discrepancy between the present-day rates of the use of *can* under *hope*, and the use of *may* under verbs of hoping in our 1425–1520 sample.

For the present-day distribution, we can use the estimates shown in Table 8.3, featuring data from the Corpus of Contemporary American English (COCA, Davies 2008), covering 1990–2012, with 450 million words. The table provides the number of occurrences of strings *hope, hopes, hoped* followed by the strings *can, will, 'll,* and *shall*, within a 5-word right window. They can serve as estimates for the overall proportion of *can* vs. the future forms in COCA. Not all of the examples counted would feature a genuine embedding of a modal or a future marker under verb *hope*, as we only conducted an adjacency search, not a structural search. But a brief examination of a small sample of the found examples shows that the sought constructions are frequent enough among the results that we can use the obtained frequencies as reasonable estimates.

Table 8.4 provides the results of identical searches within the Corpus of American Soap Operas (CASO, Davies 2012), covering 2001–2012, with 100 million words. In that corpus, consisting of scripted dialogues intended to imitate everyday speech, the prevalence of *can* in the relevant context is even higher than in the multi-genre COCA.

If we now compare the present-day data to the similar data from the 15th century, the difference becomes apparent, as Table 8.5 shows.

TABLE 8.3 Estimates of *can* vs. future markers in COCA (1990–2012)

	hope, hopes, hoped
can	2,890
will	9,348
'll	1,690
shall	28
TOTAL	13,956

TABLE 8.4 Estimates of *can* vs. future markers in CASO (2001–2012)

	hope, hopes, hoped
can	2,505
will	1,345
'll	1,306
shall	3
TOTAL	5,159

TABLE 8.5 15-century *may* vs. present-day *can* under verbs of hoping

	PCEEC 1425–1520	COCA 1990–2012	CASO 2001–2012
can/may	*may*: 2%	*can*: 21%	*can*: 49%
will, shall, 'll	98%	79%	51%

1. The figures for COCA and CASO are estimates.
2. 100% is the examples of *may, can, will, shall,* and *'ll*. Examples with other modals are excluded from the count.

When we have such discrepancy in usage, there can be several explanations. One would be semantic: if the meanings of 15th-century *may* and *can* were very different from those of Present-Day *can*, we would not expect similar distributions in the first place. But we have already ruled out this possibility, having shown that the semantics of the two types of items in the language as a whole is in fact very similar.

Another explanation would be that for some reason, 15th-century English speakers expressed very different hopes than Present-Day speakers do. This could be due to either of two possibilities: (i) 15th-century speakers expressed hopes about very different situations from Present-Day speakers, and/or (ii) 15th-century speakers expressed hopes about different types of propositions than Present-Day speakers.

The first possibility is highly implausible, as a considerable number of hoping examples without *may* or *can* from our 1425–1520 subcorpus of PCEEC may be rendered into Present-Day English with *can*:

(32)   I tryste to God **ye schall com home to London or Crystemese.**

CELY,65.050.1088

≈ 'I hope you **can** come home to London before Christmas.'

The second possibility cannot be ruled out, as we cannot ask a 15th-century speaker what exactly they meant when they said (32). But other things being equal, the principle of uniformity in historical-linguistic explanations entails that positing distinct linguistic behaviors for past and present speakers should only be used as a last resort.

In fact, such last resort is not necessary here. It is well known in variationist sociolinguistics that semantics alone cannot fully explain the observed distributions of usage—in fact, we have already seen in section 8.4.2 that the distribution of *will/would* in our data cannot be explained by semantic factors alone.

So the third explanation for why *may* is absent from the complements of verbs of hoping is that there is a non-semantic, most likely usage-based factor that prevented the modal from appearing in this context:

(33) Insufficiency of the semantics
The absence of *may* from the complements of verbs of hoping in PCEEC 1425–1520 is due to a non-semantic factor.

The explanation along the lines of (33) is far preferable to that in terms of 15th-century speakers mysteriously choosing to hope for different types of propositions in the same type of situations than Present-Day speakers. The former does not rely on unverifiable assumptions about discontinuity in semantic behavior between the 15th century and the present, and does not commit us to anything that we would have no independent grounds to commit to.

Under our explanation of the absence of *may* from the complements of hoping verbs, that absence was not a simple matter. In principle, nothing grammatical prevented *may* from starting to be used more frequently in this context. In the next section, we will look at a synchronic slice of English where *may* indeed took a considerable share of the complements of hoping verbs.

8.6 Modals under verbs of hoping in the 17th century

Our second synchronic slice consists of years 1630–81 of the same PCEEC corpus, containing about 356,000 words.[11] The modal and non-modal complements of verbs of hoping are distributed in that subcorpus as shown in Table 8.6.

TABLE 8.6 Complements of verbs of hoping, 1630–1681, PCEEC

may	might	can	must	shall	should	will	would	nm subj	nm other	ALL
7.5	1.2	0.9	0	12.1	1.7	47.0	2.0	0	27.7	100 (N=347)

---

[11] The subcorpus included the following collections of PCEEC (2006): BROWNE (21,000 words), CONWAY (58,000), CORIE (5,000), DUPPA (28,000), ESSEX (25,000), FLEMING (40,000), HADDOCK (6,000), MARVELL (11,000), MINETTE (8,000), OSBORNE (71,000), PEPYS (42,000), PETTY (22,000), PRIDEAU (8,000), TIXALL (12,000).

Comparing the data in Table 8.6 to the 15th-century data in Table 8.1,[12] we can note the following major changes: (1) in the middle of the 17th century the most frequent modal is *will*, while in the 15th century it was *shall*; (2) the unambiguous inflectional subjunctive is completely absent from hope reports; and (3) *may/might*, unlike in the 15th century, claim a significant share of the complements of hoping attitudes.

8.6.1 Will and shall

In the 15th-century subcorpus, *will* was mostly restricted to 2nd and 3rd person animate subjects, and *shall* was close to being a default form, compatible with all kinds of subjects. In the 1630–81 subcorpus, the situation is different: *shall* is mostly restricted to 1st person subjects (37 out of 42 instances), while *will* never occurs with such, but is frequent elsewhere. The two modals thus almost reach a complementary distribution. Besides the restrictions on their subjects, there seem to be no significant differences between the two. For instance, (34) and (35) illustrate that both *shall* and *will* may be used in hope reports that pragmatically serve as requests, and (36) and (37) both feature hopes about circumstances which the speaker has little control over.

(34) and I hope I **shall** heare of your health by the next Poste.   CONWAY,57.011.338

(35) I hope you **will** acquaint none but my sister with my wife's concernment,
                                                                       CONWAY,153.029.935

(36) I hope when our Case of Clay is broaken by Naturall Death, Wee **shall** no longer peep through its Craks and Cranyes, but then look round about us freely, and see cleerely the things which wee now do but grope after.   PETTY,10.003.66

---

[12] The distributions observed in the two time periods are globally different with statistical significance (which is not surprising given the large differences between the values). The actual counts of each modal in the complements of hoping verbs can be assumed to be produced by a multinomial distribution. The statistical test needs to check how likely it is that data from the two periods came from the same actual distribution—namely, that the linguistic rules governing that system remained the same, and the differences in counts that we observe are due to random chance. The usual χ^2 test for homogeneity of two observed samples is not appropriate here due to small counts in some cells. An exact test for homogeneity is not feasible given the enormous number of permutations involved. Thus the proper statistical procedure in this case involves computing a p-value based on Monte Carlo sampling of possible data tables: the idea is to check how frequently such divergent observed distributions would arise when they are truly generated from one and the same multinomial probability distribution. This procedure gives us the p-value of 0.0000001, which allows us to reject with great certainty the null hypothesis that the differences between the two periods are accidental. (In fact, this value means that the simulation has not produced a single table with more extreme differences.) R code for inputting the data and performing the test is as follows:

```
cent15 = c(3, 1, 1, 112, 25, 51, 12, 22, 29)
cent17 = c(26, 4, 3, 42, 6, 163, 7, 0, 96)
two.periods = matrix(c(cent15,cent17), byrow=T, nrow=2)
chisq.test(two.periods, simulate.p.value=T, B=10000000)
```

(37) But I hope all these rugged paths **will** best conduct me to my Journeyes end.
    PETTY,88.046.1194

8.6.2 Non-modal non-subjunctive forms

Non-modal non-subjunctive complements in the 1630–81 subcorpus perform more or less the same function as they did in the 15th-century corpus: they are used when the content of a hope is a past or present situation rather than a future one. Examples (38) and (39) are representative.

(38) Sir—I wrot you the 24th of December by my Lord Arlingtons special order, and doe hope **it came safe to you**. CORIE,30.009.108

(39) but hearing that he getts the better of them in the House of Lords, I hope **he is in no great danger**, CONWAY,447.087.2533

In rare cases, a present-tense non-modal form may be oriented towards the future, as in (40). It is hard to see any clear semantic import of the use of a finite form instead of a future-oriented modal in such examples.

(40) I hope **you find some Company with whom you may delight to Convers**;
    BROWNE,201.048.940

8.6.3 The absence of the subjunctive

The main difference between the non-modal complements of verbs of hoping in the 15th- and the 17th-century subcorpora of PCEEC is the complete disappearance of the inflectional subjunctive in the latter. While in the 15th-century subcorpus 8.6 per cent of the examples featured an unambiguous subjunctive, in the 1630–81 subcorpus there are no such examples whatsoever.

Hopes about good health, in which the subjunctive was so frequent in the 15th century, are still used in the 17th century. But with the disappearance of the subjunctive, its role has been taken up by other, non-specialized forms. Thus some hopes about good health feature an indicative lexical verb, (41), while others feature a modal, (42). As the forms used are no longer specialized for this context, hopes about health no longer form a distinguished category. The existence of examples like (43) suggests as much: there we see a hope concerning the addressee's health and his chariot at the same time.

(41) Soe hopeing that you **are** all well and with my duty to your selfe, and my loue to my brothers and sisters I rest Sr Your dutifull Son, Henry Fleming.
    FLEMING,266.101.1691

(42) and I hope in God that you **will** now recover your health
    CONWAY,265.069.1965

(43) I hope your health and chariot too **will** be settled in that due proportion and improvement as either you or Sir John Werden can covet.   PETTY,54.027.741

8.6.4 Can

With only 3 occurrences out of the 347 complements of verbs of hoping in the subcorpus, *can* remains a very rare modal in this context. When it is used, it has the expected meaning of internal ability or circumstantial possibility.

8.6.5 May

Unlike in the 15th-century subcorpus, where it was almost absent, *may* (together with *might*) is used in 8.6 per cent of cases in the 1630–81 subcorpus.[13] Semantically, examples with *may* do not form a single group, exhibiting instead a wide range of meanings for the modal. Example (44) illustrates the meaning of circumstantial possibility (and features the past-tense form *might* apparently agreeing with the past-tense form *could* from the higher clause). In (45), the modal can be interpreted as conveying either circumstantial possibility or perhaps epistemic possibility. In (46), the modal might have been a genuine deontic, or perhaps a less semanticized instance of *may* in an indirect request having the form of a hope report.

(44) and in Earnest if I could hope **it might ever bee in my power to serve him** I would promise somthing for my self;

OSBORNE,76.034.1765

(45) I hope travayling and taking the fresh ayre and surceasing some time from my studyes, **may recruitt my spiritts so much and chauff the mass of my blood that this coolness and obstructedness of my arme may be dissipated**,

CONWAY,208.048.1446

(46) Dearest Unkle, I hope **now I may venter to say something for myself**.

TIXALL,59.022.406

Despite the difficulty of confidently assigning the modal to a single semantic category in each of these examples (and others like them in the sample), it should be clear from (44–46) that in our 1630–81 dataset *may* in the complements of verbs of hoping can have a range of modal flavors mostly similar to those available for *may* elsewhere at the time.

However, what is unexpected given the semantics of the modal in other contexts is *may*'s contribution in 10 examples (out of the total 30) that feature a precursor of the Present-Day English construction in (1) and (3):

---

[13] Visser (1963–73: §1,678) implies that *may* was once very frequent under *hope*, and then replaced in later English by *will* and non-modal forms. Our data show that actually there was never a stage when *may* was more frequent than *will* or non-modal forms.

(47) But I hope **in time your Ladiship may at least recover to that measure of health** you had before you went into Ireland.   CONWAY,231.062.1811

(48) I hope y^t [=that *(IY)*] **our next interview may be with the greater ioy and comfort.**   HADDOCK,1.001.6

Three of these examples, including (47), describe hopes regarding someone's good health. The other seven, including (48), concern other subjects, but exhibit at least some degree of ceremoniality/elevatedness: they not only report a hope, but seem to do it in a solemn and relatively formal way.

8.7 Hypothesis: *may* replaced the subjunctive in elevated hopes about good health

Consider the differences shown in Table 8.7.

I propose a hypothesis which takes the changes in Table 8.7 to be related to each other. Namely, I propose that *may* initially became prominent under verbs of hoping thanks to its taking over the function that the subjunctive performed.

(49) The good-health hypothesis for *may* under *hope*

 Stage 1. The subjunctive has almost disappeared from under verbs of hoping. It is only retained in hopes about good health.

 Stage 2. The subjunctive dies out even in hopes about good health. As the speakers still perceive the need to use distinctive marking in place of the disappeared subjunctive, they choose *may*.

 The distributional replacement is the primary change, and the lexical meaning of the modal gets deduced by the speakers based on the meaning of the construction as a whole (cf. "meaning equations" of Eckardt 2006). The reconstructed meaning for the modal in this syntactic context does not contain existential quantification over worlds, since the old construction as a whole did not.

 Stage 3. The elevated construction with non-quantificational *may* generalizes its meaning from hopes about good health to all high-register hopes about serious matters. At the same time, the rise of *may* under *hope* with special semantics

TABLE 8.7 Changes in the complements of hoping attitudes

15th century	Mid-17th century
May is almost absent.	*May* is prominent.
The subjunctive is prominent.	The subjunctive is absent.
The subjunctive is used in hopes about good health.	*May* is used in elevated hopes, including hopes about good health.

makes it easier for the speakers to use all semantic variants of *may* in that syntactic context, leading to an across-the-board rise in prominence, bringing about the distribution of the mid-17th century.

In the data, we directly observe Stage 1 and the end result of Stage 3. Stage 2 was not directly registered in the data we discussed above. At the moment there is no solid evidence either for or against that stage's actual existence due to lack of data. Therefore (49) is only a hypothesis. Below I discuss what kind of evidence is lacking in order to prove or disprove it.

The strong points of the hypothesis are as follows. The disappearance of the subjunctive in English has happened in different contexts at different times, so it is safe to assume there was an external reason that drove it from under hope attitudes as well. Note that such disappearance, as it proceeded gradually, cannot be tied to drastic changes in the semantic or syntactic capabilities of the subjunctive.

That it was specifically *may* that replaced the subjunctive in hopes about good health gets support from two kinds of facts. First, *may* often replaced the subjunctive throughout the history of English; cf. (50), based on Visser (1963–73).[14] Note that those replacements occur at different times, and cannot be associated with a single sweeping change. Consequently they cannot be tied to a takeover by *may* of a single particular semantic function of the subjunctive.

(50) *May* replacing the subjunctive in different contexts:
    a. Matrix wishes and prayers
        i. The subjunctive: Old English through the 17th century, and in isolated fossils after that (Visser 1963–73: §841)
        ii. *may*: isolated examples in Middle English, well-established since the 16th century (Visser 1963–73: §1,680)
    b. Concessive clauses (without a concessive conjunction)
        i. The subjunctive: "with great frequency in all periods, with the exception of Present-Day English" (Visser 1963–73: §884)
        ii. *may*: starting in the 14th century (Visser 1963–73: §1,666)
    c. Relative clauses "with final import" (e.g. *to find a salve which **may** her life preserve*)
        i. The subjunctive: common in Old English and Middle English, but no examples after Shakespeare (Visser 1963–73: §876)
        ii. *May*: examples throughout all the periods, including Early and Late Modern English (Visser 1963–73: §1,677)

---

[14] One should be cautious using Visser's conclusions, as they come from the pre-corpus era when it was prohibitively hard to rigorously test statements about the rise and disappearance of particular forms (cf. n. 13). Still, Visser's data serves as a useful first approximation.

Second, *may* was not used under hoping verbs. As a form accidentally absent from such complements (see the preceding section), it was a perfect choice for a new marked form.

One point requiring explanation in this story is that the new *may* under hoping verbs did not have its usual possibility import. While it is puzzling why such developments can occur, the case of hoping attitudes would not be the only case where *may* replaced the subjunctive despite the fact that no possibility meaning was involved: in none of the constructions in (50) is possibility involved either.

Under our hypothesis, the new syntactically restricted meaning of *may* arises because speakers preserve the old meaning of the construction as a whole, and solve the equation (see Eckardt 2006) to deduce the import of *may* in the new construction, which turns out to be close to assertively empty. While this story may sound unlikely, the alternative story is actually much more implausible. The alternative in this case would be as follows: *may* generally acquires a new assertively empty meaning, and then for some reason that meaning gets restricted to a particular type of syntactic context. This is clearly not a very likely scenario, as we do not see evidence for close-to-empty *may* popping up everywhere in the language, outside of a few special syntactic contexts.[15]

A major weak point of our hypothesis is that we do not have direct evidence that the new *may* directly replaced the subjunctive in hopes about good health, even though there is no evidence to the contrary either. The best possible type of evidence would be to find specific individuals who earlier in their lives used the subjunctive in hopes about good health, but then switched to *may*. The next best thing would be to find a family or another tightly knit circle of authors who show the same progression from the subjunctive to *may* across generations, with younger authors switching to the innovative form (see Raumolin-Brunberg 2005 for an example of how one may find such kind of evidence). Unfortunately, the data in PCEEC (2006) do not seem to include either of those throughout the 16th century, for which the evidence of personal letters is generally less varied and abundant than for other periods. We thus have to wait for more data, whether from letters or elsewhere, to properly test the proposed hypothesis.

---

[15] As Portner (1997) discusses, there are actually several restricted non-plain-possibility variants of *may* in Present-Day English. Under the semantic-equation story, it is not surprising that *may* associated with different constructions would have different meanings: those meanings are just deduced from the meanings of whole constructions. Without such equation-based reanalysis, it is hard to explain why *several* different marginal variants of *may* could arise.

Part II

Middle modality

9

In an imperfect world: Deriving the typology of counterfactual marking

BRONWYN M. BJORKMAN AND CLAIRE HALPERT

9.1 Introduction

The complex interaction between temporal and modal semantics has been the focus of much work, including Condoravdi (2002), Arregui (2005), and Ippolito (2006). Chen et al. (chapter 12 in this volume) approach the compositional semantics of tense and modality from a cross-linguistic perspective, investigating the scope interactions of overtly marked tense and modality.

This chapter focuses instead on contexts where temporal morphology appears not to contribute its usual interpretation, but instead appears to be involved in the expression of modal meanings. Counterfactual conditionals (CFs) in many languages are marked by "fake" temporal inflection, tense or aspect markers that do not contribute their standard temporal meanings but instead seem to be necessary for the interpretation of counterfactual modality. The two types of temporal morphology that have been widely documented as playing a role in CFs are past tense and imperfective aspect (e.g. Anderson 1951, Hale 1969, Isard 1974, Steele 1975, Lyons 1977, James 1982, Palmer 1986, Fleischman 1989, Iatridou 2000, Van Linden and Verstraete 2008). In (1), we can see that verbs in CF conditional antecedents are marked with past-tense inflection even though the tense interpretation that they convey is non-past, as the present- and future-oriented time adverbs indicate.

(1) English: CF marked by **past**
    a. If I **knew** the answer **now**, I would tell you.
    b. If I **left tomorrow**, I would arrive next week.[1]

---

[1] This example is technically not a counterfactual conditional, but a "future less vivid" (FLV). These future-oriented conditionals share morphological and syntactic properties with true counterfactuals, and the two will be treated together here.

Modality Across Syntactic Categories. First edition. Ana Arregui, María Luisa Rivero, and Andrés Salanova (eds.).
This chapter © Bronwyn M. Bjorkman and Claire Halpert 2017. First published 2017 by Oxford University Press.

Similarly, in (2), not only does Greek require past-tense inflection on verbs in future-oriented CFs, but it also employs imperfective aspect morphology, even in contexts where perfective aspect is conveyed:

(2) Greek: CF marked by **past imperfective**
    a. An efevɣes   avrio   θa   eftanes   eki   tin ali
       if   leave.PST.IMPF   tomorrow   FUT   arrive.PST.IMPF   there   the   other
       evδomaδa
       week
       'If you left tomorrow, you would get there next week.'
    b. *An efiɣes   avrio   θa   eftases   tin ali   evδomaδa
       if   leave.PST.PFV   tomorrow   FUT   arrive.PST.PFV   the   other   week
       (Iatridou 2000: ex. (21))

These patterns raise the question of how tense and aspect morphology contributes to counterfactual interpretations, if it in fact does. Until recently it has been assumed that languages that use a fake imperfective to mark CFs are a subset of those languages that use a fake past—and that past and imperfective are the only temporal markers to be used in CF marking (see e.g. Iatridou 2009 for a typological summary). In this chapter, we build on our previous research to broaden the typology of temporal marking in CFs, arguing for a more complex picture of the relationship between CF modality and tense/aspect morphology (Bjorkman and Halpert 2013, Halpert and Karawani 2012).

Though our expanded typological picture introduces additional patterns that must be accommodated by the theory of temporal marking in CFs, we argue that the result is in fact a simpler profile: all languages that employ a temporal CF strategy use a single temporal CF operator, either past tense or imperfective aspect.[2] We argue that all cases where multiple temporal specifications appear to be involved in CF marking are illusory, arising out of syntactic underspecification for temporal morphology that may appear to convey complex meanings.

The broader typology that we propose is summarized in (3). Within each temporal CF type (past and imperfective), several different surface patterns (subtypes) are possible; we will see evidence throughout the chapter in favor of these characterizations.

---

[2] For the purposes of this study, we focus only on CFs marked by otherwise temporal morphology, setting aside other components, such as subjunctive mood or specialized CF complementizers, that may also be required. We also focus on the morphological marking in the antecedent clause of CFs: though many languages employ identical temporal marking in both antecedent and consequent clauses, some languages show different marking in these two contexts. We set aside for the moment e.g. the presence of future morphology in the consequent of CFs in many languages (e.g. English *would*).

(3) Broader temporal CF typology: two main types of languages
  1. Past CF languages: require past tense—and nothing else—as a CF marker.
     Three subtypes:
     (i) languages that appear to also require imperfective (French, Zulu) (Iatridou 2000, Arregui 2009, Ippolito 2004, Halpert and Karawani 2012);
     (ii) languages that appear to also require perfective (Palestinian Arabic) (Halpert and Karawani 2012, Karawani and Zeijlstra 2010);
     (iii) Languages that allow either perfective or imperfective (Russian) (Iatridou 2009).
  2. Imperfective CF languages: require imperfective aspect as a CF marker—and nothing else.
     Two subtypes:
     (i) languages that appear to also require past tense (Persian);
     (ii) languages that do not appear to require past tense (Hindi).

The remainder of this chapter is organized as follows: in section 9.2, we discuss some earlier approaches to temporally marked CFs and briefly introduce the concept of temporal underspecification, which will be crucial to how we organize our typology of temporal CFs. Then, in section 9.3, we turn to past CF languages, which have formed the basis of much previous work on the typology of temporal CF marking. We show that despite a variety of apparent aspectual specifications, these languages all share a requirement for a syntactically specified past in CFs. We argue from independent evidence that all apparent aspectual requirements in these languages are in fact an illusion. In section 9.4, we turn to a second set of languages, those that share imperfective as a common component in CF marking. We argue that in these languages, the imperfective aspect is the necessary ingredient to yield a CF meaning, and that any apparent requirement for (past) tense is illusory. In section 9.5, we return to the question of how these morphemes yield CF meanings. We show that the new, expanded typology provides a powerful metric to evaluate existing proposals regarding the use of temporal morphemes in CFs. Finally, in section 9.6, we present our conclusions.

9.2 Background: morphological marking in CFs

As mentioned in the introduction, many languages mark counterfactual conditionals with morphology that in other contexts conveys purely temporal meanings. Tense and aspect marking in CFs that does not seem to result in its ordinary temporal interpretation has been called *fake* to distinguish it from its typical temporal use (Iatridou 2000).

Fake past morphology has been well documented and widely investigated (Anderson 1951, Hale 1969, Steele 1975, James 1982, Palmer 1986, Fleischman 1989,

Iatridou 2000, Van Linden and Verstraete 2008). A number of authors have argued that fake past is the locus of CF semantics. Some have proposed that CF meaning can be derived directly from the semantics of temporal past (Ippolito 2002, Arregui 2009). For others, past tense is merely one possible meaning of a more generalized remoteness or exclusion operator. On this type of view, past marking can indicate that an event is either temporally remote (i.e. at a past time) or modally remote: holding true not in the world of the speaker but in some other possible world (Steele 1975, Iatridou 2000, Ritter and Wiltschko 2010). Schulz (2014) provides the most detailed formal implementation of the modal remoteness approach, generalizing the anteriority relation of past tense to an ordering imposed on possible worlds based on their likelihood with respect to the epistemic center of a proposition.

Fake imperfective in CFs has also been reported (Iatridou 2000, 2009, Van Linden and Verstraete 2008). In contrast to fake tense, however, this fake aspect has received much less attention, and its role in CFs is much less well understood. It has been argued that imperfective occurs in CFs simply because it is a cross-linguistically default aspect (Iatridou 2009); because perfective is incompatible with CFs (Arregui 2005); or because imperfective (like past) contributes to the semantics of CFs (Ferreira 2014). All of these claims rest on the assumption that when fake aspect occurs in CFs, it is always imperfective. Following Iatridou (2000), Arregui and Ippolito assume that in languages that mark CFs with fake past, if any aspect appears in CFs, it is fake imperfective. While Iatridou (2009) observes that some languages (e.g. Russian, Polish) allow real aspect in CFs, she maintains that all fake aspect in CFs is imperfective.

More recent work on the morphological marking of CFs, however, has shown that the full cross-linguistic typology includes languages with fake perfective aspect in CFs. In this chapter, we not only incorporate these languages with apparently perfective-marked CFs into the typology of temporal CF marking, we also introduce languages that mark CFs with imperfective aspect independently, without any use of past tense. As we discuss in section 9.5, this typology motivates a new approach to aspectual morphology in CFs.

9.2.1 Syntactic underspecification of temporal morphology

We argue in this chapter that despite diverse surface patterns in temporal CF marking, all temporal marking in CFs arises from a single CF operator, which can be realized as either (past) tense or (imperfective) aspect. We therefore must provide some account of the fact that some languages do appear to require specific tense and aspect morphology in CF contexts.

We propose that the illusion that both tense and aspect are required to compose a CF meaning in certain languages arises when temporal morphology is underspecified for either tense or aspect. In other words, while a morpheme that tends to yield a complex meaning, e.g. "past imperfective" could be specified for both tense and aspect, it may instead be specified for only one of these categories. Example (4) illustrates three possible underlying specifications that could be associated with a morpheme that occurs in contexts with a past imperfective meaning:

(4) Possible syntactic specifications for a "past imperfective" morpheme

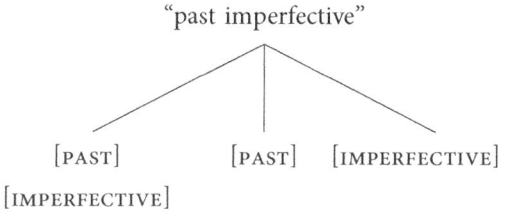

"past imperfective"

[PAST]　　　　[PAST]　　[IMPERFECTIVE]
[IMPERFECTIVE]

An accurate typology of temporal marking in CFs, then, requires that we examine the temporal morphology of languages that use temporal CF marking to independently determine the syntactic specification of the morphemes involved in CF marking. The remaining sections of this chapter demonstrate that in every case where CFs have been described as requiring both a particular tense and a particular aspect, closer examination reveals that the relevant morphology is in fact specified for only one or the other.

9.3 Past CF languages

The apparent puzzle of fake imperfective—the question of why imperfective aspect must sometimes appear in CFs in addition to fake past—has arisen largely on the basis of CF marking in Greek and in Romance languages, particularly French and Italian. In these languages, CFs are always marked with complex past imperfective morphology. The real temporal interpretation of the sentence is not morphologically expressed. Example (5) illustrates this for French, where, though the predicate does not receive the continuous or habitual interpretation typically conveyed by the French imperfective, the imperfective form of the verb is nevertheless required:

(5) French CFs: past imperfective (no real tense/aspect)
   a. Si Pierre partait   demain,   il arriverait   là-bas le
      if Pierre left.PST.IMPF tomorrow he would.arrive there the
      lendemain
      next.day
      'If Pierre left tomorrow, he would arrive there the next day'
   b. *Si Pierre est parti   demain,   il serait arrivé là-bas le
      if Pierre is left.PFV tomorrow he would arrive there the
      lendemain
      next.day

The suppression of real perfective aspect in favor of the imperfective in these CF forms leads to the conclusion that the imperfective is directly implicated in CFs. In a broader typology, however, this direct association between CF and imperfective breaks down.

In Zulu, for example, we find that all CFs are marked by the past imperfective morpheme *be-*, regardless of whether or not the predicate is interpreted as a habitual, continuous, or progressive event, as (6) shows. While the past imperfective is the only aspect marker to appear on the imperfectively interpreted predicate in (6a), the perfective suffix *-ile* appears in addition to the past imperfective in perfectively interpreted CFs in (6b) (Halpert and Karawani 2012). In other words, we learn from Zulu that while imperfective may be implicated in CFs, it is not the case that it arises solely because perfective is incompatible with CF contexts.

(6) Zulu CFs: past imperfective required (real perfective possible)
    a. [ukuba be-   ngi- gula   ] be-ngi-zo-thimula
       if   PST.IMPF- 1SG- be.sick   IMPF-1SG-FUT-sneeze
       'If I had been sick, I would have sneezed'
    b. [ukuba be-   ngi- thimul- **ile**] be-ngi-zo-dinga   ithishi
       if   PST.IMPF- 1SG- sneeze- PFV   IMPF-1SG-FUT-need 5tissue
       'If I had sneezed, I would have needed a tissue'   (H&K 2012: ex. (5))

This conclusion is pushed even further when we examine Palestinian Arabic (PA). In PA we find that past perfective morphology marks CFs (7a)—though real aspectual morphology can also appear in imperfectively interpreted CFs. In other words, PA appears to be the reverse of Zulu: both allow real aspect to appear in addition to the required CF fake aspect, but the CF aspect required in Zulu is imperfective, while the CF aspect in PA is perfective:

(7) Palestinian Arabic CFs: past perfective (real imperfective possible)
    a. [iza **ṭileʕ**   halaʔ,] kaan   b-iwsal   ʕal waʔt   la
       if   leave.PST.PFV now,   be.PST.PFV B-arrive.IMPF on the-time for
       l-muħaadara
       the-lecture
       'If he left now, he would arrive on time for the lecture'
           (Halpert and Karawani 2012: ex. (6a))
    b. [iza **kanno**   b-yitlaʕ   bakkeer kul   yom,] kaan
       if   be.PST.PFV B-leave.IMPF early   every day,   be.PST.PFV
       b-iwsal   ʕa l-waʔt   la l-muħadaraat
       B-arrive.IMPF on the-time to the-lectures
       'If he were in the habit of leaving early, he would arrive to the lectures on time'
           (H&K 2012: ex. (19a))

The clearest indication that fake aspect in CFs does not depend on cross-linguistic properties of particular aspectual specifications comes from Russian. In Russian (and other Slavic languages), past-marked CFs allow both imperfective and perfective, corresponding to the real aspectual interpretation of the sentence (Iatridou 2009):

(8) Russian CFs: past (real aspect possible)
    a. Esli by Džon umer, my poxoroni-l-i by ego na
       if SUBJ John die.PFV.PST we bury.PFV-PST-PL SUBJ he.ACC on
       gor-e.
       mountain-LOC
       'If John died, we would bury him on the mountain'
    b. Esli by Džon umira-l, s nim by-l by doktor.
       if SUBJ John die.IMPF-PST with he.INSTR be-PST SUBJ doctor
       'If John were dying, the doctor would be with him' (Sergei Tatevosov, p.c.)

The common thread across these four different patterns—suppression of real aspect in favor of fake imperfective, appearance of fake imperfective in addition to real aspect, appearance of fake perfective in addition to real aspect, and appearance of real aspect only—is the appearance of fake past tense. We argue in this section for a unified approach to all of these languages: we propose that they all mark CFs solely with a syntactically specified feature [PAST]—and not with imperfective.

The apparent requirement for a fixed aspectual marking in CFs that emerges in languages like French, Zulu, or PA is illusory. It arises simply because the fake aspectual value that we associate with the required form is in fact unspecified in the temporal morphology of the language.

Our argument proceeds in three parts. First, we return to the simple cases, illustrated by Russian, where tense and aspect are clearly morphologically distinct. In these cases, it is surface-apparent that only past morphology is required in CFs. Second, we turn to a more complex case, arguing that "past perfective" morphology is in fact underspecified for aspect in PA. Finally, we extend this underspecification analysis to the languages that were originally noted to require a fake past imperfective. We argue that in languages like French, "past imperfective" morphology is similarly underspecified for aspect.

9.3.1 Simple cases: morphologically distinct tense and aspect

We have already seen that languages like Russian show full aspectual contrasts in CFs, as repeated in (9):

(9) a. Esli by Džon umer, my poxoroni-l-i by ego na
      if SUBJ John die.PFV.PST we bury.PFV-PST-PL SUBJ he.ACC on
      gor-e.
      mountain-LOC
      'If John died, we would bury him on the mountain'

b. Esli by Džon umira-l,   s   nim   by-l   by   doktor.
   if   SUBJ John die.IMPF-PST with he.INSTR be-PST SUBJ doctor
   'If John were dying, the doctor would be with him'   (Sergei Tatevosov, p.c.)

In (9), past-tense morphology appears in both CF constructions, though neither receives a past-tense interpretation. The first is future-oriented, which is expected for perfective verbs in the absence of semantic past orientation (morphologically present perfectives in Russian being restricted to future reference).[3] The second is a present CF, as expected given the presence of imperfective aspect. These interpretations indicate that the past in these constructions is fake. The aspect that each bears, however, does correspond to the actual aspectual interpretation of the antecedent, and contributes to the temporal interpretation as expected for the combination of aspect with semantic present tense. This pattern is what we expect for all languages, if past tense is the only temporal marking required in CFs. We propose that this ability to mark real aspect in conjunction with fake tense in Russian CFs arises from the morphological independence of tense and aspect morphology. Aspectual contrasts in Russian are determined by a system of affixes, distinct from the realization of tense morphology.[4]

We find a similar independence in Zulu temporal morphology. Past-marked CFs in Zulu require the prefix *be-*, which is traditionally described as a past imperfective morpheme:

(10) [ukuba **be**-ngi-gula   ] be-gi-zo-thimula
        if   IMPF-1SG-be.sick IMPF-1SG-FUT-sneeze
      "If I had been sick, I would have sneezed."

This past imperfective morphology is generally in opposition to a past perfective suffix, *-ile*. These two affixes are typically in complementary distribution, as (11) illustrates:

(11) *Be-   ngi- thimul- ile   izolo.
      PST.IMPF- 1SG- sneeze- PFV   yesterday
      intended meaning: "I sneezed yesterday."   (HK 2012, ex. (19a))

---

[3] Being future-oriented, the sentence in (9a) is not truly counterfactual; as mentioned in the introduction, we nonetheless treat such FLV sentences together with true counterfactuals, given the consistent crosslinguistic similarities of the two types of conditional.

[4] We abstract away from the contribution of the subjunctive particle *by*. As in many languages, the subjunctive is required for counterfactual interpretations in Russian; our concern here, however, is with the co-occurrence of past inflection with the particle *by*, despite the absence of past-oriented interpretations. The role of the subjunctive in modal contexts has received much attention in the literature, but lies beyond the scope of this chapter.

In CFs, however, Zulu does allow these morphemes to co-occur. Specifically, as we see in (12), a CF with a perfective interpretation includes both the past imperfective prefix and past perfective suffix:

(12) [ukuba be-   ngi- thimul- **ile**] be-ngi-zo-dinga   ithishi
      if   PAST.IMPF- 1SG- sneeze- PFV   IMPF-1SG-FUT-need 5tissue
    'If I had sneezed, I would have needed a tissue.'   (HK 2012, ex. (5))

If both of these morphemes were in fact specified for past tense, we might expect Zulu to look like Russian, with either one able to mark CFs. It appears, however, that neither of these morphemes is fully specified: Bjorkman and Halpert (2013) and Halpert and Karawani (2012) conclude that the past imperfective morpheme in Zulu realizes only a [PAST] feature, while Botne and Kerchner (2000) suggest that the past perfective suffix is merely a perfective marker. Indeed, just as the "past imperfective" morpheme can correspond with non-imperfective interpretations in CFs in Zulu, the "past perfective" can correspond to non-past interpretations with verbs of instantaneous action:

(13) ngi- shabal-   ele manje
     1SG- disappear- PFV now
    'I disappear now.'   (H&K 2012: ex. (17a))

Like Russian, then, Zulu allows real aspect to appear on CF verbs in addition to fake CF past. Unlike Russian, which has a full complement of temporal morphemes, Zulu has two underspecified morphemes: one that realizes [PAST] and one that realizes [PERFECTIVE]. Since perfective verbs typically receive a default past tense interpretation across languages (Dahl 1985), the [PERFECTIVE] morpheme is associated with a past perfective meaning, in turn giving rise to the association of imperfective interpretations with the [PAST] morpheme, in the absence of a specified [PERFECTIVE]. The systems of temporal morphology for both languages is summarized in (14):

(14)

	Description	Tense	Aspect	Marks CFs?
Russian	"past"	PAST	(IMPF/PFV)	yes
Zulu	"past imperfective"	PAST	Ø	yes
	"past perfective"	Ø	PFV	no

9.3.2 A more complex case

In section 9.3.1 we saw how in languages like Russian, with fully distinct tense and aspect morphology, only tense is implicated in CF marking. We also saw the role that temporal underspecification can play: in a language like Zulu, an underspecified morpheme that realizes a [PAST] feature gives rise to the illusion of a fully specified past imperfective. When this morpheme is used to mark CFs, however, we see that just as in Russian, it can combine with (underspecifed) perfective aspect.

In this section, we'll turn to a somewhat different case of underspecification: that of Palestinian Arabic. We'll show that PA marks CFs with an underspecified past morpheme that yields a past perfective interpretation, in opposition to an underspecifed imperfective morpheme (Halpert and Karawani 2012, Bjorkman and Halpert 2013).

As we have already seen, PA requires "past perfective" morphology in CFs:

(15) [iza **tileʕ** halaʔ,] kaan b-iwsal ʕal waʔt la
       if leave.PST.PFV now, be.PST.PFV B-arrive.IMPF on the-time for
       l-muħaadara
       the-lecture
       'If he left now, he would arrive on time for the lecture'   (H&K 2012: ex. (6a))

Just as we saw in Zulu, PA can also express real aspect in CFs,[5] in which case fake CF past is marked via the auxiliary *kaan*. In these constructions, the auxiliary *kaan* is always inflected as though it were perfective, while the main verb bears real aspectual morphology.

(16) [iza **kanno** **b-yitlaʕ** bakkeer kul yom,] kaan
       if be.PST.PFV B-leave.IMPF early every day, be.PST.PFV
       b-iwsal ʕa l-waʔt la l-muħadaraat
       B-arrive.IMPF on the-time to the-lectures
       'If he were in the habit of leaving early, he would arrive at the lectures on time'
       (H&K 2012: ex. (19a))

In PA, then, it is perfective, rather than imperfective, that appears to be required alongside past in all CF constructions. PA is thus notable for the fact that the aspect implicated in past-marked CFs is not imperfective—contradicting the claims of authors such as Iatridou (2000, 2009) and Van Linden and Verstraete (2008), discussed earlier, that fake aspect in CFs is always imperfective.

Building on previous work (Halpert and Karawani 2012, Bjorkman and Halpert 2013), we take the same approach to PA as we did to Zulu—and Russian—in section 9.3.1: CFs in PA are marked by [PAST] alone. In contrast to a language like Zulu, however, in PA it is perfective aspect that is illusory in past contexts: past perfective morphology in PA corresponds to a simple [PAST] specification. Its perfective interpretation arises only from the absence of any additional [IMPERFECTIVE] features in the syntax.

Karawani and Zeijlstra (2010) argue that past perfective morphology in PA corresponds simply to a tense operator, and contains no aspectual specification. Bjorkman (2011) makes a similar claim about the past perfective across multiple varieties of Arabic, based on patterns of auxiliary use. One way in which we can observe this underspecification is in the inflection on the past auxiliary *kaan* itself. Though Arabic

---

[5] PA can also mark real (non-CF) tense, by using a second instance of auxiliary *kaan*.

languages have a simple past perfective form of the verb, they generally require an auxiliary to form the past imperfective (the reverse of the French situation we will see in the next section). The form of this auxiliary (*kaan* 'be') in PA is morphologically perfective, as illustrated in (17), despite the fact that there is no perfective meaning conveyed in such past imperfective clauses (Halpert and Karawani 2012).

(17) kaanat tuktub
 be.PST.PFV write.IMPF
 'She used to write.' (H&K 2012: ex. (12a))

Standing in opposition to this [PAST] morpheme that typically receives a past perfective interpretation in PA is an [IMPERFECTIVE] morpheme that is underspecified for tense. Benmamoun (2000) claims that present imperfective predicates, which receive no independent tense morphology, behave as if no tense is present in several varieties of Arabic.[6] If [PAST] is the crucial ingredient for CF marking in PA, then it is unsurprising that imperfective morphology, which is not associated with past tense, is not implicated in CF constructions.

In the next section, we will see how this type of underspecification approach required for PA can be extended to account for the original puzzle of fake imperfective in Greek and Romance CFs.

9.3.3 Extending the underspecification analysis

Recall the puzzle of fake imperfective marking in CFs that we saw at the start of this chapter:

(18) French CFs: past imperfective (no real tense/aspect)
 a. Si Pierre partait demain, il arriverait là-bas le
 if Pierre left.PST.IMPF tomorrow he would.arrive there the
 lendemain
 next.day
 'If Pierre left tomorrow, he would arrive there the next day.'
 b. *Si Pierre est parti demain, il serait arrivé là-bas le
 if Pierre is left.PST.PFV tomorrow he would arrive there the
 lendemain
 next.day

This puzzle arises from the assumption that all temporal morphology in languages like French and Greek is fully specified for both tense and aspect. Note, however, that just as in Zulu and PA—and unlike in Russian—French uses a single form,

---

[6] Specifically, Benmamoun (2000) argues that present imperfective verbs in Arabic do not raise to T, citing as evidence their interaction with negation and preference for SVO word order. Based on the absence of movement to T, Benmamoun argues that present-tense features are not syntactically active.

rather than two separate morphemes, to convey past imperfective. We argue that this complex meaning does not stem from fully specified PAST IMPERFECTIVE morphology, but rather from an underspecified past morpheme (realizing a feature [PAST] in the absence of perfective), just as in Zulu. Again, an imperfective interpretation arises due to the opposition between morphemes underspecified for [PAST] and [PERFECTIVE], both of which typically receive a past interpretation.

Just as in Zulu and PA, evidence for this approach comes from the occurrence of past imperfective morphology in contexts where we would expect either perfective aspect or no aspect at all. In French, the pluperfect (past perfect) construction provides just such a context. The auxiliaries that appear in the pluperfect standardly bear past imperfective morphology, as shown in (19):

(19) French pluperfects: perfective interpretation, morphologically imperfective auxiliary
    a. Les élèves avaient étudié
       The students have.PST.IMPF study.PTCP
       'The students had studied'
    b. L'hiver était arrivé
       The-winter be.PST.IMPF come.PTCP
       'Winter had come'

Crucially, these constructions receive a perfective interpretation, despite the appearance of past imperfective morphology. This pattern suggests that the morphological imperfective comes for free with past-tense morphology.[7]

We are now in a position to understand the difference in CF strategies between French and PA: while each language has a single specified aspect that stands in opposition to specified [PAST], the specified aspect is perfective in French and imperfective in PA. The temporal specification of French matches that of Zulu, with the crucial difference that Zulu (like PA) has a grammatical strategy to realize real (specified) aspect in CFs—in addition to CF [PAST] morphology—while French does not.

9.3.4 Interim summary

The table in (20) summarizes the claims of this section:

---

[7] The literary *passé antérieur* (*les élèves eurent etudié*), and the *passé surcomposé* (*les élèves ont eu étudié*) in French do involve apparently perfective auxiliaries. These forms, however, are limited to temporal adjuncts: consequently, we argue such auxiliaries could receive perfective features from a higher syntactic source, unlike the morphologically imperfective auxiliaries in (19).

(20)

	Description	Syntax Tense	Aspect	Marks CFs?
Russian	"past"	PAST	(+IMPF/PFV)	yes
Zulu and French	"past imperfective"	PAST	∅	yes
	"past perfective"	∅[8]	PFV	no
Palestinian Arabic	"past imperfective"	∅	IMPF	no
	"past perfective"	PAST	∅	yes

This table is a simplified typology of the temporal marking seen in CFs thus far: in all of these languages, despite the variation in surface interpretation of temporal morphology, only [PAST] is required to mark CFs. Aspect is implicated in CF marking only to the extent that certain tense morphemes may be underspecified for aspect while being associated with a canonical aspectual interpretation. By investigating the actual syntactic specifications of temporal morphology in these languages, we can show that even when particular aspectual meanings appear to co-occur with the required [PAST] feature, this aspect is not actually specified in the syntax.

9.4 Imperfective CF languages

In the previous section, we saw a number of languages in which a [PAST] morpheme was implicated in the marking of CFs. In all of the languages, we discovered that true, specified aspect was never implicated, even in cases when morphology that typically corresponded with a particular aspect was required. Though we demonstrated in the previous section that we are able to factor out aspect as a necessary ingredient in CFs in some languages, nothing that we have seen so far rules out the possibility that some languages could use true syntactic aspectual marking in CFs.

In this section, we address this possibility. We show that we do find languages for which syntactically specified aspect is required in CFs, in contrast to the languages discussed in the previous section. We argue that in these languages fake aspect alone is implicated in CF marking—and not tense. Strikingly, in the languages that we have found thus far in this category, it is imperfective aspect that is used as a CF marker.

As with the past CF languages, these languages also display variation in surface aspectual interpretations, which can mask the underlying temporal specifications. First we will see that in Hindi, which like Russian has separate, fully specified tense and aspect morphology, aspect alone is used in CFs. Then we will turn to Persian, which appears to use imperfective aspect in conjunction with past tense in CFs.

---

[8] Given the present-tense form of the past perfective auxiliary in many Romance languages, it may be that the past perfective is actually syntactically specified for present tense, rather than no tense at all.

9.4.1 Hindi: imperfective aspect, no apparent past tense

In Hindi, CFs are marked using habitual morphology, with no apparent past tense:

(21) a. Agar vo macchlii khaa-taa ho-taa, to use yeh biimaarii
      if   he fish   eat-HAB be-HAB then he.DAT this illness
      nahiiN ho-tii
      NEG   be-HAB.FEM
      'If he ate fish (on a regular basis), then he would not have this disease.'

   b. Agar vo gaa rahaa ho-taa, to log wah wah kar rahe
      if   he sing PROG be-HAB then people wow wow do PROG
      ho-te
      be-HAB
      'If he were singing, people would be going "wow wow".'

                                            (Iatridou 2009: (15), (12))

As Iatridou (2009) and Bhatt (1997) discuss, the habitual marker -taa appears in all CF constructions in Hindi. This morpheme is clearly specified for aspect but not for tense: outside of CF conditionals, -taa must co-occur with either a past or present tense auxiliary:

(22) a. Ram roj   ghar jaa-taa hai
        Ram every.day home go-HAB PRES
        'Ram goes home every day'

   b. Ram roj   ghar jaa-taa thaa
      Ram every.day home go-HAB PST
      'Ram used to go home every day'

   c. *Ram roj   ghar jaa-taa
       Ram every.day home go-HAB   (Bhatt 1997: (11d))

Iatridou (2009), following Bhatt (1997), assumes that Hindi is a language that requires (a covert) fake past in CFs, but as the data above show, it is not clear that this is the case. Rather, Hindi seems to be a language like Russian, where tense and aspect are fully independent and realized using separate morphemes. There is therefore no morphological correspondent to a past-tense operator, and no independent means of motivating a covert operator. It appears, then, that Hindi is a language that marks CFs with imperfective (habitual) aspect alone.

9.4.2 Persian: imperfective aspect, illusory past tense

In Persian, CFs are marked with the imperfective verbal prefix *mi-* (Iatridou 2009, data p.c. from Arsalan Kahnemuyipour):

(23) a. age fardaa   mi-raft   hafte-ye ba'd mi-resid
        if tomorrow DUR-go.PST   week-EZ   next DUR-arrive.PST
        'If he left tomorrow, he would arrive next week'
    b. age alaan javaab-e   so'aal-o   mi-dunest-am,   xeyli eftexaar
        If now   answer-EZ question-acc.   DUR-know.PST-1SG, a lot pride
        mi-kard-am
        DUR-do.PST-1SG
        'If I knew the answer now, I would be very proud' (lit. 'take pride a lot')

This morphology also occurs in non-counterfactual imperfectives and appears to be independent of any particular tense interpretation:

(24) a. man har   ruz raah mi-rav-am
        I   every day path DUR-go.NONPST-1sg
        'I walk every day'
    b. man daar-am raah mi-rav-am
        I   have-1sg path DUR-go.NONPST-1sg
        'I am walking (now)'

While Hindi showed no evidence of [PAST] morphology in CFs, Persian does appear to implicate past tense in CF marking. In particular, Persian requires the so-called past-stem form of the verb in CFs (23). It is clear, moreover, that this form of the stem is not generally required with imperfective morphology, as the non-CF forms in (24), which involve a non-past stem, illustrate.

Based on this pattern, we could draw two possible conclusions about Persian. First, the use of the past stem in CFs might suggest that Persian is a language in which CFs require both [PAST] and syntactically specified (non-illusory) [IMPERFECTIVE] features, as has been previously assumed for languages like French. On the other hand, just as we saw illusory aspect in Past CF languages like French, it could be that the past stem here may have only illusory pastness.

Though more work is needed on these temporal patterns in Persian CFs, we will here note some preliminary evidence that the past in these constructions is indeed illusory. Specifically, we find that the past stem does occur in some limited non-past contexts in Persian. Farahani (1990) notes that the infinitive form of verbs is formed from the past stem, as are perfect participles. Another instance of past stems in non-past constructions is the so-called formal future form in (25):

(25) "Past stem" in formal future form
    a. Sârâ daru-hâ-yaš râ   xâh-ad   xord
       S.   medicine-PL her-ACC   want.3SG   eat.PST
       'Sârâ will have her medicine'   (Taleghani 2008, ex. (30))

b. xâh-am raft
   want-1SG go.PST
   'I will go' (Maziar Toosarvandani, p.c.)

In addition to the formal future, we also find colloquial constructions where a simple past stem can receive a prospective (non-past) interpretation, as in (26):

(26) "Past stem" with prospective interpretation (colloquial Farsi)
   a. raft-am
      go.PST-1SG
      'I went'/'I'm about to go' (Maziar Toosarvandani, p.c.)

In these constructions, a past stem of the main verb combines with an agreement-bearing 'want,' yielding a future interpretation. While in PA and French we saw morphological aspect appear on auxiliary forms that clashed with the actual aspectual interpretation, here we find a similar circumstance where apparent tense on the main verb clashes with the actual tense interpretation of the construction. The use of the past stem in these contexts thus suggests that this stem may not actually indicate the syntactic presence of a [PAST] feature.

A question that emerges from all of these unusual instances of the past stem—including CFs, formal future, and colloquial prospective—is why the past stem is required in these situations. In particular, we are faced with the following puzzle about CFs: even if the so-called past stem does not in fact encode syntactic [PAST], some factor must still account for its necessity in CF conditionals. The appearance of past-stem forms in conditionals is not limited to CFs, however: non-past, non-CF conditionals may also be formed using the past stem (Farahani 1990; Maziar Toosarvandani, p.c.). It therefore seems likely that the explanation of the past stem in CFs lies in the more generalized use of past stems in Persian conditional constructions and cannot be tied directly to counterfactuality, though this remains a question for future research.

9.4.3 Interim summary and typological update

In section 9.4, we have expanded the typology of temporal marking in CFs. In addition to the languages that require syntactically specified [PAST] to mark CFs, which we saw in the previous section, we have now introduced languages that require syntactically specified [IMPERFECTIVE] aspect. In these languages, we have hypothesized that a syntactic [PAST] feature plays no role in CFs: this conclusion is straightforward in a language like Hindi, but requires more investigation into the temporal system of a language like Persian. Based on these patterns, we can conclude that in all of the languages encountered so far, a single temporal marker is required to mark CFs:

(27) New temporal CF typology
   a. Past CF languages: require past tense—and nothing else—as a CF marker.
   Three subtypes:
      (i) languages that appear to also require imperfective (Iatridou 2000, Ippolito 2004, Arregui 2009);
      (ii) languages that appear to also require perfective (Karawani and Zeijlstra 2010, Halpert and Karawani 2012);
      (iii) languages that allow either perfective or imperfective (Iatridou 2009).
   b. Imperfective CF languages: require imperfective as a CF marker—and nothing else.
   Two subtypes:
      (i) languages that appear to also require past tense;
      (ii) languages that do not appear to require past tense.

In the next section, we will examine the consequences of this expanded typology for theoretical approaches to CFs.

9.5 CF typology and the theoretical landscape

What we have shown so far in this chapter is that languages that use temporal morphology to mark CFs either require [PAST] or [IMPERFECTIVE]—but upon close inspection, no language appears to require both. This conclusion diverges from previous claims that some languages do in fact require both past tense and imperfective aspect to express CF meanings. We have argued that the illusion of both tense and aspect marking in CFs arises from independent properties of a language's morphological system, specifically from underspecification in a language's temporal morphology.

The typology of CF marking we have presented here has further implications for investigations of CF marking, and for our understanding of the interaction between modality and temporal inflection more generally. We have seen not only that there is no single tense or aspect that is required across all languages that use fake temporal morphology to mark CFs, but also that in languages like Zulu, PA, and Hindi, CFs can mark real tense and aspect even in the presence of fake morphology (in contrast to Greek and French). Taken together, these generalizations have important implications for the theory of CF marking, discussed in the next two subsections.

More broadly, this study illustrates the fact that the ability to express real tense and aspect in modal contexts is at least to some extent independent of a language's morphological resources in non-counterfactual clauses. That is to say, work on CF inflection has often adopted the view, sometimes implicitly, that real tense and aspect in CFs is limited to whatever inflection is left over after some morphology has been repurposed to express counterfactuality. We see from languages like PA, where more layers of tense auxiliaries are possible in counterfactual clauses than elsewhere (Karawani and Zeijlstra 2010, Karawani 2014), that some independent explanation must be found for why a multiple-auxiliary strategy is not used in other languages to express both real and fake tense. The ability to express real tense is also independent of whether particular modal elements are morphologically compatible with tense inflection. In the languages that we discuss here, counterfactuality is marked in CF antecedents without the presence of a dedicated modal operator; instead, temporal morphology appears to be coopted to express modal meanings. Despite the absence of a modal operator, we nevertheless find that the expression of tense or aspect (or both) is constrained within these modal CF contexts. This echoes work such as Stowell (2004), which establishes that modal interpretation (e.g. epistemic versus root) has effects on the ability to express tense and aspect beyond simple morphological compatibility.

9.5.1 Analyses incompatible with revised typology

The patterns of CF marking identified in this chapter are incompatible with certain approaches to temporal CF marking. In particular, our typology is largely incompatible with analyses in which counterfactuality is derived directly from a past-tense meaning (Ippolito 2004, Arregui 2009, Ferreira 2014). These analyses seek to tie specific properties of temporal past-tense meaning to the creation of a CF meaning. As we have now seen, languages such as Hindi and Persian, which mark CFs with [IMPERFECTIVE] alone, demonstrate that past-tense semantics cannot be crucial to the generation of CF interpretations.

The typology developed here is similarly incompatible with the view that imperfective aspect makes a semantic contribution—in addition to the contribution of past—in CF semantics, a proposal articulated in greatest detail by Ferreira (2014). The fact that languages like PA and Russian allow perfective aspect—illusory or interpreted—in CFs further eliminates the weaker position that imperfective surfaces in CFs because CF interpretations are incompatible with perfective viewpoint, as proposed by Arregui (2005).

Finally, the typology developed in this chapter clearly demonstrates that CF clauses do allow real tense and aspect marking. Authors such as Ferreira (2014) and Arregui (2009) have proposed that ordinary temporal semantics are entirely overridden in CF contexts. Languages like Zulu, Arabic, Russian, and Hindi are all counterexamples to this: all allow real temporal marking, in some cases doubled with fake CF morphology. The typology we have seen is more compatible with accounts in which fake past occurs structurally higher than real temporal past, so the two can potentially co-occur. This type of account is explicitly developed by Ippolito (2008), who argues for (some) CFs with past perfect inflection that they exhibit two layers of past: one linked to counterfactuality and realized by the simple past, the other linked to a temporal past interpretation and realized by perfect inflection.

9.5.2 Analyses favored by revised typology

The typology of CF marking developed here also makes a positive contribution to the theoretical analysis of CFs, favouring approaches that identify commonalities between CF and temporal semantics without directly composing the former from the latter.

The fact that in all languages investigated, only one temporal category (tense or aspect, but not both) is used to mark CFs suggests that there is a single syntactic position associated with the composition of CF semantics. This is in line with the possibility that there is a CF operator in the relevant clauses, which can be spelled out either by a dedicated CF morpheme or else by a morpheme that in other contexts spells out [PAST] or [IMPERFECTIVE]. Once this single choice has been made for a particular language, other properties of CF morphology—e.g. the illusion of secondary marking, compatibility between CF marking and real inflection—should fall out from broader properties of the language's inflectional morphosyntax.

From the fact that Zulu, Arabic, and Hindi allow CF inflection to co-occur with real tense/aspect, we can further conclude that CF inflection is associated with a position that is distinct from either T^0 or Asp^0. There is, moreover, reason to think that this position is higher than both T^0 and Asp^0, given that fake CF marking in both Arabic and Hindi occurs on the highest verb or auxiliary, while real temporal marking occurs lower, on the main verb.[9]

Independently of such doubling, there is evidence from Turkish that fake CF morphology is associated with a high—potentially left-peripheral—position. In Turkish, the interpretation of a conditional depends in part on the relative order of the past and the conditional suffixes: the past morpheme appears to be structurally higher when CF-linked than when temporally interpreted in indicative conditionals (Aygen 2004). Thus, while this morpheme occurs to the left of the conditional morpheme -*sa* when it has a temporal interpretation (28), it occurs to the right of the same morpheme in CF contexts (29). Assuming some version of the Mirror Principle (Baker 1985), this morphological contrast suggests that CF-linked past is structurally higher than temporal past.

(28) Indicative: V-PAST-COND
    a. Dün gece Can erken yat-dı-ysa sabah erken
       Last night John early sleep-PST-COND morning early
       kalk-abil-ir
       get-up-MOD-IMPF
       'If John went to bed early last night, he can get up early this morning'
                                          (Ulutas 2006: 3, ex. 6a)

---

[9] In English, similarly, if we view the perfect as realizing temporal past in CF contexts, the CF past occurs higher than the morphological perfect.

(29) Counterfactual: V-COND-PAST
   a. Dün gece Can erken yat-**sa**-ydı sabah erken
      Last night John early sleep-COND-PST morning early
      kalk-ar-dı
      get-up-AOR-PST
      'If John had gone to bed early last night, he would have got up early in the morning' (Ulutas 2006: 3, ex. 6b)

In a similar vein, Iatridou and Embick (1994) show that conditional inversion—the marking of conditional antecedents by inversion of the finite verb to C^0, as in *had I known*...—shows a cross-linguistic link to CFs. Indeed, they demonstrate that outside the verb-second Germanic languages, conditional inversion is possible only in CF antecedents. This pattern again suggests that CFs have some link to a left-peripheral position, potentially the same position that is the source of fake tense/aspect.

The typology developed here is, lastly, compatible with the idea that a CF operator—whatever its structural position—shares featural content with temporally interpreted [PAST]. Many authors have suggested that CFs share some abstract meaning with past tense, at least metaphorically (e.g. Steele 1975, James 1982, Fleischman 1989). Some have suggested more concretely that CF and past tense share a feature in common (Iatridou 2000, Wiltschko 2009, Ritter and Wiltschko 2010); such a feature could form the basis of post-syntactic insertion of a single morpheme in both contexts.

More concretely, Ritter and Wiltschko (2009, 2010) propose that what we think of as tense is really a general function of clausal anchoring ([±coincidence]). They propose that this feature heads clauses in all languages, but may index different deictic properties in different languages. In familiar European languages, this feature indexes the time of situations, resulting in tense systems, but in (Halkomelem) Salish it indexes the location of situations, resulting in obligatory marking of proximal/distal relations, and in Blackfoot it indexes the participants in situations, resulting in obligatory marking of so-called local/non-local contrasts. Ritter and Wiltschko propose to extend this to CF marking, proposing that [– coincidence] in C^0 establishes non-coincidence of the world of the clause, rather than its time (or location, or participants).

This approach raises the question of whether imperfective, like past, could be somehow understood as the realization of a [– coincidence] feature, in order to account for the fact that Hindi and Persian appear to use [IMPERFECTIVE]—and not [PAST]—to mark CFs. There appear to be significant obstacles to such a unification, however: Mezhevich (2006) proposes an analysis of aspect in Russian in terms of [±coincidence], but argues that imperfective is represented as [+coincidence]. It thus remains an issue for future research how the presence of imperfective aspect, in the absence of any featural representation of [PAST], can give rise to counterfactual interpretations.

Any analysis of CF marking that appeals to a more generalized notion of temporal markers as elements that can yield different interpretations when they appear in different categories, along the lines sketched above, ties into more general work proposing that the interpretation of syntactic elements depends not only on their content but also on their position, as in Aboh (2009)'s analysis of certain serial verb constructions. Aboh argues that in languages like Gungbe, lexical verb roots can be Merged—and interpreted—in higher functional positions, yielding temporal meanings instead of their typical lexical content. This type of process clearly parallels the emerging CF picture, where the same elements that yield temporal meanings when inserted lower in the (functional) structure can yield modal meanings when inserted higher.

9.6 Conclusion

The general goal of this chapter has been to broaden the descriptive typology of tense and aspect marking in clauses expressing CF modal meanings. We have demonstrated that languages can use either [PAST] or [IMPERFECTIVE] to mark CFs, but not both. In cases where specific languages have been claimed to require both past and imperfective marking in CFs, we have demonstrated that this double requirement is illusory, arising from the underspecification of individual morphological forms. In other words, though a past morpheme may, outside of CFs, occur only in imperfective contexts (due to the presence elsewhere in the language of a more specified past perfective form), this does not mean that such a morpheme always reflects the syntactic presence of imperfective features.

In identifying languages that appear to truly require the presence of imperfective morphology, our typology casts doubt on approaches that have linked CF semantics too closely to past-temporal interpretations, while also raising questions for more abstract views of fake CF inflection. Though much work has been done suggesting a metaphorical or featural link between CF and past semantics, an analogous link between CF and imperfective remains to be discovered. Even once such a link has been found, however, for languages that have both past and imperfective morphology, it remains to be discovered what determines which of these morphemes appears in CFs.

In addition, if it is correct that [PAST] and [IMPERFECTIVE] features receive a CF interpretation only when they occur in a specific left-peripheral position, rather than in T^0 or Asp^0, the further question arises of why real temporal morphology is barred in CF antecedents in so many languages. What prevents these features from occurring, and being morphologically realized, twice in a single clause—more curiously, why is this possible in some languages but not in others?

Even with these questions outstanding, however, the expanded typology developed in this chapter represents progress in the project of accounting for the inflectional morphological properties of CF clauses. Though a broader range of possibilities exist than was previously thought, we have demonstrated that this surface complexity can in fact simplify the description of those possibilities, offering the potential for an ultimately more satisfying account of CF morphosyntax.

Acknowledgments

Many thanks for helpful comments, discussion, and data to Sabine Iatridou, Hadil Karawani, Sergei Tatevosov, Maziar Toosarvandani, and two anonymous reviewers. Thanks as well to the audiences at the MIT Syntax Square, NELS 40, and GLOW 35, where earlier versions of this work were presented.

10
Dimensions of variation in Old English modals

REMUS GERGEL

10.1 Introduction

There is perhaps hardly a class of linguistic elements about which more has been written—without necessarily having a full understanding of their syntax and semantics yet—than the (Old) English modals. Aside from making certain observations on facts that have been under-researched in the rich field, the main goal of this chapter is to view—in tandem, rather than in isolation—aspects of variation that are of interest at the syntax–semantics interface. To do so, I will take recourse to philological and theoretical lines of investigation and put their insights to the test on a selection of data from Old English. In line with the topic of the present volume, the categorial status of the modals will be investigated. As far as syntactic height goes, the argument will be that an aspectual head, Asp°, is a better underlying approximation for the properties of the Old English modals than the traditional generative categorization of the class as a plain verbal head, V°.

The class of elements to be investigated, also known as "premodals" in the wake of Lightfoot (1979), has been the subject of a good deal of research from different theoretical angles (cf. e.g. Traugott 1972, 1992; Lightfoot 1979; Plank 1984; Roberts 1985, 1993; Denison 1993; Warner 1992, 1993; van Gelderen 2003; Roberts and Roussou 2003; Fischer 2010). While an exhaustive presentation is not possible, certain claims have played an essential role in the discussion, with respect not only to the modals themselves but also to questions of categorial status and clausal architecture. The present chapter will focus on the discussion of such issues in combination with the issue of potential interaction with modal meanings. The goal will be to make a case for a more nuanced alternative to one of the strongest syntactic proposals on the market and to investigate aspects of variation in meaning. A key observation will also be made in the course of the discussion with regard to the Old English aspectual prefix *ge-*.

Modality Across Syntactic Categories. First edition. Ana Arregui, María Luisa Rivero, and Andrés Salanova (eds.).
This chapter © Remus Gergel 2017. First published 2017 by Oxford University Press.

In short, the chapter will assess the morphosyntactic and semantic building blocks available in connection with the Old English modals, as well as address questions pertaining to categorial status, modal base, and modal force. Additionally, the issue of actuality entailments will be discussed (in a brief comparison with German). The inquiry is structured as follows: after a brief background given on issues that arise in diachronic linguistics and the choice of data for the present study, which are explained in section 10.2, the subsequent sections pursue the questions raised above, i.e. categorial status in section 10.3, followed by modal bases and modal force in sections 10.4 and 10.5, respectively. The possibility of event realizations or actuality entailments in the context of the modals is dealt with in section 10.6, preceding the concluding remarks offered in section 10.7.

10.2 Methodology

Given the breadth of the field and to keep the discussion manageable, I will focus on modals with apparent existential force in Old English, viz. *cunnan, magan, motan*— i.e. the cognates of *can, may, must*, where the latter modal underwent a change in its modal force (having universal force today). These modals show the maximum range of variation that one can get from Old English modals, with respect to both semantic and syntactic factors. I will refer to the modals by using the aforementioned infinitive forms even if the infinitive form is sometimes reconstructed rather than attested in the Old English varieties.

In my utilization of the data pool, I will relate the investigation to claims made in previous literature and I will draw on two lines of empirical enquiry. The first is based on two Old English collections of homilies, the second concerns the YCOE corpus (Taylor et al. 2003). The former data source is rather homogeneous in terms of register (and comparatively speaking, also timing) of composition. The homilies under scrutiny are believed to have been written some time during the tenth century. They were designed mainly as preaching texts for an uneducated audience. This data source is helpful when it comes to having a practical degree of certainty regarding nuances of modal meanings at particular times, as well as in individual texts and text types, which can be better controlled for than in the case of the entire period and diversity of Old English. However, the data source given by the YCOE is highly advantageous when it comes to maximizing the data set available. In particular, if we run into claims regarding the very low frequency of certain syntactic patterns (potentially ungrammatical structures, if a structure is not available at all), it will be useful to check such claims against a broader data pool. In the remainder of this section, some background will be given on the two types of source for readers who do not usually work on English historical linguistics.

The genre of the homilies is interesting for two reasons. One is that a wealth of such texts are available from Old English, i.e. the genre obeys a well-established and influential tradition of the time. Fewer errors of transmission may be the result. At the same time, the homilies were to a large extent intended to be transmitted orally, so that they could be understood by an audience that was in most cases illiterate. This brings them closer to natural language usage than other texts. The two volumes chosen for the present investigation are each available in multiple editions. The first one also constitutes the first volume (sometimes referred to as "series") of Ælfric's Catholic homilies. The second volume has anonymous authorship. Its homilies are referred to as "the Blickling Homilies" in the philological literature, on account of Blickling Hall, where they were once located. Ælfric was an abbot who left a considerable number of well-known writings in Old English. Combining a volume of his writings with a further volume maintains a certain consistency with respect to genre while not tying any findings too closely to potentially just one speaker/writer. While it is not known who wrote the Blickling Homilies, the writing process of the extant manuscript has been conducted by two scribes, one of whom seems to have had an editing function over the other (Kelly 2009). Philological, historical, and other issues may still remain to be elucidated with the presently available editions of the homilies. However, for our purposes they form a helpful textual base for the grammar of the modals. Data retrieved from the homilies will be reported by mentioning the collection of homilies, the edition used together with the independent philological translation (e.g. Morris, Thorpe, Kelly[1]), the chapter, and the page number.

The second source of evidence that I have made use of, the YCOE corpus (Taylor et al. 2003), combines a wide selection of Old English philological sources with structural annotation. The database is part of a larger project on historical corpora of English and other languages, lending itself well to work on syntactic questions. Using the *Corpussearch* software, designed by Beth Randall,[2] allows searches on the basis of structural annotation. It will hence come as no surprise that whenever stating that a particular syntactic pattern existed or was unlikely to have existed in Old English, reference to this source will be made. The tokens that I have retrieved from the YCOE corpus are reported by their usual corpus identifiers.

10.3 Syntax

In this section, I introduce a widely assumed analysis of the development of the modals, which takes them to have been main verbs prior to the modern period (e.g. Lightfoot 1979; Roberts 1993). According to the view, the modals underwent a diachronic reanalysis, which effectively transformed them into functional T heads

---

[1] Translations cannot guarantee the exact meaning, but they are a useful auxiliary means customary in historical linguistics. In difficult cases, multiple translations were consulted, e.g. when multiple meanings seemed to be available and such translations were available (to me). The translations followed are indicated throughout the chapter (as are possible comparisons when relevant).
[2] Cf. http://corpussearch.sourceforge.net/

"cataclysmically" during the transition from Middle to Modern English, i.e. long after the Old English period (see e.g. Plank 1984 and Denison 1993 for a critical assessment). On the syntactic side, I propose a partial correction of the assumed view to the effect that: (i) the items used as modals in Old English already displayed evidence of functional status, and in particular (ii) a plausible analysis of the modals' categorial status in Old English is under a functional head, which corresponds to Aspect rather than falling under a lexical verbal head.

10.3.1 Background on Old English clause structure

Before discussing the standard generative syntactic view, I will introduce a set of basic facts to ease the understanding of the issues and put aside potential confounds that may arise in diachronic data for readers less well-versed in the structure of earlier English.

A first clarification has to do with the directionality of the structures headed by premodals: they vary between head-final and head-initial. This is shown in (1–3) for *cunnan*, *magan*, and *motan*, respectively. The syntactic contexts of the data, which are given with their YCOE notation (see Taylor et al. 2003), are deliberately chosen as embedded clauses here in order to control for the Old English version of the Germanic verb-second constraint.[3]

(1) a. nænne geleaffulne mann þe   [hi læren] *cuþe*
      no   faithful   man who her teach could
      '([B]ecause she did not have) any faithful man in town to teach her.'
                                                        (coaelive,+ALS_[Eugenia]: 30.208)

    b. hwæðer he *cuðe* [gan].
       whether he could go   (coaelive,+ALS[Peter's_Chair]: 32.2284)

(2) a. þæt menn [hit gehyran] *mihton*.
      that men it   hear   could
      'that men could hear it.'   (coaelhom,+AHom_1: 451.233)

    b. Ic wene ðæt we *mægen* [ðis openlicor   gecyðan]...
       I believe that we may   this more.openly announce
       'I think we may make this known more clearly...'
                                                     (cocura,CP: 40.291.12.1912)

(3) a. þæt he [hine geseon] *moste*
      that he him see   could
      'that he was allowed to see him (God).'
                                      (cocathom1,+ACHom_I,_9: 250.31.1594)

---

[3] A finite element that has moved to a higher functional projection such as C would not be useful in determining whether its complement was right- or left-branching in the pre-movement position. This fact is largely orthogonal to the auxiliary vs. main verb issue, but it needs to be controlled for.

b. *þæt Samson* **moste** *[him macian sum gamen].*
   that Samson might them make some pleasure
   'that Samson might make some sport for them.' (cootest, Judg: 16.25.5805)

The examples illustrate that Old English VPs—and IPs/TPs—can be either head-initial or head-final. This fact is naturally also systematically documented independently of the modals (see especially Susan Pintzuk's and related work; cf. Pintzuk 1999; Pintzuk and Taylor 2008), and we may take it here as a datum of the language.[4]

As a second clarification, the premodals constitute preterite presents possessing morphological forms which were originally past tenses and hence do not fully match the inflectional paradigms of the present. However, they are already linked with a present-tense semantics in Old English. Secondary past tenses are available in Old English. Old English has a few additional preterite presents (e.g. *witan* 'know'), but only the modals survived. While one cannot take the outstanding morphological heritage of the premodals as preterite presents to be necessarily an argument for functional status on theoretical grounds, it is descriptively one of the features that set the premodals apart from the majority of the verbs in the paradigms.

A third point pertaining to the syntax of the premodals is their argument structure. In this chapter I focus on propositional arguments, i.e. essentially infinitival complements selected by the modals. However, the Old English modals also display alternative selectional patterns. In particular, the presence of objects that are selected by cognates of the modals without the addition of a verb is attested. For a comparison that is imperfect yet illustrates the point for speakers of Modern English, consider how today's *need* seems to be available both as a verb that takes direct objects and a modal, i.e. as a head taking infinitival complements. I take such early uses of the modals, e.g. taking direct objects and crucially lacking propositional arguments, to be plain verbs (which typically do not have modal meanings; cf. e.g. 'know,' 'have power,' and 'have something measured out' for *cunnan*, *magan*, and *motan* respectively (*OED*)). Therefore, I assume that such items carrying non-modal meanings are main verbs and develop as separate lexical items during Old English. Notice also that we are dealing with the same forms. The parsed corpora (e.g. Taylor et al. 2003) generally use the label MD indiscriminately.[5]

It is important to note that modal meanings and infinitive-selecting patterns are already available in Old English. They are associated with the propositional—rather than individual-denoting—complements. (Relevant aspects of variation with respect to the category of the complements of the modals will be re-examined in section 10.4.)

---

[4] Whether the variation is viewed as competition between coexisting options in the grammar in the sense of Kroch (1989) or via Kaynian evacuation of the complement for those phrases that appear as head-final on the surface (see e.g. Biberauer et al. 2008) is orthogonal to whether an item is an auxiliary or a verb in the base.

[5] However, the corpora offer the possibility of searching e.g. for infinitival complements of the items that are labeled as modal. I will discuss these estimates in section 10.4.

I will now turn to the heart of the matter with regard to the categorial status of the modals themselves.

10.3.2 Locating the reanalysis of the premodals in syntactic representation

The prevalent generative view of early English modals is that all the modals preceding the Modern period (i.e. including Old and Middle English) behave as main verbs (Lightfoot 1979; Roberts 1985, 1993; Roberts and Roussou 2003). Following Lightfoot's work, Old English modals are often called "premodals" (I continue to use the term descriptively, to indicate the early character). The core of the standard claim can be represented as follows:

(4) Reanalysis of the English modals: received view (simplified)
  a. Old/Middle English: => b. Modern English:

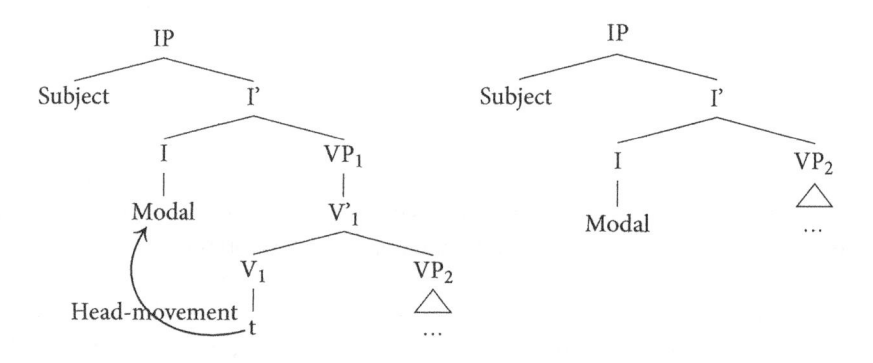

```
         IP                              IP
       /    \                          /    \
   Subject   I'                    Subject   I'
            /  \                            /  \
           I   VP₁                          I   VP₂
           |                                |    △
         Modal  V'₁                       Modal  ...
          ↑    /   \
          |  V₁    VP₂
     Head-movement  △
              t    ...
```

The specific standard claim is that the relevant head, to which the modals are reanalyzed, is in the traditional auxiliary of I(nfl) domain (e.g. 'T' in Roberts and Roussou 2003). I will adopt this part, i.e. the *output* of the reanalysis schematized in (4b), as a useful phrase-structural approximation. However, the analysis I propose differs with respect to the input of the reanalysis. I will argue that the modals were not under V, but already functional under a node at the structural height of Asp(ect) in Old English.

The traditional generative reanalysis view, as depicted above, has the potential of explaining several changes in the verbal and auxiliary system of English at the transition from Middle to Modern English. Moreover, it is also taken to apply to auxiliary *do*. However, Warner (1992, 1993) has already pointed out that although an auxiliarization tendency can be observed increasingly through the history of the language, the Old English modals already show initial indication of auxiliary-like behavior. While the framework in which Warner develops his proposal is distinct, I intend to follow and expand his observation with respect to ellipsis next. My goal is to strengthen what I take to be Warner's main argument for functional-category status, viz. the one based on VP ellipsis, and subsequently to suggest two new arguments.

I assume a simple phrase structure consisting of the heads C°, T°, Asp°, and V°, and that they are lined up in exactly this structurally decreasing order. Such heads are needed for the purposes of both syntactic and semantic representation, and I will take their presence to be uncontroversial without motivating it further here. However, I will not resort to richer, so-called Split-Infl or Split-C projections. I argue that in a phrase structure such as the one previously mentioned, the modals reanalyzed from a position corresponding to Asp° to T° (rather than from V° to T°) in syntactic terms.

A first syntactic argument for functional status of the premodals is connected to ellipsis—more specifically, VP ellipsis (VPE). The Old English modals could license VPE, a phenomenon that is taken to indicate functional status of its licenser (cf. e.g. Lobeck 1995; Johnson 2001; Winkler 2005; Gergel 2009a). I first illustrate the point with examples from Ælfric's homilies and the Blickling Homilies (example (6) is extracted via the YCOE corpus):

(5) cwæð þæt he **wolde** genealæcan his hulce, gif he **mihte_**.
    said that he wished reach   his hut,   if he could.
    '[H]e said he wished to reach his hut, if he could.' (Ælf.Hom.Thorpe XXIII: 336)

(6) Forþon we **sceolan** nu geþencean, þa hwile þe we **magan** &
    therefore we must   now consider   there while that we may   and
    motan_, ure saula þearfe, þe læs we foryldon þas alyfdon tid   &
    can   our souls' need   lest we put-off this permitted time, and
    þonne willon þonne we ne magon.
    then   want   then we not can
    'Therefore, we should now consider the need of our souls while we may and are able to, lest we put off this permitted time and wish to repent when we no longer can.'
    (coblick,HomS_26_[BlHom_7]:95.230.1239, B.Hom.Kelly 66: 194)

(7) Gif **ge cunnon_**, þa   ðe yfele sind, [syllan ða gódnysse eowrum
    if you can   who that evil are   give   the good   your
    bearnum],...
    children
    'If ye can, who are evil, give to your children what is good,...'
    (Ælf.Hom.Thorpe XVIII: 252)

The sentence in (5) contains a VPE site under the modal *mihte* (preterite of *magan*). This example obeys parallelism, and the overt antecedent is under a contrasting volitional modal *wolde*, cf. *genealæcan his hulce* 'reach his hut.' Example (6) is slightly more involved. The object of the verb in the antecedent (*ure saula þearfe* 'our souls' need') is extraposed, and the ellipsis site intervenes between the in situ and extraposed part of the antecedent. Furthermore, there are two conjoined modals under the licensing node, *magan* and *motan*, a fact which may point to the similar syntactic status of the two modals.[6] Finally, the example in (7) features a VPE site licensed by *cunnan*. All the modals under scrutiny here had the ability to license VPE. Sites containing non-expressed predicates are also available in Old English texts beyond the homilies. For example, a search for silent verbs in the YCOE corpus returned 90 examples, 82 of which were licensed by modals.[7]

Nonetheless, the argument based on VPE needs to be strengthened, since one cannot assume, a priori, that the modals have a similar status in Old English as they do in contemporary varieties of English, where VPE is taken as an indicator of auxiliaryhood (see e.g. Denison 1993). It is worth observing, from a cross-linguistic perspective, that an element's quality of licensing VPE, i.e. deletion of its complement, does not necessarily qualify it for functional status in and of itself. Lexical verbs can undergo V-to-T movement and *then* license ellipsis from the position they have moved to in some languages (cf. McCloskey 1991; Ngonyani 1996; Cyrino and Matos 2002; Goldberg 2005). Such cases usually require the fulfillment of two conditions, viz. V-to-T and licensing of VPE. For example, French has V-to-T, but no general VPE mechanism that would allow deletion in the scope of a plain verb moved to T.[8] What about early English? To make sure that the argument based on VPE is informative, we must make sure that we are not dealing with the option based on licensing after verb movement. While early English had movement of verbs to higher functional projections (Roberts 1985; Kroch 1989), it did not seem to produce the appearance of complement deletion under verbs in general with the distinctive agreement patterns that are known from the cross-linguistic research of VPE (see Goldberg 2005 and the literature reviewed there).[9]

A second argument for functional status of the premodals can be culled from VP topicalization. If we assume, e.g. with Johnson (2001), that there is some similarity in the mechanics of VP topicalization and VP ellipsis, then the availability of topicalization is expected. While topicalization is infrequent in the Old English data, it is still present. Examples (8) and (9) feature two different types of example, only the first one of which I argue to be indicative of topicalization:

---

[6] There is arguably yet one more ellipsis site at the end of the fragment, but I will not go further into its details.

[7] In addition to the ellipses licensed by modals, there were two examples of a predicate ellipsis licensed by *beon* 'be', and six examples licensed by the hortative verb *uton* 'let us.'

[8] While the existence of VPE—if VPE appears only with a restricted class of elements—could be used as one indication of auxiliaryhood, this is not the only diagnostic. For German, for example, the issue of whether the modals are auxiliaries or not is a highly debated one, and the notion of syntactic coherence a relevant diagnostic (see e.g. Haider 1997; Reis 2001; Wurmbrand 2001; Sternefeld 2006; Axel-Tober and Gergel to appear).

[9] More research on the possibilities of VPE in Old English, independently of the modals, would be required to gain fuller insight into this domain.

(8) *[Sprecan] he mihte_, gif he wolde*;
 speak   he might if he wanted
 'He could have spoken, had he been willing.' (Ælf.Hom.Thorpe IX: 142)

(9) *þeah ðe sume men [singan] ne cunnon*
 though some men sing not can
 'Though some men cannot sing, (they can, nevertheless, bear the light in their hands)' (Ælf.Hom.Thorpe IX: 150)

In (8), the subject can be assumed to occupy a high position such as Spec-TP, since it is a pronoun (cf. Fischer et al. 2000; Kroch et al. 2000, for the indicative syntax of subject pronouns). The verbal infinitive *sprecan* 'speak' is hence topicalized, since it surfaces to the left of the high subject. However, in (9) a different syntactic parse is plausible. The subject is non-pronominal and situated in its low (in situ) position, which was possible in early English. I take this position to be Spec-VP on simplest assumptions; see e.g. Haeberli (2000), Gergel (2008). The modal together with the possibly cliticized negation has its complement to the left. Thus, even though there is a contrast involved in example (9), we cannot assume such examples—unlike the type in (8)—to be in a topic position in the left periphery on syntactic grounds.[10]

A third argument for assuming functional-category status for Old English modals makes it plausible to take them to occupy Asp° territory in clause structure. This argument is based on a particular co-occurrence restriction that has escaped attention in discussions of categorial status so far. While Old English is not usually considered to have had a pervasive perfective/imperfective distinction in its suffixed paradigms, it had the verbal prefix *ge-*. The contribution of the prefix is that of a perfective (see e.g. van Gelderen 2003; McFadden 2011). To avoid confusion, the Old English version of the prefix is distinct from the distribution of the cognate *ge-* in modern languages like German. In the latter, when available, *ge-* is a (largely obligatory) morphological concord marker, marking past participles (e.g. in addition to auxiliaries such as *haben/sein* 'have/be' in the construction of the perfect). Moreover, the productive version of the German prefix *ge-* never appears in the forms of the present, the

---

[10] The status of verbal topicalization in early English remains interesting. E.g. the example in (8) combines topicalization and ellipsis (the antecedent of an ellipsis site is topicalized). Furthermore, remnants of the lexical VP can be left behind, as shown in (i).

(i) Hleotan man mot mid geleafan swa þeah on woruldðingum butan wiccecræfte,
 cast.lots one may with belief so though in worldly things without witchcraft
 'Nevertheless a man may cast lots, in faith, in worldly things, without witchcraft'
   (coaelive,+ALS_[Auguries]:84.3567, translation by Skeat, p. 371)

Independently of the technical analysis of such topicalization (e.g. one can envisage the mechanism that produces them as closer to pseudogapping, in allowing part of the VP to be pre-emptied—or perhaps something quite different; see Trinh 2009 for recent theoretical options of different fronting strategies), it appears to set the modals, with which it occurs, apart from lexical verbs, and it does so on a par with VP ellipsis, hence potentially similarly to Modern English.

preterite, or the infinitive. By contrast, the prefix *ge-* in Old English appears both in the present and in the preterite, but does not have to appear on either. Moreover, it is available on infinitives. Crucially for our object of investigation, *ge-* does not co-occur with *magan*, *cunnan*, or *motan*, and more generally with any Old English modal (with the orthogonal exception of a particular participial/adjectival use etymologically related to *cunnan*, on which see section 10.4.2). This is surprising given the general availability of the prefix with verbs in general, also e.g. with *be*. Furthermore, the restriction cannot be blamed on the preterite-present nature of the modals either. For instance, a preterite present that is not a modal, such as *witan* 'know', is well attested in the data co-occurring with *ge-*. I take the co-occurrence restriction between perfective *ge-* and the modals as evidence for the fact that they occupy the same syntactic area, namely the head Asp°.[11]

To conclude the subsection, there is evidence indicating that the modals of Old English were different from other verbs and already had the status of a functional category. The particular approximation suggested has been that the modals were inserted in the position in which aspectual heads usually join the derivation.

10.4 Modal at the syntax–semantics interface and the question of modal bases

Three types of modality are relevant for current purposes: epistemic, deontic, and circumstantial. Circumstantial modality is common in semantic treatments of modality (e.g. Kratzer 1991). It is important to note that circumstantial modality has not played a role in philological and syntactic investigations of the Old English premodals. While much of the research on the history of the modals has concentrated on the question of whether epistemic readings were available or not and how they could have developed out of *deontic* modals, I propose that circumstantial readings are decisive concerning reconstructing the origins of the epistemic modals.

The question of whether Old English has epistemic modals relates to categorial status, structural height, and the syntactic reanalysis introduced in section 10.3. The implicit logic beyond the connection is as follows. If the modals have been reanalyzed to a higher position in the syntactic tree much later than during the Old English period (Roberts 1993; compare, once again, the discussion in the previous section) and if epistemic modals are associated with high structural positions (e.g. Cinque 1999;

---

[11] Van Gelderen (2003) discusses the possibilities of *ge-* in the complements of Old English modals (not in relationship to attachment to the modals themselves). While the picture emerging in that domain may be more intricate, as van Gelderen points out, I use in this chapter the new evidence to argue for her overall suggestion (for Old English, not for Modern English), namely that the modals join the syntactic derivation in the area of an aspectual head. Finally, I will have to leave it to further research to what extent the modern tendency in German to avoid *ge-*based participial forms on the modals via suppletion (the so-called *infinitivus pro participio* rule) can be related to the earlier Germanic conditioning of the *ge-* prefix.

Drubig 2001; Butler 2003), then the *lack* of epistemic readings at a time when the modals were not yet "high enough" in terms of their syntactic position may fall intp place. However, it is important to consider if and exactly how this is reflected in the Old English data under consideration.

Epistemic occurrences of modals in Old English are infrequent in the preserved written texts. This impression has led some researchers to minimize, or even deny, their existence in Old English in different theoretical camps and to different degrees. In the generative tradition, the claim that epistemic readings are attested only late historically is interpreted in terms of an upward development in the tree-geometric sense. The idea is as simple as it may be attractive—the modals originate as main verbs at early times and end up in functional projections in Modern English only. Since epistemic modals are considered to occupy high structural positions, this is interpreted as at least compatible with the fact that they only arise after the Old English period. Even a study as careful as Roberts and Roussou (1999: 45) seems to take it for granted that epistemic readings only appear in Middle English (cf. Goosens 1982; Traugott 1989; Denison 1993; van Gelderen 2003 for cautionary notes). I will survey the allowed modal bases for *cunnan*, *magan*, and *motan* in Old English and argue that epistemic readings are possible in some cases. Since there are important differences between the modals under investigation, I will consider them individually (some cross-references will be made for ease of comparison).[12]

10.4.1 Magan/may

The variants of *magan* have the highest incidence in the Old English data.[13] The premodal has a total of over 5,400 examples in the YCOE (Taylor et al. 2003). This is more than six times the recorded incidence of *motan* and almost nine times that of *cunnan* in the same corpus (cf. 4.2 and 4.3). The proportion of infinitives selected by *magan* is also particularly high at an absolute of over 5,000 examples, including c.601 instances of infinitival 'be' and 102 of infinitival 'have'. At a total of c.92%, the proportion is very close to that of *motan*, but much higher than that of *cunnan*, as we will see in the next two subsections.[14]

---

[12] A further problem in associating epistemic modals with high structural positions in Old English is independent of our immediate concerns. Given that the premodals can move to a high position such as C (as any verb in most Germanic languages) and given the Head Movement Constraint (Travis 1984), one would have to stipulate that epistemic readings are only associated with high structural positions when they are not derived via the otherwise frequent movement to C in the language.

[13] The Old English modals and the Modern cognates are listed together for quick reference. A number of differences in their meanings will be discussed in what follows.

[14] For practical purposes stemming from the partially flat corpus annotation in the verbal domain, the relevant structural condition in the search was approached as sisterhood of a modal with an infinitival verbal head, rather than as a mother-daughter structural relationship of a modal with a VP complement. Regardless, the results are equivalent in practice. The two main conditions for the final query used for this study are given in (i):

(i) query: (MD* hasSister *VB) AND (MD* iDoms "modal_forms")

Magan, the predecessor of *may*, is often translated as 'can'. The original occurrences sometimes also appear as 'be able to' and 'may' in translations. Furthermore, the *Dictionary of Old English* offers non-modal senses such as 'to be strong, to have power, or influence'. Like *cunnan* and *motan*, *magan* seems to have had a past as a main verb. What the premodal also shares in Old English with the two other modals investigated is the possibility of allowing a circumstantial modal base when used with a further verb. However, circumstantial readings are broad and not restricted to mentally relevant circumstances in the case of *magan* (compare 4.2. and 4.3). Similar and more specific circumstances were properly included in the range of possibilities, as the following examples illustrate:

(10) Cristes þegnas þeossa worda nan ongeotan ne **mehton**
 Christ's disciples of.these words not understand not could
 'Christ's disciples were not able to understand any of these sayings.'
 (Blick.Hom.Morr. 15: 14)

(11) þa gewende he to Rome, be ðæs caseres hæse, þæt he
 there went he to Rome by the emperor's command that he
 hine betealde, gif he **mihte**
 himself exculpate if he might.
 'He therefore went, by the emperor's command, to Rome, so that he might clear himself, if he could.' (Ælf.Hom.Thorpe V: 80)

While the salient reading of (10) is circumstantial, (11) could also be plausibly interpreted deontically. In this example, the clearance referred to is only possible in the context if granted by the authorities.

Furthermore, *magan* allows for certain epistemic readings in Old English. The reason why I state this cautiously is that claims about the intended meaning cannot be made in many cases. Nonetheless, the meanings that *can* arise from the context are just as relevant when it comes to historical processes (cf. Eckardt 2006). Even if the premodals are not often necessarily intended to convey epistemic readings, in the written genres that are available to us, there is evidence of examples that could give

---

The wild card suffixed to the modal head (MD*) is necessary to incorporate modal forms in the past, as well as other forms. The wild card prefixed to the verbal head (*VB) is necessary to include verbal items with preceding particles, which would otherwise be missed due to the annotation scheme. However, a wild card prefixed to MD returns no additional hits. Additionally, a wild card suffixed to VB brings in erroneous data, in the sense that they will not be infinitives as desired any longer, rather other verbal forms that are not complements of the modals and often overlap with data from searches on forms of *be* and *have*. Hence these possibilities are not implemented above. In addition to items annotated as verbs, I have also searched, exactly as for *VB, for instances of infinitival forms of *have* (i.e. *HV) and *be* (*BE). Further searches for inflected infinitives, which existed in Old English in general, returned no hits in the complement position of the modals searched for. The searches for the other modals were conducted under the same structural conditions.

rise to such readings. This point is possibly shared with *motan* (cf. 10.4.3), but there are more types of context available for *magan*. Consider the following examples from the Blickling Homilies:

(12) þeos circe   mid þys portice **mihte** hu   hwego   fif hund
     this church with the porch   might how what/some five hundred
     manna befón   ond behabban
     men   contain and hold
     'This church with the portico might contain and hold some five hundred men.'
                                                    (Blick.Hom.Kel. 142)

(13) on sumre stowe he wæs þæt man mid his hánda **nealice** geræcean
     in some place it was that man with his hands nearly reach
     mihte,
     could
     '[I]n one place a man might hardly reach it [the roof] with his hand.'
                                                    (Blick.Hom.Kel. 142)

Such examples are circumstantial, with a potential for being reinterpreted epistemically. The narrative passage, including the sentences provided above, provides ample description and evidence regarding the capacity of the church and the unusual shape of the roof (constructed at various levels), respectively. Furthermore, the sentences above contain approximators in the expressions for 'nearly' and 'some' (the latter word being used in the approximating sense). Such contexts are compatible with circumstantial readings. However, some of them seem to also allow epistemic interpretations. The effect of not knowing whether something held true exactly as it is phrased may have originally stemmed from the approximators in such examples. Such uncertainties may have reasonably been (re)interpreted as also being associated, at least partly, with the modals. We may hypothesize that uncertainty played a role in why some modals had a potential to be interpreted epistemically, which, among other means, could be introduced via approximators. The fact that this is shown most clearly by *magan* rather than by other modals is most easily explained by its higher frequency. By this I mean that if a premodal is not frequent enough, it is less likely to appear in contexts containing elements of uncertainty, which seem to be necessary for natural-language epistemic modality. A relevant and slightly different type of example that could be interpreted epistemically is the following one from Ælfric:

(14) [A]nd hi   ða   ealle sæton, swa swa **mihte** beon fif ðusend   wera.
     and they there all   sat   such as might be five thousand men
     '[A]nd they then all sat, about five thousand men.' (Ælf.Hom.Thorpe XII: 182)

The translation of the sequence (originally adopted from Thorpe, also adopted as such in Denison 1993: 298) involves an approximating construction. The sitting event of the group was such that it produced the appearance of there being 5,000 men. The first sentence thus gives the source of the evidence in this case (viz. the sitting event). The speaker/writer might have meant a sheer circumstantial reading. However, there is a modal used, and nothing seems to be able to stop such contexts from being interpreted under an epistemic/evidential reading.

Conditionals represent yet another context in which the notion of uncertainty may have contributed to the grammaticalization of epistemic readings. In the following example, retrieved from a similar type of text via the YCOE corpus, it is interesting to note that the truth of the core proposition is under debate:

(15) Eac ða arfæstan beoð wolice   gearwurðode, **gif** þæt soð beon **mæg**
     also the virtuous are unjustly honored   it that true be may
     þæt him swa gesceapen wæs;
     that it so created   was
     'Likewise the good are unjustly honoured, if it can be true that it was so determined for them.'
     (coaelive,+ALS_[Auguries]: 233.3638; translation from Skeat 1881: 381)

For example (16), an additional note is in order regarding complementation: *magan* could take CP complements in Old English:

(16) Eaðe **mæg** þæt me Drihten þurh   his geearnung miltsigan   wille
     easily may that me God   through his earning   show.mercy wants
     'It may well be that God will show mercy through his merit.'
     (cobede,Bede_3: 11.192.5.1929)

That modal constructions with CP complements allowed epistemic readings has been observed, e.g. in Denison (1993) and Fischer (2010). To sharpen the view with respect to the modals of interest here, we may add to this observation the fact that *cunnan* and *motan* did interestingly *not* seem to display such complementation possibilities.

It may be tempting to attribute the presence of epistemic readings to the fact that the propositional argument is expressed through a finite clause. In terms of clausal architecture, the modal itself will be beyond the C domain, if one assumes the same clausal domain. However, there are two issues. The first is that the aforementioned pattern is particularly infrequent. The second, according to Denison as well as Fischer, is that a broader generalization can be culled, namely by considering impersonal constructions. Accordingly, modals with CP complements would be a part of the pattern of impersonal constructions. A typical example of an impersonal is given in (17), cited here from Fischer (2010):

(17) þonne **mæg hine**   scamigan þære brædinge his hlisan   (Bo 19.46.5)
     then can him.ACC shame   of-the spreading his fame
     'then he may be ashamed of the extent of his fame'

To sum up the key points of this subsection, *magan* is the most frequent modal in Old English, it prevails with infinitives, and it is the one that shows the clearest cases of epistemic readings, presumably under the influence of factors of uncertainty.

10.4.2 Cunnan/can

The YCOE corpus contains 615 examples of *cunnan*'s variant forms. Out of this total, only 161 tokens occur in conjunction with an overt infinitive of another verb, which is usually a main verb. There is only one instance of 'be' in the complement of *cunnan* and none of 'have'. This stands in a conspicuous contrast with *magan* (see section 10.4.1). That is, only a small proportion of the tokens containing the premodals, approximately 26%, appear with the infinitive. This estimation is already indicative of the fact that establishing the relationship of *cunnan* to modality arises. *Cunnan* is the predecessor of the modal *can*, but the distribution of its early occurrences appears to be the furthest away from Modern English modals when compared to the other modals of Old English. This holds both for argument structures, since it can frequently take nominal direct objects, and its range of meanings. The latter is rendered by the *Oxford English Dictionary* (*OED* 2013, *can* v.1) as 'to know' on its first meaning, a fact which potentially explains the presence of its selected direct objects. This seems to be a principal pattern in Old English (see e.g. (19) for an example from the Blickling Homilies below). Given that it was a preterite present, it is likely that *cunnan* was derived from learning (i.e. it meant 'know', perhaps originally 'know due to *having* learnt'). Other listed lexical entries in the *OED* are 'to have learned (a thing),' 'to have skill (in),' 'to have knowledge (in),' and a few others that appear to be related.

None of the meanings mentioned is modal *per se*. However, they can be regarded as close to a circumstantial sense of intellectual ability. A sense of being mentally able to experience or do something seems to have been prevalent in the meanings of the early occurrences. The *OED* gives one attestation of *cunnan*, from 1154, which is labeled as a modal auxiliary and still falls into the (late) Old English period. The other examples in the *OED* that are labeled auxiliary are from the Middle English period. Nonetheless, as we will see, some sense of '(originally intellectually based) ability,' and hence genuine modality, must have previously been available in the Old English period, coupled with infinitival complementation.

To gain insight into the behavior of *cunnan* on a specific textual basis, consider the Blickling instances. They contain many instances of participle/adjectival uses of *cuþ* and related forms, which had meanings along the lines of '(well) known,' 'familiar'; cf. (18) in a predicative construction *be known (to someone) that ...*). Additionally, there are six examples of *cunnan* used as a (finite) verb, which are listed in the Blickling concordance (Kelly 2009). Some of the finite instances are indeed used in the sense of 'know,' as (19) illustrates.[15]

---

[15] If it were not for the frequent participial examples, *cunnan* might appear as the least frequent candidate for a modal in this collection from the range of modals introduced in section 10.2.

(18) oþþe hwanan sceal me **cuþ** beon þæt ic, mid lichomolicum eagum,
or whence will me known be that I with bodily eyes
geseon ne mæg?
see not can
'[O]r in what manner will it be manifested to me which, with human eyes, I am
unable to see?' (Blick.Hom.Kelly 14: 100)

(19) ond þone weg ic ne **con**
and the way I not know
'[A]nd I don't know the route.' (Blick.Hom.Kelly 158: 33)

Such uses did not require a further verb, and taking them to be main verbs is the simplest hypothesis.[16] However, *cunnan* can also be used as a modal. That is, it could take infinitive-headed complements—the examples in (20a,b) are occurrences with an infinitival VP from the same homilies:

(20) a. & þa lareowas sceolan synnfullum mannum eadmodlice tæcan
and the teachers shall sinful.dat men.dat humbly present
& læran þæt hie heora synna **cunnon** [onrihtlice **geandettan**];
and teach that they their sins can rightly confess
'The teachers must humbly teach and instruct sinful men so that they may know how to properly confess their sins,' (Blick.Hom.Kelly 28: 60)

b. þæt hie [þæt **ongeotan**] ne **cuðan** þæt hie þær gehyrdon
that they that understand not could that they there heard
'[That] they were not able to recognize what they heard there.'
(Blick.Hom.Kelly 74: 19)

The relationship between genuine modal meanings and the ability meanings in the sense of 'know' can still be regarded as being in flux even in the infinitive-taking instances of *cunnan*. While example (20a) may allow an alternative construal to the one of ability (i.e. one still in the sense of 'know'; cf. the option taken in the translation via 'know how to'), (20b) brings out the circumstantial modality more clearly. Similarly, Ælfric's homilies contain a majority of examples in which *cunnan* is used as a main verb. However, examples of its use as a modal in the narrow sense, i.e. with an infinitive, also appear (cf. (9)). An example with an infinitive and a modal meaning is (21).

(21) þæt ge **cunnon** þæt ece lif geearnian
that you can that eternal life earn
'that ye may be able to earn the eternal life' (Ælf.Hom.Thorpe XXXII: 488)

---

[16] We cannot exclude entirely that e.g. a meaning along the lines of 'I am not able to state the route' might have been understood. It is entailed by the simpler meaning we assume, with the translation, in (19).

The context of (21) is about earning eternal life. The more specific modal meaning could be either circumstantial or deontic. It is important to note that an epistemic reading is less likely given that the message is conveyed as a matter of fact. *Cunnan* with infinitives and modal meanings constituted, then, a small but extant pattern in Old English. A further indication that modal *cunnan* did not behave differently in structural terms from the other Old English modals when it took infinitive complements is that it could be coordinated with the other modals. The following example from the YCOE corpus illustrates this fact:

(22) Nis   se   man on life þe   **mæge** oððe **cunne** swa yfel hit asecgan
      not-is the man in life that may   or   can   as   evil it   say
      swa hit sceal geweorðan on þam deoflican timan
      as   it   shall become   on that devilish   time
      'There is no one alive who may say or can say how evil it will be in that devilish time.'
      (cowulf,WHom_5: 97.228; translation from Joyce Tally Lionarons's edition, http://webpages.ursinus.edu/jlionarons/wulfstan/Wulfstan.html)

In (22), *magan* and *cunnan* are coordinated. Recall from section 10.4.1 that *magan* is relatively well developed as a modal already in Old English and even shows epistemic readings. In fact, this pattern of coordination is the most frequent pattern in the YCOE corpus: 8 out of a total of 49 tokens of modals in a structural sisterhood relationship have the combination consisting of *magan* and *cunnan*.

A few combinations with three modal items are also attested: see (23), with *motan* in addition to *magan* and *cunnan*. The entire series of 'possibility' modals could then be lined up in Old English. One possibility is that there are semantic distinctions in such cases. Another possibility is that the items reinforce one another to some extent. For example, they could be used as a rhetoric device (cf. Hiyama 2005: 187, who—using the example for different purposes—translates the entire series of three modals simply with one 'may').

(23) ...þæt we ure lif mid soðe &   mid rihte lifigan **moton** &
      that   we our life with truth and with justice live   must   and
      magon & **cunnan**
      may   and can
      'So that we may, are able to, and know how to live our lives truly and justly.'
      (coverhom,HomS_2_[ScraggVerc_16]: 93.2090)

How did *cunnan* behave with respect to the co-occurrence restriction with the perfective marker *ge-*, which was held with other modals but not with lexical verbs (cf. section 10.2)? A form *ge-cunnan* was available in Old English. However, it only had non-modal meanings that were in the range of 'to know, to be familiar with a fact, to understand a mystery, to know someone.' There are no co-occurrences of *cunnan* used as a modal with the prefix *ge-* in either of the homily groups studied or the entire YCOE corpus. By this I mean that the two uses of *cunnan* as a verb and a premodal, are clearly distinguishable. This reinforces the current assumption that they are already distinct lexical items in Old English.

Cunnan is an emerging modal in Old English. In the course of Old English it widens its uses from a particular version of preterite-present based verb with the original meaning along the lines of 'know' towards a particular version of premodal 'be able.' Concerning the modal readings, this early development only allows for circumstantial readings, more specifically, for a subset of them that are related to intellectual abilities. It may seem cogent to hypothesize that intellectual abilities have been transferred from the lexical entry of the earliest verb 'know' to be incorporated into the background function of the later modal. Conversely, there is no reliable epistemic attestation of this modal despite the possible connection between knowledge and epistemic states of affairs. This apparently easy connection may also have been the biggest impediment. The missing portion of *un*certainty that is usually part of epistemic modals may have been the reason why only circumstantial readings are widely attested in Old English. (Recall from 10.4.1 that *magan* 'may' displayed the relevant uncertainty contexts.)

10.4.3 Motan/must

There are 864 examples of *motan* that are labeled as modal in the YCOE. This is considerably lower than the prevalent presence of *magan* (cf. 10.4.1) in the corpus, and only slightly higher than that for *cunnan*, which displayed a total of 615 examples. Moreover, there is a considerable difference between *cunnan* and *motan* when we take into account the incidence of infinitives selected as complements. *Motan* in the YCOE appeared in 809 cases in this configuration (i.e. c.93% of cases). Out of the total of infinitives, 77 were instances of (the cognates of) 'have' and 45 of the infinitives were of 'be.' The original meaning of *motan* may have been 'have something measured out,' as is hypothesized by the *OED* via reconstruction. As in the case of *cunnan*, when the item is used as a modal, most readings are easily construed as circumstantial:

(24) þa   he hit for manna teonan begrecan ne   **moste**
     then he it for men's anger break   not could
     When **he was not able**, on account of men's anger, to break it, ...
                                         (Blick.Hom.Morr. XVIII: 221)

Unlike in the case of *cunnan* a narrowly restricted circumstantial modal base is not the only interpretive option. First, while the example in (24) had a circumstantial reading, it was not about a necessarily intellectual ability (or lack thereof due to negation).

Second, the range of meanings is not limited to clearly circumstantial cases. Consider (25), in which the modal by itself seems to be ambiguous between a circumstantial and a deontic reading. The latter is prevalent due to the embedding under a lexical item that explicitly indicates permission, viz. the noun *leafnesse* 'leave,' taking a CP which in turn contains the modal:

(25) *þæt wif   he onfeng fram hyre yldrum þære arednesse þæt hio his*
     that woman he took from her parents the condition that she his
     leafnesse hæfde þæt heo þone þeaw   þæs   Cristenan geleafan &
     leave   had   that she the custom the-of Christian belief   and
     hyre æfestnesse ungewemmedne healdan moste....
     her religion   unhindered   hold   might
     'That woman he took from her parents under the condition that she would have his permission to keep unhindered the practice of Christian belief and her religion [. . .]'   (cobede,Bede: 14.58.13.544)

A clear deontic reading for *motan* in a matrix environment is shown in (26), from Ælfric, where permission in the context is granted for certain actions (and not for others):

(26) *Ealra þæra þinga þe on neorxna-wange sindon þu most brucan....*
     all.of the things that in paradise   are   you may eat
     buton anum treowe
     except one tree
     Of all the things that are in paradise you may eat (except one tree)
     'Of all the things which are in Paradise thou mayest eat, . . . save one tree . . . '
                                                          (Ælf.Hom.Thorpe I: 12)

On closer inspection, it appears that there was even a potential for epistemic readings to arise:

(27) *þa   blissode heo micclum þæt heo hit beon moste*
     then rejoiced she much   that she it be   might
     'Then she greatly rejoiced that she might be it.'   (Ælf.Hom.Thorpe II: 42)

(27) is ambiguous between a deontic, a circumstantial, and potentially an epistemic reading. The context is one of Mary having received the news that she might bear a child. The hearsay evidence of the news, which is explicitly mentioned, could give rise to an evidential reading. Of course, the joy expressed in the sentence could also be about the permission to become the chosen one (deontic), or simply about the relevant circumstances.

Another type of context which could induce evidentially colored modality with *motan* are verbs of saying, as illustrated in (28):

(28) **Sægd is** þæt se ilca wiþerwearda þe him ær þa sinna lærde
said is that the same adversary that them before the sins taught
þæt se hi **mote** eft mid mycclum witum wítnian buton hie hit
that he them must after with great pain punish except they it
ær gebeton willon.
before amend want
'It is **said** that the same adversary that previously instructed them to sin **will** afterwards torment them with great suffering, unless they previously amend their ways.' (B.Hom.Kelly 42; similarly Morris p. 60)

Standing alone, the modal *will* which is used in the two translations, does not seem sufficient to indicate epistemic modality—although it could indicate some sort of epistemic uncertainty. The key point here is that it is under a verb that indicates reportative evidence. Here, the narrator takes a precaution in reporting on the devil and sinners, not claiming direct evidence, but contending that the information originates from an unspecified source.

To conclude the section, the three premodals inspected allowed infinitival complements, but *cunnan* displayed this option only as a minority pattern, while for *magan* and *motan* it was prevalent. *Magan* also shows the clearest examples that could give rise to epistemic readings (*cunnan* virtually never does). The potential for epistemic readings may have been enhanced by a series of factors including CP complementation (as has been previously proposed), as well as the sheer predominant frequency of the modal and the availability of a range of co-occurring expressions of uncertainty. All three items when used as modals in Old English are incompatible with perfective *ge-* prefixation. The latter fact is predicted if we assume that the modals were merged under Asp° themselves.

10.5 Modal force

In this section I will discuss potential oscillations of modal force of the same items, which is especially relevant in the case of *motan*. Although its modern cognate, *must*, has clear universal quantificational force, *motan* has a less clear status with respect to modal force, i.e. often as an apparent existential modal, as pointedly observed in the philological tradition (cf. e.g. Ono 1958; see Bech 1951 for a history of the German modals, where a similar phenomenon has been attested for *müssen*, and more generally van der Auwera and Plungian 1998 for typological considerations)

The oscillation displayed by *motan*, the cognate of *must*, in Old (and partly Middle) English is fundamentally and genuinely one of modal force. There are cases that may be translated systematically by *may* (or other exponents of existential modal force), and yet other examples that are best rendered by a modal of universal force in Modern English. I do not have a general method for translations and I am not suggesting anything new by noting this variation. Nonetheless, I will ultimately seek to determine two points: (i) To what extent did *motan* show variation in the texts under consideration? (ii) In a general sense, how does the variation relate to other parameters of variation? In the course of the inquiry, I will test to what extent Yanovich's (2013) proposal made for Alfredian prose can account for the current data.

The key point of variation is easy to illustrate. For instance, out of the 35 instances of the modal *motan* counted for the Blickling Homilies, only two are translated by *must* and a further one by *should* in Kelly's edition. A total of 22 cases are translated by using a clear expression of existential modal force (*may can be able to*). Interestingly, the translations of 10 examples (all of which are in the past tense) have no clear modal force in their Modern English counterparts (e.g. the following items are utilized in the translations: *to, will, -ing,* and *let*). Such translation-based quick facts are not semantic arguments. However, they indicate that the modal shows variation, when viewed from the perspective of modal force of Modern English. *Motan* is clearly not an ideal exponent of a modal of possibility throughout. Furthermore, examples translated with the universal counterpart *must* exist.Consider (29) and (30).

(29) *Gif him mon   þonne hyran nelle,   þonne mot se   mæssepreost*
     if him someone then listen not.will, then   must the mass priest
     hit wrecan swa hit her   bebodan   is.
     it avenge so it here commanded is
     'But if anyone will not listen to him, the priest **must** punish him as it is here decreed.'   (B.Hom.Kelly IV: 30/32)

(30) *þæt se Godes man ne sceolde be þan morgendæge þencean, þylæs þæt wære þæt he þurh þæt ænig þara goda, forylde þe he þonne þy dæge gedón mihte, ond ða wéninge hweðer he eft þæs mergendæges gebidan **moste**.*
     'The man of God should not be concerned about tomorrow, lest it should happen that he thereby put off any of the good things that he might do on that present day, and **must** then await the expectation of the next day.'
     (B.Hom.Kelly XVII: 146)

It is likely that in these examples, the universal *must* is appropriate. In principle, (29) could also be a case of granting permission (to the priest) to enforce punishment; but given the command referred to, this is less likely, and the requirement for the priest to act seems to be the much more probable reading. Somewhat similar considerations may hold for (30) and make the universal an appropriate rendering in these cases.

In regards to recent research on modality in non-Indo-European languages, an idea that offers itself to consideration for an analysis of variation in modal force is that one may be dealing with a bona fide variable-force modal. Since a recent explicit proposal exists for *motan* as it was attested in Alfredian prose (Yanovich 2013), I will begin by discussing it and then test if it can be transferred to the texts under current attention. Traditional research characterizes *motan* as a modal which diachronically changes from possibility to necessity. Yanovich (2013) takes a substantial body of philological literature into consideration and, by analyzing Old English Alfredian (i.e. King Alfred's) prose, offers a proposal that is distinct from the previous literature on English. This research is close in spirit to the analyses of variable-force modals as in Rullmann et al. (2008) and others for languages of the Pacific Northwest. In this chapter, I will not discuss proposals for variable-force modals in other languages (see Yanovich 2013: 4.3.2 for a comparison with the ultimate argument that they do not carry over). Instead I will directly address the fresh proposal made by Yanovich.

In essence, *motan* is analyzed by Yanovich as a modal conveying a possibility with a distinctive flavor of inevitability. As shown in (31) and (32), the entry suggested distinguishes between a crucial presuppositional layer and the assertive contribution of *motan*. Informally, *motan*(p) asserts that p is an open possibility. More importantly, it presupposes that if p is given a chance to be actualized, it will. The latter technical part achieves the collapse of possibility and necessity. The two parts of the formalized definition are given below (Yanovich 2013: 155–7):

(31) $[[motan]]^{w,t}(p)$ **presupposes** that $(\exists w': R_{met}(w, w', t) \wedge AT(p, w', [t, \infty))) \rightarrow$
$(\forall w': R_{met}(w, w', t) \rightarrow AT(p, w', [t, \infty)))$, where p is a property of events;
$R_{met}(w, w', t)$ holds *iff* w and w are identical up until time t;
and the interpretation of $AT(p, w', [t, \infty))$ depends on whether p is stative or eventive: for a stative p, $AT(p, w', [t, \infty))$ holds *iff* there is a p-event the running time of which intersects with $[t, \infty)$, and moreover, includes t; and for an eventive p, $AT(p, w', [t, \infty))$ *iff* there is a p-event whose running time is included into $[t, \infty)$.

(32) $[[motan]]^{w,t}(p)$ **asserts** that $\exists w': R_{met}(w, w', t) \wedge AT(p, w', [t, \infty))$, $R_{met}(w, w', t)$ holds *iff* w and w' are identical up until time t.

This is not the place to engage in all the details of the proposal (see also Condoravdi 2002 for some of the background and technicalities on which Yanovich's interesting suggestion rests). However, a number of points are relevant from a descriptive vantage point. I will organize the rest of the discussion by considering what advantages such a proposal would have over an analysis of *motan* as an existential modal, while keeping in mind that the majority of the examples in the homilies seem to have been possibility expressions.

Yanovich's (2013) conclusions integrate a range of interesting observations culled from Alfredian prose and earlier literature. However, there are reasons not to adopt it for the data I have considered. What I claim instead is that we are dealing with a modal of possibility—presumably at the beginning of a competition with a modal of necessity in the sense of Kroch (1989). The view is motivated by the fact that Yanovich's arguably strongest argument for Alfredian prose cannot be transferred to the data at hand.[17]

First, unlike in the Alfredian prose, there is no evidence for inevitability in the homilies I have considered. On the contrary, *motan* is used in contexts that indicate quite avoidable courses of events. One example was e.g. (26), where—a priori—there was both a possibility to eat and not to eat (of all the fruits except for the forbidden one). Another example that brings out non-determinism even more explicitly is the following:

(33) *Se Ælmihtiga Scyppend gesceop englas þurh his godcundan mihte,*
the almighty creator created angels through his divine power
and for his micclan rihtwisnysse forgeaf him agene cyre, þæt
and for his great righteousness granted them own free-choice that
hí **moston** *ðurhwunian on ecere gesælðe ðurh gehyrsumnysse,*
they might continue in eternal happiness through obedience
and mihton eac ða gesælða forleosan na for gewyrde ac for
and might also that happiness lose not for destiny but for
ungehyrsumnysse
disobedience
'The Almighty Creator created angels by his divine power, and in his great righteousness gave them their own choice, that they **might continue in eternal happiness** through obedience, and **might also lose that happiness**, not through destiny, but for disobedience.' (Ælf.Hom.Thorpe VII: 110)

The examples and the passages surrounding them make clear that Ælfric did not intend to convey a sense of inevitability in such cases involving *motan*, but rather possibility and free will.

A second argument is that if the 'Alfredian' entry is adopted for the homilies discussed here, then the consequent and the conditional, in examples such as (34), should be non-informative and partly misplaced, since the sequence 'the devil MOT slay us' should—according to the presuppositional semantics—express exactly that the devil will slay the relevant first person plural entity including the speaker/writer, if he can do so.

(34) *God us fett and gefrefrað and deofol us wile ofslean, gif he* **mót**;
God us feeds and comforts and devil us will slay if he may;
'God feeds and comforts us, and the devil will slay us if he may;'
(Ælf.Hom.Thorpe XIX: 270)

---

[17] Yanovich lucidly points out that none of the arguments offered enforces the conclusions drawn on its own. I believe the scope restriction relative to negation observed holds. What I take to be the strongest argument is the semantics of inevitability captured in the presupposition. We will see, however, that it cannot be upheld in the homiletic texts (Yanovich does not make the claim that his semantics should hold for all Old English texts).

Thirdly, while I could not find clear-cut scaling effects between the modals (confirming Yanovich on this), there are cases of *motan* occurring in negative conjunction with *magan* and disjunction with *sculan* 'shall':

(35) we **ne** *magon* ne ne *motan* na furðor embe þis smeagan, gif we
 we not may nor not must no further about this reflect if we
 nellað us sylfe forpæran
 not-want us selves lose
 '[W]e may not, and we must not, enquire further concerning this, if we would not lose ourselves.'
 (coaelive,+ALS_[Christmas]: 72.59; translation from Skeat 1881: 15)

(36) Ac ic þe bidde, þæt þu me secge, hwæðer he **sceolde** oððe **moste**
 but I you ask that you me say whether he should or must
 forlætan þa broðro, þe he æne underfeng.
 let.go the brothers that he once accepted
 (cogregdH,GD_2_[H]: 3.108.23.1080)

Finally, and somewhat more generally, there may be conceptual and practical reasons not to posit a complex entry on the basis of a dead language alone (given that e.g. the presupposition can hardly be tested in it). Instead, I suggest, on the basis of the data I have considered, that *motan* is a possibility modal in the grammar(s) that produced the homiletic texts. The mechanism by which such an entry began to widen its quantificational domain may well be plurigenetic, and presuppositions may have played a role as well. Nonetheless, the semantics offered cannot be endorsed for the data inspected. In the next section, I will offer an additional general argument—drawing on the connection to actuality entailments—why the very precise entry proposed by Yanovich for Alfredian prose cannot capture the semantics of *motan* for Old English.

If a universal meaning can arise from an existential, so that two meanings can compete over time, then this tendency should be observable in more cases. As mentioned, other Germanic languages such as German underwent a similar trajectory. Furthermore, what about the other elements under scrutiny in this study? I was unable to find examples of *cunnan* that could possibly be reinterpreted as universal (keeping in mind that in the majority of instances, this item lacks a modal meaning altogether). However, there was one example of *magan* in the data I considered that allows an alternative interpretation as a universal. Consider (37), from Blickling:

(37) Forþon hine **mæg** nu ælc mon oforswiþan.
 therefore him may now every man overcome
 'Every one of us **must** now overcome him.' (B.Hom. Kelly III: 20)

Kelly's translation suggests a universal meaning (as indicated), while Morris' (generally more archaically rendered translation) renders the modal as *may*. A priori, the sentence could refer to either the possibility or necessity for humans to overcome evil. The particular context is that Jesus has overcome evil, and everyone else should do so or would be able to do so, too. On one reading, a translation via *may* appears plausible; but given that the task is not presented as an easy one, the alternative reading as a(n appropriately restricted) universal cannot be excluded entirely either (i.e. that everybody should follow the example and do likewise). While such examples that are open to interpretation seem to be very sporadic with *magan*, changing the restriction of the modal quantifier contextually should not be too surprising. Additionally, two more ingredients are also likely to have been conducive to a change in modal force in the space occupied by the modals in the paradigm. On the one hand, *sculan* itself (the more standard universal in Old English) started to be used in non-deontic cases (e.g. to mark the future later on, but also potentially epistemic meanings as early as in Old English; cf. Denison 1993). The potential deontic space vacated could not be filled by *cunnan*, since the item was not used deontically. On the other, *magan* was a very frequent modal, as we have seen. Winning a competition on this territory would have been much costlier for a universal meaning. Consequently, *motan* appears to have been just the best choice from the series that was susceptible to a change in meaning. It was frequent enough with modal meanings, but not quite as broadly established as an existential as *magan*.

10.6 Event (non-)realizations under modals

If the connection between aspect and modality is as strong as it is sometimes claimed to be when it comes to the realization of events in the scope of modals (cf. Hacquard 2006), then this yields an additional area from which to cull more specific evidence for the categorial status of the modals in relationship to aspect. Depending on the results of the interaction in Old English, a potential argument for aspectual properties of the modals could be derived. This section hence discusses the status of event realizations under modals in the actual world, which are also known as actuality entailments. I begin by briefly introducing the generally assumed mechanics of the phenomenon in aspect-marking languages, to then make the observation that Germanic modals can show actuality entailments even though the modals are not marked for aspect. I draw on German to illustrate this point. Subsequently, I will report on how Old English modals behaved in this respect, as well as showing that they had a broader range of variation than their German cognates in this area.

In languages that mark aspect morphologically, modals with perfective morphology have been observed to induce an interpretation which favors the realization of the event in their scope (so-called actuality entailments) in conjunction with perfective morphology on the modal. For observations, especially with respect to languages, that make use of aspectual morphology, see e.g. Bhatt (1999), Laca (2005), Haquard (2006), Soare (2008), and Gergel and Cunha (2009). The basic correlation usually observed is quickly summarized: while a modal in the past perfective induces actuality entailments, one in the past imperfective does not. The latter fact is usually attributed to a generic operator that can be conveyed by imperfective morphology. Bhatt claims the reading implying event realization to be a reading close to 'manage to' in the case of ability modals. However, Haquard points out that the phenomenon is more general in the sense that it applies to more items than just the ability modals (focusing on French and Italian). I am not aware of a systematic investigation of this phenomenon in German(ic). Since German, for example, does not mark aspect overtly in the morphological paradigms of (modal) verbs (at least not as inflectional morphemes), this may perhaps seem unsurprising.

Bhatt's work already shows that the phenomenon of actuality entailments is worth investigating beyond aspect-marking languages. It can be tied to more than morphosyntactic correlates. It can also appear, for example, with the semi-modal *be able to* in English, which does not encode any aspectual morphology (cf. Gergel 2009b for effects in English in connection with the modality of *rather*). By this I mean that investigating it in the case of German(ic) modals may turn out to be no less interesting. While this is not the space to engage in a fuller investigation of the phenomenon, it is important to point out that actuality entailments are easy to observe with the modals of the language. Consider first the possibility modals in (38, 39).[18]

(38) *Tatsächlich* **durfte** *ich einmal beobachten, wie der Professor*
 indeed was.allowed.past I once observe how the professor
 eine Dose Ölsardinen durch bloßes Nachdenken geöffnet hat.
 a can sardines.in.oil through sheer thinking opened has.
 (# *aber ich habe das nicht beobachtet.*) (DWDS-Corpus; continuation added)
 'I was indeed once allowed to observe how the professor opened up a can of sardines through his sheer thinking (... but I didn't observe that).'

(39) *Die Feuerwehr konnte den Brand unter Kontrolle bringen.* (#*sie*
 the fire department could the fire under control bring (she
 hat es aber nicht getan)
 has it but not done)
 (adapted from DWDS-Corpus; continuation added)
 'The fire department could bring the fire under control (but it didn't do so).'

---

[18] I introduce possibility modals to stay closer to the focus set up for the Old English modals. However, a necessity modal such as *müssen* 'must' can show the effect as well. It is less clear to what extent *sollen* 'shall' can show such effects. It has several limitations. One of them is that its preterite coincides with the second subjunctive form (also known as the past subjunctive or the *Konjunktiv II*).

The events under *durfte* and *konnte* above are interpreted as realized in the actual world and relevant situation, i.e. as actualized. Retracting the realization is infelicitous. Furthermore, epistemic modals—expectedly from the perspective of aspect-marking languages—do not induce actuality entailments; cf. e.g. *mochte* on an epistemic use below (which incidentally has genuine past tense reference):

(40) Dr. Kerner **mochte** so   um die 50 sein.(after M. Suter, *Der Koch*)
      Dr. Kerner might around at the 50 be
      'Dr. Kerner might have been in his 50s (but he later turned out to be younger).'

What one might be tempted to conclude from such examples is that non-epistemic modals in the past tend to come with actuality entailments in German.[19] If the correlation posited by Haquard is on the right track, then we could claim that such examples involve a silent perfective on the modal in the language.

Returning to Old English: did the language induce obligatory event realization in the scope of a modal? I suggest that eventualities in the scope of a modal could be conveyed as factual, but they could also appear as counter-to-fact. Unlike in modern Germanic languages such as English or German, the latter type of reading did not require the introduction of specific counterfactual constructions (cf. *might have, could have*, etc. which developed in Middle English, or the counterfactual construction with reverse linearization that developed in German, i.e. the subjunctive past *hätte* + modal). Rather, I maintain that in Old English, a modal in the past by itself could convey (non-)realization, depending primarily on the context. By this I mean that Old English modals behaved differently from (Modern) German modals. Examples of actualized and counterfactual Old English modals are shown in (41, 42) (the latter repeated from the previous discussion):

(41) and þancode georne   Gode þæt he hine geseon **moste**.
      and thanked fervently God that he him   see   could
      'and thanked God fervently God that he could see him.'
                                                  (Ælf.Hom.Thorpe IX: 136)

(42) Sprecan he **mihte**, gif he wolde;
      speak   he might   if he wanted
      'He could have spoken, had he been willing.'   (Ælf.Hom.Thorpe IX: 142)

---

[19] I point out the availability of the relevant entailments, but can certainly not fully address the extent to which the phenomenon is available in German within this chapter and leave it to further research. E.g. the form *sollte* 'should' (in which the past indicative and subjunctive also coincide) is clearly less likely to induce the entailments. Similarly, the interaction with certain adverbs (e.g. *eigentlich* 'actually') and particles (e.g. the positive polarity particle *schon* 'indeed') can produce modalized non-epistemic readings without the entailments.

Such possibilities are available for all three modals under consideration (as well as for others). Relevantly, *motan* seems to be infrequently found with counterfactual meanings (a point which would confirm Yanovich's prediction towards realization of events as a tendency in Old English). Nonetheless, counterfactual examples exist in Old English, as the following token retrieved from the YCOE corpus illustrates:

(43) And gif Petrus **moste**   þone man fulslean þonne ne
     and if Peter must/may(past) the man kill   then not
     hete   Crist   hine behydan þa sweord
     commanded Christ him hide   the sword
     'If Peter had been allowed to kill the man, then Christ wouldn't have asked him to put his sword back.'   (colwstan1,+ALet_[Wulfstan_1]: 197.267)

To summarize the section: Old English modals are not tied to actuality entailments when used in the past. Rather, they display the whole gamut of variation. The event in their scope can be presented as realized, left as open, or as counterfactual. This distinguishes Old English modals from Modern German, where modals can entail realization of the event but do not convey counterfactual meanings by themselves. This means that we can assume neither that a perfective nor that an imperfective silent morpheme invariably combines with the Old English modals. This is compatible with the conclusion that the Old English modals occupy a position at the height of aspect themselves in term of structural height.

10.7 Concluding remarks

Let us review the main facts investigated for Old English by focusing on the issue of potential functional status and the readings available in Table 10.1.

The table summarizes some of the observations made in the course of the investigation. The categorial status argued for is that of a functional head in the area of aspect,

TABLE 10.1 Status and readings

	cunnan/can	*magan/may*	*motan/must*
Infinitive complements	✓ (minority pattern)	✓	✓
CP complements	–	✓	–
Licensing of VPE of the complement	✓	✓	✓
Attachment of perf. *ge-* (to the modal forms of the item)	*	*	*
Epistemic readings	–	✓	(possible)
Variation in modal force	–	(sporadic)	✓
Perspective on event realization	Open/factual/ counterfactual	Open/factual/ counterfactual	Open/factual/ counterfactual

noting the incompatibility of the early modals with perfective prefixation. Semantically, we have observed the prevalent use of circumstantial readings. While much research has focused on the transition from deontic to epistemic, we noted that circumstantial modals could also give rise to epistemic readings directly, for example via uncertainty contexts. In terms of modal base, complementation and readings do not correlate one-to-one. Nominal argument structure seems independent of the modal base insofar as all modals could show non-propositional argument patterns (in their original, non-modal uses) but only *cunnan* shows a clearer lack of epistemic readings. It remains remarkable that (i) *cunnan* still had the broadest use of non-propositional arguments in the Old English inspected, and (ii) *magan* shows epistemic readings, as well as CP complements (in addition to nominal and infinitival complements – even if epistemic readings could arise in conjunction with infinitival complements as well, i.e. the CP complementation pattern was not required for the readings).

From the modals inspected, only *motan* has been a good candidate for showing broader effects of variation in terms of modal force in Old English. Sporadic oscillations may appear in more cases, but—whether this is simply noise of the data considered and, for example, the translations or not—it cannot be too surprising if the dimension of modal force can change diachronically. Moreover, we have only considered possibility modals, and such possibilities are not unique (cf. Bech 1951; van der Auwera and Plungian 1998). Regarding *motan*, I have suggested extending the framework of grammar competition, in the sense of Kroch (1989), to the area of meaning. The competition was between the still primarily possibility reading shown in the texts I have considered and the emerging widening use of the necessity reading. This eliminates issues that arise if one tries to import the entry suggested for different types of Old English texts by Yanovich (2013). At the same time, it is fair to state that the notorious actuation problem of language change (i.e. the question of when exactly and why a new form arises; cf. Weinreich et al. 1968) remains here, as in general. Finally, I have argued that in the data considered, actuality entailments were not enforced with *motan* and, generally, event realization under Old English modals is not particularly prominent compared, for example, to Modern High German.

Acknowledgments

I am grateful to the audiences of the modality workshops in Jena and Ottawa, where parts of the material leading to this chapter were discussed. Thanks to Werner Abraham, Ana Arregui, Katrin Axel-Tober, Volker Gast, Martin Kopf, Ekkehard König, Angelika Kratzer, Remo Nitschke, Marga Reis, and Igor Yanovich for questions and input along the way. Many thanks to an anonymous reviewer for detailed comments. Thanks to Danielle Giammanco and Lyra Magloughlin for careful textual and editorial suggestions. The usual disclaimers apply.

Part III

High modality

11

Aspect and tense in evidentials

ANA ARREGUI, MARÍA LUISA RIVERO,
AND ANDRÉS SALANOVA

11.1 A tense-independent approach to evidentials

Traditionally, evidential categories are said to express information regarding the source of evidence for a proposition (e.g. Boas 1947; Jakobson 1957; Chafe and Nichols 1986; Willet 1988; Aikhenvald and Dixon 2003). Classifications of evidentials establish distinctions between, for instance, direct, reported, and inferred sources of evidence, and speaker (un)certainty ("illocutionary" evidentials in Quechua (Faller 2002, 2011), Cheyenne (Murray 2010), and Japanese (McCready and Ogata 2007), and "modal" evidentials that indicate epistemic uncertainty, as in St'át'imcets (Matthewson et al. 2007)). From a morphosyntactic perspective, evidentials can be encoded by a wide array of categories, including particles, aspectual and temporal morphology, modals, verbs, and adverbs.

The goal of this chapter is to investigate the interaction between evidential categories and temporal anchoring. With this aim in mind, we compare Bulgarian, Mẽbengokre, and Matses, whose evidential systems seem to differ in the complexity of temporal dimensions. Bulgarian is a South Slavic language with a system of evidentiality morphologically infused by tense and aspect. Mẽbengokre is a Jê language in central Brazil whose evidential markers do not interact with temporal and aspectual categories. Matses, a Panoan language in the Amazon region in Brazil and Peru, has an evidential system with a high degree of temporal complexity described by Fleck (2003, 2007). We argue for an analysis of the interaction between temporal and evidential markers on the basis of Bulgarian, where the matter has long been studied. We extend our proposal to Mẽbengokre and Matses, which we discuss more briefly given the sparseness of the literature, and conclude that it provides a successful account for very varied evidential systems.

Temporal matters have attracted previous attention in the literature on evidentials (Nikolaeva 1999; Fleck 2003, 2007; Aikhenvald 2004; Speas 2010), but interest on the topic has experienced considerable growth in formal semantics in recent years. Some analyses mainly in the context of Korean and Bulgarian argue that evidential constructions are in need of a particular temporal relation—an additional "evidential tense"—which takes the time of the acquisition of the evidence as evaluation time, and situates the described event in relation to the time the information was acquired (Lee 2011, 2013; Lim 2010; Koev 2011; Smirnova 2011, 2013).

In investigating the interaction of temporal, aspectual, and evidential categories in Bulgarian, Mẽbengokre, and Matses, we address questions such as the following: (a) To what extent do temporal categories affect the interpretation of evidentials? Can the temporal perspective of evidentials be displaced from the speech time? (b) To what extent do evidentials affect the interpretation of temporal categories? Does the interpretation of aspect and tense change in the scope of evidentials? Our conclusion is that temporal categories retain their usual interpretation in evidential contexts both in languages with evidential systems that seem independent from tense such as Mẽbengokre, and in systems where evidential markers are fused with temporal categories such as Bulgarian and Matses. There is no need to postulate an independent "evidential" system of temporal reference in these languages. Standard interpretations of temporal categories suffice to account for temporal dimensions in evidential constructions in a uniform manner in languages that, as we will see, have very different evidential and temporal systems.

Bulgarian, on the one hand, has rich tense and aspectual systems, and it is our view that aspectual morphology is crucial in signaling evidentiality. Matses also appears to encode complex relations by combining temporal and evidential markers. Bulgarian now counts amongst languages where it is claimed that tense displaces the interpretation of evidentials (Koev 2011; Smirnova 2011, 2013), and parallel claims exist about Matses (Fleck 2003, 2007). Mẽbengokre, on the other hand, has a relatively impoverished tense system. There is no formal literature on evidentials in this language, and no claims relating evidentials and tense. Our studies of the evidential systems of these languages support the following preliminary conclusions. Bulgarian, Matses, and Mẽbengokre are parallel insofar as temporal operators do not manipulate the time at which the evidence is acquired in evidentials. Both tense and aspect maintain parallel interpretations in evidential and non-evidential (indicative) contexts. Temporal operators in the scope of evidentials receive their usual speech-time anchored interpretation. These conclusions suggest that there is no need to postulate an independent "evidential tense" in Mẽbengokre, whose evidential particles are independent from tense or aspect markers, in Bulgarian, whose evidential verbal paradigm is infused by tense and aspect, or in Matses, whose evidential system seems based on complex interactions with temporal markers.

In our discussion, we simplify the interpretation of evidentials, and assume that evidential marking corresponds to an operator (EV) characterized as an epistemic/evidential modal[1] within a situations framework in the sense of Kratzer (1989, 2011b), with the semantics in (1):

(1) $[\![EV]\!]^c = \lambda p_{<s,t>}.\forall s' : s'$ is compatible with the knowledge/evidence available in $s^*, \exists s : s<s' \& p(s) = 1$(where s^* is the utterance situation corresponding to c).

According to (1), EV is a universal modal quantifier over situations compatible with the particular body of knowledge/evidence available in the utterance context; i.e. its domain of quantification will only include situations in which everything that is known is true.[2] In combination with a proposition p, the modal will deliver truth *iff* all situations compatible with what is known in the utterance context include a situation in which p is true.

The structure of the chapter is as follows. In section 11.2 we discuss Bulgarian, arguing that its evidential system is rooted in aspect. Section 11.3 examines Mẽbengokre. Section 11.4 examines Matses, arguing that its evidential system also exploits aspect, which dispenses with the need for an extra temporal relation particular to evidentials. Section 11.5 concludes.

11.2 Bulgarian

The evidential system of Bulgarian, which Scatton (1983) labels the Renarrated Mood (RM), is infused with tense and aspect. Based on Arregui et al. (2014), in sections 11.2.1 and 11.2.2 we develop an analysis that assigns a major role to Viewpoint Aspect in capturing what appear to purely be its temporal relations, and also addresses its 'modal' relations. In section 11.2.3, we briefly compare our proposal to an alternative by Smirnova (2013), who argues in favor of additional temporal relations particular to evidentials defined in relation to the Evidence Acquisition Time (EAT). We show that our viewpoint hypothesis offers advantages over the EAT hypothesis, since it successfully captures the temporal relations adduced in support of EAT and also temporal and "modal" relations that fall outside of the scope of, and constitute problems for, EAT. We conclude that a successful account of the Bulgarian RM must crucially rely on aspect and not on temporal relations specific to evidentials.

---

[1] The characterization of evidentials has been the subject of much debate. For e.g. Matthewson et al. (2007), McCready and Ogata (2007), von Fintel and Gillies (2010), and Lee (2011), they are modal. Arguments against this view are presented in e.g. Faller (2002, 2011) and Murray (2010).
[2] Following Izvorski (1997), this is the body of knowledge corresponding to what the speaker has evidence for, but we leave this aside. As noted, we make some simplifying assumptions (Gillies and von Fintel 2007; von Fintel and Gillies 2010, for discussion), and assume that EV is anchored to the utterance situation.

11.2.1 Introducing the Renarrated Mood

Bulgarian has a RM evidential verb paradigm illustrated in (2a–c), which, for simplicity, we translate into English with 'apparently.'

(2) a. Ivan **svirel** na piano.
Ivan **play.RM** on piano
'Apparently, Ivan plays/played the piano.'
b. Ivan **izjal** tsjalata banitsa.
Ivan **eat.RM** whole.the cheese pie
'Ivan apparently ate the whole cheese.pie.'
c. Ivan **bil** **izjal** tsjalata banitsa.
Ivan **be.RM** eat.PPLE whole.the cheese pie
'Ivan has/had apparently eaten the whole cheese.pie.'

The RM has been a topic of considerable attention in the Bulgarian tradition (e.g. Andrejčin 1944; Maslov 1959; Pašov 1989, 2005), was brought to the attention of the linguistic public by Roman Jakobson (1957), and has attracted recent interest in formal semantics (Izvorski 1997; Sauerland and Schenner 2007, 2013; Koev 2011; Smirnova 2011, 2013).

The RM is used in reports where the speaker has not witnessed the described events (e.g. Maslov 1959), and can also express inferential meanings (e.g. Izvorski 1997; Smirnova 2011, 2013; Koev 2011). By contrast, the Indicative Mood is usually understood as based on direct evidence justifying belief, and serves for generally accepted truths.

The RM exhibits a paradigm of tenses (e.g. Scatton 1983; Pašov 1989, 2005; Rivero 2005) partially illustrated in Table 11.1 for 3rd person masculine singular forms, and can allude to present, past, and future.

TABLE 11.1 The indicative and the evidential paradigms

	Indicative Mood	Renarrated Mood
Present '(he) writes, is writing'	*piše*	*piše-l*
Imperfect '(he) was writing, etc.'	*pišeše*	*pisa-l*
Aorist '(he) wrote'	*pisa*	
Present Perfect '(he) has written'	*e pisal / pišel*	*bi-l pisal / pišel*
Past Perfect '(he) had written'	*beše pisal / pišel*	

RM forms are characterized by participles (PPLE) with L-morphology. Some RM 1st/2nd person forms overlap in morphology with Indicative Present Perfects. The received view, however, is that the two paradigms contrast in the 3rd person, with RM (2a) lacking the *be*-auxiliary of the Present Perfect (3).[3]

(3) Ivan e svirel na piano. Indicative Present Perfect
    Ivan be.Present play.PPLE on piano
    'Ivan has played the piano.'

A syncretism important for our purposes is that only two RM forms compete with the three simple tenses in the Indicative. That is, the traditional imperfective participle *pišel* and the perfective participle *pisal* of the RM compete with Indicative Present *piše* '(He/she) writes, is writing,' Aorist *pisa*, roughly 'He/she wrote,' and Imperfect *pišeše* with the interpretations discussed in Arregui et al. (2014). In section 11.2.2 we argue that such a syncretism indicates that the (semantic) system behind morphological "tenses" in the RM depends on Viewpoint Aspect (Smith 1991), and is crucially driven by the opposition labeled Imperfective (IMPF) vs. Perfective (PERF).

11.2.2 *Viewpoint in the RM*

To justify Viewpoint Aspect as a driving force in the RM, we begin with the connection between morphology and semantics in RM participles. As to morphology, we adopt a traditional position. Table 11.1 shows that RM *pišel* and *pisal* are identical in form to the two participles available to Indicative Present Perfects. Given such an identity, we consider RM *pišel* a tenseless morphologically imperfective (imp) form and RM *pisal* a morphological perfective (pf) form, parallel to Indicative participles. We characterize RM *pišel* as semantically imperfective (IMPF), making it aspectually parallel to the (semantically imperfective) Indicative Imperfect *pišeše*. RM *pišel*, imperfect *pišeše*, and present *piše* oppose Indicative aorist *pisa* and perfective RM *pisal*, which we characterize as semantically perfective (i.e. PERF).

Following Arregui et al. (2014), we propose that imperfective RM *pišel* reflects the presence of a modal imperfective operator IMPF, which quantifies universally over situations identified by a "modal base" MB, as in (4):

---

[3] Both RM morphology and semantics have proven controversial. For Pašov (2005: 190), RM forms and Indicative Present Perfects have evidential meanings, but such meanings differ. RM patterns without 3rd person aux are reportative: (2a-c). Present Perfects with a 3rd aux display an inferential reading among other interpretations: (3). By contrast, for Izvorski (1997) and Smirnova (2011, 2013) the RM has both reportative and inferential readings. For Friedman (1986, and related work), (a) Present Perfects have a "non-confirmative" reading in reportative contexts, (b) 3rd person present auxiliaries are optional, and (c) Bulgarian lacks an independent evidential system. In our view, the RM and the Indicative Mood are morphologically distinct in several tenses including futures. Reportative readings are not under dispute in the RM, and they prove sufficient for our claims, so we omit discussion of inferential readings.

(4) $[\![\text{IMPF}]\!]^c = \lambda P_{<l,<s,t>>} . \lambda s. \forall s': MB_\alpha(s)(s') = 1, \exists e: P(e)(s') = 1$,
defined only if there is a contextually or linguistically determined salient modal base (MB) of type α.

IMPF in (4) quantifies over situations corresponding to a given MB (technically, an accessibility relation), and in combination with a predicate of events P claims that all situations s' compatible with the relevant MB include a P-event. According to this proposal, flavors in imperfective readings are due to the different MBs available to IMPF. In Bulgarian, those MBs are identical in the RM and Indicative systems, but are hosted by different morphologies. IMPF is hosted by present and imperfect tense inflections in the Indicative, and by imperfective verb stems such as *pišel* in the RM.

The flexible semantics of IMPF in (4) allows temporal reference to be past, present, or future. Thus, imperfective *pišel* in (5) may be felicitously disambiguated towards the past (5a), the present, or the future (5b,c), by deictic adverbs.

(5) (Spored   dobre osvedomeni iztočnitsi,)
    (According.to well informed   sources,)
    a. ... Ivan **pišel**   kniga včera.
       ... Ivan write.RM.imp book yesterday
       '... Ivan was writing a book yesterday.'
    b. ... Ivan **pišel**   kniga dnes.
       ... Ivan write.RM.imp book today
       '... Ivan {a. was/is in the process of writing a book today / b. was supposed to be writing a book (later) today}.'
    c. ... Ivan **pišel**   kniga utre.
       ... Ivan write.RM.imp book tomorrow
       '... Ivan was (supposed to be) writing a book tomorrow.'

An instance with IMPF in the (non-evidential) Indicative is (6), where an adjunct clause disambiguates the matrix verb in the imperfect tense towards the past.

(6) Kogato Petar **vleze**   v   stajata,   Ivan **pišeše**   kniga.
    When   Peter enter.Aorist in room.the, Ivan write.Imperfect book
    'When Peter entered the room, Ivan was writing a book.'

Regarding perfectives, we propose that aorist inflectional morphology on Indicative *pisa* and perfective morphology on RM *pisal* do not reflect a modal quantifier over situations. Instead, we follow a traditional view according to which aorists/perfectives locate eventualities in the past with respect to Speech Time, with a PERF operator receiving the (simplified) temporal semantics in (7):

(7) $[\![\text{PERF}]\!]^c = \lambda p_{<s,t>} . \lambda s_s: s \text{ precedes } s^* \ \& \ p(s) = 1$.

Given (7), PERF combines with a property of situations to restrict the domain of the function to situations that are past with respect to the speech situation (s*). An instance of PERF in an Indicative is the Aorist in (8).

(8)　Ivan **pisa**　　　včera/　　*utre.
　　　Ivan write.Aorist yesterday/ *tomorrow
　　　'Ivan wrote yesterday/*tomorrow.'

In section 11.2.3 we demonstrate that when IMPF is under the scope of the operator EV, the modal semantics in (4) suffice to derive both temporal and modal interpretations, and that PERF in RM *pisal* always situates events in the past, indicating that the event is over by Speech Time.

11.2.3 *Imperfectives vs. perfectives in the RM*

11.2.3.1 Imperfectives　Imperfective RM forms allow for reported events to be situated towards the past, present, or future, and also report on the modal dimensions of events that were interrupted or habitual.

In our proposal, different flavors in imperfectives depend on the identical MBs available to IMPF in the RM and the Indicative, so let us introduce some flavors of IMPF when embedded under EV, with examples borrowed or adapted from Arregui et al. (2014) and Rivero and Slavkov (2014).

A reading familiar in discussions of imperfectives is known as "ongoing"/ "processual." In (9a), imperfective RM *govorela*—a feminine participle that agrees with a feminine subject—reports on an eventuality ongoing in a (salient) past situation. We propose that here IMPF is interpreted in relation to an Ongoing MB (9c).

(9)　a.　(Spored　　dobre osvedomeni iztočnitsi,) Maria **govorela**　　s
　　　　　(According.to well　informed　　sources,)　Mary talk.RM.imp to
　　　　　priyatelya　si　včera.
　　　　　boyfriend.the her yesterday
　　　　　'(According to well informed sources,) Mary **was talking** to her boyfriend yesterday.'

　　　b.　[EV [IMPF [Maria **govorela** s priyatelya si včera]]]
　　　c.　⟦(9b)⟧^{c} = 1 *iff*
　　　　　$\forall s': s'$ is compatible with the knowledge available in s^*,
　　　　　$\exists s: s < s'$ & $\forall s''$: MB$_{Ongoing}(s)(s'') = 1$,
　　　　　$\exists e$: e is an event of Maria talking to her boyfriend yesterday in s'',
　　　　　where for any two situations s and s'', MB$_{Ongoig}(s)(s'') = 1$ *iff* $s'' < s$.[4]

---

[4] See Arregui et al. (2014) and Cipria and Roberts (2000) for further discussion. In (9c) we appeal to proper parts <, but remain agnostic regarding the advantage of using 'regular' parts ≤.

According to (9c), (9b) will be true *iff* in all situations compatible with what is known at the utterance situation there is some situation such that Maria is talking to her boyfriend (yesterday) throughout that situation. Depending on the "size" of *s*, this MB will result either in an interpretation in which there was an event of Maria speaking to her boyfriend in the past or in a continuous, 'repetitive', reading.

Deictic adverbs may disambiguate imperfective RM forms towards the past. Adjunct clauses with perfective RM forms such as *došla* in (10) have a similar effect. Again, perfective RM forms parallel Indicative Aorists (compare (10) to (6)).

(10) Kogato Olga **došla** v stayata, Mary **govorela** s
  When Olga enter.RM.pf in room.the Mary speak.RM.imp with
  priyatelya si.
  boyfriend.the her.
  'Apparently, when Olga entered the room, Mary was talking to her boyfriend.'

Second, the "event-in-progress" reading of imperfectives familiar in non-evidential contexts is brought out in so-called "imperfective paradox" contexts with accomplishment Vs, and speaks of events that began but were interrupted in some past time. Imperfective RM participles may host such modal reading, as in (11), and involve the (simplified) MB in (12b), which appeals to events that continue in the situations quantified over.

(11) Šaxmatistăt **pečelel** igrata, kogato bil udaren po
  Chess.player.the win.RM.imp game.the when be.RM hit.PPLE on
  glavata i igrata bila prekăsnata.
  head.the and game.the be.RM interrupted.PPLE
  'Apparently, the chess player **was winning** the game, when he was hit on the head and the game was interrupted.'

(12) a. [EV [IMPF [šaxmatistăt pečelel igrata]]]
  b. $[\![(12b)]\!]^c = 1$ *iff*
    $\forall s': s'$ is compatible with the knowledge available in s^*,
    $\exists s: s < s'$ & $\forall s''$: $MB_{Event\text{-}inertia}(s)(s'') = 1$,
    $\exists e$: e is an event of the chess player winning the game in s'',
  where for any two situations s and s'', $MB_{Event\text{-}inertia}(s)(s'') = 1$ *iff* all the events that have actually started in s continue in s'' as they would if there were no interruptions.

Third, another reading familiar in imperfectives is the generic/habitual type. A RM with such a reading is (13), with a MB based on characteristic situations, as in (14a,b).

(13) (Spored dobre osvedomeni iztočnitsi,) Ivan četjal ot
(According.to well informed sources,) Ivan read.RM.imp from
sutrim do večer.
morning to evening
'According to well informed sources, Ivan used to read from morning to evening.'

(14) a. [EV [IMPF [Ivan četjal ot sutrim do večer]]]
b. $[\![(14a)]\!]^c = 1$ *iff*
$\forall s'$: s' is compatible with the knowledge available in s^*,
$\exists s$: $s < s'$ & $\forall s''$: $MB_{Generic}(s)(s'') = 1$,
$\exists e$: e is an event of Ivan reading from morning till evening in s'',
where for any two situations s and s'', $MB_{Generic}(s)(s'') = 1$ *iff* s is a characteristic part of s''.

We now conclude by reconsidering ambiguous (5b). This may report on a past or present event, but may also speak of a plan to write a book later today, as in (15a) (or also tomorrow, as in (5c)). In the last case, IMPF reports on past plans for events to happen today or tomorrow, appealing to "inertia situations" of a preparatory type (a modal dimension). Following Arregui et al. (2014), IMPF in (15a) is interpreted relative to a MB that identifies the domain of quantification in terms of situations in which plans are carried out, with the Logical Form in (15b), and the truth-conditions in (15c):

(15) a. (Spored dobre osvedomeni iztočnitsi,) Ivan **pišel** kniga dnes.
'(According to well informed sources,) Ivan was/is (supposed to be) writing a book (later) today.'
b. [EV [IMPF [Ivan pišel kniga dnes]]]
c. $[\![(15b)]\!]^c = 1$ *iff*
$\forall s'$: s' is compatible with the knowledge available in s^*,
$\exists s$: $s < s'$ & $\forall s''$: $MB_{prep\text{-}inertia}(s)(s'') = 1$,
$\exists e$: e is an event of Ivan writing a book (later) today in s'',
where for any two situations s and s'', $MB_{prep\text{-}inertia}(s)(s'') = 1$ *iff* all the events that are in preparatory stages in s continue in s'' as they would if there were no interruptions.

According to (15c), (15b) will be true *iff* in all situations compatible with what is known in the utterance, there is a situation in which plans have been made for Ivan to write a book later today (no claim is made as to whether he actually did or not). Given the (simplified) definition of the MB in terms of continuations in which plans reach fruition, the situation where plans are made has to temporally precede the situation of Ivan writing a book (in all the situations quantified over that are compatible with what is known).

In brief, IMPF is encoded in imperfective RM participles such as *pišel* in (5) and (15), *govorela* in (9,10), *pečelel* in (11,12), and *četjal* in (14). The MBs available to this IMPF operator in Bulgarian cut across the Indicative vs. RM distinction, and include an Ongoing type, an Event-Inertia type, a Generic type, and a Preparatory-Inertia type. Such MBs account for temporal and modal flavors of imperfective participles in RM constructions.

11.2.3.2 Perfectives   As to perfective RMs, *vzela* in (16) is the RM counterpart of imperfective RM *vzimala*.[5] In the temporal semantics in (7), PERF combines with a property of situations to restrict the domain of the function to situations that are past with respect to the speech situation (s^*). Thus, the perfective verb embedded under EV in (16) gives rise to past readings.

(16)   Maria (veče) **vzela** lekarstvoto.
Maria (already) Pr.take.RM.pf medicine.the
'Apparently, Maria (already) took the medicine.'

The proposal accounts for why PERF cannot combine with future-oriented adverbs in (17a–c).

(17)   a. *(Spored dobre osvedomeni iztočnitsi,) Ivan **pisal** kniga utre.
'*(According to well-informed sources), Ivan wrote a book tomorrow.'
b. [EV [PERF [Ival pisal kniga utre]]]
c. $[\![(17b)]\!]^c = 1$ *iff*
$\forall s': s'$ is compatible with the knowledge available in s^*,
$\exists s: s < s'$ & s precedes s^* &
$\exists e: e$ is an event of Ivan writing a book tomorrow in s.

According to (17b,c), (17a) will be true *iff* in all situations compatible with what is known there is a situation that precedes the speech event that includes a situation of Ivan writing a book tomorrow. Given the incompatibility of the temporal specification, (17a) cannot be true and sounds contradictory.

In sum, taking a position that we dub a "Viewpoint hypothesis," we analyzed a variety of RM constructions, arguing that their temporal anchoring depends on aspect. Imperfective RM participles may lead to past or prospective readings in parallel to Indicative verbs in the Imperfect. By contrast, perfective RM participles are always past, like Indicative verbs in the Aorist. The temporal and the modal

---

[5] Both perfective *vzela* and imperfective *vizmala* are prefixed participles. Thus, the IMPF-PERF viewpoint contrast does not crucially depend on absence/presence of prefixes (and see Rivero and Slavkov 2014 for relevant discussion).

flexibility available to imperfective RM participles are due to their IMPF operator. In particular, the temporal orientation of RMs is a side effect of the choice of modal flavor (accessibility relation) for this operator, without the need for extra temporal relations specific to the RM.

11.2.4 Dispensing with Evidence Acquisition Time (EAT)

The relation between temporal and evidential categories in Bulgarian has always concerned grammarians, and has recently been taken up by Smirnova (2011, 2013) and Koev (2011) under new lights. Smirnova in particular argues for a specialized tense for evidentials based on the Evidence Acquisition Time (EAT), characterizing the semantic contrast between the reportative RM forms in (18) and (19) as a difference in tense. Both are claimed to be imperfective, but (feminine) *pisala* in (18) is past, and (feminine) *pišela* in (19) is present. By contrast, we argued in sections 11.2.2 and 11.2.3 that *pisal/pisala* encodes PERF and *pišel/pišela* encodes IMPF, making them aspectually parallel to Indicative Aorist and Imperfect/Present tenses.

(18) Reportative context: Last month Ivan told you that Maria, your former classmate, spent last year writing a book and that the book has just been published. You believe Ivan. Today, your friend asks you what Maria was doing last year. You say:
Maria pisala/# pišela kniga.
'Maria was writing a book, [I heard].'

(19) Reportative context: Last month at the class reunion Ivan told you that Maria is busy writing a book. You believe Ivan. Today your old friend asks you what kept Maria from coming to the class reunion last month. You say:
Maria #pisala/pišela kniga.
'Maria was writing a book, [I heard].'

Smirnova goes on to argue that (18) and (19) provide evidence in favor of tenses specific to evidentials. These tenses order the event reference time with respect to the time of acquisition of information (EAT), differing from Indicative tenses that establish an order relative to Speech Time. On Smirnova's view, past RM forms claim that the event reference time precedes the time the evidence was acquired, while present forms claim that the event reference time and evidence acquisition time coincide. Thus, *pisala* in (18) indicates that the reference time for the writing event precedes the time at which the speaker acquired the information about this event: i.e. it had happened before the speaker heard about it. By contrast, *pišela* in (19) claims that the reference time for the writing event overlaps the time at which the speaker acquired the information: i.e. it was ongoing when the speaker heard about it. Smirnova explicitly opposes (traditional) aspectual characterizations of the RM forms in (18,19), and instead favors a view in terms of tense.

In section 11.2.2 and 11.2.3 we developed a proposal that relies on Viewpoint Aspect to capture temporal relations in the RM, without appealing to a specialized tense operator specific to evidentials. In this section, we argue that our proposal easily accommodates the RM patterns adduced in support of the EAT hypothesis, and offers the advantage of also accounting for RM patterns that run foul of the EAT hypothesis.

To motivate our claim, we first reconsider (18,19) from the perspective of our earlier proposals. Our claim is that it is possible to account for such RM examples within a view where *pisala* and *pišela* encode a semantic contrast between the viewpoint operators PERF and IMPF, without specialized tense operators appealing to EAT.

Smirnova provides an informal context for (18) that builds up the available information in several steps. We propose that such a context constitutes a body of information that makes salient a background where the described event culminated, not where the event was still in progress. That is, it presents the situation as "perfective" in a way roughly comparable to *Mary wrote a book and she (or somebody else) published it last year*, with a sequencing/advancing effect. Given this body of indirect information where the completion of the book is the salient dimension, a suitable reportative answer is with a perfective RM *pisala*, namely one that intuitively speaking encodes that the report is about an activity that has reached its end. By contrast, the context in (19) provides a body of indirect information that leaves the described event open, the traditional definition of imperfectivity, and this can be felicitously reported by means of an imperfective *pišela*, for example appealing to the Event-Inertia MB discussed in section 11.2.3.

Smirnova's proposal that RM *pišela* is a present form that indicates that the reported event was ongoing at the time the evidence was acquired is problematic. On this view, several interpretations familiar in the literature on imperfectives should be infelicitous when encoded in RM *pišela*, which is an incorrect prediction. To illustrate, (20) is a felicitous report of a writing activity that ceased, and thus could not be ongoing as the information was acquired. On Smirnova's approach, such an event should be reported with *pisala*—the form we consider perfective and not imperfective—which is not the case.

(20) (Minalata godina) Marija **pišela/** #**pisala** (kniga) no
    (Last.the year), Maria write.RMimp/ #write.RMpf (book) but
    sprjala (da piše) prez dekemvri.
    stop.RMpf (to write) during December
    'Apparently, (last year) Mary was writing a book but stopped (writing) in December.'

Examples of type (20) seem to lead to contradiction under the EAT approach. They would indicate that the activity had stopped in view of perfective *sprjala*, while also being ongoing while the evidence was acquired in view of *pišela*. Similar problems arise with 'imperfective paradox' examples of type (11), which display imperfective

RM forms in the main clause: *Šaxmatistăt pečelel igrata, kogato bil udaren po glavata i igrata bila prekăsnata*. 'Apparently, the chess player was winning the game, when he was hit on the head and the game was interrupted.'

In addition, the last example raises the issue of the role of adjunct clauses within evidential constructions, which Smirnova does not mention. When they are added as in (11), they specify temporal and modal relations internal to the structure under the scope of the EV operator. These relations replicate familiar behaviors of imperfectives and perfectives in non-evidential contexts, suggesting that extra relations such as EAT play no role in them.

The pattern in (20) represents a standard case in discussions of IMPF vs. PERF in the literature. However, Smirnova's views are also problematic when less standard interpretations are considered, as in those including modal dimensions in types such as so-called "habitual" and "futurate" imperfectives.

On the one hand, habitual readings do not easily fit within the EAT view, but are renarrated with imperfective participles, as in (13). Thus, we proposed a familiar analysis of the IMPF operator leading to generic/habitual readings embedded under the EV operator.

On the other hand, the idea that RM verbs such as *pišela* are present forms that indicate that the reported event was ongoing at the time at which the evidence was acquired cannot account for "futurate" examples such as (15a), *Spored dobre osvedomeni iztočnitsi, Ivan pišel kniga dnes* 'According to well-informed sources, Ivan was supposed to be writing a book (later) today.' In our approach, these are unproblematic with the analysis in (15b,c), where IMPF accesses the same preparatory inertia MB as in Indicative Imperfect verbs.

All the above correlations, then, are easily captured by our analysis where viewpoint IMPF is contained in imperfective (imp) RM participles and PERF in perfective (pf) RM participles, and where IMPF and PERF receive interpretations familiar in many languages. On our approach, no reference is made to the time the evidence was acquired in the RM, which is similar in this respect to the Indicative.

An advantage of the Viewpoint hypothesis is that it allows for a unified perspective on temporal systems that interact with evidentials in a crucial way, such as Bulgarian, and those that seemingly lack interactions, as in Mẽbengokre (section 11.3).

11.3 Mẽbengokre

11.3.1 Evidentials

Mẽbengokre modal or aspectual notions are expressed by optional left-peripheral particles or post-verbal elements, both in bold in (21):[6,7]

---

[6] Abbreviations for Mẽbengokre are NFUT = non-future, NOM = nominative pronoun, PL = plural, V = finite verb, N = non-finite verb, WE = evidential, DJA = conjectural evidential. Morpheme boundaries are not indicated.

[7] Mẽbengokre data were collected by Salanova in the field unless otherwise indicated.

(21) Karinhô **nẽ** ba akôr onhỹ.
     tobacco NFUT 1NOM 3.blow.N sit.V
     'I am smoking some tobacco.'

Left particles include *nẽ* (nonfuture) in (21), *dja* (future or conjectural), evidentials, frustratives (indicating an initiated but unaccomplished action), and completive and continuative aspect. Postverbal elements include items with progressive meanings such as *nhỹ* in (21), *nẽ* (result state), *mã* (prospective), *kadjy* (purposive), and manner modifiers.

Left particles have a different morphosyntactic behavior from postverbal elements. While the latter combine with the nominalized lexical verb N (e.g. *akôr* in (21)), left particles may appear with all types of predicates, including non-nominalized V, as in (22) with *nẽ*.

(22) Kajtire **nẽ** arỳm mã tẽ.
     Kajtire NFUT already away go.V
     'Kajtire has left already.'

Mẽbengokre normally marks propositions that are learned through indirect evidence with *we*, called "hearsay evidential" in other work (e.g. Arregui et al. 2014). This particle can attach to any type of predicate, and seems to have no restrictions regarding co-ocurrence with other particles. We illustrate its various flavors, before we discuss its interaction with temporal markers.

We is very frequent in narratives, where it often occurs in almost every sentence, as in (23a,b) from myths, and (24a,b) elicited with everyday contexts.

(23) a. Onija kàjkwa krax kam **we** mẽ ari ba.
        far heaven beginning in WE PL constantly stay
        'They lived, it is said, far away towards the beginning of heaven [i.e. the east].'

     b. Kam mẽ'õ **we** arirẽnh'ã tẽn **we** kẽn kam màt kre
        so someone WE hunting went.and WE rock in maccaw hole
        pumũ.
        see
        'So someone went hunting, it is said, and saw a macaw's nest on the side of a rock, it is said.'

(24) a. Gorotire nẽ **we** kato.
        Gorotire NFUT WE win
        'Gorotire won [the tournament], it is said.'

     b. Mỳj kadjỳ nẽ jã?– **we** mesa kadjy.
        what for NFUT this?– WE table for
        'What is this for?– It is for the table, it is said.'

The primary use of *we* in narrative is hearsay, as in (23a,b). In elicited (24a,b), both hearsay and inferential readings are possible. If one controls contexts carefully, however, one may find clear instances where *we* could not be hearsay and has to be inferential, as in (25a,b).

(25) I am looking for Bep in his house. He is not around. His son-in-law has not seen him and does not know where he went, but notices that his gun is not where it normally is. He tells me:
  a. **We** bàkam tẽ.
     WE hunt go
     'Apparently he has gone hunting.'
     Or, if the basket is missing:
  b. **We** puru mã nẽ tẽ.
     WE garden to NFUT go
     'Apparently it is to the garden that he has gone.'

As expected, (25a,b) are equally fine in a hearsay use, i.e., in contexts where I have been told rather than inferred the proposition myself. We can therefore conclude that *we* may be used in both hearsay contexts and contexts of inference.

Our interest is in temporal matters, so we characterize *we* simply as an evidential operator as in (1) [EV]. Temporal markers provide information regarding the location of events relevant to the embedded proposition. Generally, evidentials in Mẽbengokre are speaker-oriented. They are often translated into Portuguese as propositional attitude verbs with first person subjects ('I believe that ...,' 'I heard that'), or with the evidential *diz que* of colloquial Portuguese and Spanish,[8] which may be both a hearsay and an inferential evidential.

One final evidential category of Mẽbengokre is the conjectural, which cannot be used as a reportative. A statement made on the basis of a belief in things happening according to a plan will be marked with the future particle *dja* in (26). In previous work, this particle has been glossed as future (a reading it also encodes) or irrealis (a term that is intended to cover both future and conjectural uses).

(26) Kajtire **dja** arỳm ũrũkwã kam bôx.
     Kajtire DJA already 3.house in arrive
     'Kajtire should have already arrived at his house.'

This usage is not unlike the conjectural use of the Spanish future (cf. Rivero 2014):

(27) Habrá llegado a casa.
     Will.have arrived to house
     'S/he has likely arrived home.'

---

[8] See Travis (2006) and Demonte and Fernández-Soriano (2013) for Spanish *dizque*.

Though it is possible to have both *dja* and *we* in the same sentence, the former will only get its non-evidential future interpretation in those cases. In other words, it is impossible to combine conjectural evidentiality with inferential or hearsay evidentiality in a single clause.

As far as we have been able to ascertain, it is impossible to combine conjectural *dja* with hearsay *we* (e.g. *dja* always gets a future interpretation if *we* is also present).

11.3.2 Temporal markers in evidentials

As noted above, evidential *we* can co-occur with other particles. In (28), it co-occurs with the non-future tense *nẽ*:

(28) Gorotire **nẽ** **we** kato.
 Gorotire NFUT WE win
 'Gorotire won the tournament, it is said.'

We follow Salanova (2013) in the claim that finite forms such as (28) include a category-forming *v*-head that projects below tense responsible for quantifying over events, as in (29) (modified for the situations framework):

(29) $[\![v]\!]^c = \lambda P_{<l,<s,t>>} . \lambda s_s. \exists e: P(e)(s) = 1.$ (adapted from Salanova 2013)

The role of tense is to place restrictions on the temporal location of embedded propositions. We adopt a referential approach to tense according to which tense is a referential expression that picks out the topic situation the claim is about (see Kratzer 2011b; Arregui et al. 2014). As a situation "pronoun," tense is interpreted via the given variable assignment. The general pattern for the interpretation of topic situations pronouns is given in (30):

(30) Where s_i is a pronoun ranging over situations,
 $[\![s_i]\!]^c = g(i) = s_i$, where g is the variable assignment salient in c.

Tense features introduce presuppositions that restrict felicitous interpretations of the situation pronoun (situating the running time of the topic situation ($\tau(s_i)$) in the past, present, or future, with respect to Speech Time). The Non-future tense in (28) is interpreted as in (31), so is restricted to non-future situations:

(31) $[\![nẽ_i]\!]^c = g(i) = s_i$, where g is the variable assignment salient in c.
 Defined only if the variable assignment g salient in c is such that $\tau(s_i)$ either precedes or overlaps Speech Time in c (i.e. if s_i is non-future with respect to Speech Time).

The EV operator corresponding to *we* takes propositional arguments, so, following Heim and Kratzer (1998), we propose that an index abstracts over the tense pronoun to generate a property of situations embedded under the evidential, as in (32):

Aspect and tense in evidentials 227

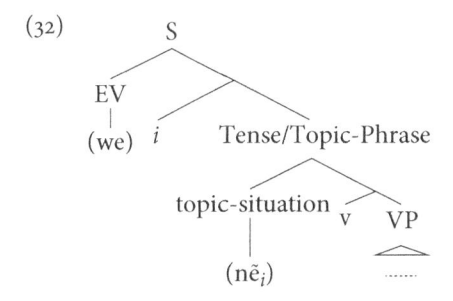

(32)
```
            S
           / \
         EV   \
         |    Tense/Topic-Phrase
        (we) i    / \
           topic-situation  \
                |        v   VP
              (nẽᵢ)
```

Given the above assumptions, (28) receives the (simplified) Logical Form in (33a) and the truth-conditions in (33b):

(33) a. [we [nẽ [v [Gorotire kato]]]]
  b. $[\![(33a)]\!]^c = 1$ *iff*
   $\forall s': s'$ is compatible with the speaker's beliefs in s^*
   $\exists s_i: s_i < s'$ & $\exists e : e$ is an event of Gorotire winning the tournament in s_i,
   defined only if s_i precedes s^* or s_i overlaps s^*.

According to (33b), the interpretation of (33a) will only be defined if $s_i < s'$ as the denotation of nẽᵢ is not future. If the interpretation is defined, the sentence will be true *iff* all situations compatible with the speaker's beliefs in the utterance situation include a non-future situation s_i in which there is an event of Gorotire winning the tournament. In this proposal, there is no interaction between the temporal specification of such an event and the temporal anchoring of the evidential, which is always evaluated in relation to the speaker's beliefs in the utterance context. In other words, the temporal operator locates the eventuality corresponding to the clause embedded under the evidential in relation to the utterance situation.

The intuitions reported by native speakers support the hypothesis that *we* scopes over *nẽ* in (33a), which can only be interpreted in terms of the speaker's current beliefs about a past event and not in relation to the speaker's past beliefs. That is, (33a) cannot mean that according to what the speaker used to believe, Djudjêkô is/was the winner (compare (33b) with the interpretations in non-evidential (21) and (22)).

In our view, Mẽbengokre provides another example of a system where there is nothing special about temporal operators in evidential contexts (as opposed to non-evidential contexts). In evidentials, temporal operators provide the temporal parameter for the location of the eventuality corresponding to the clause embedded under EV. The evidential itself is interpreted in relation to the utterance situation (current knowledge/evidence).

One corollary of our analysis is that the time of acquisition of evidence (EAT) has no status in the grammar of Mẽbengokre. In the case of direct evidence, EAT is determined pragmatically: by necessity, it has to coincide with the reference time, as it is from that time that the speaker is "viewing" the event. In the case of indirect evidence, EAT is left undetermined. In Mẽbengokre, then, there is no way of modifying a proposition marked with evidential *we* to indicate the time of acquisition of evidence.

11.4 An apparent counterexample: Evidence Acquisition Time in Matses?

11.4.1 A Viewpoint "aspectual" hypothesis

A language with interesting interactions between tense and evidentiality is Panoan Matses (Fleck 2003, 2007; Munro et al. 2012). Fleck (2003, 2007) argues that the Matses sentences in (34a,b), which we label "Inferentials" from now on, are "double tense" constructions that support the postulation of a temporal relation particular to evidentials.[9]

(34) a. mayu-n　　　　　　　bëste-wa-**nëdak**-o-şh.
　　　non.Matses.Indian-ERG　hut-make-dist.past.inf- recent.past.exp-3
　　　'Non-Matses Indians (had) made a hut.' [an old hut was discovered by the speaker a short time ago]　　　　　　　　　　　　(Fleck 2007: (1a))

b. şhëktenamë　　　　　　kuen-**nëdak**-o-şh.
　　white.lipped.peccary　pass.by-distant.past.inf-recent.past-3
　　'White-lipped peccaries (evidently) passed by.' [old tracks were discovered a short time ago at a distant location]　　　　　　(Fleck 2007: (1b))

Roughly, Inferentials are felicitous when describing events the speaker did not experience directly, but whose results the speaker can relate to the event so as to justify the deduction. Fleck tells us that (34a,b) encode both the time an inference was made (-o- as recent past) and the period between the inference and the described event, indicated by -**nëdak**- as a portmanteau morpheme that simultaneously encodes distant past and evidentiality.

Based on the rich materials and discussion of Fleck (2003, 2007), we would like to explore an alternative analysis for Inferentials. While we aim to dispense with the extra temporal relation particular to them, which bears a resemblance to EAT in Bulgarian, our proposal is deeply indebted to Fleck's.

Let us sketch our general idea. Oversimplifying, our morphology-rooted proposal consists in arguing that the Inferentials in (34a,b) are characterized by an overt morpheme for evidentiality that is independent from tense: -**ak**-. Such a morpheme encodes an EV operator, which scopes over two additional morphemes with, roughly speaking, "temporal" flavors: -**o**- and -**nëd**-. On the one hand, -**o**- is under the scope of inferential EV -**ak**-, and encodes the topic/reference time of the described event. On the other hand, -**nëd**- is a resultative also under the scope of EV, and

---

[9] Fleck labels (34a,b) "Recent experiential with a distant inferential."

establishes an aspectual-like relation with the topic/reference time. On this view, then, the complex temporal relations in Inferentials result from the interaction of topic-time and aspectual-like resultative morphemes under the scope of an evidential operator with its own distinct morphology.

Fleck proposes (2007: 589): "All evidential markers are portmanteau verbal inflectional suffixes that simultaneously mark evidentiality and tense." He analyzes constructions of type (35), which he labels Experientials, treating -o- as a marker for both evidentiality (experiential) and tense (recent past).

(35) nid-   o-   şh   tumi-o.
      go-   rec.past.exp- 3   man's.name-abs
      'Tumi went.'

As stated above, we differ from Fleck in considering that evidentiality is marked by morphemes that are independent of temporal markers. In the case of (35), we consider -o- the same independent temporal marker of recent past also observed in (34a) and (34b). On our view, (35) is overtly marked only for tense, but not for evidentiality. Depending on analysis, (35) could (a) be semantically unmarked, implying direct perception as one option, or (b) contain a covert operator for (direct) evidentiality, whose denotation would differ from the one we later propose for -ak- in (34a,b).

11.4.2 The structure of inferentials

We propose that (34a) and (34b) are evidential constructions with the structure in (36), where an operator EV scopes over a tense/topic phrase (TP), a resultative phrase, and a VP that encodes event properties. Inferentials are interpreted in relation to the moment of speech, i.e. anchored on evidence available at the speech time.

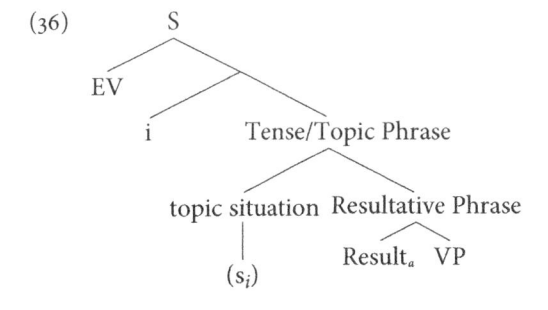

(36)
```
              S
            /   \
          EV     \
         /  \     \
        i    Tense/Topic Phrase
             /        \
    topic situation  Resultative Phrase
         |              /      \
        (s_i)       Result_a   VP
```

Let us add detail to (36). As mentioned in section 11.3 for Mẽbengokre (see the discussion concerning (30)), EV embeds a clause headed by a Tense/Topic head. This Tense head hosts a topic situation pronoun s_i that identifies the situation the claim is "about." The situation pronoun bears an index bound by a c-commanding index i, which generates a property of situations abstracting over the topic situation. Matses has several topic-situation pronouns partially mentioned later, and the features of each of those pronouns are treated as presuppositions. The Tense Phrase in (36) embeds a Resultative Phrase identifying a result state. Temporal anchoring in result states is also morphologically encoded in Matses, so this language also displays an inventory of resultative-like morphemes/situation pronouns mentioned later.

11.4.3 Applying the analysis

With (36) in place, we illustrate in (37a–c) possible temporal combinations in Inferentials in addition to those in (34):

(37) a. şhëktenamë   kuen-nëdak-onda-şh.
       white.lipped.peccary pass.by-rec.past.inf-rem.past.exp-3
       'White-lipped peccaries (evidently) passed by.' [old tracks were discovered a long time ago at a distant location]   (Fleck 2007: (18b))

   b. şhëktenamë   kuen-ak-o-şh.
      white.lipped.peccary pass.by-rec.past.inf-rec.past.exp-3
      'White-lipped peccaries (evidently) passed by.' [fresh tracks were discovered a short time ago at a distant location]   (Fleck 2007: (18a))

   c. şhëktenamë   kuen-ak-onda-şh.
      white.lipped.peccary pass.by-rec.past.inf-dist.past.exp-3
      'White-lipped peccaries (evidently) passed by.' [fresh tracks were discovered a long time ago at a distant location]   (Fleck 2007: (18d))

Given (36), the morpheme templates we propose for (34a) and (34b) are given in (38a) and (38b) respectively.

(38) a. *Verb*   *Resultative*   *Evidential* *Topic situation*
        1   2   3   4
        bëste.wa- -nëd-   -ak-   -o-   (+person)
        'hut.make' Distant past   EV   Recent past

     b. **kuen-**   -nëd-   -ak-   -o-   (+person)
        'pass.by'   Distant past   EV   Recent past

In our proposal,[10] Inferentials contain three independent layers of semantic and morphological relevance to the analysis, with the evidential one being the only layer that is systematically overt:

11.4.3.1 *(i) The evidential operator in (36)*   As stated, this systematically corresponds to an overt morpheme (a)k/(i)k, which scopes over the two temporal-like elements in the structure, which may be phonologically null. The evidential tells us what kind

---

[10] Note that we differ from Fleck and consider position [2] **nëd** in (38a,b) an (independent) distant past resultative, with **ak** standing for EV. To repeat, we do not adopt the idea that evidentiality and tense combine in a portmanteau morpheme.

of indirect evidence is relevant/where the evidence is coming from. In Inferentials, it also involves reasons, causes, or results related to the event.

11.4.3.2 *(ii) The topic-situation morpheme in (36)* This morpheme treated as a pronoun ranging over situations adds a temporal dimension to the result state of the VP eventuality. In Matses, topic situations for different pasts are encoded by different morphemes or pronouns. The morpheme **o** in (34a,b) stands for a recent past, in contrast with **onda** in (37a) for a distant past. Another option is remote past **denne**, mentioned by Fleck but not illustrated here (the encoding of topic situations, however, can also be covert/phonologically null).

For recent past -**o**- in (34a,b), the interpretation is (39).

(39) $[\![o_i]\!]^c = g(i) = s_i$, where g is the variable assignment salient in c.
Defined only if $\tau(s_i)$ is in the recent past of the speech time in c.

11.4.3.3 *(iii) The resultative morpheme in (36)* This item introduces a result state of a building event in (34a), or a peccary-passing event in (34b), and adds another temporal dimension to Inferentials. Similarly to tense pronouns, resultative morphemes may encode different pasts, and can also be null as in (37b,c) (Fleck also mentions forms for more remote pasts, which we omit).

Inspired by Parsons (1990) and Kratzer (2000), we propose to capture the second temporal-like relation in Inferentials by means of the Resultative Phrase in (36), with (40) providing the semantics for **nëd** in (34a,b):

(40) $[\![\text{nëd}]\!]^c = \lambda p_{<s,t>} . \lambda s_s . \exists s' . p(s') = 1$ & distant-result$(s')(s) = 1$.
Where for any two situations s and s', distant-result$(s')(s) = 1$ iff s is a result of s' and $\tau(s')$ is in the distant past with respect to $\tau(s)$.[11]

According to (40), **nëd** takes as argument a property of situations p. It will provide as value a proposition true in a situation s *iff* (a) there is some situation s' such that p is true in s', (b) s is a result of s', and (c) the running time of s' [$\tau(s')$] is temporally in the distant past with respect to the running time of s [$\tau(s)$].

We do not provide a formal characterization of when a situation s is a result of a situation s', a complex issue. It should minimally be the case that s' temporally precedes s, but there will presumably be other constraints. The proposal in (40) can be understood as a "tensed" resultative characterizing distant results, with the constraint being that the running time of the result situation s [$\tau(s)$] remotely/distantly precedes the running time of the situation corresponding to the VP eventuality.

With the above ingredients, let us compose the interpretation of (34b) repeated as (41) with the morphemic segmentation we assume.

---

[11] For simplicity, we assume that the distant-result situation only holds between world-mate situations.

(41) shëktenamë   kuen-   nëd-   ak-   o-   -sh.
     white.lipped.peccary pass.by- distant.past- evidential- recent.past -3
     'White-lipped peccaries (evidently) passed by.' [old tracks were discovered a short time ago]

On the above view, (41) has the structure in (42), and the truth conditions in (43).

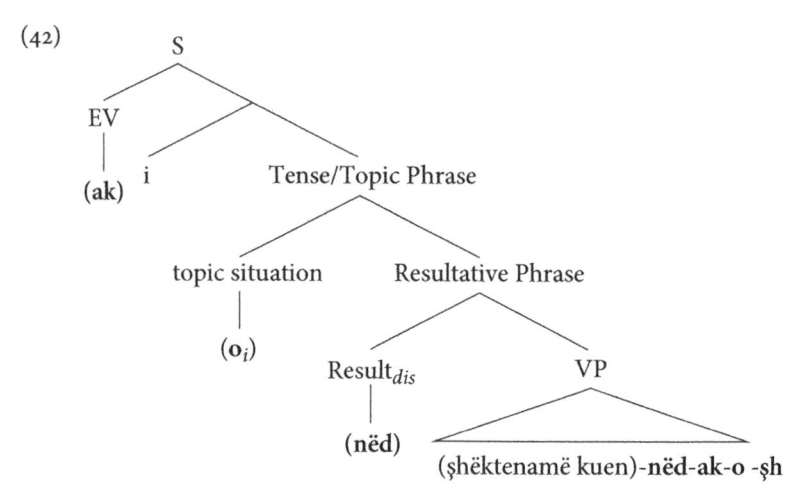

(42)
```
        S
       / \
     EV   \
      |    \
     (ak) i  Tense/Topic Phrase
             /        \
      topic situation  Resultative Phrase
            |           /        \
           (o_i)    Result_dis   VP
                       |
                     (nëd)   (shëktenamë kuen)-nëd-ak-o-sh
```

(43) a. [ak [i [o_i [nëd [shëktenamë kuen]]]]]
     b. $[\![(43a)]\!]^c = 1$ iff
        $\forall s'': s''$ is compatible with the knowledge/evidence available in s^*,
        $\exists s: s<s''$ & $\exists s'$.white-lipped peccaries pass by in s' & <u>distant-result</u>$(s')(s) = 1$,
        defined only if $\tau(s)$ is in the recent past of the speech event in c.

According to (43b), (43a) is true *iff* every situation s'' compatible with the knowledge/evidence available at the speech time (s^*) includes a situation s ($s < s''$) such that there is a situation s' in which white-lipped peccaries pass by and s is the distant result of s' (i.e. s is the result of s', and s' temporally is in the distant past of s). The truth-conditions are only defined if the temporal location of s is in the recent past of the speech event in c.

Now consider (37a) repeated in (44a). It contains the distant past topic-situation marker -onda- instead of recent past -o- in (34a,b). The analysis is (44b,c).

(44) a. shëktenamë   kuen-   nëd-   ak-   onda- sh.
        white.lipped.peccary pass.by -distant.past- evidential- distant.past-3
        'White-lipped peccaries (evidently) passed by.' [old tracks were discovered a long time ago]
     b. [ak [i [onda_i [nëd [shëktenamë kuen]]]]]

c. $[\![(44b)]\!]^c = 1$ *iff*
   $\forall s''$: s'' is compatible with the knowledge/evidence available in s^*,
   $\exists s : s < s''$ & $\exists s'$.white-lipped peccaries pass by in s' & distant-result$(s')(s)$
   $= 1$, defined only if $\tau(s)$ is in the distant past of the speech event in c.

Given our proposals, Inferentials include both an eventive component (hut-building, bird-passing) and a stative/resultant component (the state of the hut having been built, the prints on the ground having been made), and each is assigned a different time interval. In (36), the resultative head mediates between the VP and the topic time, functioning as a kind of aspectual projection reminiscent of a resultative perfect. In morphology, temporal resultant relations are encoded in position [2] in (38a,b).

In our analysis, the evidential operator in Inferentials is always an overt independent morpheme: **ak**. However, the temporal morphemes for TP and RP in (36), or positions [4] and [2] in (38a,b), may be headed by null items (under specifiable conditions). To briefly illustrate, consider Inferential (45a) (=Fleck 2007: (1a)) with our morphemic segmentation (45b). This represents a case where the Resultative Phrase lacks phonological content, so evidential -**ak**- attaches to the verb, and is followed by topic-situation -**onda**.

(45) a. Mayu-n   bëste-   wa-   ak- onda- sh.
        non.Matses.Indian-ERG make.hut- rec.past- ev- dist.past -3
        'Non-Matses Indians (had) made a hut.' [a recently made hut was discovered by the speaker a long time ago]
    b. *Verb*   *Resultative* *Evidential* *Topic situation*
       1   2   3   4
       bëste.wa-   ∅ -   -ak-   -onda (+person)
       'hut.make' Recent past   EV   Distant past

We can now briefly compare our analysis with Fleck's (2007) proposal (Fig. 11.1).

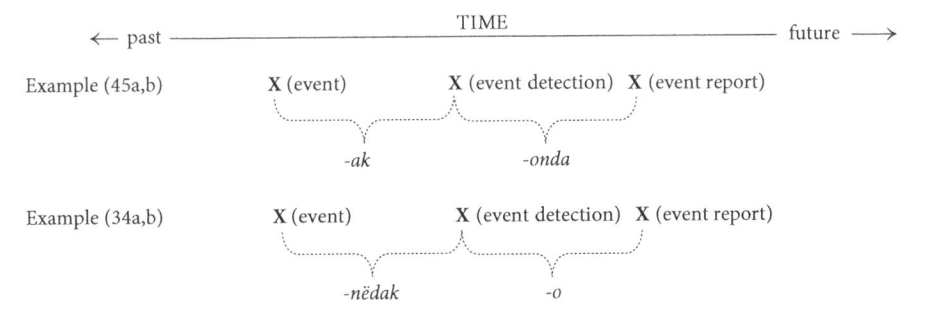

```
                    ← past ————————————— TIME ————————————— future →

Example (45a,b)        X (event)        X (event detection)  X (event report)
                           ⎵_____⎵  ⎵_____⎵
                                -ak                   -onda

Example (34a,b)        X (event)        X (event detection)  X (event report)
                           ⎵_____⎵  ⎵_____⎵
                               -nëdak                 -o
```

FIG. 11.1 'Temporal reference points for the suffixes that Fleck labels "inferential" and "experiential" respectively (see Fleck 2007: 590, table 1)'

The main difference between the two proposals is that we contemplate three relations while Fleck contemplates only two. First, our analysis proposes a resultative relation encoded in an independent temporal-like morpheme that can be phonologically null in (45a,b) or overt in (34a,b). Second, it identifies an independent evidential marker **ak** in all Inferentials. Third, it identifies a topic-situation morpheme that provides the result-state situation as the "clue" for detecting the event given what we know; this corresponds to Fleck's "detection." The topic-situation pronoun can be **onda**, a distant past with respect to Speech Time, or **o**, understood as a recent past.

In sum, Matses Inferentials contain an overt evidential morpheme **ak** independent from tense markers; this corresponds to EV in (36) and semantically scopes over the construction. Second, they also display a temporal morpheme for a result state/topic time for the described event; this corresponds to TP in (36), is overt for distant and remote pasts, and can be covert for recent pasts. Third, Inferentials display a Resultative morpheme—RP in (36)—which interacts with the topic situation morpheme, encodes temporal information, and may also be overt or covert under specifiable conditions.

11.5 Conclusion

Our goal in this chapter has been to investigate the interpretation of temporal markers in evidentials. There has been much recent interest in the semantics of evidentials, and proposals have been made that temporal operators have special "evidential-specific" interpretations in evidential contexts. We have argued against this view on the basis of three languages with very diverse evidential and temporal systems. Our overall hypothesis is that temporal operators retain their usual interpretation in evidential contexts. A careful analysis of the role of tense and aspect, paying particular attention to the richness of aspectual interpretations, can account for cases in which temporal interpretations appear to shift in evidential contexts without positing an independent "evidential-specific" paradigm.

Acknowledgments

We would like to thank our reviewers for detailed comments on the chapter. We also owe many thanks to Galia Dukova-Zheleva and Nikolay Slavkov for help with Bulgarian, and to Bepkamrêk Kayapó, Ikrô Kayapó, and the Djudjêkô community for Mẽbengokre. Research for this work was carried out with partial support from the Social Sciences and Humanities Research Council of Canada (Research Grant 410-2010-2040 to A. Arregui (PI), M. L. Rivero and A. Salanova (co-investigators), and Research Grant 410-2009-0828 to M. L. Rivero). The usual disclaimers apply.

12

Past possibility cross-linguistically: Evidence from twelve languages

SIHWEI CHEN, VERA HOHAUS, REBECCA LATURNUS, MEAGAN LOUIE, LISA MATTHEWSON, HOTZE RULLMANN, ORI SIMCHEN, CLAIRE K. TURNER, AND JOZINA VANDER KLOK

12.1 Introduction

The goal of this chapter is to subject Condoravdi's (2002) groundbreaking analysis of English modal–temporal interactions to cross-linguistic testing, a task which has not so far been attempted in the literature. We test a generalized version of Condoravdi's proposals on twelve languages from seven families. We show that a core architecture can be retained, while allowing language-specific differences in tense and aspect to influence the available interpretations in predictable ways.

12.1.1 Background

Condoravdi (2002) observes that the English sentence in (1) has two distinct readings.

(1)   He might have won the game.

On an epistemic reading, (1) asserts that it is compatible with the speaker's utterance-time knowledge that he won the game in the past. The modal *might* has a present temporal perspective and a past temporal orientation. A continuation asserting that the prejacent is false is infelicitous, as shown in (2).

(2)   He might have (already) won the game (# but he didn't).

On the second reading, which Condoravdi calls "metaphysical," (1) asserts that it was compatible with the facts at some past time that he would win the game after that time. The modal has a past temporal perspective, and a future temporal orientation. Under this reading, it is possible for the speaker to know at the utterance time that the prejacent is false.

Modality Across Syntactic Categories. First edition. Ana Arregui, María Luisa Rivero, and Andrés Salanova (eds.).
This chapter © Sihwei Chen, Vera Hohaus, Rebecca Laturnus, Meagan Louie, Lisa Matthewson, Hotze Rullmann, Ori Simchen, Claire K. Turner, and Jozina Vander Klok 2017. First published 2017 by Oxford University Press.

(3) At that point he might (still) have won the game, but he didn't in the end.

Condoravdi proposes an analysis whereby the perfect auxiliary *have* optionally raises to scope over the modal. The scope ordering *might* > *have* gives rise to the first reading, and the scope ordering *have* > *might* gives rise to the second reading. This information is summarized in Table 12.1. Following Abusch (2012), we will henceforth assume that the 'metaphysical' reading is a type of circumstantial reading (relying on a realistic modal base representing relevant facts about the evaluation world, but not requiring the entire history of all the worlds in the modal base to be identical).

Subsequent literature has debated various aspects of Condoravdi's analysis (see e.g. Arregui 2005, Hacquard 2006, Laca 2008). Analytical issues include the question of how the readings are compositionally derived—is the *have*-raising operation justified? There are also empirical questions, including whether (1) has readings other than the two identified by Condoravdi. This question is important because Condoravdi's framework does not actually rule out an additional set of readings for *might have* sentences, namely those with an epistemic conversational background and a past temporal perspective. These potential readings are listed in Table 12.2.

Example (4) is an example of Reading C-present: it was epistemically possible at some past time t that there was ice cream in the freezer at t.

(4) **Context:** Sophie is looking for some ice cream and checks the freezer. There is none in there. Asked why she opened the freezer, she replies:
There might have been ice cream in the freezer. (von Fintel and Gillies 2008: 87)

TABLE 12.1 Readings of *might have*

Reading	Conversational background	Temporal perspective (T.P.)	T.P. given by	Temporal orientation (T.O.)	T.O. given by
A	epistemic	present	present tense	past	low *have*
B	circumstantial	past	raised *have*	future	*might*

(Condoravdi 2002)

TABLE 12.2 Extra potential readings for *might have* sentences

Reading	Conversational background	Temporal perspective	Temporal orientation
C-past	epistemic	past	past
C-present	epistemic	past	present
C-future	epistemic	past	future

Although many authors have claimed that epistemic modals do not allow past temporal perspectives (see e.g. Groenendijk and Stokhof 1975, Cinque 1999, Drubig 2001, Condoravdi 2002, Stowell 2004, Hacquard 2006, Borgonovo and Cummins 2007, Demirdache and Uribe-Etxebarria 2008, Laca 2008), other researchers have argued that C-readings exist in various languages (Eide 2003, Boogaart 2007, von Fintel and Gillies 2008, Homer 2010, Martin 2011, Matthewson and Rullmann 2012, Rullmann and Matthewson 2012, 2015; and see Iatridou 1990, Portner 2009: 222–36 for discussion).

12.1.2 Preview of proposals

In this study we bring a cross-linguistic perspective to the issue of possibility modals with some kind of "pastness." We present and discuss data on Readings A, B, and C from twelve languages (see Table 12.3).

Our general null hypothesis, inspired by Condoravdi, is that modal–temporal interactions are restricted only by independent language-internal properties of the tense and aspect systems. We thus pursue a fully decompositional approach to modal–temporal interactions, whereby neither the temporal perspective nor the orientation is contributed by the lexical entry of the modal itself. More precisely, our null expectations are as in (5):

(5) The null hypothesis
 (i) Temporal perspective is provided by tense.
 (ii) Temporal orientation is provided by viewpoint and lexical aspect.

There are two important things to note about (5). First, it is a corollary of (5i) that there should be no special constraints on the temporal perspective of epistemic modals. We therefore expect epistemic modals to be able to have past temporal perspectives; C-readings will exist. With respect to (5ii), there is one systematic exception to the

TABLE 12.3 Languages discussed

Language	Family
English	Germanic (Indo-European)
Dutch	Germanic (Indo-European)
German	Germanic (Indo-European)
Mandarin	Sino-Tibetan
St'át'imcets	Northern Interior Salish
Northern Straits Salish	Central Salish
Halkomelem	Central Salish
Gitksan	Tsimshianic
Blackfoot	Algonquian
Ktunaxa	Isolate
Atayal	Austronesian (Formosan area)
Javanese	Western Malayo-Polynesian (Austronesian)

expectation that temporal orientation is provided by aspect. This has to do with the cross-linguistically stable observation that circumstantial modals have a special affinity with future temporal orientation (see e.g. Enç 1996, Condoravdi 2002, Stowell 2004, Laca 2008, Thomas 2014). Condoravdi captures this correlation with her Diversity Condition, which states that metaphysical modal claims are only possible when the modal base contains both worlds where the prejacent is true, and worlds where it is false. Assuming a branching-futures model, the past is settled but the future is not. Events that occurred in the past occurred in all metaphysically accessible worlds. A modal claim asserting the circumstantial possibility of an event prior to the temporal perspective is thus ruled out.[1] Given this, circumstantial modals are an exception to the null hypothesis that temporal orientation is given by aspect; they can only occur with non-past temporal orientations. We will see various ways in which this restriction plays out in different languages.

The final thing to note about our null hypothesis is that it leaves room for variation based on language-internal features of the tense and aspect systems. For example, we expect that languages will vary in whether the distinction between present and past temporal perspective is overtly marked. Languages which do not distinguish past from present tense will be expected to display systematic ambiguity with respect to the temporal perspective of modals. We also expect the expression of future temporal orientation to be influenced by how each language independently marks future time reference.

This chapter is organized as follows. In the remainder of the introduction, we provide background information on the languages discussed and describe our methodology. Section 12.2 presents data from seven languages which exemplify our null hypotheses: Dutch, German, Gitksan, St'át'imcets, Javanese, Mandarin, and Ktunaxa. Section 12.3 presents data from four additional languages which at least partially diverge from the predictions of our null hypothesis: Blackfoot, the SENĆOŦEN dialect of Northern Straits Salish, the Hul'q'umi'num' dialect of Halkomelem, and Atayal; and section 12.4 discusses how these divergences can be accounted for. Section 12.5 concludes.

12.1.3 Languages and methodology

Although much work has been done on modal–temporal interactions, almost all formal research in this area has concentrated on a handful of Indo-European languages, primarily in Germanic and Romance. The languages investigated in the current study come from seven language families, as outlined in Table 12.3. Seven of the languages are endangered, and almost all have modal–temporal systems which are understudied from a formal perspective. Here we provide a brief introduction to the less familiar languages we discuss.

---

[1] Thomas (2014) argues that Diversity Condition effects extend to non-priority circumstantial modals more generally.

St'át'imcets (a.k.a. Lillooet) is a Northern Interior Salish language spoken in the southwest interior of British Columbia, with fewer than 100 speakers. Data and generalizations come from fieldwork with speakers of both the Upper St'át'imcets dialect (Carl Alexander, the late Beverley Frank, the late Gertrude Ned, and the late Rose Agnes Whitley) and the Lower St'át'imcets dialect (Laura Thevarge).

Gitksan is the term conventionally used to cover that part of the Nass–Gitksan dialect continuum spoken along the upper drainage of the Skeena River in northwestern interior British Columbia. It has fewer than 400 speakers. The data presented here come from speakers of the dialects spoken in Ansbayaxw/Kispiox (Barbara Sennott), Git-anyaaw/Kitwancool (Vincent Gogag), and Gijigyukwhla/Gitsegukla (Hector Hill).

Ktunaxa is a language isolate spoken in southeastern British Columbia, northern Idaho, and northwestern Montana. Fewer than 50 native speakers are estimated to be remaining from the two known dialects, Lower and Upper Kootenay. The data presented here are from a speaker of Upper Kootenay.

Javanese is an Austronesian language of the Western Malayo-Polynesian branch spoken in Indonesia by over 90 million people. There are three main dialectal groups: West, Central, and East Javanese (Hatley 1984). The data presented here are from speakers of East Javanese, as spoken in the village of Paciran, East Java (Dhifa Ariffudin, Fina Aksanah, Titis Subekti, Bahrul Ulum, and Nashrulloh Khoyrun Nashr).

Blackfoot is a Plains Algonquian language spoken on three reserves in southern Alberta (the Siksika, Blood/Kainaa, and Piegan reserves), and the Blackfeet reservation in Montana. The data presented here are from a speaker of the Blood dialect (the late Beatrice Bullshields).

SENĆOTEN and *Hul'q'umi'num'* are dialects of two closely related languages of the Central branch of the Salish language family. The two dialects are spoken adjacent to each other on Southeastern Vancouver Island, British Columbia. SENĆOTEN is the Saanich dialect of Northern Straits Salish. Examples come from fieldwork with Ivan Morris, Sr., Raymond Sam, Mary Jack, and Anne Jimmy. Hul'q'umi'num' is the Vancouver Island dialect of Halkomelem. Examples come from fieldwork with Ruby Peter from Quamichan.

Atayal is an Austronesian language spoken in northern Taiwan. There are two major dialects, Squliq Atayal and C'uli' Atayal. The data presented here come from speakers of Squliq Atayal spoken in Hsinchu County of Taiwan (Heitay Payan, Tintin Payan, Buya' Bawnay).

Information on the orthographies used for each language, and on abbreviations used in glosses, is given in the Appendix.

Our data were gathered by means of semantic fieldwork, as well as by introspection in the cases of languages spoken natively by an author. Our semantic fieldwork methodology includes (i) elicited production tasks, in which speakers produce object-language utterances in contexts provided by the researcher; (ii) acceptability judgment tasks, in which speakers judge the acceptability of utterances in discourse contexts provided by the researcher; and (iii) targeted construction storyboard tasks, in which speakers tell stories in their language based on pictorial representations, which are designed to elicit particular constructions or elements (www.totemfieldstoryboards.org; Burton and Matthewson 2015). See Matthewson (2004) and Krifka (2011) for further discussion of methodologies used and the rationale behind them.

12.2 Results compatible with the null hypothesis

In this section, we show that various languages have modals that satisfy our null hypothesis. We show that Dutch, German, Gitksan, St'át'imcets, Javanese, Mandarin, and Ktunaxa all have modals whose temporal perspective behaves as if determined by tense (and thus, epistemic possibility modals can have past temporal perspectives) and whose temporal orientation behaves as if determined by aspect, except where this is tempered by Diversity Condition effects.

12.2.1 Dutch and German

12.2.1.1 Tense and aspect
German and Dutch are closely related (their non-standard dialects form a geographic continuum) and their tense/aspect systems are very similar (and similar to English).[2] As far as tense is concerned, there is a basic opposition between non-past and past, which semantically we will assume correspond to the non-past operator N in (6) and the past operator P in (7):

(6) $[\![N]\!] = \lambda t.\lambda p_{<i,t>}.\exists t'[\neg(t' < t) \& p(t')] = \lambda t.\lambda p_{<i,t>}.\exists t'[t' \geq t \& p(t')]$

(7) $[\![P]\!] = \lambda t.\lambda p_{<i,t>}.\exists t'[t' < t \& p(t')]$

There is some variation in the way these operators are expressed in the morphosyntax. In both languages, N is realized as a morphological present tense, but whereas P is realized in Dutch and some (western) dialects of German as a morphological past tense, in other (southern) varieties of German, P is realized as a periphrastic perfect form with *haben* ('to have') or *sein* ('to be') plus a past participle. (German examples below do not take this variation into consideration and are from High German.) In Dutch and varieties of German that use a morphological past tense for P, periphrastic perfect forms express some kind of perfect aspect (although there are differences in the meaning and use of the perfect, both compared to English and between Dutch and the German varieties). The perfect forms may either share the semantics of (7) or be the realization of an extended-now temporal operator,[3] but a real analysis of the semantics and pragmatics of the perfect in German and Dutch is beyond the scope of this chapter.

Future can be expressed by means of a modal auxiliary (*zullen* in Dutch, *werden* in German), but this is often optional. The languages do not have an overt

---

[2] For a basic introduction to tense and aspect in German and a comparison with English, we refer the reader to e.g. von Stechow (2009) or Beck and Gergel (2014: 214–91).
[3] See Kratzer (1998), von Stechow (1999, 2009), Klein (2000), Musan (2002), and Alexiadou et al. (2003).

perfective/imperfective contrast, and eventive verbs can get an "in-progress" interpretation without any overt aspectual marking. We assume the two phonologically null aspectual operators from Kratzer (1998) in (8,9):

(8) ⟦ IPFV ⟧ = λt.λp_<v,t>. ∃e [p(e) & τ(e) ⊇ t]

(9) ⟦ PFV ⟧ = λt.λp_<v,t>. ∃e [p(e) & τ(e) ⊆ t]

Both languages have various progressive-like constructions, but these are much less commonly used than the English progressive and are never obligatory.

12.2.1.2 Temporal perspective given by tense, and availability of Reading C In our examples we will mostly focus on the epistemic interpretation of the Dutch modal *kunnen* and its German cognate *können* ('can, could, may, might'), but these can have non-epistemic readings as well (see e.g. Kratzer 1991: 649–50 for further discussion.)

German and Dutch modals are morphosyntactically just like main verbs in that they inflect for tense. Based on our null hypothesis we therefore expect that the tense inflection on the modal will determine its temporal perspective. We also predict that Reading C will be available for epistemic modals with past tense inflection. These predictions are borne out. The modal *kunnen/können* can combine either with the N operator, yielding a present (or future) temporal perspective, as in (10a), or with the P operator for a past temporal perspective, as in (10b):

(10) a. De sleutel-s *kunn-en* in de la ligg-en. (Dutch)
     the key-PL can-PRS.PL in the drawer lie-INF
     'The keys may/might be in the drawer.' (PRESENT T.P., PRESENT/FUTURE T.O.)

   b. De sleutel-s *kon-den* in de la ligg-en. (Dutch)
      the key-PL can-PST.PL in the drawer lie-INF
      'The keys might have been in the drawer.' (PAST T.P., PRESENT/FUTURE T.O.)

Example (10a) says that it is epistemically possible at the speech time that the keys are in the drawer. (10b) can be paraphrased as follows: At a (contextually salient) time *t* preceding the speech time, it was epistemically possible that the keys were in the drawer (either at *t*, making this an instantiation of Reading C-present, or after *t*, making it C-future).

German examples showing present and past T.P. are given in (11,12). Crucially, as shown by the temporal adverbs, (11) cannot be interpreted with past temporal perspective and (12) cannot have a present temporal perspective:

(11) Der FC Chelsea *kann* {zum jetzigen Zeitpunkt / #damals} die
     the FC Chelsea can.PRS.SG at+the now time.point / #then(PST) the
     Champions League noch gewinn-en.
     Champions League still win-INF (German)
     'Right now/#Back then, FC Chelsea can still win the Champions League.'
                                              (PRESENT T.P., FUTURE T.O.)

(12) Borussia Dortmund *konn-te* {zu diesem Zeitpunkt / #zum jetzigen
Borussia Dortmund *can*-PST.SG at this time.point / at+the now
Zeitpunkt} sogar noch gewinn-en.
time.point even still win-INF (German)
'At this point in the game /#Right now, Borussia Dortmund could still win.'
(PAST T.P., FUTURE T.O.)

A past temporal perspective for epistemic modals (Reading C) is somewhat more difficult to obtain than a present one, but these readings can be facilitated by an appropriate discourse context. Here is a context for (10b) in which the past epistemic perspective is very natural:

(13) **Context for (10b):** When I arrived at work yesterday, I discovered that I didn't have my keys on me. I called my wife and asked if I had left them somewhere at home by any chance. She asked me where she should look. I tried to remember where I might have left them the previous night. They might have been in the drawer, but perhaps they were still in the pocket of my pants.

Past temporal perspective can also be expressed by putting the modal in the past perfect (the German analogue of this would be the past subjunctive):[4]

(14) De sleutel-s *hadd-en* in de la *kunn-en* ligg-en. (Dutch)
the key-PL *have*-PST.PL in the drawer *can*-INF lie-INF
'The keys might have been in the drawer.' (PAST T.P., PRESENT T.O.)

Example (14) is ambiguous. In addition to a past counterfactual (circumstantial) interpretation, it can also express epistemic modality with past temporal perspective (and present orientation). The past-perspective reading of (14) is very similar to that of the modal in the simple past, as in (10b), but there is a subtle difference. Example (14) expresses "hindsight" knowledge, in the sense that at the utterance time, the speaker knows that the prejacent was false. Example (15) would be an appropriate context:

(15) Context for (14)
A: Why did you turn the whole drawer upside down? Your keys were on the counter, weren't they?
B: Yes, but I didn't know that then. I had to find them, but I had no idea where I had left them. They might have been in the drawer.

---

[4] The modal in (14) is an infinitive instead of a past participle, as would normally be expected for a verb in the perfect. This is a well-known morphosyntactic quirk, which need not concern us here.

Here the speaker knows at the speech time that the keys were not in the drawer, but at the reference time (the time that she was looking for her keys) they could have been in the drawer for all she knew then. We assume that this difference between an epistemic modal in the simple past (as in (10b)) and in the past perfect (as in (14)) is due to the fact that the past perfect has an additional counterfactual component (i.e. a presupposition or implicature to the effect that the prejacent is false at the utterance time), but analyzing this further is beyond the scope of this chapter, given the wide range of variation in the morphosyntactic expression of counterfactuals cross-linguistically.

12.2.1.3 Temporal orientation given by aspect and the Diversity Condition As predicted by our null hypothesis, the temporal orientation of Dutch and German modals is determined by temporal (aspectual) operators that scope below the modal (in combination with the lexical aspect of the predicate). The prejacent proposition can feature either of the temporal operators in (6) and (7), in addition to the choice of imperfective versus perfective, as sketched in (16).

(16) $[_{<s,t>} \lambda w \, [\, [_{<<i,t>,t>} \{N/P\} \, t' \,] \, [_{<i,t>} \lambda t \, [_{<<v,t>,t>} \{PFV/IPFV\} \, t]$
$[_{<v,t>} \lambda e \, (\text{verb phrase})_{w,e} \,]\,]\,]$

Let us first consider cases where the non-past operator N appears below the modal. Because N is phonologically empty, the prejacent predicate lacks any overt temporal or aspectual marking. If the predicate is stative, the temporal orientation is present (as in the most common interpretation of (10a,b)) or future, as in (17):

(17) Als   je   thuis-kom-t,   (Dutch)
      when   you   home-come-PRS.2SG
      kunn-en   de   sleutel-s   in   de   la   ligg-en.
      can-PRS.PL   the   key-PL   in   the   drawer   lie-INF
      'When you come home, the keys might be in the drawer.'
                                                  (PRESENT T.P., <u>FUTURE T.O.</u>)

We assume for concreteness that if the prejacent predicate is stative, the imperfective operator is always selected. If the predicate is eventive, we assume the perfective operator is normally selected (unless it is possible to give the verb an imperfective interpretation; see below), and we get future temporal orientation, just as in English. In that case, the modal can be interpreted epistemically or non-epistemically. German examples were given in (11,12); (18) is a Dutch case:

(18) We   {*kunn-en / kon-den*}   winn-en.   (Dutch)
      we   can-PRS.PL / can-PST.PL   win-INF
      'We are / were able to win.'   (PRESENT/PAST T.P., <u>FUTURE T.O.</u>)

However, here there is one relevant difference between Dutch and German on the one hand and English on the other. In Dutch/German, bare activity verbs in the complement of an epistemic modal often allow for present temporal orientation, whereas their English counterparts can only have future orientation. This contrast is illustrated in (19–21).[5]

(19) a. It might rain {*right now / tomorrow}.
b. It might be raining {right now / tomorrow}.

(20) Het kan   {op dit   moment/morgen} regen-en.   (Dutch)
     it   can.PRS.SG at   this moment/tomorrow rain-INF
     'It might be raining right now' OR 'It might rain tomorrow.'

(21) Es könnte   ja   {gerade / morgen}   regn-en.   (German)
     it can.SBJV.PRS.SG   DISC right.now / tomorrow rain-INF
     'It might be raining right now.' OR 'It might rain tomorrow.'
                                    (PRESENT T.P., PRESENT/FUTURE T.O.)

This difference between the Dutch/German and English aspectual systems exists independently of modality. Exactly the same contrast is observed in *non*-modal sentences. In Dutch and German, an activity verb in the simple present tense can have an "in-progress" interpretation (as in (22)), whereas English requires the use of the present progressive in such cases.

(22) Het regen-t   op dit   moment.   (Dutch)
     Es   regne-t   in diesem Moment.   (German)
     it   rain-PRS.3SG   at this   moment
     'It is raining right now.'

This suggests that (some) eventive verbs in Dutch and German that lack overt viewpoint aspect can optionally have the IPFV operator and therefore allow an imperfective interpretation, unlike English, which requires them to be overtly marked with progressive aspect.

In order to get a *past* temporal orientation, the P operator is selected in the scope of the modal. This is illustrated for Dutch in (23). In this case, an epistemic interpretation is the only possible one, because of Condoravdi's Diversity Condition, which rules out past-oriented circumstantial modals.

(23) Hij kan   / kon   gewonnen   hebb-en.   (Dutch)
     he   can.PRS.3SG / can.PST.3SG   win.PST.PTCP have-INF
     'It is/was possible that he won.'   (PAST/PRESENT T.P., PAST T.O.)

Morphologically, P scoping below the modal is expressed by marking the modal's complement with the periphrastic perfect, much as in English. This is independent

---

[5] (21) uses the subjunctive to weaken the modal claim. Since it is not immediately relevant to the null hypothesis, we do not explore the semantic contribution of the subjunctive further.

of whether the particular variety of Dutch/German uses the periphrastic perfect to express past tense. That is, even those varieties (like Standard Dutch and western dialects of German) that in non-modal sentences use a morphological past tense to express P, uniformly use the periphrastic perfect to express P when it scopes below the modal. The explanation, of course, is that for morphosyntactic reasons the complement of the modal has to be in the infinitive form, and hence cannot be inflected for tense, leaving the periphrastic perfect as the only available temporal operator that can shift the temporal orientation backwards. We conjecture that in the scope of a modal the semantic/pragmatic contrast between the morphological past and the periphrastic perfect is neutralized. (The same thing seems to happen in the pluperfect, in Dutch/German as well as English.)

Note again that in English the facts are essentially the same (i.e. English uses the periphrastic perfect to express P scoping below the modal), except for one wrinkle. Because (present-day) English modals cannot be inflected for tense, *have* in the complement of certain modals (including *might*, but not *must* and *may*) can also express past temporal *perspective* rather than past temporal *orientation*, which leads to the ambiguity that Condoravdi analyzed in terms of the relative scope of *have* and the modal. In this regard, Dutch and German are "better behaved" languages, which express past temporal perspective by means of a tense operator (either the morphological past or the periphrastic perfect) scoping over the modal, and past orientation by means of perfect aspect with the semantics of P in the complement of the modal.

Finally, note that it is possible to have both past T.P. and past T.O. Here is an example in both languages:

(24) **Context:** Polina is about to leave for work. As she leaves her apartment, her neighbor's son runs past her through the hallway. She then hears a loud bang. She fears that the boy might have fired a gun and calls the police. The next day, the boy's mother tells her that the boy only used a firecracker. She is quite upset because she had to deal with the police and a youth welfare officer. She wants to know why Polina even called the police. Polina justifies herself:

a. Ihr   Sohn *hätte*   ja   jemand   [erschossen   *hab-en*]
   your   son   have.SUBJ.PST.SG   DISC somebody shot.PST.PTCP   have-INF
   *könn-*en.
   can-INF   (German)

b. Uw   zoon   *had*   immers iemand   neergeschoten   *kunn-*en
   your son   have.PST.SG   DISC   somebody   shot.PST.PTCP   can-INF
   *hebb-*en.
   have-INF   (Dutch)
   'Your son could have shot somebody.'   (PAST T.P., PAST T.O.)

Note that (24) additionally employs counterfactual marking (encoded in German by the past subjunctive *hätte können* and in Dutch by the past perfect *had kunnen*).

Again, we hypothesize that this counterfactual form is required to indicate that, at the utterance time, Polina knows for a fact that her neighbor's son has not shot somebody.

12.2.2 Gitksan

In this section we illustrate modal–temporal interactions in Gitksan with respect to two representative modals, epistemic *ima('a)* and the circumstantial possibility modal *da'akhlxw*. These modals are lexically specialized for epistemic and circumstantial conversational backgrounds respectively; for evidence, see Peterson (2010) and Matthewson (2013).

12.2.2.1 Tense and aspect Gitksan does not overtly mark past or present tense, but has obligatory marking for future eventualities (Jóhannsdóttir and Matthewson 2007; Matthewson 2013). Example (25) shows that eventive and stative predicates can be interpreted with either past or present time reference, in the absence of overt temporal marking.

(25) a. Bax=t Yoko.
   run=DM Yoko
   'Yoko ran.' / 'Yoko is running.'   (Jóhannsdóttir and Matthewson 2007)
 b. Siipxw=t James.
   sick=DM James
   'James was sick.' / 'James is sick.'

Examples (26,27) show that the prospective aspect marker *dim* is necessary and sufficient for a future interpretation. See Rigsby (1986: 279), Jóhannsdóttir and Matthewson (2007), Matthewson (2013) for further data and discussion.

(26) *(*Dim*) ha'w=t James t'aahlakw.
   *(PROSP) go.home=DM James tomorrow
   'James will go home tomorrow.'

(27) *(*Dim*) siipxw=t James t'aahlakw.
   *(PROSP) sick=DM James tomorrow
   'James will be sick tomorrow.'

Following Jóhannsdóttir and Matthewson (2007) and Matthewson (2012, 2013), we assume that Gitksan possesses a phonologically null non-future tense morpheme, as in (28); this tense refers to the contextually salient reference time provided by the assignment function g, and presupposes that this time interval does not follow the utterance time. The obligatory presence of the non-future tense morpheme restricts the temporal reference to non-future in sentences like (25a,b).[6]

---

[6] The fact that (28) adopts a referential analysis of tense, while (7) above adopts an existential analysis, is an artifact of prior analyses of the respective languages and has no import for our main claims.

(28) $[\![\text{NON-FUT}_i]\!]^{g,c}$ is only defined if no part of $g(i)$ is after t_c.
If defined, $[\![\text{NON-FUT}_i]\!]^{g,c} = g(i)$.

In cases of future time reference, the null tense co-occurs with prospective *dim*, just as proposed by Abusch (1985) for English WOLL (the element which surfaces either as *will* or *would*, depending on whether it combines with present or past tense). *Dim* is thus an aspect marker, not a tense: it co-occurs with tense, and orders event time with respect to reference time (cf. Klein 1994). This correctly predicts that *dim* allows "past future" readings, where the event precedes the utterance time, as in (29).

(29) Hlaa gilbil=hl ganuutxw lhi-daa-t mahl-is Diana *dim*
INCEP two=CN week NMLZ-SPT-3SG.II tell-PN Diana PROSP
yee-t goo=hl Winnipeg ji hlaa k'i'ihl ganuutxw.
go-3SG.II LOC=CN Winnipeg HYP INCEP one week
'Two weeks ago Diana said that she would go to Winnipeg in a week.'
(adapted from Jóhannsdóttir and Matthewson 2007)

There does not appear to be a dedicated marker for perfect aspect in Gitksan. Present perfect meanings are often rendered without any overt marking, as shown in (30).

(30) 'Witxw=hl ts'awat.
arrive=CN smart
'The smart one has arrived.'

The analysis just sketched of the Gitksan temporal system leads us to expect the following: modals should receive their T.P. from the null non-future tense, thus being able to have either past or present temporal perspective without overt marking. Future T.O. should be marked by *dim* below the modal. Past T.O. should be possible without any overt aspectual marking.

12.2.2.2 Temporal perspective given by tense, and availability of Reading C As we predict, the temporal perspective of Gitksan modals may be either present or past, without any overt temporal marking. Representative examples are given in (31,32). (31a) talks about a sickness which is epistemically possible at the utterance time (present T.P.), while (31b) has a past T.P. The speaker of (31b) is aware at the utterance time that the animal in question is not (and never was) a rabbit. The sentence asserts that it was compatible with the speaker's epistemic state at some past time that he was a rabbit. (31b) is thus a clear case of Reading C.

(31) a. **Context:** Why isn't Joe here?
Yugw=*imaa/ima'*=hl siipxw-t.
IPFV=*EPIS*=CN sick-3SG.II
'He might be sick.' (Matthewson 2013: 365)

b. Context: Stacey bought food to feed Pat's pet, but she didn't know what kind of pet he had, so she bought all the wrong kinds of food. Later she finds out Pat's pet is a snake. Pat asks "Why did you buy a carrot?" Stacey replies:
Yugw=*imaa*=hl ga̱x.
IPFV=*EPIS*=CN rabbit-3SG.II
'He might have been a rabbit.' (TFS 2012, "Feeding Fluffy")

Examples of present and past T.P. with circumstantial *da'a̱khlxw* are given in (32). In (32a), the speaker is talking about her utterance-time abilities (present T.P.), and in (32b), the speaker is reporting a girl's past ability (past T.P.).

(32) a. Nee=dii=n   *da'ak̲xw*   #(dim)   xsaw-i'y/xsaxw-i'y.
        NEG=CNTR=1SG.I CIRC.POS #(PROSP) go.out-1SG.II
        'I am not able to go out.' (TFS 2011, "Chore Girl")
    b. Ii   nee=dii-t   *da'ak̲xw* dim   ma'us-t.
        and NEG=CNTR-3SG.II CIRC.POS PROSP play-3SG.II
        'And she was not able to play.' (TFS 2011, "Sick Girl")

12.2.2.3 *Temporal orientation given by aspect and the Diversity Condition*   Our null hypothesis predicts that future T.O. will appear with the prospective marker *dim*, and this is what we find, as shown in (33,34) for epistemic *ima(')a*. The *dim*-less version is only acceptable in contexts which support a past or present T.O., and the version with *dim* is only acceptable with future T.O.

(33) Yugw=*ima'*=hl siipxw-t.
     IPFV=*EPIS*=CN sick-3SG.II
     'He might have been sick.' / 'He might be sick (now).' / ≠'He might be sick (in future).'
     Contexts:
     √ Why wasn't Joe at the meeting yesterday? (PAST T.O.)
     √ Why isn't Joe here? (PRESENT T.O.)
     # He's wearing no coat in the rain, he might get sick. (FUTURE T.O.)

(34) Yugw=*ima'*=hl *dim*   siipxw-t.
     IPFV=*EPIS*=CN PROSP sick-3SG.II
     ≠ 'He might have been sick.' / ≠'He might be sick (now).' /
     'He might be sick (in future).
     Contexts:
     # Why wasn't Joe at the meeting yesterday? (PAST T.O.)
     # Why isn't Joe here? (PRESENT T.O.)
     √ He's wearing no coat in the rain, he might get sick.
                                            (FUTURE T.O.) (Matthewson 2013: 365)

With the circumstantial modal *da'akhlxw*, we get a slightly different result. Future T.O. is still marked by *dim*, as predicted by the null hypothesis, but *dim* is obligatory, as shown in (35).

(35) *Da'akhlxw*-i-s   Henry #(dim)   jam-t.
CIRC.POS-TRA-PN Henry #(PROSP) cook-3SG.II
'Henry is able to cook.' / 'Henry was able to cook.'   (Matthewson 2013)

The obligatoriness of *dim* with *da' akhlxw*, and indeed with all circumstantial modals in Gitksan (Matthewson 2013), is a straightforward Diversity Condition effect. The language enforces obligatory prospective aspect to ensure that circumstantial modals are always future-oriented.

12.2.3 St'át'imcets

12.2.3.1 Tense and aspect St'át'imcets is another language which lexically restricts the conversational background of modals (Rullmann et al. 2008, Davis et al. 2009). The language does not obligatorily overtly encode a distinction between present and past tense, but obligatorily overtly marks prospective aspect (Matthewson 2006; see also van Eijk 1997). This is shown in (36–38); the possible temporal interpretations are the same for stative predicates.

(36) K'ác-an'=lhkan.
dry-DIR=1SG.SU
'I dried it.' / 'I am drying it.' / ≠ 'I will dry it.'

(37) *K'ác-an'=lhkan   natcw / zánucwem.
dry-DIR=1SG.SU one.day.away / next.year
'I will dry it tomorrow / next year.'   (Matthewson 2006: 677)

(38) K'ac-an'-lhkán=*kelh*.
dry-DIR=1SG.SU=PROSP
'≠ I dried it' / ≠ 'I am drying it' / 'I will dry it.'   (Matthewson 2006: 678)

Kelh is a prospective aspect which gives rise to "past future" interpretations when the reference time is in the past; this is shown in (39). *Kelh* is therefore parallel to Gitksan *dim* and English WOLL.

(39) **Context:** Mike Leech is currently chief of T'ít'q'et. His (deceased) mother was called Julianne.
Zwát-en-as   s=Julianne   [k=wa=s   kúkwpi7=*kelh*
know-DIR-3ERG NMLZ=Julianne [DET-IPFV-3POSS chief=PROSP
ta=skúza7=s=a]   i=kwís=as.
DET=child-3POSS=EXIS] when.PST=fall=3SBJV
'Julianne knew when he was born that her child would become chief.'

We adopt a non-future tense analysis of St'át'imcets, just as in (28), following Matthewson (2006).

12.2.3.2 Temporal perspective is given by tense, and availability of reading C As St'át'imcets lacks overt tense marking, we predict that all its modals will allow both present and past temporal perspectives, without overt marking. This is upheld, as shown in (40) and (41) for an epistemic and a circumstantial modal respectively. In each case, the (a) example has present T.P. and the (b) example has past T.P. Example (40b) shows that St'át'imcets allows Reading C, as the epistemic modal here has a past temporal perspective.

(40) a. Wa7=*k'a* séna7 qwenúxw.
   IPFV=*EPIS* COUNTER sick
   'He may be sick.' (Context: Maybe that's why he's not here.)
   (Rullmann et al. 2008: 321)

   b. **Context:** The Canucks were playing last night. You weren't watching the game, but you heard your son sounding excited from the other room, where he was watching. You thought the Canucks were winning, and you called up your friend and said: "Good sports news!" But after the game, you found out that the Canucks had actually lost, and your son was excited about something his friend was telling him on his cellphone. The next day, you see your friend and he asks you why you had told him there was good sports news when the Canucks had lost. You say:
   Wá7=*k'a* t'cum i=Canucks=a.
   IPFV=*EPIS* win PL.DET=Canucks=EXIS
   'The Canucks might have been winning.'

(41) a. Wá7=lhkan *ka*-cát-s-*a* ta-két'h=a.
   IPFV=1SG.SU *CIRC*-lift-CAUS-*CIRC* DET=rock=EXIS
   'I can lift the rock.'

   b. Qwenúxw=kan i=nátcw=as, t'u7
   sick=1SG.SU when.PST=day=3SBJV but
   ka-tsunam'-cal=lhkán-*a*=t'u7.
   CIRC-teach-ACT=1SG.SU-*CIRC*=ADD
   'I was sick yesterday, but I still was able to teach.' (Davis et al. 2009)

12.2.3.3 Temporal orientation given by aspect and the Diversity Condition As prospective marking is obligatory whenever the event time follows the reference time, we predict the obligatory presence of *kelh* under modals when they are future-oriented (and the absence of *kelh* when the modals are past- or present-oriented). This is correct for epistemic modals, as shown in (42,43). In (42), the T.O. is past, and there is no prospective; in (43), the T.O. is future, and *kelh* appears.

(42) **Context:** You've been watching the gold medal hockey game, but in the middle of it the power went off, so you had no TV. My power is out too, so I call up and ask: "Did the Canadians win?"
T'cúm=wit=k'a skánas, cw7aoz kw=s=áts'x-en=an.
win=3PL=EPIS YNQ NEG DET=NMLZ=see-TR=1SG.SBJV
'They might have won, I didn't see it.'

(43) **Context:** Your grandson is celebrating a Canadian victory, but the game is only half over and so you say : "The Americans might win."
Sxek tc'úm=kelh=tu7 i=telh-álqw-emc=a.
EPIS win=PROSP=then DET.PL=line-mass-people=EXIS
'The Americans might win.'

These data are broadly in accordance with the null hypothesis, but two things must be noted. First, (42) lacks any aspectual marking, rather than having the marking one would usually expect for a perfect meaning in St'át'imcets, the auxiliary *plan*, as in (44) (see Davis 2012).

(44) Plán=lhkan t'cum.
PRF=1SG.SU win
'I have / had (already) won.'

This suggests that past T.O. may in some languages be given by a lower past (or in this case, non-future) tense, rather than by perfect aspect, as in English. The second thing to note is that future temporal orientation is not overtly marked for circumstantial modals in St'át'imcets; this can be seen in (41a,b) and (45), which are future-oriented.

(45) Lán=lhkacw=ka áts'x-en ti=kwtámts-sw=a.
PRF=2SG.SU=CIRC see-DIR DET=husband-2SG.POSS=EXIS
'You may go to see your husband.'

This is again a Diversity Condition effect, but it is the inverse of the Gitksan pattern, where prospective aspect was obligatory with circumstantial modals. We see that in some languages, the inherent future T.O. of circumstantials is overtly marked by prospective aspect, while in other languages, the circumstantial modals themselves are perhaps inherently future-oriented and thus require no overt marking. We will see other instances of the latter type of case in following sections.

12.2.4 *Javanese*

In this section we investigate the Javanese epistemic possibility modal *paleng* and the circumstantial possibility modal *iso*, which both lexically restrict their respective modal base (Vander Klok 2013).

12.2.4.1 Tense and aspect Verbs in Javanese are not marked for tense or aspect (Horne 1961: 50, Robson 2002: 54). All clauses are compatible with past, present, or future reference times, as shown in the following dialogue; the same facts hold for stative predicates.

(46) a. Wingi/ sa'iki/ sesok ewoh opo?
yesterday/ now/ tomorrow busy what
'Yesterday what [were you] doing?'
'Now what [are you] doing?'
'Tomorrow what [will you be] doing?'

b. Aku marut kelopo.
1SG AV.grate coconut
'I shaved / was shaving / am shaving / will be shaving / coconut.'

We assume a tenseless analysis of Javanese, where only context and temporal expressions serve to restrict the temporal reference (in matrix clauses) (cf. Tonhauser 2011 for Paraguayan Guaraní).[7] This is different from St'át'imcets or Gitksan, which we analyzed as having a covert non-future tense morpheme.

While temporal marking is not required in Javanese, optional aspectual auxiliaries or adverbial/nominal temporal expressions can explicitly indicate the reference time. Future reference in Paciran Javanese for both eventive and stative predicates can be indicated by a prospective aspect auxiliary *ape* or by temporal adverbs like *sesok* 'tomorrow; in the future'. See Vander Klok (2012) for further discussion.

(47) a. Pak Bambang *wingi-nan-e* loro.
Mr. Bambang *yesterday*-NMLZ-DEF sick
'Mr. Bambang was sick in the past.'

b. Bocah Paciran podho *ape* dolan nok WBL.
child Paciran PL PROSP visit at WBL
'Paciran children will play at WBL (*Wisata Bahari Lamongan*).'

Evidence that *ape* is a prospective aspect marker is given in (48), which shows a 'past future' interpretation when the reference time is in the past.

(48) **Context:** *Dino iki April 20*. Today is April 20.
Sak wulan kepungkor kepala sekolah ngomong *ape* ono prei
one month ago head school AV.say PROSP EXIS holiday
tanggal 1 April. Tapi gak sido.
date 1 April but NEG go.ahead
'One month ago, the school headmaster said that there would be a holiday on April 1st. But it never happened.'

---

[7] In out-of-the-blue contexts or in translations to English, only present temporal reference is felicitous. This suggests that when the context does not provide an antecedent temporal reference time, the default is to fix the reference time to the utterance time.

12.2.4.2 Temporal perspective given by tense, and availability of Reading C Assuming a tenseless analysis for Javanese, we expect that possibility modals will be compatible with past, present, or future temporal perspective, given by the context or optional temporal markers. This prediction is borne out for the circumstantial modal *iso*, as shown in (49–51).

(49) **Context:** BG is talking to BZ about a deceased family member.
Rondok ra *iso* obah iku wes patang dino.
around NEG CIRC.POS move DEM already four day
'She couldn't move for already four days.' (PAST T.P., PRESENT T.O.)

(50) **Context:** Mary's friends are asking her to go out and play now.
Aku mari tibo, gak *iso*.
1SG finish fall NEG CIRC.POS
'I fell; [I] cannot [play].' (TFS 2011, "Chore Girl") (PRESENT T.P., PRESENT T.O.)

(51) **Context:** *Bu Yani ora iso melaku sa'iki. Dokter ngomong nek sa'wise operasi...*
Mrs. Yani cannot walk now. The doctor said that after the operation...
Bu Yani *iso* melaku.
Mrs. Yani CIRC.POS walk
'Bu Yani will be able to walk.' (FUTURE T.P., FUTURE T.O.)

(52–54) show that the epistemic possibility modal *paleng* also allows for past, present, and future T.P. Importantly, (52) illustrates the availability of past temporal perspective with epistemic possibility (here, Reading C-past). Additional examples of C-readings are given in (55–57).

(52) **Context:** When you looked outside earlier this morning, the ground was wet. But later, you found out that Bunga was playing with water. You thought before that:
Paleng (wes) mari udan.
EPIS.POS (already) finish rain
'It might have rained.' (PAST T.P., PAST T.O.)

(53) **Context:** You were watching the football game with Surabaya Muda but you fell asleep when the game was tied 2:2. They might have won (but you're not sure).
Surabaya Muda *paleng* sing (wes) menang (tapi aku durung
Surabaya Muda EPIS.POS REL (already) win (but 1SG not.yet
weroh).
know)
'Surabaya Muda might have won.' (PRESENT T.P., PAST T.O.)

(54) **Context:** Tomo's family are fishermen. But Tomo is an elementary school teacher. He likes teaching. Tomo doesn't want to fish now. But because fishing is Tomo's family's tradition, . . .

Paleng Tomo pengen dadi wong miang.
EPIS.POS Tomo want become person fisher
'Tomo might want to be a fisherman.' (FUTURE T.P., FUTURE T.O.)

12.2.4.3 *Temporal orientation given by aspect and the Diversity Condition* Our null hypothesis predicts that temporal orientation is given by aspect; a split is found between epistemic and circumstantial modals in Javanese, which follows from the Diversity Condition. The epistemic modal *paleng* can have past and present T.O. with no embedded aspectual or temporal markers. Past T.O. was illustrated in (52), and present T.O. (Reading C-present) is given in (55):

(55) **Context:** Ayu bought food to feed Joni's pet, but she didn't know what kind of pet he had, so she bought all the wrong kinds of food. Later she finds out Joni's pet is a snake. Joni asks: "Why did you buy some fish?" Ayu replies:
Paleng Fluffy iku kucing.
EPIS.POS Fluffy DEM cat
'Fluffy might have been a cat.' (TFS 2012, "Feeding Fluffy")
(PAST T.P., PRESENT T.O.)

In order to indicate future T.O. with the epistemic modal *paleng*, the prospective aspect *ape* is obligatory in Paciran Javanese, as shown in (56), an example of Reading C-future.

(56) **Context:** This morning when you looked outside, it was cloudy, so you took an umbrella with you when you went to work. Later, you explain to your father why you took an umbrella (when you get home after "Ashar," the third call to prayer).
Paleng *(ape) udan
EPIS.POS *(PROSP) rain
'It might have rained.' (PAST T.P., FUTURE T.O.)

The circumstantial modal *iso* is different from epistemic *paleng* with respect to T.O. Like St'át'imcets circumstantial modals, *iso* is future-oriented and does not require overt future marking, as shown in (57). This pattern illustrates one way languages meet the Diversity Condition.

(57) **Context:** You were watching the Persela Lamongan game, and at one point in the first half, Persela Lamongan was winning 3–1. But the referee made a bad call, and the other team won.
Persela Lamongan ranjene iso menang, tapi kalah.
Persela Lamongan actually CIRC.POS win but lose
'Persela Lamongan could have won, but they lost.'
(PAST T.P., FUTURE T.O.; READING B)

12.2.5 Mandarin

12.2.5.1 Tense and aspect The data presented here represent Mandarin as spoken in Taiwan. This language lacks overt tense morphology, but it has been argued that viewpoint aspect and the telicity of the predicate interact to determine temporal interpretations (Smith and Erbaugh 2005, Lin 2006). Stative predicates can be interpreted as either past or present without additional morphology, as in (58).

(58) Tāmen hěn jǐnzhāng.
    3PL   very   nervous
    'They are / were very nervous.'

Atelic eventive predicates can be aspectually unmarked and interpreted as present or past habitual, as in (59a). Most eventives can either take the progressive maker *zài*, yielding a present or past interpretation, as in (59b), or the perfective aspect *-le*, yielding the past only, as in (59c). Achievements, however, cannot take progressive *zài*, as shown in (60a), but can optionally take the perfective *-le* and have a past interpretation, as in (60b). (A present reading is the default in (59a) and (59b), and a past interpretation usually requires rich context or a temporal adverbial to make the past referent time salient.)

(59) a. Tāmen chàng gē.
       3PL   sing   song
       'They sing songs.' / 'They used to sing songs.'

   b. Tāmen zài   chàng gē.
      3PL   PROG sing song
      'They are singing songs.' / 'They were singing songs.'

   c. Tāmen chàng-*le* gē.
      3PL   sing-PFV song
      ≠ 'They sing songs.' / 'They sang songs.'

(60) a. *Tā zài   dǎ-pò   bēizǐ.
       3SG PROG break   cup
       Intended: 'He is breaking cups.'

   b. Tā dǎ-pò(-*le*) bēizǐ.
      3SG break(-PFV) cup
      'He broke cups.'

Future reference relies on the prospective aspect *huì*, as shown in (61).[8] Example (62) shows that *huì* can also order the future relative to a past reference time.

---

[8] *Huì* has been regarded as a modal as it can also express ability, epistemic and metaphysical interpretations (Ren 2008). We limit ourselves to the temporal use of *huì* here.

(61) a. Tāmen *(huì)   hěn máng.
       3PL   *(PROSP) very busy
       'They will be very busy.'

   b. Tāmen *(huì)   chàng gē.
       3PL   *(PROSP) sing song
       'They will sing songs.'

(62) Zhāngsān shuō tā huì hěn máng.
     Zhangsan say 3SG PROSP very busy
     'Zhangsan said that he would be busy.'   (Lin 2006: 18)

We assume that Mandarin possesses a null non-future tense, which can refer to the present or past depending on context and interaction with lexical and viewpoint aspect; see Sun (2014) for such an analysis. The prospective *huì* combines with the null tense, giving rise to a future (in the present) or future in the past.

12.2.5.2 Temporal perspective given by tense, and availability of Reading C Mandarin modals lexically encode conversational background (except for one weak necessity modal, which allows both epistemic and circumstantial interpretations) (see Ren 2008, Chen 2014). In this section, we show that the temporal perspective of two representative possibility modals, circumstantial *kěyǐ* and epistemic *kěnéng*, is given by tense.

Given that tense is covert and underspecified for present vs. past, the null hypothesis predicts that Mandarin modals allow present and past TPs without overt marking. This is borne out. The circumstantial modal *kěyǐ* can be interpreted with a present or past temporal perspective without additional morphology, as shown in (63–64). Example (63) says that according to the hearer's goal at the utterance time, consuming more vegetables is possible. Example (64) talks about a possibility at a past time that the traffic lights were still green and the speaker caught the bus, which is however not true in the actual world. It is thus a counterfactual reading.

(63) Nǐ   kěyǐ   duā chī shūcài.
     2SG CIRC.POS more eat vegetable
     '(To have a balanced diet) you can eat more vegetables.'

(64) **Context:** You are late for an appointment with your friend. You are explaining to him the reason. You could have caught the last bus but the traffic lights on your way just turned red and stopped you from crossing the street to the bus stop while the bus was arriving.
     Wǒ kěyǐ   dādào gōngchē de   (dànshì wǒ méi gǎn-shàng).
     1SG CIRC.POS catch bus   PART but   1SG NEG catch-up
     'I could have caught the bus (but I didn't).'

Like circumstantial *kěyǐ*, the epistemic modal *kěnéng* is compatible with present or past temporal perspective with no extra marking. Examples (65) and (66–68) illustrate present and past T.P. respectively. Example (65) states that winning the game is epistemically possible at the utterance time, whereas in (66–68) the prejacents are compatible with the evidence available at some past time, but not with the utterance-time evidence. We see that Mandarin exemplifies the corollary of our null hypothesis that past epistemic temporal perspectives (C-readings) are possible.

(65) Context: You were watching the Canucks but you fell asleep when the game was tied. They might have won (but you're not sure) (adapted from Matthewson 2013: 364):
Tāmen *kěnéng* dǎ-yíng-le.
3PL EPIS.POS play-win-PFV
'They might have won the game.' (PRESENT T.P., PAST T.O.)

(66) Context: You and your friend agreed to meet at the 7-11 on 41st St., but you didn't see him at the appointed time. The 7-11 clerk told you there's another 7-11 on 41st St., so you hastened to go there but still didn't find him. When you came home, you got a call from him. He says, "Why didn't you wait for me? I was only 15 minutes late! " You reply:
Wǒ zěnme zhīdào! Nǐ *kěnéng* qù-le lìngwài yī-jiā 7-11.
1SG how know 2SG EPIS.POS go-PFV another one-CLF 7-11
'How could I know! You might have gone to another 7-11.'
(PAST T.P., PAST T.O.)

(67) Context: Stacey bought food to feed Pat's pet, but she didn't know what kind of pet he had, so she bought all the wrong kinds of food. Later she finds out that Pat's pet is a snake. Pat asks "Why did you buy a bone?" Stacey replies (TFS 2012, "Feeding Fluffy"):
Wǒ zěnme zhīdào! Nǐ yǎng-de *kěnéng* shì yī-zhī gǒu.
1SG how know 2SG raise-NMLZ EPIS.POS be one-CLF dog
'How could I know! What you raise might have been a dog.'
(PAST T.P., PRESENT T.O.)

(68) Context: You thought you were going to meet your friend at the 7–11 on 41st St., but you didn't see him at the appointed time. You didn't have a cellphone with you so you only waited there but never found him. Later when you came home, you got a call from him, saying: "Why didn't you go find a booth and call me? I was waiting for you at the 7–11 on 44th St. for an hour! " You reply:
Rúguǒ wǒ zǒu-le, nǐ *kěnéng* huì zhǎo-bú-dào wǒ.
if 1SG leave-PFV 2SG EPIS.POS PROSP find-NEG-out 1SG
'If I left the 7–11 (and you arrived while I was gone), you might not have been able to find me.' (PAST T.P., FUTURE T.O.)

12.2.5.3 *Temporal orientation given by aspect and the Diversity Condition* Recall that the prospective *huì* is required to give futurity in unembedded sentences. We predict that *huì* under modals yields future orientation, and the absence of *huì* yields only present or past orientation, with predictable aspectual restriction. This is straightforwardly upheld for the epistemic modal *kěnéng*. *Huì* is always present under *kěnéng* with future T.O., irrespective of event type and the telicity of the prejacent. We show this for an atelic eventive predicate in (69).

(69) Context: Your friend caught a cockroach. He tells you he is going to show it to his sister because she is afraid of cockroaches. You persuade him not to do this:
Tā kěnéng *(huì) kū.
3SG EPIS.POS *(PROSP) cry
'She might cry.'

In the absence of *huì*, *kěnéng* is restricted to non-future T.O. Prejacents with statives and progressive-marked eventives can receive either present or past T.O., as exemplified with progressives in (70–71). *Kěnéng* cannot embed a bare eventive verb; past T.O. for *kěnéng* with an eventive prejacent requires the perfective aspect *-le*, as in (72).

(70) Context: You hear the uproar and clink of bottles from the living room.
Tāmen kěnéng zài hē jiǔ.
3PL EPIS.POS PROG drink wine
'They might be drinking wine.'

(71) Context: You called your neighbour friend but she didn't sound right. One hour later, she comes to your place with red and swollen eyes. You think:
Tā kěnéng zài kū.
3SG EPIS.POS PROG cry
'She might have been crying (when I was calling).'

(72) Context: You come home finding some pieces of glass-like fragments on the floor. You suspect that your children broke something.
Tāmen kěnéng dǎpò*(-le) dōngxī.
3PL EPIS.POS break-*(PFV) stuff
'They might have broken something.'

Turning to circumstantial modals, we find that the T.O. of the circumstantial modal *kěyǐ* is restricted due to the Diversity Condition. Unlike the epistemic modal, circumstantial *kěyǐ* allows a future T.O. with a bare eventive prejacent. This is shown in (73). In fact, the overt prospective aspect *huì*, which marks a future T.O. with the epistemic modal, is not allowed on either stative or eventive prejacents with *kěyǐ*.

(73) Context: You acquire a piece of land in a faraway country and discover that the soil and climate are very much like at home, where hydrangeas prosper

everywhere. Since hydrangeas are your favourite plants, you wonder whether they would grow in this place and inquire about it. (Kratzer 1991: 646)

Xiùqiúhuā *kěyǐ* (*huì) shēngzhǎng zài zhèlǐ.
hydrangea CIRC.POS (*PROSP) grow LOC here
'Hydrangeas can grow here.'

The circumstantial modal is inherently future-oriented, and thus requires no overt marking. This is a manifestation of the Diversity Condition.

12.2.6 Ktunaxa

12.2.6.1 Tense and aspect   Like Gitksan and St'át'imcets, Ktunaxa does not obligatorily distinguish between past and present tense, but obligatorily marks future time reference. As shown in (74a,b), unmarked predicates may not be interpreted as future. Ktunaxa has two prospective aspect markers, *¢xaɬ* and *¢*, which are compatible with modal meanings (see Laturnus 2014 on the difference between them). In order for a predicate to have a future reading, it must be marked with one of them, as shown in (74b).

(74) a. xaqwiɬ-ni ¢an.
    dance-IND John
    'John danced.' / 'John is dancing.' / *'John will dance.'

  b. *(¢xaɬ/ ¢) xaqwiɬ-ni kanmiyit-s ¢an.
    *(PROSP / PROSP) dance-IND tomorrow-OBV John
    'John will dance tomorrow.'

This pattern of temporal interpretation can be accounted for by proposing a phonologically null non-future tense, following Matthewson (2006) for St'át'imcets, and Jóhannsdóttir and Matthewson (2007), Matthewson (2012, 2013) for Gitksan.

12.2.6.2 Temporal perspective given by tense, and availability of Reading C   Ktunaxa lexically distinguishes between epistemic and circumstantial modality. We restrict ourselves here to the unambiguously epistemic modal *ɬin*, and an unambiguously circumstantial modal, *taɬ*, both of which have variable modal force.

As predicted by our null hypothesis, the T.P. of Ktunaxa epistemic modals can be present or past without any overt tense marking; this is shown in (75). Example (75a) has a present T.P., while the TPs in (75b–d) are past. The data in (75b–d) show that Readings C-past, -present, and -future are available in Ktunaxa.

(75) a. **Context:** Mary wasn't looking well yesterday and now she's not in class.
    ɬin saniɬxuʔ-ni maɬi.
    EPIS sick-IND Mary
    'Mary might be sick.'   (PRESENT T.P., PRESENT T.O.)

b. **Context:** My brother blew up a pipe bomb in our mailbox one morning. The neighbour called the cops. Later, my extremely embarrassed mother asked the neighbour why he called the police. He had thought someone had been shot.
qała łin mitx-ił!
someone EPIS shoot-PASS
'Someone might have been shot!' (PAST T.P., PAST T.O.)

c. **Context:** Your neighbour doesn't show up for work and you know there's been a flu going around. You send your son to bring her hot soup. She actually took the day off because her apartment flooded, so she asks why you sent her soup in the middle of the day.
łin hin saniłxuʔ-ni.
EPIS 2 sick-IND
'You might have been sick.' (PAST T.P., PRESENT T.O.)

d. **Context:** Why did you salt the driveway?[9]
łin ma ȼxał wałinkʼałaʔ-ni.
EPIS PFV PROSP snow-IND
'It might have been going to snow.' (PAST T.P., FUTURE T.O.)

Circumstantial modals may also have a present or past T.P., as in (76a,b).

(76) a. hu qa tał ȼinax-i.
      1 NEG CIRC go-IND
      'I can't go out.'   (TFS 2011, "Chore Girl") (PRESENT T.P., PRESENT T.O.)

   b. qa tał kłinqʼuymu-ni watʼqum-s.
      NEG CIRC play-IND   ball-OBV
      'She was not able to play ball.'
                              (TFS 2011, "Sick Girl") (PAST T.P., PRESENT T.O.)

12.2.6.3 Temporal orientation given by aspect and the Diversity Condition Because prospective marking is required whenever the event time follows the reference time in Ktunaxa, we predict it will be necessary under modals when future-oriented. This is true for the epistemic modal *łin*. Without *ȼxał*, (77) is not compatible with a future reading; with it, as in (78), the sentence is not compatible with a non-future reading.

(77) **Context:** You were watching the Canucks but you fell asleep when the game was tied. They might have won (but you're not sure).
łin hukakaʔ-ni (#miksan qa   hukakaʔ-ni).
EPIS win-IND   but   NEG win-IND
'They might have won (#but they didn't).' (PAST T.O.)

---

[9] The perfective marker *ma* is necessary in past-future contexts to mark anteriority.

(78) **Context:** The Canucks are winning by two goals halfway through the third period. Your friend calls to ask how the game's going. You know they could lose their lead and let the other team win.
ɬin ȼxaɬ hukaka?-ni.
EPIS PROSP win-IND
'They might win.' (FUTURE T.O.)

With circumstantial modals, no prospective aspect marking is required to get a future T.O., just like in St'át'imcets, Javanese, and Mandarin; circumstantial modals are inherently future-oriented in Ktunaxa. Unmarked sentences like (79) are compatible with all three temporal perspectives, but in each case the temporal orientation is future. This is a Diversity Condition effect.

(79) taɬ q'umni?-ni ȼan.
CIRC sleep-IND John
'John can sleep.' / 'John was able to sleep.' / 'John will be able to sleep.'

12.2.7 Summary

In this section we have tested a generalized version of Condoravdi's proposals—one which retains her core architecture, but allows for language-specific differences in tense and aspect systems—on seven languages from six families. It is striking that in all these languages, we see evidence for our null hypothesis that the temporal perspective of the modals is given by tense, while the temporal orientation is given by aspect, or at least by some lower-scoping temporal operator.

In each of these seven languages we found support for Condoravdi's Diversity Condition, which restricts the temporal orientation of circumstantial modals to non-past. We saw that languages apply different strategies to enforce Diversity Condition effects. In Gitksan, the inherent future T.O. of circumstantials is obligatorily overtly marked by prospective aspect, while in St'át'imcets, Javanese, Mandarin, and Ktunaxa, the circumstantial modals themselves are inherently future-oriented and thus require no overt marking. Alternatively, non-future temporal orientations can trigger a shift in the modal flavour from circumstantial to epistemic (Dutch, German, and English).[10]

The next section discusses the remaining four languages: Blackfoot, Northern Straits Salish, Halkomelem, and Atayal. We will show how the languages do and do not behave as expected given the null hypothesis.

---

[10] María Luisa Rivero asks (p.c.) whether there is a principled distinction between the languages in which circumstantial modals are inherently future-oriented and those in which additional prospective markers are required. We have to leave this question for future research.

12.3 Languages which only partially obey the null hypothesis

Recall that we departed from Condoravdi in our null hypothesis: we hypothesized that epistemic modals would be able to have past temporal perspectives (C-readings). In support of this, we found C-readings for at least one epistemic modal in seven languages (eight, including English). This section shows that the remaining four languages, Blackfoot, Northern Straits Salish, Halkomelem, and Atayal, all have epistemic modals that lack C-readings, and hence appear to be exceptions to our null hypothesis. However, we argue that this divergence from the null hypothesis actually follows either from a reformulation of the hypothesis that relies on the structural position of the temporal operators in question, as opposed to their categorization as a tense or aspect, or from independently motivated language-specific properties.

12.3.1 Blackfoot

In this section, we show that the Blackfoot (variable-force) epistemic modal *aahkam-* behaves (for the most part) as our null hypothesis predicts—its temporal perspective patterns like tense interpretations in non-modal clauses, and its temporal orientation patterns like aspect in non-modal clauses. We also show that Blackfoot's circumstantial modals *aahkama'p-* 'might' and *ohkott-* 'able to' have temporal perspectives that pattern like tense, and that they display predictable restrictions in temporal orientation, given the Diversity Condition. In section 12.3.1.4 we address the areas where Blackfoot modals deviate from the null hypothesis.

12.3.1.1 Tense and aspect Although Blackfoot lacks overt tense morphemes (Ritter and Wiltschko 2004, 2005, Reis Silva and Matthewson 2007), the temporal interpretation of non-modal Blackfoot claims is semi-predictable given the aspectual properties of the predicate. Reis Silva and Matthewson (2007) observe that stative predicates (or predicates "stativized" by means of an imperfective or perfect) can be interpreted as either past or present, with no additional morphology, but eventive predicates can only be interpreted as past (unless first "stativized" by the aforementioned aspectual morphology).

These generalizations are exemplified by the following data. Example (80a) shows that an aspectually unmarked stative predicate can have either a past or present interpretation; (80b) shows that an aspectually unmarked eventive predicate, in contrast, is only compatible with a past interpretation.

(80) a. Anna mai'stoo-wa *isttso'kini*-wa.
　　　 DEM raven-3PROX *be.hungry*.VAI-3
　　　 'Mai'stoo is hungry.' OR 'Mai'stoo was hungry.'　　　　　　　　　　STATIVE

　　 b. Anna mai'stoo-wa *ihpiyi*-wa.
　　　 DEM raven-3PROX *dance*.VAI-3
　　　 'Mai'stoo danced.' (≠ 'Mai'stoo is dancing.')　　　　　　　　　　　EVENTIVE

TABLE 12.4 Temporal interpretation of Blackfoot non-modal predicates

Temporal interpretation	Eventive predicate		Stative predicate
	PFV	IPFV	
Past	✓	✓	✓
Present	×	✓	✓

Example (81) shows that predicates temporally "stativized" by the imperfective *á-* are compatible with either a past or present interpretation. Past interpretations are generally only accepted, however, if additional context makes such a reading salient. The facts are summarized in Table 12.4.

(81) Anna mai'stoo-wa á-íhpiyi-wa.
      DEM raven-3PROX *IPFV*-dance.VAI-3
      'Mai'stoo is/was dancing.'

Reis Silva and Matthewson (2007), following Dunham (2008), assume that the absence of morphological aspect in Blackfoot non-modal claims is always interpreted as perfective. They also assume, following Bennett and Partee (1978), that (i) eventive predicates are inherently dynamic and (ii) present tense is instantaneous. With these assumptions, they derive the temporal pattern observed above as follows: eventive predicates, being inherently dynamic and involving change, can only hold true of non-instantaneous evaluation times. Under the standard assumption that perfective places the run-time of the event within the evaluation time, a perfective eventive is incompatible with an instantaneous present evaluation time. Thus, perfective eventives like (80b) cannot be interpreted as present. Stative or stativized predicates, on the other hand, can hold true of instantaneous evaluation times, and thus can be interpreted with respect to an instantaneous present evaluation time, or with respect to a (non-instantaneous) past evaluation time. With this analysis, we arrive at the following picture of Blackfoot's tense/aspect inventory:

(82) The Blackfoot tense/aspect inventory (non-modal claims)
      Tenses   Aspects
      $\emptyset_{PRESENT}$ *á-*$_{IPFV}$
      $\emptyset_{PAST}$ *ikaa-* ~ *akaa-*$_{PRF}$
                  $\emptyset_{PFV}$

12.3.1.2 Temporal perspective given by tense, and availability of Reading C In this section, we first discuss the temporal perspective of *aahkam-*, an epistemic modal, and show the availability of a past temporal perspective for this modal (Reading C).

We then discuss the temporal perspective of circumstantial modals (the ability modal *ohkott-* and *aahkama'p-* 'might').

The following data show that the epistemic modal *aahkam-* is compatible with a past temporal perspective. In (83), Tiny's stealing the painting was compatible with the evidence I had available to me yesterday, but is no longer compatible with the current evidence. Thus this must be a past temporal perspective.

(83) Context: Someone stole a famous painting from a museum three days ago. Yesterday I had it narrowed down to three suspects: Blue-eyes, Eagle, and Tiny, and I had them all brought in for questioning. Today, however, I found a blond hair at the scene of the crime, which rules out the dark-haired Tiny as a suspect. When my supervisor reviews the evidence and asks me why I bothered bringing in Tiny for questioning yesterday, I explain: "Yesterday Tiny might have still stolen the painting."

Matónni *aahkam*-ikamo'sat-yii-wa annisk sinááksin.
yesterday EPIS-steal.VTA-3>3'-3 DEM painting
'Yesterday she might have stolen that painting.' (PAST T.P., PAST T.O.)

The context in (84) is similarly one where the prejacent is only compatible with evidence that the speaker had at a previous epistemic state; it is not compatible with the speaker's current epistemic state. On the basis of these data, we conclude that *aahkam-* is compatible with an epistemic past temporal perspective. Note that (84) has a present temporal orientation, while (83) has a past temporal orientation.

(84) Context: Pat asked Stacey to take care of his pet, Fluffy, while he was away. Stacey, being unaware of what kind of pet Fluffy was, bought some dog food. When Pat asks Stacey why she bought dog food for his pet snake, she says:
aahkam-omitaa-wa.
EPIS-be_dog.VAI-3PROX
'He might have been a dog.' (TFS 2012, "Feeding Fluffy")

(PAST T.P., PRESENT T.O.)

The modal *aahkam-* is also compatible with a present temporal perspective, as shown in (85) and (86), which have a past and present temporal orientation respectively.

(85) Context: I'm watching the security feed for the museum, which has a very famous painting on display. At one point, I see a man walk into the screen, then the video security feed goes fuzzy. When the feed comes back on, everything looks to be in place. But later I learn that the man I saw on the video feed is a famous art thief and counterfeit artist. Even though everything looked to be in place when the feed came back on, for all I know, the painting that's there now might be a forgery. Stunned, I realize: "He might have stolen the painting."/ "Maybe he stole the painting."

Oma nínaa *aahkam*-ikamo'sat-yii-wa annisk sinááksin.
DEM man EPIS-steal.VTA-3>3'-3 DEM painting
'That man might have stolen that one painting.' (PRESENT T.P., PAST T.O.)

(86) **Context:** I don't see my dad around anywhere, but I notice his running shoes are missing.
Aahkam-á-ipi-okska'si-wa.
EPIS-IPFV-far-run.VAI-3PROX
'He must be going for a long run.' (PRESENT T.P., PRESENT T.O.)

To summarize, *aahkam*- is compatible with both a past and present temporal perspective. This is what we expect if the temporal perspective is provided by tense.

We now turn to the T.P. of Blackfoot circumstantial modals: the ability modal *ohkott*- and the modal *aahkama'p*- 'might'. These modals are both compatible with either a past or present temporal perspective, but differ in whether the modal requires additional aspectual morphology in order to be interpreted with a present temporal perspective.

Blackfoot's ability modal is, when unmarked by aspectual morphology, interpreted with a past temporal perspective. In order to be interpreted with a present T.P., the ability attribution must first be modified by imperfective aspect. This is shown in (87): (87a) shows that a bare ability modal can only be interpreted with a past T.P., while (87b) shows that an imperfective ability claim is compatible with either past or present T.P.

(87) a. *Ohkott*-ihpiyi-wa.
able-dance.VAI-3
'He was able to dance.'
≠ 'He is able to dance.'

b. *Á-ohkott*-ihpiyi-wa.
IPFV-able-dance.VAI-3
'He was able to dance (when young).'
OR 'He is able to dance.'[11]

The 'might' modal *aahkama'p*-, on the other hand, can be interpreted with either a past or present temporal perspective, with no additional aspectual morphology. This is shown in (88), and the overall results are summarized in Table 12.5.

---

[11] In the absence of overt temporal adverbials or specific context, the interpretation of an imperfective-marked ability modal, like imperfective-marked non-modal predicates, is present. The range of contexts in which an imperfective-marked ability modal with a present interpretation is accepted as felicitous, however, is narrow, as Blackfoot's imperfective is always interpreted with either an event-in-progress or habitual reading. The present-interpreted imperfective ability attribution thus requires a context where the prejacent event is already in progress, or a context where the prejacent event is habitually achieved. The more general contexts in which we would assert "He can P"—i.e. cases where "If he chooses to P, he will achieve P"—are conveyed with a future-marked ability attribution.

TABLE 12.5 Range of temporal perspectives for Blackfoot circumstantial modals

Temporal interpretation	ohkott-'can/able' PFV	ohkott-'can/able' IPFV	aahkama'p-'might'
Past perspective	✓	✓	✓
Present perspective	×	✓	✓

(88) a. **Context:** My neighbour was born with heart problems, and her mother worries about her over-exerting herself. Tomorrow is her prom, and her mom is really worried.
Aahkama'p-iik-sska-ihpiyi.
might-INTS-INTS-dance.VAI
'She *might* dance a lot.' (PRESENT T.P., FUTURE T.O.)

b. **Context:** Martina's hockey team was down a player, and they tried to get Heather as a ringer, but Heather couldn't play, and they lost.
Anna Heather waawahkaa-ohtopi aahkama'p-omo'tsaaki-yaawa
DEM Heather play.VAI-UNR *might*-win.VAI-3PL
'If Heather had played, they *might have* won.' (PAST T.P., FUTURE T.O.)

The pattern of temporal perspective represented in Table 12.5 directly parallels the pattern of tense interpretations for non-modal claims in Table 12.4. This suggests that the temporal perspective of circumstantial modal claims is determined by tense: the modal claim can combine with either the null present, or the null past, if the modal is stative-like (*aahkama'p*-), or stativized by the imperfective. These modals can thus be interpreted with either past or present TPs. If the modal is perfective and eventive-like (*ohkott*-), however, it can only combine with the null past, and thus can only be interpreted with a past temporal perspective. Louie (2015) proposes that the eventive nature of Blackfoot's ability modal is derived from a lexically encoded agentivity requirement on its prejacent.[12]

12.3.1.3 *Temporal orientation given by aspect and the Diversity Condition* The temporal orientation of Blackfoot circumstantial modals can be analyzed according to our null hypothesis, whereby T.O. is given by a lower-scoping temporal operator like aspect, modulo the Diversity Condition. Blackfoot *ohkott*- 'able to' claims, with their

---

[12] The reader may note that the examples in (88a) and (88b) are not minimal pairs; this is because without a conditional antecedent, the modal *aahkama'p*- cannot be interpreted with a past temporal perspective. This contrasts with Blackfoot's ability modal, which can be past-shifted via context and overt temporal adverbials. At this point, the authors are hesitant to hypothesize as to why this is the case.

default temporal perspective (past), can only take aspectually bare eventive complements, and these are always interpreted with a perfective/past temporal orientation.[13] This is exactly what we expect given the aspectual system discussed above; the absence of overt aspect with bare eventives is interpreted as perfective.

Blackfoot *aahkama'p-*, on the other hand, takes the instantaneous present as its default temporal perspective. We thus expect that this modal is incompatible with a perfective/past temporal orientation, which appears to be the case: bare eventive complements to *aahkama'p-* are always interpreted with future T.O., which Louie (2013) argues is provided by a null prospective aspect. When *aahkama'p-* takes stative (or stativized) prejacents, however, it is interpreted with present temporal orientation. This is shown in (89); (89a) has a lexical stative prejacent, and (89b,c) have eventive prejacents stativized by the imperfective and perfect respectively. These examples can be analyzed as epistemic, as they appear to express what is possible given the speaker's evidence; i.e. the observation that saskatoon berries are normally ripe at this time in (89a), the low rumbling sounds in (89b), and the closed eyes in (89c).[14]

(89) a. **Context:** Saskatoon berries are usually ripe this time of year, but it's been irregularly cold.
   Aahkama'p-i'tsii-yi-aawa.
   might-be_ripe.VII-3PL-DTP
   'They (saskatoon berries) might be ripe.'   (PRESENT T.P., PRESENT T.O.)

   b. **Context:** After a long shift at the hospital, my sister often falls asleep sitting up while watching TV. Right now she's sitting on the sofa, and I think I hear some low, rumbling sounds coming from her.
   Aahkama'p-á-sohk-aanistsii-wa
   might-IPFV-loud-do_sthing.VAI-3
   'She might be snoring.'   (PRESENT T.P., PRESENT T.O.)

---

[13] We use the term "perfective/past temporal orientation" instead of "past temporal orientation" for Blackfoot, to indicate that the run-time of the event is contained within the past interval taken as the modal evaluation time, rather than preceding the modal evaluation time (cf. Louie 2013).

[14] We must point out, however, that with a present temporal perspective, circumstantial and epistemic readings are empirically impossible to distinguish. Without hindsight to distinguish between a speaker's evidence regarding a state of affairs at *t* and the actual circumstances of that state of affairs at *t*, from that speaker's perspective, epistemic and circumstantial modal bases are identical. Thus while (89) could be interpreted as an epistemic claim, it could equally be interpreted as a circumstantial claim. Nevertheless, *aahkama'p-* provides the closest candidate to an existential epistemic modal in Blackfoot, and even with an alternative analysis whereby *aahkama'p-* yields solely circumstantial claims, it does not pose a problem for the main claim of this chapter: the data in (88) show that its temporal perspective behaves as if dictated by tense, and the data forthcoming in (90,91) are no longer problematic—as a dedicated circumstantial modal, we would not expect *aahkama'p* to have a Reading C interpretation.

c. **Context:** After a long shift at the hospital, my sister often falls asleep sitting up while watching TV. Her eyes are closed, and she might just be resting them, but I doubt it.
Aahkama'p-ikaa-yo'kaa-n-opii-wa
might-PRF-sleep.VAI-?-sit.VAI-3
'She might have already fallen asleep sitting up.' (PRESENT T.P., PRESENT T.O.)

The modal *aahkama'p-* thus appears to be compatible with either circumstantial or epistemic interpretations, but the various readings are temporally/aspectually conditioned: future orientations, which arise with eventive prejacents, are interpreted as circumstantial, and present orientations, which arise with stative prejacents, are interpreted as epistemic.[15] This is in accord with the predictions of the Diversity Condition, and parallels what we observed in section 12.2 with Dutch *kunnen* and German *können*.

12.3.1.4 Areas where Blackfoot deviates from the null hypothesis The temporal orientation of *aahkam-* does not behave exactly as expected given our null hypothesis. Recall that while statives in Blackfoot are compatible with evaluation times that are either instants (like the present) or intervals (like the past), eventives are only compatible with the latter. If temporal orientation is given by aspect, we predict that stative prejacents should be interpreted with a present/coinciding temporal orientation, whether the modal claim has an instantaneous/present T.P. or an interval/past T.P. This is exactly what we saw in (86) and (84) respectively. We also predict, however, that eventive prejacents with a present temporal perspective should either (i) like non-modal eventives, be interpreted as perfective and thus be impossible (as eventive perfectives and the present are incompatible in Blackfoot), or (ii) like with *áak* and *aahkama'p-*, be interpreted with a null prospective aspect and thus receive a prospective T.O. This is not the case. As shown in (83) and (85), eventives receive a past temporal orientation whether the temporal perspective is an instant (present) or interval (past). Louie (2015) proposes that Blackfoot epistemic modals are uniformly interpreted with a past-extended interval as their temporal perspective, where tense, rather than giving the temporal perspective, gives the rightmost-bound of this past-extended interval. This modification allows the data in (83) and (85) to be analyzed with perfective/past temporal orientation, where the run-time of the event is contained within the (past-extended) temporal perspective time, as predicted by our null hypothesis.

Another area where Blackfoot modals behave in ways unexpected given our null hypothesis is that the epistemic readings of *aahkama'p-* cannot take past temporal

---

[15] Given the obvious morphological similarity between *aahkam-* and *aahkama'p-*, the reader may wonder whether a derivational relationship between these two morphemes is possible. But given differences in their temporal behaviour, range of modal flavour, and uncertainty regarding the meaning of the morpheme *a'p-* (glossed as "about" in Frantz and Russell 1995), we are not in a position to propose such a relationship at this time.

perspectives, in contrast to *aahkam-* as discussed above. In other words, *aahkama'p-* fails to display Reading C. The following data show that *aahkama'p-* is infelicitous in contexts where the prejacent is only compatible with a previous epistemic state, but not the current epistemic state.[16]

(90) **Context:** The weather seems like it's been normal, and the U-Pick Berry Farms opened last week. I figure the berries must be ripe, so I plan a trip. When we get there, though, none of the berries are ripe. Afterwards, I shrug and say: "They're not ripe yet, but they might have been ripe."

Máát-omaa-i'tsii-waistaa ki *aahkama'p*-ikaa-i'tsii-yi-aawa.
NEG-YET-ripe.VII-NONAFF.PL.INAN CONJ might-PRF-ripe.VII-3PL-DTP

'They're not ripe yet, but they might have been ripe.' (PAST T.P., PRESENT T.O.)

Consultant: "You can't put those together—when you say *aahkama'pikai'tsiiyaa*, you don't know if they're ripe or not, you're just guessing."

(91) **Context:** Pat asked Stacey to take care of his pet, Fluffy, while he was away. Stacey, being unaware of what kind of pet Fluffy was, bought some dog food. When Pat asks Stacey why she bought dog food for his pet snake, she says:

Aahkama'p-omitaa-wa.
might-be_dog.VAI-3

'He might have been a dog.'

(TFS 2012, "Feeding Fluffy") (PAST T.P., PRESENT T.O.)

Consultant: "Not a clear sentence. Mind-boggling."

In order to use *aahkama'p-* with this interpretation, the modal claim must be embedded under an attitude predicate like *nisóóksst* 'I thought/used to think'—this is shown in (92).

(92) **Context:** We live in Richmond, where the largest percentage of the inhabitants are Chinese. My mom sees someone who looks Chinese, and asks her directions in Cantonese. The person turns out to be Korean, though. My mom is a bit embarrassed, but she says:

a. #Máát-wapatamsstsinimaa-waatsiksi ki
NEG-be_chinese.VAI-NONAFF.SG CONJ
Aahkama'p-wapatamsstsinimaa-wa.
might-be_chinese.VAI-3

'She's not Chinese, but she might have been Chinese.'

Consultant: "You're saying two things at once."

---

[16] Recall that *aahkama'p-* can only receive epistemic-like readings with stative or stativized prejacents. The previous data in (88) thus does not constitute an epistemic reading with a past T.P.

b. Ni-sook-sstaa   aahkama'p-wapatamsstsinimaa-wa ki
      1-used_to-think.VAI might-be_chinese.VAI-3   CONJ
      máát-wapatamsstsinimaa-waatsiksi.
      NEG-be_chinese.VAI-NONAFF.SG
      'I thought she might be Chinese, but she's not Chinese.'

This shows that while *aahkama'p-* is compatible with a past temporal perspective, this is only so for its metaphysical/counterfactual readings; when interpreted epistemically, it is restricted to a present temporal perspective. We return to possible reasons for this absence of Reading C in section 12.4.

12.3.2 SENĆOŦEN and Hul'q'umi'num'

In this section, we show that SENĆOŦEN and Hul'q'umi'num' partially fit the null hypothesis. Several lexical items of various syntactic types can be analyzed as modals in the two languages, as shown in descriptive works (including Montler 1986, Galloway 1993, Suttles 2004) and one semantic categorization in terms of modal type (Jelinek 1987). However, only one circumstantial modal and one epistemic modal have been studied in depth semantically (Turner 2013), and these are the only two considered in this chapter. We start with a discussion of tense and aspect in the two languages.

12.3.2.1 *Tense and aspect*
Tense in SENĆOŦEN and Hul'q'umi'num' is encoded by two second position clitics: *ləʔ/əɬ* indicates that the reference time is prior to the utterance time (93), while *səʔ/ceʔ* indicates that the reference time is subsequent to the utterance time (94).[17] We leave aside a modal analysis of the future here, and instead treat the future as comparable to the past tense. The data in this subsection come from SENĆOŦEN.

(93) **Context:** You see that the ground is wet, so you know that it was raining this morning.
    O ȽEMEW̱ LO.
    ʔa ɬəməxʷ=ləʔ.
    oh rain=PST
    'Oh, it rained some.'

(94) **Context:** You go outside and you see the raindrops just starting to fall.
    O ȽEMEW̱ SE.
    ʔa ɬəməxʷ=səʔ
    oh rain=FUT
    'Oh, it's going to rain.'

---

[17] The Halkomelem past tense marker is sometimes treated as a suffix. Suttles (2004: 368) notes that it behaves phonologically like a suffix and grammatically like a particle and includes it in a list of second-position particles. It is treated as a second-position clitic here, like the SENĆOŦEN cognate.

There is no morphological present tense, but in order to indicate that the reference time and utterance time overlap, the clause is uttered with no overt tense marker.

(95) ŁEM,W̱ TŦE SAKEŁ.
ɬəm̓xʷ tθə sɛqəɬ.
rain[IPFV] GNRL.DET outside
'It's raining outside.'

In SENĆOŦEN, clauses without a tense clitic can also be interpreted with past or future reference times, particularly when it is clear from adverbials or the discourse context (Montler 1986, Turner 2011).

(96) N̲EN ŁEMEW̱ E TŦE PEXSISEN̲.
ŋən ɬəməxʷ ʔə tθə pəx̌sisəŋ.
much rain OBL GNRL.DET spring
'It rained a lot in the spring.'

(97) TU ŁĆIU,S SEN *(SE)* ĆEĆÁĆELES.
tuʔ ɬčiw̓s=sən*(=səʔ)* kʷəkʷečələs.
a.bit tired[IPFV]=1SG.SBJ*(=FUT)* tomorrow
'I'll still be tired tomorrow.'

In Hul'q'umi'num' too, sentences with no past clitic can be interpreted as past (Suttles 2004: 508). This is also true for the future clitic in at least some contexts. In the literature on Halkomelem, Suttles (2004: 508, Musqueam dialect) states that the future marker "may be" obligatory, while Wiltschko (2003: 687, Upriver dialect) states that it is optional.

Other factors also affect temporal interpretation, such as predicate type in SENĆOŦEN (Kiyota 2008, Turner 2011) and locative auxiliaries in Hul'q'umi'num' (Suttles 2004: 36), but neither of these obligatorily restricts reference time. Thus, SENĆOŦEN and Hul'q'umi'num' exhibit superficial tenselessness, since past, present, or future reference times are all available without overt tense.

SENĆOŦEN contains two contrasting viewpoint aspects: perfective and imperfective (Kiyota 2008, Turner 2011). We assume that the semantics of aspect is the same in Hul'q'umi'num', since the behaviour of the two aspects in both languages appears to be identical. Perfective aspect is shown in examples (93), (94), and (96). Imperfective is shown in (95) and (97). In the glosses, verbs not glossed as imperfective (IPFV) are in the perfective aspect.

In addition, Kiyota (2008) has proposed that there is a perfect in SENĆOŦEN, indicated by the particle $k^w\mathit{ɬ}$. Kiyota shows that the range of readings associated with $k^w\mathit{ɬ}$ largely overlap those of the English perfect. The cognate in Hul'q'umi'num' is $k^w\mathit{ɬ}$ and appears to behave similarly. In some of the other languages discussed in this chapter, perfect or its future counterpart, prospective, provide temporal orientation in modal sentences. This is not the case in SENĆOŦEN and Hul'q'umi'num', where both T.P. and T.O. are provided by tense, except in the case of circumstantial modals, which have inherent future temporal orientation.

12.3.2.2 Temporal perspective is partially provided by tense SENĆOŦEN and Hul'q'umi'num' lexically distinguish circumstantial from epistemic modality; only one circumstantial modal and one epistemic modal are discussed here. The two languages partially fit the first part of our null hypothesis, since temporal perspective is provided by tense for the (variable-force) circumstantial modal x̌ʷəŋ/x̌ʷəm. Tense does not provide temporal perspective for the epistemic modal ʔiʔwawə/wəẃaʔ; this will be discussed in section 12.3.2.4.

Examples (98,99) show that when the circumstantial modal appears with tense clitics, the clitics provide temporal perspective.

(98) Hul'q'umi'num'
Context: A mother and child went and looked at some scenery next to a fence on the edge of a cliff. When they got back in the car, the mother said:
ʔəẏ   kʷə=ṅ=s   ʔəwə niʔ-əxʷ   k̇ʷiʔ ʔə   tᶿə
good DET=2SG.POSS=NMLZ NEG AUX-2SG.SUB.SBJ climb OBL GNRL.DET
q̇əlex̌əctən x̌ʷəm=əł=č   ʔiʔ hiləm.
fence   CIRC=PST=2SG.SBJ COM fall
'It's good that you didn't climb onto the fence, because you would have/might have fallen.'   (PAST T.P.)

(99) SENĆOŦEN
Context: Right now I can't walk, but the doctor says that next month I'll be able to.
AXEN   TŦE   doctor   ĆS   XEN SEN ŚE   STEN.
ʔex̌əŋ tθə   doctor   kʷ=s   x̌ʷəŋ=sən=səʔ   štəŋ.
say   GNRL.DET doctor DET=NMLZ CIRC=1SG.SBJ=FUT   walk
'The doctor said I will be able to walk.'   (FUTURE T.P.)

As predicted by the fact that overt tense marking is optional, circumstantial clauses with no overt tense can have future temporal perspective. In (100), the future clitic səʔ is optional.

(100) SENĆOŦEN
AXEN   TŦE   doctor ĆS   XEN SEN (SE)   ŚTEN
ʔex̌əŋ tθə   doctor kʷ=s   x̌ʷəŋ=sən(=səʔ)   štəŋ
say   GNRL.DET doctor DET=NMLZ   CIRC=1SG.SBJ(=FUT) walk
EĆS   YE,Á,WE   ŁḰÁLĆ.
ʔə=kʷ=s   yəʔewə   łqelč.
OBL=DET=NMLZ coming   moon
'The doctor said I will be able to walk in the next month.'   (FUTURE T.P.)

In (99,100), x̌ʷəm gets an ability reading and has future temporal perspective, since the time that the modal base will be evaluated is in the future. The speaker claims that in the future certain circumstances (she has her cast off, and her leg is healed) will allow for the possibility of walking. It is not always possible to distinguish between present and future T.P., but here the context makes it clear that the speaker does not have the ability to walk in the present. We assume that the temporal orientation is also future, as with circumstantial modals generally. Thus, it may appear possible that the future clitic in (99,100) is indicating future temporal orientation, not perspective. However, that cannot be the case, since the future clitic is infelicitous when the temporal perspective is non-future:

(101) SENĆOŦEN
X̱EN SEN SE I ŚTEṈ.
x̌ʷəŋ=sən=səʔ ʔiʔ štəŋ.
CIRC=1SG.SBJ=FUT COM walk
'I will be able to walk.' / # 'I can walk.'

Overt past tense is required to get past temporal perspective for all examples tested, as shown in (102), which cannot have past T.P.

(102) SENĆOŦEN
X̱EN I ȾWENEḴ.
x̌ʷəŋ ʔiʔ ƛ̓xʷənəq.
CIRC COM win
'They could win.' / # 'They could have won.' (PRESENT T.P. ONLY)

This may be due to the fact that all of these examples are counterfactual; further research is required to determine whether past tense is required for past T.P. in non-counterfactual circumstantial sentences.

12.3.2.3 *Temporal orientation of circumstantials* With respect to the temporal orientation of circumstantial modals, SENĆOŦEN and Hul'q'umi'num' behave like several other languages in that there is no separate marker of temporal orientation. Temporal orientation is always future, yet no marker of futurity is used in circumstantial clauses. This is a systematic Diversity Condition effect: circumstantial modals seem to be inherently future-oriented. This matches the strategy we saw in section 12.2 for St'át'imcets, Mandarin, and Ktunaxa.

(103) Hul'q'umi'num'
m̓i nəw̓-əš tᶿə pipə, x̌ʷəm ʔiʔ ɬəməxʷ ʔə tən̓a snet.
come go.in-TR DET paper CIRC COM rain OBL PROX.DEM night
'Bring the paper in, because it might rain tonight.'

12.3.2.4 *Areas where SENĆOŦEN and Hul'q'umi'num' modals do not fit the null hypothesis* There are three ways in which SENĆOŦEN and Hul'q'umi'num' do not fit the null hypothesis. First, unlike with the circumstantial modal, tense does not provide temporal perspective in clauses with the epistemic modal *ʔiʔwawə/wəẃaʔ*. Second (relatedly), Reading C is not available. And third, temporal orientation in epistemic clauses is not provided by aspect. Each of these properties is discussed here. We will argue that they all result from the fact that the epistemic modal *ʔiʔwawə/wəẃaʔ* always scopes higher than tense; i.e. there is no tense node above the modal.

First, SENĆOŦEN and Hul'q'umi'num' appear not to allow a past temporal perspective (Reading C) for epistemic modals. Instead, the epistemic modal always has a present temporal perspective. In Reading C contexts, speakers of both languages either give a non-modal sentence or embed the epistemic modal under an attitude predicate like *think*. This is shown here for past, present and future temporal orientations. (104) is a variation on von Fintel and Gillies' (2008: 81) ice-cream example from (4) above. For Hul'q'umi'num', this context prompted the use of the attitude verb *š'te:wəṅ* 'think.' The epistemic modal can but need not be used; if it is used it is embedded under this attitude verb.

(104) Hul'q'umi'num'
 Context: I can't find my keys and start looking around, including looking in the fridge. You ask me why I looked in the fridge. I reply:
 ʔi=cən š'te:wəṅ wəẃaʔ niʔ=cən   ʔiʔet̓ nəẃ-əš ʔə
 AUX=1SG.SBJ *think* EPIS AUX=1SG.SBJ expected go.in-TR OBL
 t^θə   šx̌ey̓ƛə̓ls.
 GNRL.DET fridge
 'I thought I may have put it in the fridge.'
                               (based on von Fintel and Gillies 2008: 81)

An attempted Reading C with present orientation is given in (105). If the speaker already knows that Fluffy is a snake, then the modal must be embedded under *š'te:wəṅ* 'think' (or the SENĆOŦEN equivalent).

(105) Hul'q'umi'num'
 Context: You bought a bone for your friend's pet snake, Fluffy, and he asks you why.
 ʔi=cən   š'te:wəṅ wəẃaʔ ṗeʔ sqʷəmey kʷθə   Fluffy ʔəwəteʔ
 AUX=1SG.SBJ *think* EPIS indeed dog REM.DET Fluffy not.any
 nə   š-ta~təl̓-stəxʷ   ʔəw' stem̓-əs   kʷθə   Fluffy.
 1SG.POSS NMLZ-IPFV~know-CAUS CONTR what-3SUB.SBJ REM.DET Fluffy
 'I thought that maybe Fluffy is a dog. I don't know what Fluffy is.'
                                    (TFS 2012, "Feeding Fluffy")

The attitude verb is interpreted with a past perspective in (104,105); the speaker's belief that the keys were in the fridge or that Fluffy was a dog is in the past. However, note that the past tense does not occur in the matrix clause containing the attitude verb. It is possible to use the optional past tense marker, as shown by (106), though this has not been extensively tested.[18]

(106) Hul'q'umi'num'
niɬ   kʷθə Oliver ni? kʷən-ət ɬaña sləpəs. ʔi:ɬ=cən
3EMPH DET Oliver AUX take-C.TR dem slippers AUX:PST=1SG.SBJ
šte:wəṅ kʷ=s   niɬ=s   kʷθə nəċa? sqʷəmeẏ ni? kʷən-ət
think   DET=NMLZ 3EMPH=NMLZ DET one   dog   AUX take-C.TR
ɬaña sləpəs   ʔəwə niɬ-əs   kʷθə Oliver.
DEM slippers. NEG 3EMPH-NEG DET Oliver
'It was Oliver that took my slippers. I thought that it may have been the other dog that took them, not Oliver.'

A sentence where the modal is not embedded, as in (107), is only compatible with a context where the friend still does not know what kind of animal Fluffy is.

(107) Hul'q'umi'num'
Context: You don't know what kind of animal your friend's pet is.
wəẁa? sqʷəməẏ kʷθə   Fluffy. ʔəwəteʔ nə
EPIS   dog   REM.DET Fluffy not.any 1SG.POSS
š-ta~təl̕-stəxʷ   ʔəw' stem-əs.
NMLZ-IPFV~know-CAUS CONTR what-3SUB.SBJ
'Maybe Fluffy is a dog. I don't know what he is.'   (TFS 2012, "Feeding Fluffy")

A Reading C context with future temporal orientation is given in (108); this morning it was an epistemic possibility that it would rain later in the day, based on the speaker's observation of clouds in the sky. Again, an attitude predicate is used: x̌ʷənəkʷen 'think.'

(108) SENĆOŦEN
QENNEW̱ SEN   TŦE   SNOUES   E   TI,Á   ĆEĆIL
k'ʷən-nəxʷ=sən tθə   snawəs   ʔə   tiʔə   kʷəčil
see-NC.TR=1SG.SBJ GNRL.DET clouds   OBL   PROX.DEM morning
X̱ENEĆÁN SEN ȽEMEW̱ SE ĆIL   TŦE   SḰEḰEL I   EWENE
x̌ʷənəkʷen=sən ɬəməxʷ=səʔ kʷil tθə   sqʷəqʷəl ʔi? ʔəwənə
think=1SG.SBJ rain=FUT   appear GNRL.DET sun   COM not.any
SȽEMEW̱.
s-ɬəməxʷ.
NMLZ-rain
'This morning I saw some clouds and I thought it was going to rain. Then the sun came out and it didn't rain.'

---

[18] The past tense appears on the auxiliary ʔi, rather than the verb. This is due to a syntactic property of tense in both Halkomelem and Northern Straits, which always appears on the clause-initial auxiliary, if there is one.

When tense appears in clauses containing the epistemic modal ʔiʔwawə/wəẃaʔ, it does not indicate temporal perspective. Since Reading C is unavailable, the temporal perspective is always the utterance time, or the reference time associated with an attitude predicate in a higher clause. The tense clitics instead appear—unexpectedly— to indicate temporal *orientation* when they co-occur with the epistemic modal ʔiʔwawə/wəẃaʔ. Example (109) illustrates this with past T.O., and (110) is an example with future T.O.

(109) Hul'q'umi'num'
Context: When you go out to the field, take a blanket to spread...
wəẃaʔ ʔi:ɬ   ɬəm̓əxʷ ʔə kʷəṅa   netəɬ,   ʔi=ćtwaʔ ɬəqʷ
EPIS   AUX:PST rain[IPFV] OBL REM.DEM morning AUX=EVID wet
tᶿə   saxʷəl.
GNRL.DET   grass
'... it may have been raining earlier, and the grass might be wet.'

(110) SENĆOŦEN
Context: We look outside and there are lots of dark clouds.
I WOWE JÁN SE   U   ĆEK ŁEMEW ENÁ,E.
ʔiʔwawə ćen=səʔ ʔuʔ   čəq ɬəməxʷ ʔənə<ʔə>.
EPIS   really=FUT CONTR big   rain   come<IPFV>
'A really big rainfall must be coming here.'

Both of these examples contain overt tense clitics. However, since overt tense is optional in SENĆOŦEN and Hul'q'umi'num', epistemic clauses with no overt tense clitic can also have past (111) or future (112) temporal orientation, in addition to present orientation.

(111) SENĆOŦEN
Context: I left a bowl of cherries on the table and when I got back the bowl was empty.
I WOWE NIŁ ŦE   Claire NOT   TŦE   cherries.
ʔiʔwawə niɬ θə   Claire ŋa-t tθə   cherries.
EPIS   3PRED F.DET Claire eat-C.TR GNRL.DET cherries
'Maybe it was Claire that ate the cherries.'

(112) Hul'q'umínum'
ʔəy̓   kʷə=ṅ=s   ʔiləqəls ʔə kʷθə   x̌əɬə-st-əm̓
good DET=2SG.POSS=NMLZ buy   OBL REM.DET say[IPFV]-CAUS-PASS
lottery tickets, wəẃaʔ λ̓xʷənəq=č
lottery.tickets EPIS   win=2SG.SBJ
'You better buy some lottery tickets. You might win.'

We have shown that tense indicates temporal orientation in SENĆOŦEN and Hul'q'umi'num' modal claims containing ʔiʔwawə/wəẃaʔ. This appears to go against our null hypothesis that temporal orientation is determined by aspect. However, it does not actually go against the spirit of our analysis, which states that the reason temporal orientation is normally determined by aspect is that aspect is a lower temporal operator, scoping under the modal. This will be discussed in section 12.4.

12.3.3 Atayal

Atayal has several modals, all of which lexically distinguish between modality type and quantificational strength. This section shows that the circumstantial possibility modal *blaq* fits our null hypothesis: its temporal perspective is provided by tense, and its temporal orientation is provided by aspect, with the restriction that past T.O. is not possible, following Condoravdi's (2002) Diversity Condition. In addition, Atayal has circumstantial modals specialized for deontic and ability readings, both of which behave like *blaq* except that ability modals can be marked with overt aspect, yielding predictable aspectual interpretations; see Chen (in prep.) for details. The epistemic modals in Atayal, however, use different strategies for T.P. and T.O.; this will be addressed in 12.3.3.4.

12.3.3.1 Tense and aspect   Like many other Formosan languages, Atayal exhibits a grammatical distinction between future and non-future (Zeitoun et al. 1996). Future is obligatorily indicated either by the prefix *p-* in active voice, by reduplication of the first consonant of the verb stem in non-active voice, or by means of an auxiliary *musa'*. Examples (113) and (114) illustrate the morphological strategies and the auxiliary *musa'* respectively.

(113) a. *(p-)qwalax.   ACTOR VOICE
         *(PROSP.AV-)rain
         'It will rain.'

     b. *(t-)thaygal-an   ni   Tali' laqi' qasa.   NON-ACTOR VOICE
        *(PROSP-)bully-LV ERG   Tali' child that
        'Tali' will bully that child.'

(114) a. *(musa') m-qwalax.   ACTOR VOICE
         *(PROSP) AV-rain
         'It will rain.'

     b. *(musa') thaygal-an ni Tali' laqi' qasa.   NON-ACTOR VOICE
        *(PROSP) bully-LV   ERG Tali' child that
        'Tali' will bully that child.'

Non-future tense distinctions are not overtly marked on the verb but partially depend on the viewpoint aspect. Imperfective aspect is aspectually unmarked: a stative can have a past or present interpretation, as shown in (115), and an eventive can have a past or present (non-progressive) episodic interpretation, as shown in (116).[19] A progressive reading uses an additional marker *cyux/nyux*, with different forms indicating spatial deixis, which can be interpreted as either past or present as well, as shown in (117).

(115) m'uy=saku' la. STATIVE
       tired=1S.ABS PART
       'I am tired.' / 'I was tired.'

(116) m-nbuw Tali'. EVENTIVE
       AV-drink Tali'
       'Tali' is drinking.' / 'Tali' drank.'

(117) *nyuw/cyuw*   m-nbuw Tali'.
       PROG.PROX/PROG.DIST AV-drink Tali'
       'Tali' is drinking (here/over there).' / 'Tali' was drinking (here/over there).'

Perfective aspect is overtly marked with *wal/wayal*, and perfective marked predicates are only compatible with a past interpretation, as shown in (118). There is also a dedicated marker *-in-/-n-* for experiential perfect, as shown in (119a), and for anteriority of an adverbial event, as in (119b).

(118) *wal* niq-un ni Tali' qulih qasa.
       PFV eat-PV ERG Tali' fish that
       'Tali' ate that fish.' / ≠ 'Tali' is eating that fish.'

(119) a. q<m><n>alup   mit sraral hiya'.
          hunt<AV><PRF> goat before 3S.ABS
          'He has hunted goats before.'
       b. m-<*in*>aniq=saku' kira'   lga,   p-tzyuwaw=saku'   la.
          AV-<PRF>eat=1S.ABS today.later PART.TOP PROSP.AV-work=1S.ABS PART
          'After I eat, I will work.'

We assume that Atayal possesses a phonologically null non-future tense morpheme, which can contribute either a past or present reference time, and we leave the question open whether the perfective aspect *wal/wayal* lexically encodes pastness or whether the pastness is attributed to a finer tense distinction. This covert tense can combine with prospective aspect to give a future reading. The prospective is an aspect marker

---

[19] Zeitoun et al. (1996) claim that the unmarked eventives in Squliq (Wulai variant) can have a present progressive reading. The progressive reading is, however, absent for the speakers consulted in this chapter. The unmarked form instead allows a past/present unbounded, rather than progressive, interpretation with an accomplishment or activity predicate.

rather than a tense, as it can order the event time after a present reference time, as shown in (113–114), or a past reference time, as in (120).

(120) baq-un=nya'   mha   *musa'* h<m>swa'   m-qyanux m-aki' qsahuy
      know-PV=3S.ERG COMP PROSP   how<AV>   AV-live   AV-be   inner
      na   hlahuy.
      GEN   forest
      'He knew how he would live inside the forest.'

      (Yuqih and Yupas 1991: 53, cited by Huang 2008: 30)

12.3.3.2 Temporal perspective is given by tense with circumstantial modals   In this section we focus on the circumstantial possibility modal *blaq*. This modal is usually interpreted with a present temporal perspective. For example, (121) talks about the possibility of staying here, based on relevant facts which hold at the utterance time.

(121) **Context:** You visit your friend and talk to the extent that you forget the time. Your friend offers:
      blaq   m-'abi=su'   sqa.
      CIRC.POS   AV-sleep=2S.ABS here
      'You can stay here (if you like).'

The modal *blaq* is also compatible with a past temporal perspective. In (122), the context describes what might have happened (and actually happened), given the relevant facts at some time in the past; present T.P. is not available since the speaker is no longer allowed to take the road.

(122) **Context:** You are driving to the road that you usually take but a policeman prevents you from taking the same road today.
      blaq   wah-an sa   wayal hrwa, swa' ini' baq-i
      CIRC.POS   go-LV LOC past PART   why   NEG   able-NEG
      m-usa'=misu   qa   la?
      AV-go=1S.ERG.2S.ABS   here PART
      'I could go this way before! Why can't you let me go now?'

The data in (121–122) show that, in the absence of overt marking, *blaq* is ambiguous between a present and past temporal perspective. In analogy to the present/past ambiguity of an aspectually unmarked predicate in Atayal, this is what we expect if tense provides the temporal perspective of *blaq*.

Future T.P. is overtly marked by the prospective *musa'* above the modal. Example (123) shows that *musa'* is obligatorily required when there is no possibility at the utterance time of a future event but it will become a possibility at some future time. Note that *blaq* cannot co-occur with the other overt aspects; both progressive and perfective markers are incompatible with *blaq*.

(123) **Context:** Although you don't have money, you will get a job soon, and then you will have money.
*(*musa'*) blaq m-bazi=su' sa ana nanu sawyan=su'.
*(PROSP) CIRC.POS AV-buy=2S.ABS LOC even what like-LV=1S.ERG
'You will be able to buy whatever you like (if you have a job).'

To summarize, the modal *blaq* is compatible with both a past and present temporal perspective without overt marking, and with future temporal perspective with the prospective *musa'*. This is what we expect if the temporal perspective of *blaq* is provided by tense.

12.3.3.3 Temporal orientation given by the Diversity Condition The temporal orientation of the circumstantial modal *blaq* displays a Diversity Condition effect: it is always future-oriented. Moreover, as shown in (124–125), future temporal orientation for *blaq* does not permit overt marking of futurity: neither the auxiliary *musa'* nor a morphological prospective aspect is allowed. This is a similar effect to that seen with SENĆOŦEN/Hul'q'umi'num' above, and with St'át'imcets and Mandarin in section 12.2.

(124) **Context:** Your children ask your permission to go out. You say:
aw, blaq {m-usa'/**m-awsa'*}=simu g<m>naw.
yes, CIRC.POS {AV-go/*AV-go.PROSP}=2PL.ABS play<AV>
'Sure, you can go to play.'

(125) **Context:** Given that you want to be thinner, . . .
blaq (**musa'*) spng-un cikay qa-qaniq.
CIRC.POS (*PROSP) control-PV a.bit NMLZ-eat
'You can control your food.'

12.3.3.4 Areas where Atayal modals do not fit the null hypothesis When we turn to Atayal epistemic modals, we see a departure from our null hypothesis. In this section, we show that the epistemic possibility modal *ki'a* behaves differently from circumstantial possibility modals in the language with respect to T.P. and T.O., and shows similarity to the SENĆOŦEN/Hul'q'umi'num' data. It is the temporal orientation, rather than the temporal perspective, of *ki'a* which patterns in a parallel fashion to temporal reference in non-modal claims. The temporal perspective appears to be always present (that is, C-readings do not exist).

Given our null hypothesis that tense provides the temporal perspective of modals, and the fact that tense in Atayal displays a future vs. non-future distinction, as discussed in section 12.3.3.1, we expect that the epistemic modal *ki'a* should allow present and past TPs with a null tense. Nevertheless, past temporal perspective for the epistemic modal *ki'a* (i.e. Reading C) preferably arises only if the modal is embedded under an attitude predicate, usually *maha=saku'* 'I thought'. Examples are given in

(126–128), where the prejacent is only compatible with a previous epistemic state, as the speaker is aware at the present time that the prejacent is no longer true.

(126) **Context:** It was very cloudy when I left home to go to school this morning so I brought my umbrella. But it turns out to be sunny later all the day. My classmate asks me why I brought my umbrella. I say: (adapted from Matthewson 2013: 366)
kiʔa   p-qwalax   ??(maha=sakuʔ).
EPIS.POS PROSP-rain ??(say=1S.ABS)
'I thought it might rain.'   (PAST T.P., FUTURE T.O.)

(127) **Context:** When you sat in the office earlier today, your heard water pouring, so it sounded like it was raining. But you found out later it was the operating sound of your fan. (modified from Matthewson 2013: 363)
kiʔa   cyux   m-qwalax tanux   la   ??(maha=sakuʔ).
EPIS.POS PROG.DIST AV-rain   outside PART ??(say=1S.ABS)
'I thought it might be raining.'   (PAST T.P., PRESENT T.O.)

(128) **Context:** You saw your classmate leaving the class in pouring rain and the next morning she's absent from class. You thought she might get sick from the rain and told the teacher. Later in the afternoon, she showed up and asked why you said that. (adapted from Matthewson 2013: 366)
kiʔa=suʔ   wal m-nbu' ??(maha=sakuʔ).
EPIS.POS=1S.ABS PFV AV-sick ??(say=1S.ABS)
'I thought you might have gotten sick.'   (PAST T.P., PAST T.O.)

The unavailability of past temporal perspective suggests that the T.P. of the Atayal epistemic modal *kiʔa* is not provided by tense; instead, it is always present with respect to the utterance time or the reference time of a higher attitude predicate.

Turning to temporal orientation, recall that Atayal has a covert non-future tense, which picks out either a present or past reference time. The covert tense can combine with prospective aspect to give future interpretation. This tense system is directly parallel to the temporal orientation of the epistemic modal *kiʔa*. The presence of prospective aspect under *kiʔa* obligatorily gives future T.O., as shown in (129).

(129) a. kiʔa   musaʔ   m-sʔang.
         EPIS.POS PROSP AV-scold
         'He might scold.' / ≠ 'He might be scolding.' / ≠ 'He might have scolded.'
     b. kiʔa   p-ksʔang.
         EPIS.POS PROSP.AV-scold
         'He might scold.' / ≠ 'He might be scolding.' / ≠ 'He might have scolded.'

In the absence of the prospective, an aspectually unmarked eventive prejacent allows for past T.O., as shown in (130). While present T.O. requires the progressive aspect, a progressive-marked prejacent is also compatible with a past T.O., as shown in (131–132).

(130) ki'a   m-qwalax   (ssawni'/??misu/*kira').
      EPIS.POS AV-rain   today.earlier/??now/*today.later
      'It might have rained (just now).' / ??'It might be raining (now).' /
      ≠ 'It might rain (later).'   (PRESENT T.P., PAST T.O.)

(131) **Context:** You hear pattering when you are sitting in front of your laptop.
      ki'a   cyux   m-qwalax.
      EPIS.POS PROG.DIST AV-rain
      'It might be raining.'   (PRESENT T.P., PRESENT T.O.)

(132) **Context:** You wonder why you didn't see your cousin Tali' when you came to your uncle's place yesterday.
      m-wah=saku'   shira'   ga,   ki'a   cyux   m-'abi   qu   Tali'.
      AV-come=1S.ABS yesterday TOP   EPIS.POS PROG.DIST AV-sleep ABS Tali'
      'When I came yesterday, Tali' might have been sleeping.'
                                                    (PRESENT T.P., PAST T.O.)

Moreover, perfective aspect under the modal always yields a past T.O., as shown in (133), just like with non-modal claims.

(133) **Context:** You hear that Tali' and Rimuy have a baby but you can't remember when they got married. You recall they held a party last year, which you didn't attend.
      ki'a   wal msqun   sa   kawas wayal.
      EPIS.POS PFV combine.AV   LOC year   past
      'They might have gotten married last year.'   (PRESENT T.P., PAST T.O.)

We can thus conclude that the temporal orientation of the epistemic modal *ki'a* is given by tense, rather than by aspect as predicted by our null hypothesis. We will explain that this is, however, expected, given that the syntactic position of the epistemic modal is higher than tense, and tense only scopes under the modal.

12.3.4 Summary

In this section we discussed modals in Blackfoot, SENĆOŦEN, Hul'q'umi'num', and Atayal. For the most part, the modals pattern as we expect given our null hypothesis: tense encodes temporal perspective, while aspect encodes temporal orientation. We also saw that patterns of temporal orientation differ in a predicted way from the aspectual patterns in non-modal claims, due to the influence of Condoravdi's Diversity Condition. We saw different strategies to satisfy the Diversity Condition. Blackfoot *aahkama'p-*, like Dutch *kunnen* and German *können*, avoids circumstantial modals with non-future temporal orientations by shifting to an epistemic flavour. SENĆOŦEN/Hul'q'umi'num' x̌ʷəŋ/x̌ʷəm and the Atayal modal *blaq* allow for future orientations without overt prospective/future morphology, just like the St'át'imcets modal *ka-. . . -a*, the Mandarin modal *kěyǐ*, and Ktunaxa *tał*.

We also saw several respects in which the languages deviate from our null hypothesis. We turn to discussion of these in the next section.

12.4 Diverging from the null hypothesis: tense and temporal orientation

In the previous section we saw three cases where, contrary to our null hypothesis but consistent with Condoravdi's (2002) initial assumption, epistemic modals disallow past temporal perspectives unless they are embedded under a higher attitude predicate. These modals thus do not behave as if their temporal perspective is given by tense. SENĆOŦEN *ʔiʔwawə*, Hul'q'umi'num' *wəẁaʔ*, and Atayal *kiʔa* further pattern together in that their prejacent's temporal orientation patterns as if determined by tense. We will suggest that these three deviations from the null hypothesis result from a single property of the particular epistemic modals discussed in this section: they always scope higher than tense.

In discussion of SENĆOŦEN and Hul'q'umi'num' epistemic modals, Turner (2013) suggests that the restriction on Reading C is not due to their being epistemic modals, but rather to their syntactic properties, which differ from that of the circumstantial modal *x̌ʷəŋ/x̌ʷəm*. Recall that the tense markers in SENĆOŦEN and Hul'q'umi'num' are second-position clitics. As such, they cliticize to the main verb of the clause, or, if there is an auxiliary, to the auxiliary. The circumstantial modals *x̌ʷəŋ/x̌ʷəm* are auxiliaries, and so the second position clitics, including past and future tense, cliticize to them.

(134) Hul'q'umi'num'
. . . x̌ʷəm=əł=č   ʔiʔ   hiləm
. . . CIRC-PST=2SG.SBJ COM fall
'. . . you would have/might have fallen.' (from (98))

x̌ʷəŋ/x̌ʷəm are thus similar to Dutch *kunnen* (discussed in section 12.2) in that they are directly in the scope of tense.

The epistemic modals *ʔiʔwawə/wəẁaʔ* are different. They are not verbs or auxiliaries and so never take second-position clitics. When they appear in a clause, the second position clitics are cliticized to the verb (or auxiliary).

(135) SENĆOŦEN:
. . . wəẁaʔ ɬəməxʷ = ceʔ ʔə taṅa snet.
. . . EPIS rain=FUT OBL PROX.DEM night
'. . . it might rain tonight.' (from (103))

In work on SENĆOŦEN, the epistemic modal has been termed a 'pre-predicate particle' (Montler 1986), which is a pretheoretical term capturing the fact that it always appears before the main verb/auxiliary of the clause. In terms of its semantic scope and its syntactic position, it is similar to the English modal adverbs *maybe* and *perhaps*. Notice that English *maybe* behaves like *ʔiʔwawə/wəẃaʔ* with respect to temporal perspective, too: unlike *might*, it is unable to get a past temporal perspective. This is illustrated in (136).

(136) **Context:** Sophie is looking for some ice cream and checks the freezer. There is none in there. Asked why she opened the freezer, she replies:
  a. There *might have* been ice cream in the freezer.
  (von Fintel and Gillies 2008: 87)
  b. # *Maybe* there was ice cream in the freezer.
  c. I thought maybe there was ice cream in the freezer.

One of the claims of this chapter is that modals are not inherently temporally restricted. In particular, both epistemic and circumstantial uses are compatible with past or present temporal perspective. The failure of the epistemic modals *ʔiʔwawə/wəẃaʔ* to allow past T.P. appears at first to weaken our claims; however, if the syntactic properties of the epistemic modals are taken into consideration, the facts actually support our basic framework. We have suggested that, as an adverb (or pre-predicate particle), *ʔiʔwawə/wəẃaʔ* always scopes over the entire clause and thus always scopes above tense. This means that tense will always indicate temporal orientation for *ʔiʔwawə/wəẃaʔ*. The temporal perspective of *ʔiʔwawə/wəẃaʔ* then comes from the context; it is tied to the utterance time in regular extensional contexts, the current narrative time in narrative contexts, and the reference time of the higher clause in intensional contexts. This can be achieved via a temporal index in the lexical semantics of the epistemic modal, as in Absuch's (1997) analysis of *might*; the index can be free and thus the T.P. is interpreted as present to the utterance time, or it can be bound by the temporal reference of a higher attitude predicate.

Lastly, consider temporal orientation, which appears to be provided by tense. Since *ʔiʔwawə/wəẃaʔ* is unable to scope under tense, tense scopes under the modal and over aspect. Therefore, tense performs the same role that it does in non-modal sentences: it restricts the reference time of the aspect-inflected main predicate with respect to the evaluation time t_0. This temporal location also indicates the temporal orientation because in epistemic claims containing *ʔiʔwawə/wəẃaʔ*, the temporal perspective is always at t_0. Thus, the relationship between t_0 and the reference time is the same as the relationship between the temporal perspective and the reference time (temporal orientation), and tense indicates the temporal orientation as a result. For further details, see Turner (2013).

The same explanation holds for Atayal's epistemic modal *kiʔa*, which (unlike the Atayal circumstantial modal *blaq*) resists past T.P. and has its T.O. determined by tense.

The difference can again be attributed to the syntactic positions of the two types of modals. Independent evidence for this proposal comes from the relative position of the two modals and the prospective auxiliary *musa'*. The epistemic modal *ki'a* always precedes *musa'*, as shown in (137), whereas the circumstantial modal *blaq* always follows *musa'*, as shown in (138) (repeated from (123)). Crucially, the lower-scoping *musa'* provides the epistemic modal with future T.O., while the higher-scoping *musa'* provides the circumstantials with future T.P.[20]

(137) **Context:** You are watching a game, and in the middle part, the team which was falling behind starts to score.
ki'a   musa'   l<m>aqux   la.
EPIS.POS PROSP win<AV> PART
'They might win.'   (PRESENT T.P., <u>FUTURE T.O.</u>)

(138) **Context:** Although you don't have money, you will get a job soon, and then you will have money.
musa' blaq   m-bazi=su   sa   ana   nanu sawyan=su.
PROSP CIRC.POS AV-buy=2S.ABS LOC even what like.LV=1S.ERG
'You will be able to buy whatever you like (if you have a job).'
                                                                  (<u>FUTURE T.P.</u>, FUTURE T.O.)

Finally, the same explanation for the absence of Reading C can be extended to Blackfoot *aahkama'p-*, although at this time there is no independent evidence that *aahkama'p-* differs syntactically from other modals in the language. We leave this for further research. What is clear is that while the null hypothesis holds generally, there are still syntactic/lexical restrictions on specific modals within languages.

12.5 Conclusion

Condoravdi's (2002) influential analysis of English possibility modals has inspired much subsequent research, but has so far not been systematically subjected to cross-linguistic testing. In this chapter we tested a generalized version of Condoravdi's proposal in twelve languages from seven families. Our results significantly expand the available empirical coverage in the area of modal–temporal interactions.

We advanced the hypothesis that a modal's temporal perspective is given by tense, and its temporal orientation is given by aspect. We provided evidence for this hypothesis from Dutch, German, Gitksan, St'át'imcets, Javanese, Mandarin, and Ktunaxa.

---

[20] The proposed analysis that there is a null (past/present) tense projection under epistemic modals and above aspects not only predicts past T.O. without overt tense marking and with progressive aspect (as in (130) and (132)), but also predicts the combination of past/present tense and prospective aspect, which would give rise to future T.O. with the event time either after the utterance time or after some earlier time. We expect both readings to exist, although we have so far demonstrated the first reading only (see (129)). We leave this issue for further research, and we thank an anonymous reviewer for raising the question.

In section 12.3, we showed that Blackfoot, Atayal, SENĆOŦEN, and Hul'q'umi'num' appear to diverge from our null hypothesis in some respects; however, as we argued in section 12.4, these can be accounted for under a less restrictive version of the null hypothesis—i.e. that temporal operators scoping above a modal give its temporal perspective, and temporal operators scoping below a modal give its temporal orientation.

This is in fact exactly what we expect in a fully compositional account of modal-temporal interactions: a temporal operator that scopes below a modal, but above the modal's prejacent, binds the temporal argument introduced by the modal's prejacent, giving the prejacent's run-time; a temporal operator that scopes above a modal binds the temporal argument introduced by the modal, giving the temporal perspective. While in most cases the temporal operators scoping above a modal are tenses, and the temporal operators scoping below a modal are aspects, as per the formulation of our original null hypothesis, this is not necessarily the case. Temporal operators that cannot scope below other elements will be bound by the discourse context and appear to have deictic semantics. They will thus be categorized as tenses. Temporal operators that can scope below modals and deictic temporal operators, on the other hand, are more likely to be categorized as aspects. Languages that can use the same temporal operators for both tense and aspect (i.e. for indicating both deictic and non-deictic temporal relations), however, should allow their temporal operators to encode either temporal perspective when they scope above a modal, or temporal orientation when they scope below a modal. Modal–temporal interactions are driven by the principle of compositionality: by the meaning of the temporal operators, and the way they combine with the modal, not by whether the temporal operators have been categorized as tenses or aspects.

12.6 Appendix

Gitksan data are given in the orthography developed by Hindle and Rigsby (1973). St'át'imcets data are given in the orthography developed by Jan van Eijk; see van Eijk and Williams (1981). SENĆOŦEN data are given in the community orthography and the Americanist Phonetic Alphabet. Hul'q'umi'num' data are given in the APA.

We follow the Leipzig Glossing Rules where possible. Other morpheme glosses are as follows.

I/II/III = series I/II/III pronoun, ACT = active intransitive, ADD = additive particle, ATT = attributive, AV = Actor Voice, AX = A (transitive subject) extraction, C = control, CF = counterfactual morphology, CIRC = circumstantial, CN = common noun connective, CNTR = contrastive, CONJ = conjunction, CONTR = contrastive conjunction, COUNTER = counter to expectations, DETR = detransitive, DIR = directive transitivizer, DISC = discourse particle, DM = determinate, DTP = distinct third person pronoun, EPIS = epistemic, EVID = evidential, EXIS = assertion of existence, GNRL = general, HYP = hypothetical, IMPERS = impersonal, INAN = inanimate nominal, INCEP =

inceptive, INCH = inchoative, INTS = intensifier, LV = locative voice, MED = medial, MID = middle, NC = non-control, ND = non-deictic, NECESS = necessity, NONAFF = non-affirmative verbal clitic, PART = particle, PN = proper noun, POS = possibility, PRED = predicative, PRON = pronoun, PROSP = prospective, PROX = proximal, PTCP = participle, PV = patient voice, REDUP = reduplication, REM = remote, REPORT = reportative, SPT = spatio-temporal, SUB = subordinate, T = "T" suffix, UNR = unreal clause-type, VAI = animate (subject) intransitive verb, VII = inanimate (subject) intransitive verb, VTA = animate (subject) animate (object) verb, VTI = animate (subject) inanimate (object) verb, X>Y = X acting on Y theme marker (where X,Y = {1,2,3,3',0} for 1st, 2nd, 3rd person proximate, 3rd person obviative and inanimate entities respectively), YNQ = yes/no question.

Acknowledgments

First and foremost, we would like to thank all the speakers we worked with; this research could not have taken place without them. For St'át'imcets we thank Carl Alexander, the late Beverley Frank, the late Gertrude Ned, Laura Thevarge, and the late Rose Agnes Whitley. For Gitksan we thank Barbara Sennott, Vincent Gogag, and Hector Hill. For Ktunaxa we thank Violet Birdstone. For Javanese we thank Dhifa Ariffudin, Fina Aksanah, Titis Subekti, Bahrul Ulum, and Nashrulloh Khoyrun Nashr. For Blackfoot we thank the late Beatrice Bullshields. For SENĆOŦEN we thank the late Ivan Morris Sr., the late Ray Sam, Mary Jack and the late Anne Jimmy. For Hul'q'umi'num' we thank Ruby Peter. For Atayal we thank Heitay Payan, Tintin Payan, and Buya' Bawnay.

We would like to thank audiences at the Modality@OttawaU workshop, the first Tübingen Tempus Tuesday, the Syntax-Semantics Colloquium at the University of Potsdam, the Canadian Linguistic Assocation 2013, the Northwest Linguistic Conference 2013, the University of Kentucky, and the University of Surrey. In addition we would like to thank Henry Davis, Donna Gerdts, Marianne Huijsmans, Janet Leonard, Tianhan Liu, Amélia Reis Silva, the participants in the UBC Seminar on Modality, the editors of the current volume, and two anonymous reviewers for helpful feedback. We would also like to thank Wanda Rothe for assistance in preparing the manuscript.

This research was funded in part by SSHRC (grants 756-2012-0648 and #410-2011-0431) and the Jacobs Research Fund.

13

A modest proposal for the meaning of imperatives

KAI VON FINTEL AND SABINE IATRIDOU

13.1 Introduction

In this chapter, we attempt to make a modest contribution to the understanding of the meaning of imperatives. By "imperative" we mean a verb form that is typically used to convey directive force, and is not typically used in subordinate roles (distinct from infinitives and subjunctives; but see later).

Now, one might think that there is an obvious answer to the question of what imperatives mean: imperatives are used to impose an obligation on the addressee to make the prejacent of the imperative true. A speaker who utters

(1) Read this book!

is trying to get the addressee to take on the obligation to make it true that the addressee reads this book. If the imperative is successful, the addressee now has the obligation to read this book.

So, it's unsurprising that "command" is often taken to be the basic function of the imperative verb. In fact, in many languages, even the (folk-)linguistic name of the form is based on a verb that means "command":

- Romance *imperative* from Latin *imperare* 'to command'
- Greek *prostaktiki* from *prostazo* 'to command'
- Turkish *emir kipi* 'command' (noun)
- Slovenian *velelnik* from *veleti* 'to command'
- Hebrew *civuy* 'to command'
- Albanian *urdherore* from *me urdheru* 'to command'
- Arabic *fi'l ?amr* 'to command'

Modality Across Syntactic Categories. First edition. Ana Arregui, María Luisa Rivero, and Andrés Salanova (eds.).
This chapter © Kai von Fintel and Sabine Iatridou 2017. First published 2017 by Oxford University Press.

Are we done then? Well, no, even if the idea that imperatives express commands or impose obligations were entirely correct, which as we'll see, it isn't, we would still have to figure out what the morphosyntax of imperatives is, how the meaning of imperatives arises compositionally, and what the division of labor between semantics and pragmatics is. The latter two questions are what we focus on here.

In the syntactic literature it is often assumed that there is a functional projection whose content is the semantics (whatever this may prove to be) associated with the verb form and with which the verb merges. For example, Rivero and Terzi (1995) postulate an imperative mood feature which can appear at different heights of the tree in different languages and which attracts the verb. This analysis is meant to capture, among other phenomena, the fact that the imperative verb always precedes the clitic in a number of languages, even though the tensed verb normally follows it (see also Han 1998, and many others). The following examples are from Greek:

(2) i   Maria to dhiavazi
    the Mary it read-prog
    'Mary is reading it'

(3) dhiavase to!
    read-imp it!
    'Read it!'

(4) *to dhiavase! (* as an imperative)
    It read-imp

Though no project on the imperative can count as complete if it does not address syntactic phenomena like (3, 4), we will not undertake this here. The hope is that a proper understanding of the interpretation of imperative forms will also provide an answer to the question of the target of verb movement in (3). We leave this issue for a future occasion, even though we need to admit at the outset that if our conclusions here are correct, the functional projection in question has less content than is assumed in most syntactic work on imperatives.

Since imperatives are clearly expressions whose use changes the world (in the stereotypical case, they bring about obligations), a full theory of their meaning needs to specify both a denotational semantics and a model of how their denotation is used to change the context, including what exactly in the context is being changed. So, theory choice in this case is quite intricate. At the level of denotational semantics, we can distinguish "strong" theories that build something like obligation into the denotation and "minimal" theories which are non-modal in their denotation. Let us look at three proposals in particular.[1]

---

[1] For further alternatives, we refer the reader to surveys by Han (2011) and Charlow (2014). We think that the two empirical domains we explore here constitute serious problems for any strong semantics for imperatives.

Kaufmann (2012) proposes a rich denotational semantics, according to which imperatives denote modal propositions. In effect, *read this book!* gets a semantics very close to *you should/must read this book*. In addition, there are presuppositions that ensure that imperatives are not used as statements about what is required but only as performatives that (attempt to) change what's required.

Condoravdi and Lauer (2012) propose that imperatives convey the speaker's "effective preference." They are agnostic about whether this meaning comes directly from the semantics or "later" from the pragmatics.

Portner (2007), following Hausser (1980), proposes a rather minimal denotational semantics, according to which imperatives denote a property that is restricted to the addressee:

(5) ⟦read this book⟧ $= \lambda x : x$ is the addressee. x reads this book

Any serious proposal about the denotation of imperatives needs to be accompanied by a theory of the dynamic pragmatics: what is it in the context that uses of imperatives change and how do they change it? Here again there are a variety of proposals, interconnected with proposals about the denotational semantics. What the proposals have in common is that there is a separate discourse component that the clause type of imperatives specializes in updating.[2] The particular proposals about what the discourse component is that imperatives affect include the to-do-lists (TDLs) of Portner (2007), the plan sets of Han (2000), the permissibility spheres of Lewis (1979), or the effective preference structures of Condoravdi and Lauer (2012).

In the end, then, proposals about the meaning of imperatives are package deals of a denotational semantics and a dynamic pragmatics. We need to decide how much of that meaning is encoded in the compositional semantics and how much is due to higher-level pragmatics. The less of the directive, context-affecting force is built into the denotational semantics of imperatives, the more needs to be done at the pragmatic level. There is no question that the typical meaning of an imperative is to express a command. The question is where this is achieved, in the syntax-semantics or in the pragmatics.

In this chapter, we will argue for a particular package deal that combines Hausser's and Portner's minimal semantics with a modified version of Portner's dynamic pragmatics. In Portner's view, imperatives, like the other two main sentence types, introduce a distinctive type of denotation: declaratives denote propositions, interrogatives denote sets of propositions, and imperatives denote addressee-restricted properties. There is a uniform pragmatics: an utterance of a sentence is used to update the appropriate component of the context. Declaratives are used to add a proposition to the common ground, interrogatives are used to add a question to the stack of questions

---

[2] Just as declaratives update the common ground and interrogatives update the stack of questions under discussion.

under discussion, and imperatives are used to add a property to the addressee's TDL. For every individual, the TDL contains a list of properties that the individual "should" make true of themselves (the particular meta-modality involved in embedding the TDL in a theory of context is explored in detail in Portner 2007).[3] For Portner, then, the heavy lifting is done in the pragmatics: the sense of "obligation" that we associate with imperatives is not encoded in the syntax-semantics but is part and parcel of the relevant discourse component. It is not the case, in other words, that Portner's account of imperatives is "modality-free"; the modality is there, but just not in the syntax.

As we have said, we will call Portner's proposal (and similar ones) a "minimal semantics" for imperatives and we will use the term "strong semantics" for Kaufmann's proposal and the version of Condoravdi and Lauer's proposal that builds preference into the semantics. These accounts, minimal or strong, all in the end deliver something like a command-force meaning, but differ in how much of that is encoded in the semantics of the imperative vs. the pragmatics. So how can we choose between these accounts and others in this neighborhood?[4]

We will use two kinds of uses of imperatives to argue for a minimal (non-modal, non-attitude) denotational semantics: (i) acquiescence and indifference uses and (ii) the use of imperatives in conditional conjunctions.

13.2 Weak imperatives: acquiescence and indifference

There are two "weak" uses of imperatives that constitute a serious problem for any theory that encodes some kind of modal strength (or speaker preference) in the semantics of imperatives. Consider:

(6) A: It's getting warm. Can I open the window?
     B: Sure. Go ahead. Open it!

(7) Go left! Go right! I don't care.

We call the first use an "acquiescence" imperative and the second an "indifference" imperative. The first is often called a "permission" use, but we find something slightly inaccurate in that terminology. It seems to us that what the imperative in (6) really conveys is that the hearer can rest assured that the speaker will not object to the

---

[3] There are, of course, as always, problems with the TDL way of modeling the contextual effect of imperatives, many of which are canvassed by Condoravdi and Lauer (2012). We stress that the main thrust of our chapter is that we need a minimal denotational semantics of imperatives. While we adopt the TDL view of the dynamic pragmatics for concreteness, we are open to alternative context models.

[4] Condoravdi and Lauer float the intriguing possibility that there is "no fact of the matter about what the denotation of imperatives is" because the limited range of embedded uses of imperatives imposes too few constraints on the language learner. Indeed, it seems entirely plausible that sometimes the data underdetermine the semantics of an expression or construction and we may find populations that differ in their semantic "theories" of that expression or construction. Nevertheless, we believe that in the case of imperatives there is, in fact, a fact of the matter.

window being opened, that they can expect that they will not have a problem with the speaker if they open the window.[5]

These weak readings are cross-linguistically common. We have found them in all of the Mediterranean[6] and Western European languages that we've surveyed.

How can a strong semantics for imperatives deal with acquiescence readings? That is, if anything like "command" or "obligation" is part of the denotation of the imperative verb, how can we derive the acquiescence reading? One appealing possibility would be that something in the context interacts with the semantics to weaken its force. So, we would have to identify what that something is and how it interacts with the strong semantics of imperatives to give the weak acquiescence meaning. The first question is perhaps easily answered: acquiescence readings are facilitated in contexts where it is obvious or at least possible that the hearer actually wants to carry out the relevant action. This has been observed by many people (Wilson and Sperber 1988, Portner 2012, Kaufmann 2012, Condoravdi and Lauer 2012).[7]

The second question is harder. An intriguing idea, first floated by Wilson and Sperber (1988) and spelled out in detail by Kaufmann (2012: sect. 5.1), is that the modality expressed by an acquiescence imperative is relativized not to the speaker's desires, as usual, but to the hearer's desires. Kaufmann sketches her proposal as follows: an acquiescence imperative expresses that " 'it is best that you p' where 'it is best' is understood as 'according to what you want/according to what your goals are.' " Further assumptions about the context then lead to an inference that the speaker (who is ostensibly saying that the hearer's desires entail p) is conveying that they are permitting p.

Here's our problem with this analysis (and others along similar lines): if contextual weakening of this sort were possible, then we would expect it to occur not just with the modal/attitudinal proposition putatively expressed by imperatives but also with

---

[5] One might wonder whether the modal *may*, the typical permission modal of English, can have the same range of uses as "permission" imperatives, i.e. whether it also can have mere acquiescence uses. Consider:

(i) Can I open the window?
    Sure, go ahead, you may open the window!

To us, (i) carries an air of an authority giving permission. Using *can* here would perhaps correspond more closely to the acquiescence meaning. But getting involved in the question of deontic *may* vs. *can*, so fraught with prescriptive ardor, is not part of our mission here.

[6] An early stage of this chapter was presented in October 2010 at a conference on the syntax of Mediterranean languages in Athens. For that occasion, data on imperatives were collected in many languages spoken around the Mediterranean Sea.

[7] We hasten to note that hearer desire may be necessary but is not sufficient:

(i) A: I want to write a novel.
    B: So, write a novel!

The exasperated life coach uttering this imperative is not giving permission but instructing the hearer to write the novel he wants to write. Once one is in the life coach mode, it becomes easy to hear even imperatives like *Do whatever you want!*, which are at first glance prime examples of acquiescence imperatives, as strong commands.

related expressions, other directives, desideratives, or deontics. Instead, what we find is that no other expression is subject to such a weakening in context.

For those who believe that imperatives contain a strong modal, it is a problem that performative deontic modals cannot be used to express acquiescence:

(8) A: May I open the door?
     B: Sure, go ahead, open it!
     B': Sure, go ahead, #you must open it.
     B": Yes, in fact: you must open it!
     C: Sure, go ahead, you *should* open it.

In (8B'/B") *must* is clearly stronger than the acquiescence imperative, and attempts to bestow an obligation which in the context in B' does not quite work. Even the weaker *should* in (8C) conveys speaker endorsement in a way that the acquiescence imperative does not.

For those who believe that imperatives express a speaker's preference, it is a problem that desideratives cannot convey mere acquiescence either:

(9) A: Can I go out and play?
     B: Okay, go out!
     B': Okay, I want you to go out.

Again, the desiderative in (9B') expresses speaker endorsement in a way that the acquiescence imperative does not.

Lest you think that this difference in the availability of acquiescence readings is due to a difference between explicitly strong directives and the almost covert nature of imperative marking: many languages have other verb forms that can be used as directives. Examples include infinitives, participles, subjunctives. Cross-linguistically, some non-imperative directives can only be used as strong directives, not allowing the putative contextual weakening to express acquiescence. Hebrew is a case in point. It has an infinitive that can only be used to give commands and it has a future form, which can be used to convey both commands and acquiescence:

(10) la-   shevet!
     INF-   sit
     'Sit!' (command only)

(11) te-   xabek   ot-   o!
     FUT.2- hug(sg.M)   ACC-   3sg.M
     'Hug him! (command, acquiescence)

If contextual weakening is what brings about acquiescence readings, why wouldn't it be able to apply to the Hebrew infinitive?

Similarly, German has in addition to its imperative (which has acquiescence uses) an infinitive that when used directively can only express commands, not acquiescence:

(12) Geh raus!   imperative (command, acquiescence)
      go.IMP out

(13) Rausgehen!   infinitive (command only)
      out-go.INF

(14) A: Kann ich rausgehen und spielen?
         can I out-go and play
      B: Na klar, geh raus!   acquiescence reading
         PRT clear go.IMP out
      B': Na klar, rausgehen!   no acquiescence reading
         PRT clear out-go.INF

So the Hebrew and German infinitives are bare verb forms that have a command use but cannot be weakened to acquiescence in context. We find the same pattern with subjunctives. Slovenian has a subjunctive that can be used to convey command, but not acquiescence:[8]

(15) *da mi greš domov*
      DA me.dat go.2nd.sg.pres home
      'Go home!'

So if contextual weakening is what permits a strongly directive form to be interpreted as acquiescence, it should always be possible. But this is not always so, neither with overtly modalized forms nor with covertly marked verb forms.

The issue with indifference uses is the same: no overt directive/desiderative/deontic expression that gets close to what the strong theory of imperatives says is their meaning can be used in an indifference context. Compare:

(16) Go left! Go right! Either way is fine with me.

(17) #You must go left. You must go right. Either way is fine with me.

(18) #I want you to go left. I want you to go right. I don't care.

Note also that acquiescence imperatives can be followed by an expression of indifference, but an explicit priority modal cannot:

(19) Sure, open the window! I don't care.

(20) #Sure, you should open the window. I don't care.

The upshot then is that imperatives (and, as we will see, a subset of their non-imperative cousins) allow weak acquiescence and indifference uses, unlike overtly

---

[8] *da* is the Balkan subjunctive INFL/COMP particle.

marked strong directives (and some covertly marked ones). This would be unexpected if imperatives had a strong directive *semantics* that could be predictably weakened in context.

What we have seen so far is that accounts that build a strong directive meaning into the imperative face serious challenges with the acquiescence and indifference readings. What about Portner's account? Recall that Portner gives a minimal semantics to imperatives and proposes a pragmatics according to which the utterance of an imperative amounts to putting the property that the imperative denotes on the addressee's TDL. Now, a to-do list is just that: a list of things that a person is to do—in other words, a list of their obligations. This means that this analysis also is faced with the problem of acquiescence imperatives: saying *Sure, go ahead, open the window* doesn't put opening the window on the addressee's to-do list. Or so it seems.

Portner (2012) recognizes the problem posed by the weaker readings of the imperative, and proposes that an imperative p! has a permission reading in the presence of a prior prohibition against p (or prior command of some q that is inconsistent with p). Portner associates with the TDL a Kratzerian mechanism for calculating what is permitted and what is required (see Kratzer 1991 for an overview). One crucial property of that mechanism is that the presence of conflicting instructions leads to choice. If both p and q are on the TDL and they are inconsistent (perhaps because q is not-p or because of some constellation of facts), the best the agent can do is to realize one of them (that's still better than neither of them, of course), but there is no built-in preference for one of them, which means that the agent can choose which one to realize. That, Portner suggests, is a way towards permission or choice imperatives.

There is a serious problem with this approach (actually, both for the Kratzerian view about deontic conflicts and for Portner's use of it for permission imperatives): conflicting requirements do not, in fact, give rise to choice. Consider:

(21) It's April 15, tax day. I have to finish my tax return.

(22) It's April 15. I have to send in my letter of recommendation.

Imagine that there's no way I can both finish the tax return and the letter of recommendation. Confronted with the dire truth that both these requirements hold, it is simply not so that I would rejoice and declare that luckily, I now have a choice and that I may choose to not do my tax return since I also have to send in the letter.[9]

Portner does recognize the issue and illustrates it with imperatives:

(23) [Party host to guest at 5pm]: Bring beer to the party!

(24) [Party host to same guest at 6pm]: Bring wine to the party!

Again, imagine that it is either impossible or uncalled-for to bring more than one beverage. The guest will not conclude that they now have free choice between bringing

---

[9] See von Fintel (2012) for further discussion of deontic conflicts.

beer or wine to the party. They will either take the most recent command to override the earlier one or they will ask for clarification: which does the host actually want?

Portner's response to this difficulty is to try and maintain that permission can result from conflicting imperatives but that in the default case, this doesn't happen. Permission imperatives need to be marked with an element that indicates that we are in a context where the conflicting requirements result in choice. We will not go into the details of his proposal, some of which are unclear to us. Suffice it to say that in the end, Portner embraces something like an ambiguity approach: imperatives convey commands unless they are explicitly marked to give rise to permission readings. But this, to some extent, pulls the rug from under the minimal approach, which Portner himself advocates.

We will return at the end of the chapter to our own view on how to derive the acquiescence reading within a minimal semantics for the imperative. Here we would like to address one more possibility. One could imagine that imperatives do have a modal semantics but that they are systematically ambiguous between possibility and necessity meanings.[10]

A possibility/necessity ambiguity for imperatives is, in fact, what Grosz (2009) proposes, based on distributional facts of the German adverbs *bloß* and *ruhig*. The adverb *bloß* goes with the command reading of imperatives, and the adverb *ruhig* goes with the acquiescence/indifference reading, a pattern that replicates how these adverbs combine with overt deontic modals.

(25) a. *Iß *bloß/ruhig den Spinat! Das stört mich nicht.*
    eat bloß/ruhig the spinach that disturbs me not
    'Eat bloß/ruhig the spinach! That doesn't disturb me.'

   b. *Iß bloß/*ruhig den Spinat! Sonst wirst du bestraft.*
    eat bloß/ruhig the spinach or.else will.be you punished
    'Eat bloss/ruhig the spinach! Or else you'll be punished.'

While we are in principle sympathetic to this possibility, we do not think it will work. There is in fact a serious problem for the idea that imperatives can express a possibility modal meaning. Consider our example of an indifference use and the obvious way in which a Grosz-style analysis could account for it:

(26) a. Go left! Go right! I don't care.
   b. You could go left. You could go right. I don't care.

---

[10] Such ∃/∀ ambiguities are, of course, attested in natural language: bare plurals appear to have both existential and (quasi-)universal readings (although, of course, where the duplicity of meaning comes from is controversial); modals in several languages have recently been described as being underspecified for modal force (Rullmann et al. 2008, Deal 2011); infinitival relative clauses appear to have two readings: *this is the/a man to consult* (Hackl and Nissenbaum 2012). NB: Crnič and Trinh (2008) propose an adaptation of the Rullmann et al. (2008) selection function approach to account for the variable force of imperatives. We believe that their account faces the same issues that we discuss in the main text for Grosz's account.

The idea would be that the two imperatives, which would be contradictory under a strong semantics, have a possibility meaning, paraphrasable with something like *could*. But this idea would incorrectly predict that we could conjoin two such "contradictory" imperatives just like we can conjoin two "contradictory" *could*-statements. But that is not so:

(27) a. #Go left and go right! I don't care.
     b. You could go left and you could go right. I don't care.

If the imperative had an ∃-reading, why would the conjunction of contradictory imperatives in (27a) not be possible, since one would think it should get a reading as in (27b)? How can the minimal semantics approach explain the contrast between (26) and (27)? In (27a), we have a contradictory conjunction of properties, which is then to be added to the TDL, which, of course, is absurd: no addressee can logically make this contradiction true of themselves. In contrast, (26a) can be expected to be good, since it involves two separate speech acts, each of which is merely conveying acquiescence with respect to the prejacent of the two imperatives. The modal semantics cannot make use of the fact that there are two separate imperatives in (26) and a conjunction of two imperatives in (27), since under the modal semantics, there are two modals introduced in either case, with each imperative morpheme. To make (26a) good, the two modals have to be weak ones, but then (27a) would incorrectly be predicted to be as good as (27b). We submit, then, that there is no plausible story here under a modal semantics.[11]

We conclude that a strong directive *semantics* for imperatives is in serious trouble. Even a Grosz-style ambiguity analysis is in trouble. Portner's minimal semantics is looking better and better. But we hasten to repeat that we would need to explain how it can get mapped onto both strong and weak readings (depending on context and clues). In the meantime, we will raise a second serious problem for strong imperative semantics.[12]

13.3 Imperatives in certain conjunctions

In this somewhat sprawling section, we will explore some issues arising from the use of the imperative in certain conjunctions, a construction succinctly called "IaDs" (Imperative and Declarative) by Kaufmann. Here are three examples:

(28) a. Study hard and you will pass the class.
     b. Ignore your homework and you will fail this class.
     c. Open the paper and you will find five mistakes on every page.[13]

---

[11] To explain the distinction, a modal semantics for imperatives might try to say that even though there are two imperatives being conjoined in (27a), there is only one imperative modal taking scope over conjoined verb phrases. We doubt that this is a promising avenue.

[12] The problem we're about to discuss is a problem for ambiguity theories like Grosz's as well.

[13] This is a version of an example from Clark (1993).

We note a clear distinction between two kinds of readings of IaDs: the first example, (28a), is naturally interpreted as coming with an endorsement from the speaker about the advisability of studying hard, while the other two examples, (28b,c), do not seem to come naturally with such an endorsement. We therefore suggest distinguishing between two kinds of interpretations of IaDs:

- endorsing IaDs ("e-IaDs")
- non-endorsing IaDs ("n-IaDs")

IaDs are very common in our survey of languages spoken around the Mediterranean. Here are examples of n-IaDs from Greek, Palestinian Arabic, French, Albanian:

(29) *Fae   ena apo afta ke   tha pethanis mesa se 24 ores*
     Eat.IMP one from these and FUT die   within   24 hours
     'Eat one of these and you will die within 24 hours' (Greek)

(30) *Ilmis-ha   w   b-tindam   tool 'omr-ak*
     touchIMP-it and b-regret.2sgm all life-your
     'Touch it and you will regret it the rest of your life' (Palestinian Arabic)

(31) *ignore tes   devoirs   et   tu   échoueras*
     ignore your homework and you fail-FUT
     'Ignore your homework and you will fail' (French)

(32) *haje kete dhe do   te   vdesesh brenda 24 oresh*
     eat this and you will die   within 24 hours
     'Eat this and you will die within 24 hours' (Albanian)

We have found one set of languages that does not have IaDs (either e- or n-IaDs), which we represent here by Turkish:

(33) ??/*Cok   CalIS   ve   baSarI-lI   ol-ur   -sun!
     much work (imp.) and success-with be-aor -2.sg
     'Study hard and you'll succeed'

(34) ??/*Ev   Odev-in   -i   unut   ve   baSarI   -sIz
     home work-2.sg.poss -acc. forget (imp.) and success -without
     ol-ur-sun!
     be-aor.-2.sg
     'Ignore your homework and you will fail'

Other languages that, according to informal reports, behave like Turkish in not allowing IaDs are Hindi, Bangla, and Persian. (One suspects an areal/historical connection.)

We will return later to the question of where these languages differ from those that do have IaDs.

There is a very tempting approach to IaDs (adopted, e.g. by Kaufmann 2012 and Russell 2007), according to which (i) e-IaDs are a conjunctive sequence of two speech acts: an imperative endorsing the prejacent followed by a declarative stating a modal claim about what will happen *if* the prejacent is made true; and (ii) n-IaDs do not involve an imperative at all but are an instance of a more widely attested construction called "conditional conjunction" (Keshet 2012) or "left subordinating *and*" (Culicover and Jackendoff 1997).

Our plot gets a bit convoluted now. We first embark on a somewhat inconclusive (but hopefully fun) excursus about e-IaDs, which will inject some useful data and thoughts into the debate about their nature. We then turn to n-IaDs, which provide us with our second argument for a minimal, non-modal semantics for imperatives.

13.3.1 e-IaDs

e-IaDs are IaDs where the prejacent of the imperative is felt to be endorsed by the speaker. The question is why this is so. One obvious answer is that, duh, there's an imperative there and thus someone uttering such an IaD of course endorses the prejacent, since that's what imperatives mean. The competing answer is that there is no imperative issued but that we have here an instance of conditional conjunction. Let's call the analysis that involves a true imperative speech act the "Type I" analysis and the analysis that treats the IaD as a pure conditional the "Type II" analysis. So, our example of an e-IaD would be analyzed as follows by the two approaches:

(35) Type I analysis of e-IaDs
Study hard and you will pass.
Study hard!$_{command}$ and [*if you study hard*$_{silent}$ you will pass]$_{modal\ subordination}$

(36) Type II analysis of e-IaDs (works for n-IaDs as well)
Study hard and you will pass.
If you study hard, you will pass.

Under the Type II analysis, the endorsing nature of e-IaDs is not part of their semantics but is an inferred component of meaning: passing the class is likely a positive outcome, so saying that studying hard will lead to that outcome is naturally taken to be an endorsement of that course of action. Under the Type I analysis, the endorsement component follows straightforwardly, since the speaker of an e-IaD is actually using an imperative. Note that there is a kind of inclusion relation between the Type I and Type II analyses: both say that a conditional proposition is asserted, but the Type I analysis adds to this that, before that, the imperative is actually issued. Moreover, in the Type II analysis, the conditional antecedent is the first conjunct, while in the Type I analysis, the antecedent is provided silently in the second conjunct via modal subordination.

We will discuss later how the Type II analysis gets the IaD to assert a conditional (since this is needed for the n-IaDs in any case), but for now let's focus on how the Type I analysis deals with the second component of the meaning it assigns to e-IaDs. The idea is that we're dealing with an instance of "modal subordination," the process by which a modalized sentence can be implicitly restricted to scenarios made salient by a previous utterance. Consider the canonical example from Roberts (1989):

(37) A wolf might walk in. It would eat us both.

The first sentence in (37) asserts that it is epistemically possible for a wolf to walk in. It thereby raises to salience the set of possible worlds where a wolf walks in. The modal *would* in the second sentence is then understood to quantify over worlds in that salient set. In effect, the second sentence thus means 'if a wolf walked in, it would eat us both.'[14] The modal in the first sentence doesn't have to be epistemic; it can also be a deontic/priority modal or desiderative:

(38) a. You { must / have to / should } invest in this company! You will become rich.
      b. I want you to invest in this company! You will become rich!

Perhaps unsurprisingly, we can construct sequences of an imperative followed by a modal sentence where the modal is restricted to the worlds where the prejacent of the imperative is made true:

(39) Invest in this company! You will become rich.

So, the Type I idea of how e-IaDs work is that they are just like (39) but have *and* conjoining the two speech acts:

(40) Invest in this company and you will become rich.
      ≈ Invest in this company! (and) (if you do,) you will become rich.

One worry one might have about this analysis is that conjunction of unlike speech acts isn't exactly a widely attested option (#*You are very handsome and can I have your*

---

[14] This is as good a place as any to point out what should be obvious: a conditional "meaning" is not the same as the *if p, q* "syntactic structure," a common enough confusion. A variety of syntactic structures can map to a conditional meaning, and *if p, q* is but one of those; it has no privileged status. (37) shows that we can have implicitly restricted modals that convey conditional meanings, and the cases of conditional conjunction discussed later show that there are further ways of conveying conditionality. Even so, we will be using *if p, q* as a natural language paraphrase of a conditional meaning. Confusing the syntactic structure *if p, q* with conditional semantics happens often enough, including in Culicover and Jackendoff (1997). See Iatridou (2014) for discussion.

phone number?). But we will not dwell on this, and assume that conjoining an imperative speech act with an assertion is, in principle, possible. What we will point out is that if an imperative contains strong directive semantics, and modal subordination is involved in the derivation of IaDs (i.e. the Type I analysis), it has quite different properties from cases of modal subordination with overt strong directive modals.

Let us start with pointing out that inserting a conjunction into sequences of speech acts is not an innocent operation.

The paradigm example of modal subordination with an epistemic modal in the first conjunct, as in (37), does seem to allow insertion of conjunction:

(41) [Let me tell you why we shouldn't open the door]
A wolf might walk in and it would eat us both.

However, deontic modals do not behave the same way as epistemic ones. A deontic/priority modal or desiderative in the first conjunct are to various degrees degraded:[15]

(42) ?? You $\left\{\begin{array}{l}\text{must}\\ \text{have to}\\ \text{should}\end{array}\right\}$ invest in this company and you will become rich.

(43) ?? I want you to invest in this company and you will become rich.

On the other hand, the e-IaD in (40) is impeccable, as we saw. This asymmetry between overt strong modals and the imperative is unexpected under a Type I analysis.

We suspect that the reason why (42) and (43) are degraded is that conjunction is actually not as innocent as logicians might have thought. Bar-Lev and Palacas (1980) and Txurruka (2003) discuss contrasts like the following:

(44) a. Max fell; he broke his arm.
b. = Max fell and he broke his arm.

(45) a. Max fell; he slipped on a banana peel.
b. ≠ Max fell, and he slipped on a banana peel.

Without going into the details, it appears that *and* does not allow a (reverse) EXPLANATION relation between the two conjuncts. Further, *and* does not allow a JUSTIFICATION relation, either:[16]

(46) a. You should do the Atkins diet. It comes highly recommended.
b. ≠ You should do the Atkins diet and it comes highly recommended.

---

[15] Daniel Lassiter (p.c.) has pointed out to us that there are naturally occuring examples of the "should *p* and will *q*" type. We maintain that there is intuitively a real difference in acceptability between e-IaDs and such *should*-conjunctions.

[16] We borrow the Atkins diet scenario from Dorr and Hawthorne (2013).

This then sheds light on why there's a problem with conjunctions with any explicitly modalized statement of the sort we have seen so far in the first conjunct and a putatively modally subordinated *will*-statement in the second conjunct, which explains/justifies why the overtly modalized statement is warranted:

(47) a. You should do the Atkins diet. You will lose a lot of weight.
b. ≠ You should do the Atkins diet and you will lose a lot of weight.

Now, this inability to follow up a modal with a conjoined justification carries over to imperatives, while a sequence without conjunction is just fine:[17]

(48) a. Do the Atkins diet! It comes highly recommended.
b. # Do the Atkins diet and it comes highly recommended.

But with all this in place, it becomes mysterious why e-IaDs work so well:

(49) Do the Atkins diet and you will lose a lot of weight.

The preceding is an intricate pattern of data, and we concede that there may be a way of reconciling an analysis of the e-IaD as a conjunction of an imperative and a modally subordinated follow-up, with the restrictions we have found on when modal subordination is possible across conjunction. We await such attempts.

Another reason to be skeptical that the modal subordination account of e-IaDs (i.e. the Type I analysis) is entirely correct is that modal subordination, as expected from an anaphoric process, allows a kind of indirection that we will call "polarity switch":

(50) a. Don't park there! You will be towed.
b. = Don't park there! If you park there, you will be towed.

The modal in the second speech act is interpreted not with respect to the worlds where you don't park there (the ones that the imperative makes salient are the ones where its prejacent, *not park there*, is true) but with respect to the worlds where you, against the speaker's advice, do park there. But now consider an attempt at an e-IaD version:

(51) a. Don't park there and you will be towed.
b. ≠ Don't park there! If you park there, you will be towed.
c. = Don't park there! If you don't park there, you will be towed.

So, IaDs do not allow polarity switch while modal subordination should in principle allow it. This is a considerable problem for a Type I account of e-IaDs.

---

[17] Here's another such contrast:

(ii) a. Don't go in there! There are monsters in there.
b. #Don't go in there and there are monsters in there.

We would like to give one more reason to doubt the Type I analysis of e-IaDs. Turkish has conjunction in modal subordination exactly where English allows it as well:[18]

(52) kapıda   bir   kurt   olabilir   ve   Allah   korusun   hepimiz   yer
     door.loc a   wolf   might.be   and   God   forbid   all.of.us eat.aor
     'A wolf might be at the door and God forbid it would eat all of us'

But as we've already pointed out, Turkish has no IaDs, not even e-IaDs—an absence that would be mysterious under the Type I analysis.

Our tentative conclusion is that all IaDs, even endorsing ones, which at first blush might have appeared as easy candidates for a Type I analysis, involve conditional conjunction, rather than having a true imperative speech act followed by modal subordination across *and*. In other words, we favor a Type II analysis for *all* IaDs.

It is time to end the excursus on e-IaDs and turn to n-IaDs which are more central to the main argument of this chapter. We will return to the question of the nature of e-IaDs later on and discuss some challenges to the unified analysis of IaDs.

13.3.2 n-IaDs

Non-endorsing IaDs such as the ones in (53) more or less clearly do not come with any endorsement of the prejacent of the imperative by the speaker:

(53) a. Open the paper and you will find five mistakes on every page.
     b. Ignore your homework and you will fail this class.

Instead, the most promising idea about n-IaDs is that they convey a purely conditional proposition, that is, what we called the Type II analysis earlier. So, n-IaDs would be an instance of a more general phenomenon: that some conjunctions have a conditional interpretation. The most famous investigation of these constructions is the one in Culicover and Jackendoff (1997). A few canonical examples:

(54) Louie sees you with the loot and he puts out a contract on you.

(55) You drink one more beer and I'm out of here.

(56) One more beer and I'm out of here.

Conditional conjunctions are attested cross-linguistically. Here are some examples from the same languages we showed earlier as possessing IaDs: Greek, Palestinian Arabic, French, and Albanian.

---

[18] Speakers tell us that *Allah korusun* is necessary in (52). We do not know why this is, but it is irrelevant for our main point because the addition of this string to an (n-)IaD does not improve it.

(57) O skilos mu akui keravnus ke krivete kato apo to trapezi
the dog my hears thunder and hides under the table
'My dog hears thunder and hides under the table' (Greek)

(58) Ena lathos akoma ke tha se apoliso
One mistake more and will you fire
'One more mistake and I will fire you' (Greek)

(59) Bet-talla' fee-ha w be-hmarr wejh-o
b-look.3sgm in-her and b-redden3sgm face-his
'He looks at her and his face reddens' (Palestinian Arabic)

(60) Kamaan ghaltah w betorr-o-ok
Another mistake and b-fire.3-pl-you
'Another mistake and they'll fire you' (Palestinian Arabic)

(61) il voit son patron et il s'enerve
he sees his boss and he gets nervous
'He sees his boss and he gets nervous' (French)

(62) une bière de plus et nous vous expulserons
one beer more and we you fire
'One more beer and we will fire you' (French)

(63) Mesuesi e-cl shikon dhe ai fshihet nen tavoline
The teacher looks at him and he hides under table-the
'The teacher looks at him and he hides under the table' (Albanian)

(64) nje gabim dhe do te te pushoj (nga puna)
one mistake and fut you fire (from work)
'One mistake and I will fire you' (Albanian)

Recall that Turkish does not have IaDs. It turns out that Turkish does not allow conditional conjunctions either:

(65) *kadIn-lar-a gülümse-me -si yeter ve hemen
woman-pl-dat smile -'ing'-3.sg.poss sufficient and immediately
kendisin -e tut -ul -ur- lar
he (logophoric pronoun, 3.sg) -dat capture -(impers.) pass -aor -3.pl.
int.: 'It's enough for him to smile at women and they immediately fall for him'

(66) ??/*Bir hata daha ve sen -i iS -in -den at
one mistake more and you (sg.) -acc work -2.sg.poss -abl. throw
-ar -Im
-aor. -1.sg
int.: 'one more mistake and I'll fire you from your job'

Since Turkish has imperatives, the fact that it lacks a conditional conjunction suffices to explain the absence of IaDs, if such a conjunction is necessary for the formation of IaDs. But we also have an argument for the unified analysis of IaDs: Turkish (and Bangla, Hindi, Persian) lack both types of IaDs. If conditional conjunction was necessary only for n-IaDs and e-IaDs were derived via a Type I analysis, we would expect Turkish to lack n-IaDs but to have e-IaDs, contrary to fact. Obviously, we would like to know why Turkish does not have conditional conjunction, but we have nothing to say here about that particular puzzle.

Another reason to believe that IaDs are an instance of conditional conjunction is that they show several of the properties identified with this phenomenon in Culicover and Jackendoff (1997). For example, conditional conjunction permits inverse binding, something that is not otherwise permitted in garden-variety conjunctions:

(67) a. You give him enough opportunity and every senator, no matter how honest, will succumb to corruption. (C&J's (23a))
b. *We gave him enough opportunity and every senator, no matter how honest, succumbed to corruption. (C&J's (23d))

Inverse binding is also possible in IaDs of both types:

(68) a. Give him enough opportunity and every senator, no matter how honest, will succumb to corruption.
b. Ignore him and every senator, no matter how senior, will feel insulted.

Let us foreshadow the plot: at least n-IaDs, but maybe all IaDs, are conditional conjunctions (CCs). We will rehearse some basic facts about CCs and sketch two possible kinds of analyses. Either of these analyses can be applied to IaDs, but only if there is no modal in the first conjunct, i.e. *iff* imperatives have a minimal, non-modal semantics; QED.

13.3.3 *Approaching CCs*

Conditional conjunctions show some of the same kinds of meanings that ordinary conditionals have. For example, run-of-the-mill indicative conditionals, with appropriate tense/aspect relations, can be read as being about one particular situation or about a multi-case regularity (an ambiguity called "one case" vs. "multi-case" by Kadmon 1987):

(69) If John leaves his house before doing his homework, he's grounded.

Example (69) is ambiguous between a reading where it makes a claim about one specific time (such as tonight) and a reading where it states a family policy that applies more broadly. A conditional conjunction variant shows the same ambiguity:

(70) John leaves his house before doing his homework, and he's grounded.

Conditional conjunction can also give rise to counterfactual readings but only in a special case:

(71) a. One more beer and I would have fired you.
b. *You had drunk one more beer and I would have fired you.
c. *Drink one more beer and I would have fired you.

Three readings that ordinary conditionals allow are not possible with CCs: there are no epistemic CCs, no factual CCs, and no biscuit CCs:[19]

(72) John is not here and he's at home.
≠ If John is not here, he's at home.

(73) ??You're so smart and you should do it yourself.
≠ If you're so smart, you should do it yourself.

(74) !!You're hungry and there's biscuits on the sideboard.
≠ If you're hungry, there's biscuits on the sideboard.

As we canvass possible analyses of conditional conjunctions, we will want to keep in mind the limited set of conditional meanings that can be expressed by CCs and the cross-linguistic distribution (most languages in our sample have CCs but some, Turkish etc., do not).

There are two main kinds of approaches to CCs: positing (i) a special meaning for *and* in CCs, or (ii) a modal/conditional operator scoping over standard conjunction together with a method for taking the first conjunct to be the restriction of the operator. The first approach is exemplified by Culicover and Jackendoff (1997) and by Klinedinst and Rothschild (2012), while the second approach is advocated by Keshet (2012).

Culicover and Jackendoff (1997) argue that the conjunction *and* is transformed at a representational level they call "Conceptual Structure" into a left-subordinating conditional connective $_{LS}$*and*, whose semantics is basically the same as *if*. Klinedinst and Rothschild (2012), in effect, try to develop a less stipulative but still lexicalized meaning for $_{LS}$*and*. Their special conjunction is like regular *and* in that the first conjunct dynamically updates a modal parameter that the second conjunct can be relative to (something very much like modal subordination), but unlike regular conjunction in that its first conjunct is not asserted/entailed. For bare CCs, they need to posit a covert modal in the second conjunct (a move known from Kratzer's work on conditionals; cf. Kratzer 1986).

---

[19] Proposals like the one in Franke (2009) that derive biscuit readings pragmatically from ordinary conditional meanings may have a problem here. Or maybe this shows that conditional conjunction encodes more "true conditionality" than conditionals of the form *if p, q*.

Keshet (2012) argues that conditional conjunction is a case of internal partition. A modal takes wide scope over standard conjunction. Focus structure determines that the first conjunct restricts the modal and that the second conjunct becomes the "consequent." Consider the following CC:

(75) You come on time and you get a good seat.

As we discussed, such examples are often ambiguous between a one-case reading and a multi-case reading. Keshet posits that (75) can either have a covert *FUT* operator (for the one-case reading) or a covert *GEN*-operator. In either case, the first conjunct is de-accented, signaled as given, and thus is interpreted as the restrictor of the *FUT/GEN* operator. The second conjunct is focused and thus is interpreted as the nuclear scope/consequent of the operator. Such a focus-driven partition process is well known (Rooth 1985):

(76) [MARY]$_F$ usually takes John to the movies. [R's (3c): 165]
   = Most times of someone taking John to the movies are ones where Mary does so.

(77) Mary usually takes [JOHN]$_F$ to the movies. [R's (3d): 165]
   = Most times after Mary taking someone to the movies are ones where she takes John.

Keshet notes that sometimes operators from the second conjunct can take wide scope and supplant the *FUT/GEN* operators:

(78) You come on time and you sometimes get a good seat.

(79) You work hard for the next month and you might get a raise.

On the whole, we think that Keshet's approach should be considered the null hypothesis on how CCs work. That said, we have some worries that may in the end argue for some version of the $_{LS}and$ story. Independent evidence for the covert *FUT* operator is a bit slim. Certainly an example with narrow focus but no conjunction cannot get a conditional reading (but presumably should if *FUT* exists):

(80) You get a GOOD seat.
   ≠ If you get a seat, you'll get a GOOD seat.

Note that, in this sense, the putative covert *FUT*, and overt *will*, differ from overt *would*:

(81) a. You get a GOOD seat. (no conditional reading)
   b. You will get a GOOD seat. (no conditional reading)
   c. You would get a GOOD seat. (conditional reading)

Only the example with *would* has a conditional reading ("if you tried to get a seat, you would get a GOOD seat").

So, one might consider an elaboration of the $_{LS}and$ story to be more promising. Either story has many puzzles to address, and we will not make a choice here. Luckily, there's a clear lesson for the analysis of IaDs even without making a choice.

13.3.4 Back to IaDs

There are two properties of CCs that are of particular interest when we think about how to analyze IaDs (especially n-IaDs, but also e-IaDs if we're right that the Type I story for those is in trouble). The first property that is relevant is that CCs do not allow modals in their first conjunct to be the main operator. As we saw when we discussed Keshet's work, there is either a covert modal or an operator from the second conjunct. Consider for example:

(82) You should forget to call your mother and you (will) apologize.

This does not give rise to a sensible reading like "If you forget to call your mother, you should apologize," indicating that the *should* modal in the first conjunct can't act to create a deontic conditional. At most, a deontic modal in the first conjunct of a CC can be interpreted as part of the antecedent proposition:

(83) John has to take out the garbage and he complains endlessly.

Example (83) has a CC reading (in addition to a regular conjunction reading) that expresses the same as "if John has to take out the garbage, he complains endlessly."

The fact that imperatives can appear in the first conjunct of a CC without their putative modal force being present in the antecedent of the conditional meaning, while overt modals *must* contribute their modal force to the antecedent constitutes a serious problem for any analysis of imperatives that assigns them anything stronger than a minimal, non-modal semantics.[20]

The second property of CCs that is of relevance to IaDs is that CCs, for some reason, can have very minimal first conjuncts, famously the *one more*-phrases known from Culicover (1972):

(84) One more missed homework and you will fail this class.

So, under the minimal, non-modal semantics for imperatives, it is no surprise that imperatives can serve as the first conjunct of CCs:

(85) Ignore your homework and you will fail this class.

---

[20] A fortiori, under Kaufmann's (2012) proposal, we would expect the performativity-inducing presuppositions to be triggered in the antecedent and then to project like presuppositions from a conditional antecedent usually do. This is not good news, because there's no hint of performativity in n-IaDs.

We should note that Russell (2007) tries to isolate the semantics of imperatives from the impact of n-IaDs by arguing that they do not, in fact, contain imperatives but some other kind of minimal (but crucially non-modal) verb form.[21] This possibility arises for English because imperatives are not morphologically distinguishable from bare infinitives. The critical issue with this idea is that IaDs are widely attested and are perfectly happy in languages with unambiguous imperatives in the first conjunct. This point was made many years before Russell by Grand Old Master Jespersen (1924: 314):

As the imperative has no particular ending in English, one might perhaps feel inclined to think that these sentences contained infinitives (though how used?). Parallel uses in other languages show us, however, clearly that they contain imperatives.

We submit, then, that IaDs, and especially n-IaDs, give a compelling argument for a minimal, non-modal semantics for imperatives.

13.3.5 Some cross-linguistic explorations

We already mentioned that in addition to morphosyntactic imperatives, many languages employ other verb forms to convey directive force. We often find infinitives or subjunctives used this way, and there are others as well (participles, futures). We have conducted a survey of the languages spoken around the Mediterranean asking two questions about such forms: (i) Do they have acquiescence readings in addititon to stronger directive meanings (commands) or are they restricted to the latter only? (ii) Can they occur in the first conjunct of IaD-like conditional conjunctions? If so, can they give rise to both endorsing and non-endorsing readings?

What we found were forms that can only be used with command-like force and forms that can in addition have acquiescence meanings. We have found forms that can be used in IaDs and forms that cannot be used in IaDs.[22] An exceptionless generalization emerged:

(86) Any form that can be used in IaDs can also be used with an acquiescence reading.

In other words: no directive that can occur in the first conjunct of IaDs is unambiguously strong. We take this to be clear evidence that it is correct to link the appearance of imperatives in IaDs with their possibility of expressing acquiescence meanings. And we conclude that adopting a minimal, non-modal semantics for such forms is the best way to explain the link.

---

[21] This is reminiscent of what (Bolinger 1977: 159) wrote about IaDs such as (i):
(i) ([If] you) tell him anything, (and) he just looks at you blankly.
"[T]here has been an aphesis of the initial *if* or *if you*, which produces something with all the appearance of an imperative *and*."

[22] Strictly speaking, from this point on, "IaD" is used for "Imperative-like form and Declarative", since we're looking at forms that are not actually the imperative but are imperative-like in their relevant uses.

Let us illustrate our findings with Hebrew. Hebrew uses both infinitives and futures to express imperative-like meanings. As we saw earlier, the infinitive can only be used with command-like force, while the future can be used both to express commands and to convey acquiescence. When we look at IaDs, we find that the future can be used in all IaDs, including n-IaDs:

(87) ti-ftax ?iton ve-(ata) ti-mca xamesh
FUT.2-open(sg.M) newspaper and-you(sg.M) FUT.2-find(sg.M) five
ta?uy-ot o yoter
mistake-PL.F or more
'Open the newspaper and you will find five or more mistakes'

The infinitive, on the other hand, cannot occur in IaDs, not even e-IaDs, where the Type I analysis would have expected a strong directive to be able to occur:

(88) *la-shevet be-sheket ve-(ata) te-kabel pras
INF-sit in-quiet and-you(sg.M) FUT.2-receive(sg.M) prize
Attempted: 'Sit quietly and you will get a prize'

Here is a quick summary of specific findings:

- One pattern is for imperative-like forms to have variable force, including acquiescence readings, and to be able to appear in the first conjuncts of IaDs. This is true of *all* imperatives (except in Turkish-type languages which do not have CCs at all). It is also true of the Hebrew future, negated infinitives in Italian, Croatian, Serbian, and the subjunctive in Albanian.
- What is not attested at all is a form that can *only* express command-like force but can occur in IaDs.
- Several forms (Hebrew infinitive, Catalan infinitive, Slovenian subjunctive) can express commands but cannot express acquiescence and cannot occur in IaDs.

One might suspect at this point that the possibility to be the first conjunct of an IaD and the possibility for an acquiescence reading are biconditionally related. But this is not so; (86) is not a biconditional. If a form (infinitive, subjunctive, imperative) can appear in IaDs, it indeed also has an acquiescence reading. But we have found that the reverse is not true: there are languages which have non-imperative forms with acquiescence readings but which cannot form the equivalent of IaDs. Let us illustrate.

Palestinian Arabic does not have negative imperatives. But there is a directive form that can be negated: the present imperfective. And this form can be used as command or acquiescence:

(89) tkassel-sh
laze.2sgm-neg
'Don't be lazy'

However, even though the form can be used as acquiescence, it cannot form IaDs:[23]

(90) *tkassel-sh   w   b-tenjah
     laze.2sgm-neg and b-succeed.2sgm
     'Don't be lazy and you will succeed'

(91) *esma'-sh   en-naseeha w   b-torsob
     listen2sgm-neg the-advice and b-fail.2sgm
     'Don't listen to advice and you will fail'

Catalan provides a counterexample to the bidirectionaliy as well. It does not have negated imperatives but instead uses the subjunctive, which can be used as command or acquiescence:

(92) No   dormis!
     Not sleep-subj
     'Don't sleep!'

Our Catalan speakers are able to use the imperative substitute in e-IaDs but not in n-IaDs:[24]

(93) No vagis a fisioteràpia i t'estalviaràs diners
     'Don't go to physiotherapy and you will save money'

(94) ??/*No vagis a fisioteràpia i et quedaràs coix
     'Don't go to physiotherapy and you will stay crippled'

In other words, the following sentence is good only as long as you want Peter to win. If you want him to lose, it is not:

(95) No treguis la reina de cors i guanyarà en Pere
     'Don't throw the queen of hearts and Pere will win'

We do not know what this contrast is due to, but since it appears in the domain of the negated substitute and not the imperative as such, we will risk staying away from it

---

[23] This is different from Moroccan Arabic, where our speaker can have IaDs of both types with the negated present imperfective:

(i)   ma   t-akul   shi
      Neg you-eat.IMP Neg
      'Don't eat!'

(ii) ma   t-kasl   shi w   gha t-njaH
      Neg you-be.lazy Neg and will you-succeed
      'Don't be lazy and you will succeed'

(iii) ma   t-qra   shi w   gha t-sqT
      Neg you-study.IMP Neg and will you-fail
      'Don't study and you will fail'

[24] Greek subjunctive *na*-clauses show a similar pattern.

for now. The larger point is that while having an acquiescence reading is a necessary condition for a verb form to appear in an IaD, it is not sufficient.

Again, our tentative conclusion from this survey is that the source of acquiescence readings and the ability to occur in IaDs is the same: a minimal, non-modal semantics.

13.4 What now: conclusion and open ends

13.4.1 Conclusion

Exploring acquiescence and indifference uses of imperatives and the appearance of imperatives in the first conjunct in conditional conjunctions (IaDs) has led us to the conclusion that imperatives have a minimal, non-modal semantics à la Hausser and Portner. There are many remaining tasks on our TDL, the first one of which is to understand the acquiescence readings themselves. We have said that we follow Hausser and Portner in endowing imperative forms with a minimal semantics, but we found Portner's derivation of the acquiescence readings problematic. In the upcoming section, we first comment on what one might do to derive the weak readings. After that, we go through some other remaining questions, including some rather recalcitrant facts.

13.4.2 Open ends

13.4.2.1 Capturing weak readings The fact that imperatives appear in the antecedent of non-endorsing IaDs, to us, provides strong support for a non-modal semantics for imperatives, such as the one developed by Portner. The fact that imperatives have weak uses, to us, means that Portner's dynamic pragmatics needs to be modulated (Portner's own proposal for dealing with the weak uses was critically discussed in section 13.2). The basic insight we would like to develop is that we need to take the "proposal" aspect of contextual update moves seriously.[25] It is suggested that the core of imperative pragmatics is that the addressee-restricted property denoted by the imperative is put on the table as a *possible* addition to the addressee's TDL. How strongly the speaker endorses this addition is variable. Surely, strong speaker endorsement is the default, but weaker levels of endorsement all the way down to begrudging acquiescence are possible in the right circumstances.

We would like to point out that the level of speaker endorsement doesn't just appear to be variable in the case of imperatives. Low-endorsement assertions can be signaled by intonation and/or tags as investigated by Malamud and Stephenson (2015), and presumably by other means as well:

(96) He's home?

---

[25] As Condoravdi and Lauer (2012) point out, there are precedents to this idea in Davis (2011: 151, 154) and Farkas (2011).

(97) He's home, isn't he?

There are low-endorsement questions as well, questions where the speaker is indicating a low level of urgency for having the question be on the question stack. Consider the "conjectural questions" attested in Romanian (cf. also Greek *araye*):

(98) Oare Petru a sosit deja?
 oare Peter has arrived already
 'Has Peter arrived already?'

Farkas and Bruce (2010) write that this Romanian question "indicates that settling the issue is not necessarily a projected conversational future and therefore that answering the question is optional."

The idea, then, is that any of these core speech moves—assertion, question, imperative—by default carries full speaker endorsement: an assertion commits the speaker to the proposition asserted, a question means that the speaker wants the conversation to address this question now, and an imperative means that the speaker wants the addressee to add the prejacent to their TDL. But in the right circumstances and perhaps depending on linguistic clues, any of these speech moves can have weaker speaker endorsement levels: an assertion may just float a proposition, without much or any indication that the speaker believes it, and expect the hearer to decide whether it should be added to the common ground; a question may just be put in the room without any urge to put it on the top of the question-under-discussion stack; and an imperative may just be put out there without speaker endorsement, leaving it fully to the addressee to decide whether to add it to their TDL. We submit that the latter corresponds to acquiescence and indifference uses.

Beyond this suggestion, what would be needed to turn this into a full account of weak uses of imperatives (and ideally, the other speech moves)? The first order of business will be to specify a model of conversational dynamics that makes endorsement levels explicit. Then, we'd have to talk about compositionally interpreted expressions that manipulate endorsement levels. Finally, we'd have to put in place a mechanism to ensure that the default level of endorsement is at the strong end of the scale.

The first task is addressed by Malamud and Stephenson (2015), who build on the very influential discourse model by Farkas and Bruce (2010). According to the latter, a discourse move puts an object on "the table," records speaker commitment, and projects the future of the conversation. An assertion, for example, puts a proposition on the table, commits the speaker to the truth of the proposition, and projects that the common ground will become one where the proposition is taken for granted. To model lower levels of speaker commitment, Malamud and Stephenson (2015) add additional elements (projected speaker and hearer commitments) and allow the speaker to put an object on the table without committing themselves to that object. This is a rich model, which, therefore, may be rich enough to model weak commitments to imperatives when married with Portner's TDL system.

The second task, a compositional semantics for speech-act-weakening expressions, is something that has not yet been worked out. The systems devised by Farkas and Bruce (2010) and Malamud and Stephenson (2015) are not compositionally grounded (as they freely admit). We will not attempt here to embark on such a project.

Finally, in the absence of weakening markers, imperatives, like the other speech moves, are perceived to come with full speaker endorsement. How can that be captured? Much of the answer will of course depend on the specifics of the solutions to the first two problems. But we would like to suggest that there may be a general principle at work:[26]

(99) Default Strength of Speech Acts
When a speaker utters a sentence α, this is understood with the highest level of speaker endorsement compatible with the context and any strength/weakness markers in the sentence.

One might see this principle as related to the Strongest Meaning Hypothesis, Maximize Presupposition, and other strength-related pragmatic generalizations.

But, one might object: just because we weaken the force of speaker endorsement of an addition to the hearer's TDL, that doesn't really seem to capture acquiescence. If the hearer does decide to add the imperative property to their TDL, doesn't Portner's system now predict that the hearer is *obligated* to make that property true? And isn't that far too strong a prediction: after all, doesn't it seem like the hearer still has full choice whether to act on the imperative, even if they accept the speaker's acquiescence? This worry isn't unique to acquiescence uses, but also arises with other uses of imperatives: an advice imperative doesn't seem to result in an obligation to follow the advice. Portner is well aware of this, and what he says in Portner (2007) about advice uses (and others—but not for permission uses, where, as discussed earlier, he proposes a different approach) can be adapted here to cover acquiescence as well. First, we should be clear about what the "to do" in the TDL means: when a property is on somebody's TDL they are committed to making it true of themselves (officially: the participants in the conversation take it for granted that the individual will only be considered rational and cooperative if they endeavor to make the property true). This is not quite the same as an obligation. But still, a commitment taken on because you were commanded to is different from a commitment taken on because you got useful advice from an expert. If you don't follow through on a commitment from a command, you will be looked upon much more severely than if you don't follow through on advice; let alone, if you don't follow through on a commitment freely chosen when a speaker signaled acquiescence. Portner models this by implementing

---

[26] This principle is modeled after the principle called "Contextually Determined Speech Act Force," proposed in von Fintel (2003) for the special case of possibly epistemically weakened assertions.

a system where a TDL has "sections," subsets of properties that were put on the TDL in different ways: a command section, an advice section, and so on.[27]

Without fully advocating a wholesale adoption of this system, we do think that something along these lines may prove necessary. If this is so, then we don't see an issue with allowing a section on the TDL that contains commitments taken on freely by the individual.[28] So, a speaker who signals low endorsement levels conveys to the hearer that they can freely choose to add the imperative's prejacent to their TDL. And, the discourse model keeps track of the fact that, if added to the TDL, the addition was of the hearer's own choosing. This can cover both acquiescence and indifference.

We might also point out that keeping track of the provenance of items on the TDL seems quite parallel to the fact that we may need to keep track of the provenance of items in the common ground: some propositions are in the common ground because the participants in the conversation have very reliable first-hand evidence for them and others are there because of much weaker evidential support. This will have consequences for when we discover new facts that conflict with what's being taken for granted; some propositions are easier to give up than others. In the case of the TDL, all items on it are actions the hearer has committed to, but the ones that were put there because of a strongly endorsed imperative from an authoritative source are much harder to renege on/remove from the TDL than ones that the hearer freely chose to put on the TDL (perhaps with the license that came from a low endorsement imperative).

We realize that we have only given the bare outlines of a full account of weak uses of imperatives. What we hope to have done is convince the reader of the plausibility, if not necessity, of such an account (i.e. that previous accounts have not successfully captured weak uses) and lay out one possible avenue of further research. What follows are other open ends that call out for further work.

13.4.2.2 Understanding CCs
We need to make a decision on the best analysis of conditional conjunction, adjudicating between the $_{LS}and$ approach and Keshet's approach, or finding a third way. In addition, we need to understand why certain languages, like Turkish and Persian, lack conditional conjunction.

13.4.2.3 Intrinsic Consequence
A challenge for any theory of CCs and also IaDs is a fact pointed out by Bolinger (1967), namely that the second conjunct must be an intrinsic consequence of the first conjunct. Here are some examples from Bolinger, involving statives, that illustrate this fact:

---

[27] Though not a "permission" section, to be clear.

[28] In fact, our real-life daily to-do lists have exactly that character: they may contain items like "file tax return," which are full-blown obligations and come with severe sanctions if not made good on, and items like "watch Mad Men," which are freely put there as reminders of our evening plans, but where there are little or no sanctions if we don't make them true.

(100) a. Like her and her friends will love you.
b. *Like her and I'll introduce her to you.

(101) a. Own a piece of property and you get taxed mercilessly.
b. *Own this property and I'll buy it from you

(102) a. Understand Chinese and you can get any of these jobs.
b. *Understand Chinese and I need you for a teacher.

We do not know what this pattern is due to.

13.4.2.4 Sufficiency CCs We have seen that modals cannot appear in the first conjunct of a conditional conjunction. Yet there is a counterexample to this generalization: the case of the sufficiency conditional conjunction, illustrated in the following examples:

(103) a. You $\left\{\begin{array}{l}\text{only}\\\text{just}\end{array}\right\}$ have to look at him and he shies away in fear.

b. = If you $\left\{\begin{array}{l}\text{only}\\\text{just}\end{array}\right\}$ look at him, he shies away in fear.

c. ≠ If you $\left\{\begin{array}{l}\text{only}\\\text{just}\end{array}\right\}$ have to look at him, he shies away in fear.

The example in (103a) is special among CCs in that it contains a modal (specifically the sufficiency modal construction studied in von Fintel and Iatridou (2007)) that does not contribute to the antecedent proposition. (103a) is synonymous with (103b) and not with (103c). In other words, the paradigm in (103) shows that it is not the case that the first conjunct of a conditional conjunction has the exact same possibilities as the antecedent of the "equivalent" conditional of the *if p, q* form. We feel that fully understanding this construction would help us enormously with understanding how CCs work. Alas, we are not even close to reaching that goal.

13.4.2.5 Challenges to a unified approach of IaDs While we are generally optimistic about a uniform Type II analysis for IaDs, which treats all of them as cases of conditional conjunction, there are also a few difficulties. One that we have already seen is the case of Catalan, which permits the formation of e-IaDs with a negated subjunctive, but not of n-IaDs. But there are other potential differences, involving not imperative substitutes but the imperative itself. Greek imperatives permit second person subjects.[29] In an e-IaD, the subject can be preverbal (as well as post-verbal), in an n-IaD it must be postverbal:[30]

---

[29] Greek imperatives, in fact, permit *only* second person subjects, unlike English, which permits third person as well.

[30] Bulgarian shows the same phenomenon (Roumi Pancheva, p.c.).

(104) e-IaD
Esi kane ta mathimata su   ke ola tha pane kale
You do   the lessons your and all will go   well

(105) n-IaD
  a. ??Esi fae   ena apo afta ke tha pethanis mesa se 24 ores
       You Eat.IMP   one from these and FUT die   within   24 hours
  b. fae   esi ena apo afta ke tha pethanis mesa se 24 ores
     Eat.IMP you one from these and FUT die   within   24 hours

Other differences between e-IaDs and n-IaDs were identified by Han (1998) and Russell (2007) and experimentally confirmed by Scontras and Gibson (2011): *do*-support and overt imperative subjects favor e-IaD interpretations. Since we do not think that there are two different structures for e-IaDs and n-IaDs, we need to provide some other foothold for markers that favor an endorsing reading. The obvious thought would be that some of these markers are conventional indicators of speaker endorsement, somewhat like a hidden way of adding an appositive remark:

(106) If you invest in this company, which I strongly advise, you will become rich.

We have no worked-out analysis along these lines (and it's not clear how this might extend to the effect of having an overt subject).

13.4.2.6 *Embeddability of IaDs* Since n-IaDs, and possibly e-IaDs as well, express conditional propositions and do not seem to encode any speech act other than assertion, one would think that IaDs can be embedded wherever proposition-expressing constructions can be embedded. But while CCs in general can be embedded more or less felicitously, IaDs cannot:

(107) He doesn't believe that you look at him and he shies under the table.

(108) a. *He doesn't believe that ignore your homework and you will fail.
      b. *He doesn't believe that study and you will succeed.

IaDs have the embeddability properties of imperative forms, in that they can't be embedded in most places but can be embedded where imperatives can (see Crnič and Trinh 2008, 2009 for discussion of the embeddability of imperatives):

(109) a. John said call him.
      b. John said ignore him and you will regret it.
      c. John said talk to him and everything will be fine.

We do not have a thoroughly worked-out explanation for this, but the pattern is reminiscent of a phenomenon described in Gazdar et al. (1985) and Progovac (1998), in which we see that it is the first conjunct that satisfies the subcategorization requirements of the higher verb. The verb *depend on* subcategorizes for a DP and cannot take a CP as complement. When a DP and a CP are conjoined, that conjunction will do as a complement of *depend on* but only if the DP is the first conjunct:

(110) a. You can depend on my assistant
b. *You can depend on that he will be on time.
c. You can depend on my assistant and that he will be on time.
d. *You can depend on that my assistant will be on time and his intelligence.

It is possible then, that the contrast beween (108) and (109b,c) is due to the imperative, as the first conjunct, being visible to the subcategorization needs of the higher verb in a manner that is general for conjunctions at large. This visibility creates a problem for (108) but is fine in (109b,c) since this verb can embed imperatives, as is independently attested in (109a).

13.4.2.7 Rejections and tags Intriguingly, when one adds tags to imperatives, they use the future form *will*:

(111) a. Take out the garbage, will you?
b. Take out the garbage, won't you?

There were early proposals that took this data point to argue for an analysis of imperatives that had an underlying future morpheme (see especially Katz and Postal 1964: 74–9; and see Arbini 1969 and Huddleston 1970 for early follow-ups). One might also point out that the most idiomatic way of rejecting an imperative seems to involve *will*:

(112) a. Take out the garbage!
b. No, I won't do that.

Half of the authors thinks that this connection between imperatives and the future might motivate a rethinking of the nature of the TDL and replacing it with some kind of more future-oriented discourse component, rather than a list of direct obligations. The other half doesn't quite know what to make of this.

13.4.2.8 Imperatives and negation The position that an imperative verb form does not contain a command or force operator raises problems that one might have considered solved and that will now have to be reinvestigated. There are languages that do not have "true" negative imperatives. This means that in the presence of negation, the verb form must be taken from a non-imperative directive paradigm, typically an infinitive or a subjunctive, like, for example, in Greek:

(113) a. *mi   dhiavase   to
      NEG read.IMP   it

b. *mi   to dhiavasis!*
   NEG it read.SUBJ
   'Don't read it!'

The explanation of Han (2001) and Zeijlstra (2013) for this phenomenon crucially relies on the syntactic presence of a force operator. They argue that the syntax of languages like Greek is such that the force operator would end up in the scope of negation, and this is not a licit configuration. If there is no force operator in the syntax, we obviously need a different explanation for (113a,b).

13.4.2.9 *Conditional imperatives*   One prima facie suggestive reason to think that imperatives have a modal meaning is that there are conditional imperatives:

(114)   If he calls, tell him I'm not here!

Assuming the restrictor theory of conditionals, the easiest way to understand (114) is to say that the *if*-clause restricts the imperative modal. If imperatives have a minimal, non-modal semantics, we need a different analysis of conditional imperatives. We do not have one at the moment.

13.4.3 *One last summary*

Imperatives have a minimal, non-modal semantics. Imperatives have variable pragmatic force (but so do the other major speech moves).

Acknowledgments

This chapter has taken far too long to write. We have talked about and taught this material many times in many places. It all started with a seminar on imperatives we taught at MIT in 2008. We've also taught this material at the 2009 LSA Institute in Berkeley CA, and in subsequent classes and seminars at MIT. Kai gave related talks at Cornell, UConn, Yale, UMass, and CLS. Sabine gave relevant talks in Athens, St. Petersburg, U. of Chicago, Konstanz, EGG, LOT. We are extremely thankful to the audiences at all of these occasions. We also thank colleagues and friends who have discussed these matters with us. Finally, we thank those who have shared their native judgments with us.

References

Aboh, E. O. (2009). Clause structure and verb series. *Linguistic Inquiry* 40: 1–33.
Abusch, D. (1985). On verbs and times. Ph.D. thesis, University of Massachusetts Amherst.
Abusch, D. (1997). Sequence of tense and temporal *de re*. *Linguistics and Philosophy* 20: 1–50.
Abusch, D. (2012). Circumstantial and temporal dependence in counterfactual modals. *Natural Language Semantics* 20: 273–97.
Aikhenvald, A. Y. (2004). *Evidentiality*. Oxford: Oxford University Press.
Aikhenvald, A. Y., and R. M. W. Dixon (eds) (2003). *Studies in Evidentiality*. Amsterdam: Benjamins.
Alexiadou, A., M. Rathert, and A. von Stechow (2003). The modules of perfect constructions. In A. Alexiadou, M. Rathert, and A. von Stechow (eds), *Perfect Explorations*. Berlin: de Gruyter, v–xxxvi.
Aloni, M. (2001). Quantification under conceptual covers. Ph.D. thesis, University of Amsterdam.
Aloni, M., and A. Port (2011). On epistemic indefinites. *Sinn und Bedeutung* 16, Utrecht University.
Aloni, M., and A. Port (2013). Epistemic indefinites crosslinguistically. In Y. Fainleib, N. Cara, and Y. Park (eds), *Proceedings of the 41st Annual Meeting of the North East Linguistic Society*. Amherst, Mass.: GLSA, 29–43.
Aloni, M., and A. Port (2015). Epistemic indefinites and methods of identification. In L. Alonso-Ovalle and P. Menéndez-Benito (eds), *Epistemic Indefinites*, 116–40. Oxford: Oxford University Press.
Alonso-Ovalle, L., and P. Menéndez-Benito (2003). Some epistemic indefinites. In M. Kadowaki and S. Kawahara (eds), *Proceedings of the 33rd Annual Meeting of the North East Linguistic Society*. Amherst, Mass.: GLSA, 1–12.
Alonso-Ovalle, L., and P. Menéndez-Benito (2008). Minimal domain widening. In N. Abner and J. Bishop (eds), *Proceedings of the 27th West Coast Conference on Formal Linguistics*. Somerville, Mass.: Cascadilla, 36–44.
Alonso-Ovalle, L., and P. Menéndez-Benito (2010). Modal indefinites. *Natural Language Semantics* 18(1): 1–31.
Alonso-Ovalle, L., and P. Menéndez-Benito (2011a). Domain restrictions, modal implicatures and plurality: Spanish *algunos*. *Journal of Semantics* 28: 211–40.
Alonso-Ovalle, L., and P. Menéndez-Benito (2011b). Expressing indifference: Spanish *un NP cualquiera*. In N. Ashton, A. Chereches, and D. Lutz (eds), *Proceedings of the 21st Semantics and Linguistics Theory Conference*, 333–42. Available online at: journals.linguisticsociety.org/proceedings/index.php/SALT/issue/.../88
Alonso-Ovalle, L., and P. Menéndez-Benito (2013a). Epistemic indefinites: are we ignorant about ignorance? In M. Aloni, M. Franke, and F. Roelofsen (eds) *Proceedings of the 19th Amsterdam Colloquium*, 35–43. Available online at: http://staff.science.uva.nl/maloni/AC2013/ACproceedings.pdf

Alonso-Ovalle, L., and P. Menéndez-Benito (2013b). Two views on epistemic indefinites. *Language and Linguistics Compass* 17(2): 105–22.

Alonso-Ovalle, L., and P. Menéndez-Benito (2013c). Random choice modality: Spanish *uno cualquiera*. In E. Chemla, V. Homer, and G. Winterstein (eds), *Proceedings of Sinn und Bedeutung* 17, 27–43. Paris: ENS. Available online at: http://semanticsarchive.net/sub2012/

Alonso-Ovalle, L., and J. Shimoyama (2014). Expressing ignorance in the nominal domain: Japanese *wh-ka*. In R. E. Santana-LaBarge (ed.), *Proceedings of the 31st West Coast Conference on Formal Linguistics*, 11–20. Somerville, Mass.: Cascadilla.

Anand, P., and V. Hacquard (2013). Epistemics and attitudes. *Semantics and Pragmatics* 6: 1–59.

Anderson, A. R. (1951). A note on subjunctive and counterfactual conditionals. *Analysis* 12(2): 35–8.

Andrejčin, L. (1944). *Osnovna bulgarska gramatika*. Sofia: Hemus.

Arbini, R. (1969). Tag-questions and tag-imperatives in English. *Journal of Linguistics* 5: 205–14.

Arregui, A. (2005). On the accessibility of possible worlds: the role of tense and aspect. Ph.D. thesis, University of Massachusetts Amherst.

Arregui, A. (2009). On similarity in counterfactuals. *Linguistics and Philosophy* 32: 245–78.

Arregui, A., M. L. Rivero, and A. P. Salanova (2014). Cross-linguistic variation in imperfectivity. *Natural Language and Linguistic Theory* 32: 307–62.

Austin, J. (1962). *How to Do Things with Words*. Oxford: Clarendon Press.

Axel-Tober, K., and R. Gergel (to appear). Modality and mood in formal syntactic approaches. In J. Nuyts and J. van der Auwera (eds), *The Oxford Handbook of Modality and Mood*. Oxford: Oxford University Press.

Aygen, G. (2004). T-to-C and overt marking of counterfactuals: syntactic and semantic implications. *Harvard Working Papers in Linguistics* 10: 1–18.

Baker, M. (1985). The mirror principle and morphosyntactic explanation. *Linguistic Inquiry* 16: 373–415.

Bar-el, L., H. Davis, and L. Matthewson (2005). On non-culminating accomplishments. In *Proceedings of NELS* 35(1): 87–102. Amherst, Mass.: GLSA.

Bar-Lev, Z., and A. Palacas (1980). Semantic command over pragmatic priority. *Lingua* 51: 137–46.

Beavers, J. (2006). Argument/oblique alternations and the structure of lexical meaning. Ph.D. thesis, Stanford University,

Beavers, J. (2010). An aspectual analysis of ditransitive verbs of caused possession in English. *Journal of Semantics* 28: 1–54.

Bech, G. (1951). *Grundzüge der semantischen Entwicklungsgeschichte der hochdeutschen Modalverba* [Outline of the semantic developmental history of the High German modal verbs]. Copenhagen: Munksgaard.

Beck, S., and R. Gergel (2014). *Contrasting English and German Grammar: An Introduction to Syntax and Semantics*. Berlin: de Gruyter.

Becker, M. (1999). The *some* indefinites. In G. Storto (ed.), *Syntax at Sunset 2: UCLA Working Papers in Linguistics*, 1–13. Los Angeles: UCLA.

Bédaride, P. (2012). Raffinement du lexique des verbes français. In *Actes de TALN 2012*. Available online at: www.atala.org/taln_archives/TALN/TALN-2012/

Benmamoun, E. (2000). *The Feature Structure of Functional Categories: A Comparative Study of Arabic Dialects*. Oxford: Oxford University Press.

Bennett, M., and B. Partee (1978). *Towards the Logic of Tense and Aspect in English*. Bloomington, Ind.: Indiana Linguistics Club.

Bhatt, R. (1997). Counterfactual morphology in modern Indo-Aryan languages: semantic and typological issues. MS, University of Pennsylvania/MIT.

Bhatt, R. (1999). Covert modality in non-finite contexts. Ph.D. thesis, University of Pennsylvania.

Bhatt, R., and R. Pancheva (2006). Conditionals. In M. Everaert and H. van Riensdijk (eds), *The Blackwell Companion to Syntax*, 638–87. Oxford: Blackwell.

Biberauer, T., A. Holmberg, and I. Roberts (2008). Structure and linearization in disharmonic word orders. In C. B. Chang and H. J. Haynie (eds), *Proceedings of the 26th WCCFL*, 96–104. Somerville, Mass.: Cascadilla.

Bjorkman, B. M. (2011). *Be-ing* default: the morphosyntax of auxiliaries. Ph.D. thesis, MIT.

Bjorkman, B. M., and C. Halpert (2013). In search of (im)perfection: the illusion of counterfactual aspect. In *Proceedings of NELS 42*, 67–78. Amherst, Mass.: GLSA.

BNC (2007). *British National Corpus*. Oxford: BNC Consortium.

Boas, F. (1947). Kwakiutl grammar, with a glossary of the suffixes. *Transactions of the American Philosophical Society* 37: 201–377.

Bobaljik, J., and H. Thráinsson (1998). Two heads aren't always better than one. *Syntax* 1: 37–71.

Bolinger, D. (1967). The imperative in English. In *To honor Roman Jakobson*, vol. 1, 335–62. The Hague: Mouton.

Bolinger, D. (1977). *Meaning and Form*. Harlow: Longman.

Boogaart, R. (2007). The past and perfect of epistemic modals. In L. de Saussure, J. Moeschler and G. Puskas (eds), *Recent Advances in the Syntax and Semantics of Tense, Aspect and Modality*, 47–70. Berlin: de Gruyter.

Borgonovo, C., and S. Cummins (2007). Tensed modals. In L. Eguren and O. Fernández Soriano (eds), *Coreference, Modality, and Focus*, 1–18. Amsterdam: Benjamins.

Botne, R., and T. Kerchner (2000). Time, tense, and the perfect in Zulu. *Afrika und Übersee* 83: 161–80.

Bouchard, D.-É. (2012). Long-distance degree quantification and the grammar of subjectivity. Ph.D. thesis, McGill University.

Bouchard, D.-É. (2013). The partial factivity of opinion verbs. In *Proceedings of Sinn und Bedeutung* 17: 133–48. Available online at: semanticsarchive.net/sub2012/

Brennan, V. (1993). Root and epistemic modal auxiliary verbs in English. Ph.D. thesis, University of Massachusetts Amherst.

Büring, D. (2008). The least *at least* can do. In C. B. Chang and H. J. Haynie (eds), *Proceedings of the 26th West Coast Conference on Formal Linguistics*, 114–20. Somerville, Mass.: Cascadilla.

Burton, S., and L. Matthewson (2015). Targeted construction storyboards in semantic fieldwork. In R. Bochnak and L. Matthewson (eds), *Semantic Fieldwork Methodology*, 135–56. Oxford: Oxford University Press.

Butler, J. (2003). A minimalist treatment of modality. *Lingua* 113: 867–996.

Bybee, J., R. Perkins, and W. Pagliuca (1994). *The Evolution of Grammar: Tense, Aspect, and Modality in the Languages of the World*. Chicago: University of Chicago Press.

Castle, N., R. Chancall, and I. Yanovich (2012). Modals in the complements of verbs of asking in 15th century English. Technical report, MIT.
Chafe, W., and J. Nichols (eds) (1986). *Evidentiality: The Linguistic Coding of Epistemology*. Norwood, NJ: Ablex.
Charlow, N. (2014). The meaning of imperatives. *Philosophy Compass* 9: 540–55.
Chen, S. (2014). The temporal interpretation of modals in Mandarin Chinese. *UBC Working Papers in Linguistics* 34: 15–30.
Chen, S. (in prep.). Temporal interpretation of modals: evidence from Atayal. Ph.D. thesis, University of British Columbia.
Chierchia, G. (2013). *Logic in Grammar: Polarity, Free Choice and Intervention*. Oxford: Oxford University Press.
Choi, J. (2007). Free choice and negative polarity: a compositional analysis of Korean polarity sensitive items. Ph.D. thesis, University of Pennsylvania.
Choi, J., and M. Romero (2008). Rescuing existential free choice items in episodic sentences. In O. Bonami and P. Cabredo Hoffner (eds), *Empirical Issues in Syntax and Semantics* 7: 77–98.
Cinque, G. (1999). *Adverbs and Functional Heads: A Cross-Linguistic Perspective*. Oxford: Oxford University Press.
Cipria, A., and C. Roberts (2000). Spanish *imperfecto* and *pretérito*: truth conditions and aktionsart effects in a situation semantics. *Natural Language Semantics* 8: 297–347.
Clark, B. (1993). Relevance and 'pseudo-imperatives'. *Linguistics and Philosophy* 16: 79–121.
Coates, J. (1983). *The Semantics of the Modal Auxiliaries*. London: Croom Helm.
Condoravdi, C. (2002). Temporal interpretation of modals: modals for the present and for the past. In D. Beaver, S. Kaufmann, B. Clark, and L. Casillas (eds), *The Construction of Meaning*, 59–88. Stanford, Calif.: CSLI.
Condoravdi, C. and S. Lauer (2011). Performative verbs and performative acts. In *Proceedings of Sinn und Bedeutung 15*, 149–64. Saarbrücken: Saarland University Press.
Condoravdi, C., and S. Lauer (2012). Imperatives: meaning and illocutionary force. *Empirical Issues in Syntax and Semantics* 9: 37–58.
Crnič, L. (2011). Getting *even*. Ph.D. thesis, MIT.
Crnič, L., and T. Trinh (2008). Embedding imperatives. *North East Linguistics Society (NELS)* 39.
Crnič, L., and T. Trinh (2009). Embedding imperatives in English. *Sinn und Bedeutung* 13: 113–27.
Culicover, P. W. (1972). OM-sentences. *Foundations of Language* 8: 199–236.
Culicover, P. W., and R. S. Jackendoff (1997). Semantic subordination despite syntactic coordination. *Linguistic Inquiry* 28: 195–218.
Cyrino, S., and G. Matos (2002). VP-ellipsis in European and Brazilian Portuguese: a comparative analysis. *Journal of Portuguese Linguistics* 1: 177–95.
Dahl, Ö (1985). *Tense and Aspect Systems*. Oxford: Blackwell.
Davidson, D. (1967). The logical form of action sentences. In N. Rescher (ed.), *The Logic of Decision and Action*, 81–95. Pittsburgh: University of Pittsburgh Press.
Davies, M. (2008). The Corpus of Contemporary American English: 450 million words, 1990–present. Available online at: http://corpus.byu.edu/coca/

Davies, M. (2012). The corpus of American soap operas: 100 million words, 2001–2012. Available online at: http://corpus2.byu.edu/soap/

Davis, C. (2011). Constraining interpretation. Ph.D. thesis, University of Massachusetts Amherst.

Davis, H. (2012). A teaching grammar of Upper St'át'imcets. MS, University of British Columbia.

Davis, H., L. Matthewson, and H. Rullmann (2009). 'Out of control' marking as circumstantial modality in St'át'imcets. In L. Hogeweg, H. de Hoop, and A. Malchukov (eds), *Cross-Linguistic Semantics of Tense, Aspect and Modality*, 205–44. Amsterdam: Benjamins.

Deal, A. R. (2011). Modals without scales. *Language* 87: 559–85.

Demirdache, H. (1997). 'Out of control' in Salish and event (de)composition. MS, University of British Columbia.

Demirdache, H., and F. Martin (2015). Agent control over non-culminating events. In E. Barrajón López, J. L. Cifuentes Honrubia, and S. Rodríguez Rosique (eds), *Verb Classes and Aspect*, 185–217. Amsterdam: Benjamins.

Demirdache, H., and H. Sun (2014). On non-culminating accomplishments in Mandarin. MS, University of Nantes.

Demirdache, H., and M. Uribe-Etxebarria (2008). Scope and anaphora with time arguments: the case of 'perfect' modals. *Lingua* 118: 1790–1815.

Demonte, V., and O. Fernández-Soriano (2013). Evidentials *dizque* and *que* in Spanish: grammaticalization, parameters and the (fine) structure of Comp. *Linguística: Revista de estudos linguísticos da Universidade do Porto* 8: 211–34.

Denison, D. (1993). *English Historical Syntax*. London: Longman.

Denison, D., G. Trousdale, and L. van Bergen (1994). A corpus of Late Modern English prose (CLMEP). Corpus constructed 1992–1994 by David Denison with the very considerable assistance of Graeme Trousdale and Linda van Bergen. Distributed through the Oxford Text Archive.

Dorr, C., and J. Hawthorne (2013). Embedding epistemic modals. *Mind* 122: 867–913.

Dowty, D. (1972). Studies in the logic of verb aspect and time reference in English. Ph.D. thesis, University of Texas.

Drubig, H. B. (2001). On the syntactic form of epistemic modality. MS, Universität Tübingen.

Ducrot, O. (1975). Je trouve que. *Semantikos* 1: 63–88.

Dunham, J. (2008). A unified analysis of the habitual and in-progress readings of *á* in Blackfoot. MS, University of British Columbia.

Eckardt, R. (2006). *Meaning Change in Grammaticalization: An Enquiry into Semantic Reanalysis*. Oxford: Oxford University Press.

Egan, A., J. Hawthorne, and B. Weatherson (2005). Epistemic modals in context. In G. Preyer and P. Peter (eds), *Contextualism in Philosophy*, 131–68. Oxford: Oxford University Press.

Eide, K. (2003). Modals and tense. In M. Weisgerber (ed.), *Proceedings of Sinn und Bedeutung 7*, 120–35.

Enç, M. (1996). Tense and modality. In S. Lappin (ed.), *The Handbook of Contemporary Semantic Theory*, 345–58. Oxford: Blackwell.

Fălăuș, A. (2009). Polarity items and dependent indefinites in Romanian. Dissertation, Université de Nantes.

Fălăuş, A. (2011a). Alternatives as sources of semantic dependency. In N. Li and D. Lutz (eds), *Proceedings of SALT 20*, 406–27. Available online at:conf.ling.cornell.edu/salt/20/salt20bib.pdf

Fălăuş, A. (2011b). New challenges in the area of semantically dependent indefinites: the Romanian epistemic constraint. In J. Herschensohn (ed.), *Romance Linguistics 2010*, 287–302. Amsterdam: Benjamins.

Fălăuş, A. (2014). (Partially) free choice of alternatives. *Linguistics and Philosophy* 37(2): 121–73.

Faller, M. (2002). Semantics and pragmatics of evidentials in Cuzco Quechua. Ph.D. thesis, Stanford University.

Faller, M. (2011). A possible worlds semantics for Cuzco Quechua evidentials. Proceedings of *SALT 20*, 660–83. Ithaca, NY: CLC.

Farahani, A. A. K. (1990). A syntactic and semantic study of the tense and aspect system of modern Persian. Ph.D. thesis, University of Leeds.

Farkas, D. (2002a). Varieties of indefinites. In B. Jackson (ed.), *Proceedings of SALT 12*, 59–83. Ithaca, NY: CLC.

Farkas, D. (2002b). Extreme non-specificity in Romanian. In C. Beyssade, R. Bok-Bennema, F. Drijkoningen, and P. Monachesi (eds), *Romance Languages and Linguistic Theory*, 127–51. Amsterdam: Benjamins.

Farkas, D. F. (2011). Polarity particles in English and Romanian. In *Romance Linguistics 2010*, 303–28. Amsterdam: Benjamins.

Farkas, D. F., and K. B. Bruce (2010). On reacting to assertions and polar questions. *Journal of Semantics* 27: 81–118.

Ferreira, M. (2014). Displaced aspect in counterfactuals: towards a more unified theory of imperfectivity. In L. Crnic and U. Sauerland (eds), *The Art and Craft of Semantics: A Festschrift for Irene Heim*, 147–64. Cambridge, Mass.: MIT Working Papers in Linguistics.

Finlay, S. (2009). Oughts and ends. *Philosophical Studies* 143: 315–40.

von Fintel, K. (1994). Restrictions on quantifier domains. Ph.D. thesis, University of Massachusetts Amherst.

von Fintel, K. (1999). NPI-licensing, Strawson-entailment, and context-dependency. *Journal of Semantics* 16:97–148.

von Fintel, K. (2000). Singleton indefinites (re. Schwarzschild 2000). MS, MIT.

von Fintel, K. (2003). Epistemic modals and conditionals revisited. Handout from a colloquium talk at University of Massachusetts Amherst.

von Fintel, K. (2012). The best we can (expect to) get? Challenges to the classic semantics for deontic modals. Paper presented in a session on deontic modals at the Central APA, Feb. 17.

von Fintel, K., and A. S. Gillies (2007). An opinionated guide to epistemic modality. *Oxford Studies in Epistemology* 2: 32–62.

von Fintel, K., and A. S. Gillies (2008). CIA leaks. *Philosophical Review* 117: 77–98.

von Fintel, K., and A. S. Gillies (2010). Must...stay...strong! *Natural Language Semantics* 18: 351–83.

von Fintel, K., and I. Heim (2011). Intensional semantics. Manuscript, MIT. Available at: http://mit.edu/fintel/fintel-heim-intensional.pdf

von Fintel, K., and S. Iatridou (2003). Epistemic containment. *Linguistic Inquiry* 34: 173–98.

von Fintel, K., and S. Iatridou (2007). Anatomy of a modal construction. *Linguistic Inquiry* 38: 445–483.
von Fintel, K., and S. Iatridou (2008). How to say *ought* in foreign: the composition of weak necessity modals. In J. Guéron and J. Lecarme (eds), *Time and Modality*, 115–41. New York: Springer.
Fischer, O. (2010). On problem areas in grammaticalization: Lehmann's parameters and the issue of scope. In A. Van Linden, J. Verstraete, and K. Davidse (eds), *Formal Evidence in Grammaticalization Research*, 17–42. Amsterdam: Benjamins.
Fischer, O., A. van Kemenade, W. Koopman, W., and W. van der Wurff (2000). *The Syntax of Early English*. Cambridge: Cambridge University Press.
Fleck, D. (2003). A grammar of Matses. Ph.D. thesis. Rice University, Texas.
Fleck, D. (2007). Evidentiality and double tense in Matses. *Language* 83: 589–614.
Fleischman, S. (1989). Temporal distance: a basic linguistic metaphor. *Studies in Language* 13: 1–50.
Fox, D. (2007). Free choice and the theory of scalar implicatures. In U. Sauerland and P. Stateva (eds), *Presupposition and Implicature in Compositional Semantics*, 71–120. Basingstoke: Palgrave Macmillan.
Frana, I. (2010). Concealed questions: in search of answers. Ph.D. thesis, University of Massachusetts Amherst.
Franke, M. (2009). Signal to act. Ph.D. thesis, Institute for Logic, Language and Computation, Universiteit van Amsterdam.
Frantz, D., and N. J. Russell (1995). *Blackfoot Dictionary of Stems, Affixes and Roots*, 2nd edn. Toronto: Toronto University Press.
Friedman, V. (1986). Evidentiality in the Balkans. In Chafe, W., and J. Nichols (eds), *Evidentiality: The Linguistic Coding of Epistemology*, 168–97. Norwood, NJ: Ablex.
Fulk, R. D. (2012). *An Introduction to Middle English*. Peterborough, ON: Broadview Press.
Galloway, B. (1993). *A Grammar of Upriver Halkomelem*. Berkeley: University of California Press.
Gazdar, G., E. H. Klein, G. K. Pullum, and I. A. Sag (1985). *Generalized Phrase Structure Grammar*. Oxford: Blackwell.
Gergel, R. (2008). Comparative inversion: a diachronic study. *Journal of Comparative Germanic Linguistics* 11: 191–211.
Gergel, R. (2009a). *Modality and Ellipsis: Diachronic and Synchronic Evidence*. Berlin: Mouton de Gruyter.
Gergel, R. (2009b). *Rather*—on a modal cycle. In E. van Gelderen (ed.), *Cyclical Change*, 243–64. Amsterdam: Benjamins.
Gergel, R., and C. Cunha (2009). Modalidade e inferências do mundo real em português europeu. *Rasal Linguistica* 1/2: 111–27.
Geurts, B. (1998). Presuppositions and anaphors in attitude contexts. *Linguistics and Philosophy* 21: 545–601.
Giannakidou, A., and J. Quer (2013). Exhaustive and non-exhaustive variation with free choice and referential vagueness: evidence from Greek, Catalan, and Spanish. *Lingua* 126: 120–49.
Gillies, A., and K. von Fintel (2007). An opinionated guide to epistemic modality. In T. Gendler and J. Hawthorne (eds), *Oxford Studies in Epistemology* 2, 32–62. Oxford: Oxford University Press.

Goldberg, L. M. (2005). Verb-stranding VP ellipsis: a cross-linguistic study. Ph.D. thesis, McGill University.

Goosens, L. (1982). On the development of the modals and of the epistemic function in English. In A. Ahlqvist (ed.), *Papers from the 5th International Conference on Historical* Linguistics. Amsterdam: Benjamins.

Goosens, L. (1987). The auxiliarization of the English modals: a functional grammar view. In M. Harris and P. Ramat (eds), *Historical Development of Auxiliaries*, 111–44. Berlin: Mouton de Gruyter.

Gotti, M., M. Dossana, R. Dury, R. Facchinetti, and M. Lima (2002). *Variation in Central Modals*. Bern: Lang.

Green, G. (1974). *Semantics and Syntactic Regularity*. Bloomington: Indiana University Press.

Groenendijk, J., and M. Stokhof (1975). Modality and conversational information. *Theoretical Linguistics* 2: 61–112.

Gropen, J., S. Pinker, M. Hollander, R. Goldberg, and R. Wilson (1989). The learnability and acquisition of the dative alternation in English. *Language* 65: 203–57.

Grosz, P. (2009). German particles, modality, and the semantics of imperatives. *North East Linguistic Society (NELS)* 39: 323–36.

Hackl, M., and J. Nissenbaum (2012). A modal ambiguity in *for*-infinitival relative clauses. *Natural Language Semantics* 20: 59–81.

Hacquard, V. (2006). Aspects of modality. Ph.D. thesis, MIT.

Hacquard, V. (2010). On the event relativity of modal auxiliaries. Natural Language Semantics 18: 79–114.

Hacquard, V. (2011). Modality. In K. von Heusinger, C. Maienborn, and P. Portner (eds), *Semantics: An International Handbook of Natural Language Meaning*, vol. 2, 1484–1515. Berlin: Mouton de Gruyter.

Haeberli, E. (2000). Adjuncts and the syntax of subjects in Old and Middle English. In S. Pintzuk, G. Tsoulas, and A. Warner (eds), *Diachronic Syntax: Models and Mechanisms*, 109–31. Oxford: Oxford University Press.

Hagstrom, P. (1998). Decomposing questions. Ph.D. thesis, MIT.

Haider, H. (1997). Projective economy: on the minimal functional structure of the German clause. In *Arbeitspapiere des Sonderforschungsbereichs 340: Sprachtheoretische Grundlagen für die Computerlinguistik*, 31–54. Tübingen: Universität Tübingen.

Halbach, V., and P. Welch (2009). Necessities and necessary truths: a prolegomenon to the use of modal logic in the analysis of intensional notions. *Mind* 118: 71–100.

Hale, K. (1969). Papago /čim/. *International Journal of American Linguistics* 35: 203.

Halpert, C., and H. Karawani (2012). Aspect in counterfactuals from A(rabic) to Z(ulu). In *Proceedings of WCCFL 29*, 99–107. Somerville, Mass.: Cascadilla.

Han, C. (1998). The structure and interpretation of imperatives. Ph.D. thesis, University of Pennsylvania. Published 2000 by Garland, New York.

Han, C. (2000). *The Structure and Interpretation of Imperatives*. New York: Garland.

Han, C. (2001). Force, negation and imperatives. *Linguistic Review* 18: 289–325.

Han, C. (2011). Imperatives. In C. Maienborn, K. von Heusinger, and P. Portner (eds), *Semantics*, 1785–1804. Berlin: de Gruyter.

Haspelmath, M. (1997). *Indefinite Pronouns*. Oxford: Oxford University Press.

Hatley, R. (1984). Mapping cultural regions of Java. In R. Hatley, J. Schiller, A. Lucas, and B. Martin-Schiller (eds), *Other Javas: Away from the Kraton*, 1–32. Clayton: Monash University.

Hausser, R. R. (1980). Surface compositionality and the semantics of mood. In J. R. Searle, F. Kiefer, and M. Bierwisch (eds), *Speech Act Theory and Pragmatics*, 71–95. Dordrecht: Reidel.

Heim, I. (1979). Concealed questions. In R. Bauerle, U. Egli, and A. von Stechow (eds), *Semantics from Different Points of View*, 51–60. Berlin: Springer.

Heim, I. (1982). The semantics of definite and indefinite noun phrases. Dissertation, University of Massachusetts.

Heim, I. (1992). Presupposition projection and the semantics of attitude verbs. *Journal of Semantics* 9: 183–221.

Heim, I., and A. Kratzer (1998). *Semantics in Generative Grammar*. Malden, Mass.: Blackwell.

Higgins, R. (1979). *The Pseudo-cleft Construction in English*. New York: Garland.

Hindle, L., and B. Rigsby (1973). A short practical dictionary of the Gitksan language. *Northwest Anthropological Research Notes* 7: 1–60.

Hintikka, J. (1969). Semantics for propositional attitudes. In J. W. Davis, D. J. Hockney, and W. K. Wilson (eds), *Philosophical Logic*, 21–45. Dordrecht: Kluwer Academic.

Hiyama, S. (2005). Element order in the Vercelli homilies. *Journal of the Faculty of Foreign Languages* (Komazawa University, Tokyo) 32: 1–288.

Homer, V. (2010). Epistemic modals: high ma non troppo. In S. Kan (ed.), *Proceedings of NELS 40*, 14–28.

Homer, V. (2011). Polarity and modality. Ph.D. thesis, University of California, Los Angeles.

Horne, E. C. (1961). *Beginning Javanese*. New Haven, Conn.: Yale University Press.

Huang, L. M. (2008). Grammaticalization in Squliq Atayal. *Concentric: Studies in Linguistics* 34: 1–46.

Huddleston, R. (1970). Two approaches to the analysis of tags. *Journal of Linguistics* 6: 215–22.

Huitink, J. (2008). Scoping over epistemics in English and in Dutch. In *Current Issues in Unity and Diversity of Languages*, 2077–89. Seoul: Dongam.

Iatridou, S. (1990). The past, the possible and the evident. *Linguistic Inquiry* 21: 123–9.

Iatridou, S. (1991). Topics in conditionals. Ph.D. thesis, MIT.

Iatridou, S. (2000). The grammatical ingredients of counterfactuality. *Linguistic Inquiry* 31: 231–70.

Iatridou, S. (2009). Some thoughts about the imperfective in counterfactuals. Handout from Yale Imperfective Workshop, April 10–11, 2009. Available online at: http://web.mit.edu/linguistics/people/faculty/iatridou/publications.html

Iatridou, S. (2014). Grammar matters. In L. Walters and J. Hawthorne (eds), *Conditionals, Probability, and Paradox*. Oxford: Oxford University Press.

Iatridou, S., and D. Embick (1994). Conditional inversion. In *Proceedings of NELS* 24: 189–203.

Ippolito, M. (2002). On the semantic composition of subjunctive conditionals. MS, MIT/Universität Tübingen.

Ippolito, M. (2004). Imperfect modality. In J. Guéron and J. Lecarme (eds), *The Syntax of Time*, 359–87. Cambridge, Mass.: MIT Press.

Ippolito, M. (2006). Semantic composition and presupposition projection in subjunctive conditionals. *Linguistics and Philosophy* 29: 631–72.

Ippolito, M. (2008). Subjunctive conditionals. In *Proceedings of Sinn und Bedeutung* 12: 256–70.

Isard, S. D. (1974). What would you have done if . . . ? *Theoretical Linguistics* 1: 233–56.
Israel, M. (2000). *Some* and the pragmatics of indefinite construal. In S. S. Chang, L. Liaw, and J. Ruppenhofer (eds), *Proceedings of the 25th Annual Meeting of the Berkeley Linguistics Society*, 169–82. Available online at: linguistics.berkeley.edu/bls/previous_proceedings/bls25S.pdf
Israel, M. (n.d.). *Some* and the pragmatics of indefinite construal. MS. Quoted in Farkas (2002a).
Izvorski, R. (1997). The present perfect as an epistemic modal. *SALT* 7, 222–39. Ithaca, NY: CLC.
Jacobs, P. (2011). Control in Skwxwú7mesh. Ph.D. thesis, University of British Columbia.
Jakobson, R. (1957). *Shifters, Verbal Categories, and the Russian Verb*. Cambridge, Mass.: Harvard University Press. Repr. in *Selected Writings*, vol. 2: *Word and Language* (The Hague: Mouton, 1971), 130–47.
James, D. (1982). Past tense and the hypothetical: a cross-linguistic study. *Studies in Language* 6: 375–403.
Jayez, J., and L. Tovena (2006). Epistemic determiners. *Journal of Semantics* 23: 177–207.
Jayez, J., and L. Tovena (2008). Evidentiality and determination. In A. Grönn (ed.), *Proceedings of the 12th Sinn und Bedeutung Conference*. Oslo: University of Oslo, 271–82.
Jayez, J., and L. Tovena (2011). The meaning and (a bit of) the history of *quelque*. In L. Tovena (ed.), *French Determiners In and Across Time*. London: College Publications, 111–39.
Jayez, J., and L. Tovena (2013). Scenarios of equivalence: the case of *quelque*. In C. Ebert and S. Hinterwimmer (eds), *Different Kinds of Specificity across Languages*, 177–207. Berlin: Springer.
Jelinek, E. (1987). Possibility and necessity in Samish. In J. Dunn (ed.), *Papers from the 22nd International Conference on Salish and Neighbouring Languages*.
Jespersen, O. (1924). *The Philosophy of Grammar*. London: Allen & Unwin, 313–15.
Jóhannsdóttir, K., and L. Matthewson (2007). Zero-marked tense: the case of Gitxsan. In E. Elfner and M. Walkow (eds), *Proceedings of NELS 37*, I: 299–310.
Johnson, K. (2001). What VP ellipsis can do, and what it can't, but not why. In M. Baltin and C. Collins (eds), *The Handbook of Contemporary Syntactic Theory*, 439–79. Oxford: Blackwell.
Kadmon, N. (1987). On unique and non-unique reference and asymmetric quantification. Ph.D. thesis, University of Massachusetts Amherst.
Kadmon, N., and F. Landman (1993). Any. *Linguistics and Philosophy* 16: 353–422.
Kamp, H. (1999–2007). Intentions, plans and their execution: turning objects of thought into entities of the external world. MS, University of Stuttgart.
Kamp, H. (2013). Some remarks on the pragmatics and semantics of agentive and non-agentive *offer*. MS, University of Stuttgart and University of Texas at Austin.
Kaneko, M. (2011). DP external epistemic 'determiners' in Japanese. In O. Bonami and P. Cabredo Hofherr (eds), *Empirical Issues in Syntax and Semantics 8*, 239–66. http://www.cssp.cnrs.fr/eiss8/index_en.html
Karawani, H. (2014). The real, the fake, and the fake fake in counterfactual conditionals, crosslinguistically. Ph.D. thesis, Universiteit van Amsterdam.
Karawani, H., and H. Zeijlstra (2010). The semantic contribution of the past morpheme in Palestinian counterfactuals. Handout, Workshop on Tense and Aspect in Generative Grammar. Lisbon, Portugal, July 1–2.
Karttunen, L. (1974). Presupposition and linguistic context. *Theoretical Linguistics* 1: 181–94.

Katz, G., P. Portner, and A. Rubinstein (2012). Ordering combination for modal comparison. In A. Chereches (ed.), *Semantics and Linguistic Theory (SALT)* 22, 488–507. Available online at: https://www.researchgate.net/publication/281213866_Ordering_combination_for_modal_comparison

Katz, J. J., and P. M. Postal (1964). *An Integrated Theory of Linguistic Descriptions*. Cambridge, Mass.: MIT Press.

Kaufmann, M. (2012). *Interpreting Imperatives*. Berlin: Springer.

Kearns, K. (2007). Telic senses of deadjectival verbs. *Lingua* 117: 26–66.

Kelly, R. J. (ed.) (2003). *The Blickling Homilies: edition and translation*. London: Continuum Books.

Kelly, R. J. (2009). *The Blickling Concordance*. London: Continuum Books.

Kennedy, C. and B. Levin (2008). Measure of change: the adjectival core of verbs of variable telicity. In L. McNally and C. Kennedy (eds), *Adjectives and Adverbs: Syntax, Semantics, and Discourse*, 156–8. Oxford: Oxford University Press.

Keshet, E. (2012). Focus on conditional conjunction. *Journal of Semantics* 30: 211–56.

Kiyota, M. (2008). Situation aspect and viewpoint aspect: from Salish to Japanese. Ph.D. thesis, University of British Columbia.

Klein, W. (1994). *Time in Language*. New York: Routledge.

Klein, W. (2000). An analysis of the German *Perfekt*. *Language* 76: 358–82.

Klinedinst, N., and D. Rothschild (2012). Connectives without truth tables. *Natural Language Semantics* 20: 137–75.

Koenig, J.-P., and A. Davis (2001). Sublexical modality and the structure of lexical semantic representations. *Linguistics and Philosophy* 24(1): 71–124.

Koev, T. (2011). Evidentiality and temporal distance learning. *SALT* 21: 95–114.

Kölbel, M. (2004). Faultless disagreement. In *Proceedings of the Aristotelian Society* 104(1): 53–73.

Krasikova, S. (2008). Quantifiers in comparatives. In A. Grønn (ed.), *Proceedings of SuB12*, 337–52. Oslo: ILOS.

Kratzer, A. (1977). What 'must' and 'can' must and can mean. *Linguistics and Philosophy* 1(3): 337–56.

Kratzer, A. (1981). The notional category of modality. In H. J. Eikmeyer and H. Rieser (eds), *Words, Worlds, and Contexts: New Approaches in Word Semantics*, 38–74. Berlin: de Gruyter. Repr. in P. Portner and B. H. Partee (eds), *Formal Semantics: The Essential Readings* (Oxford: Blackwell, 2002), 289–323.

Kratzer, A. (1986). Conditionals. In *Proceedings of the Chicago Linguistics Society* 22: 1–15.

Kratzer, A. (1989). An investigation of the lumps of thought. *Linguistics and Philosophy* 12: 607–53.

Kratzer, A. (1991). Modality. In A. von Stechow and D. Wunderlich (eds), *Semantik: Ein internationales Handbuch der zeitgenössischen Forschung*, 639–50. Berlin: de Gruyter.

Kratzer, A. (1998). More structural analogies between pronouns and tenses. In D. Strolovitch and A. Lawson (eds), *Proceedings of SALT 8*, 92–110.

Kratzer, A. (2000). Building statives. *Berkeley Linguistic Society* 26: 385–99.

Kratzer, A. (2005). Indefinites and the operators they depend on: from Japanese to Salish. In G. N. Carlson and F. J. Pelletier (eds), *Reference and Quantification: The Partee Effect*, 113–142. Stanford, Calif.: CSLI.

Kratzer, A. (2011a). What 'can' can mean. Talk given at SALT 2011, Rutgers University.
Kratzer, A. (2011b). Situations in natural language semantics. *Stanford Encyclopedia of Philosophy*. Available online at: http://plato.stanford.edu/entries/situations-semantics/
Kratzer, A. (2012). *Modals and Conditionals*. Oxford: Oxford University Press.
Kratzer, A. (2013). Creating a family: construction transfer of possession verbs. Paper presented at Little v Workshop, Leiden University, 25-6 Oct.
Kratzer, A. (2014). Chasing Hook. To appear in L. Walters and J. Hawthorne (eds), *Conditionals, Probability, and Paradox: Themes from the Philosophy of Dorothy Edgington*. Oxford: Oxford University Press.
Kratzer, A., and J. Shimoyama (2002). Indeterminate pronouns: the view from Japanese. In Y. Otsu (ed.), *Proceedings of the 3rd Tokyo Conference on Psycholinguistics*, 1-25. Tokyo: Hituzi Syobo.
Krifka, M. (2011). Varieties of semantic evidence. In C. Maienborn, K. von Heusinger, and P. Portner (eds), *Semantics: An International Handbook of Natural Language Meaning*, 242-68. Berlin: de Gruyter.
Krifka, M., J. Pelletier, G. Carlson, A. ter Meulen, G. Chierchia, and G. Link (1995). Genericity: an introduction. In G. N. Carlson and F. J. Pelletier (eds), *The Generic Book*, 1-124. Chicago: University of Chicago Press.
Kroch, A. S. (1989). Reflexes of grammar in patterns of language change. *Language Variation and Change* 1: 199-244.
Kroch, A., and A. Taylor (2000). *Penn-Helsinki Parsed Corpus of Middle English*, 2nd edn. University of Pennsylvania.
Kroch, A., A. Taylor, and D. Ringe (2000). The Middle English verb-second constraint: a case study in language contact and language change. In S. Herring, P. van Reenen, and L. Schoesler (eds), *Textual Parameters in Old Language*, 353-91. Amsterdam: Benjamins.
Kuroda, S. Y. (1965). Generative grammatical studies in the Japanese language. Ph.D. thesis, MIT.
Laca, B. (2005). Tiempo, aspecto y la interpretación de los verbos modales en español. *Lingüística ALFAL* 17: 9-44.
Laca, B. (2008). On modal tenses and tensed modals. In Chiyo Nishida and C. Russi (eds), *Selected Proceedings of CHRONOS 8*.
Laca, B. (2012). On modal tenses and tensed modals. In Ch. Nishida and C. Russi (eds), *Building a Bridge between Linguistic Communities of the Old and the New World: Current Research in Tense, Aspect, Mood and Modality*, 163-98. Geneva: Rodopi, Cahiers Chronos.
Lasersohn, P. (1996). Adnominal conditionals. In *Proceedings of SALT 6*. Available online at: https://www.researchgate.net/publication/214750291_Adnominal_Conditionals
Lasersohn, P. (2005). Context dependence, disagreement, and predicates of personal taste. *Linguistics and Philosophy* 28: 643-86.
Lasersohn, P. (2009). Relative truth, speaker commitment, and control of implicit arguments. *Synthese* 166: 359-74.
Lassiter, D. (2011). Measurement and modality: the scalar basis of modal semantics. Ph.D. thesis, New York University.
Laturnus, R. (2014). Ktunaxa future modals. In H. Greene (ed.), *Proceedings of SULA 7*, 71-87.
Lauer, S. (2010). Some news about *irgendein* and *algún*. Presentation at Workshop on Epistemic Indefinites, University of Göttingen, June 10-12.

Lee, J. (2011). The Korean evidential *-te*: a modal analysis. In O. Bonami and P. Cabrero Hofherr (eds), *Empirical Issues in Syntax and Semantics* 8, 287–311. Available online at: http://www.cssp.cnrs.fr/eiss8

Lee, J. (2013). Temporal constraints on the meaning of evidentiality. *Natural Language Semantics* 21: 1–41.

Leech, G., M. Hundt, C. Mair, and N. Smith (2009). *Change in Contemporary English: A Grammatical Study*. Cambridge: Cambridge University Press.

Levin, B. (1999). Objecthood: an event structure perspective. In *Proceedings of CLS 35*, vol 1: 223–247.

Levin, B. and M. Rappaport Hovav (1995). *Unaccusativity: At the Syntax–Lexical Semantics Interface*. Cambridge, Mass: MIT Press.

Levin, B. and M. Rappaport Hovav (2013). Lexicalized meaning and manner/result complementarity. In B. Arsenijevic, B. Gehrke, and R. Marín (eds), *Studies in the Composition and Decomposition of Event Predicates*, 49–70. Dordrecht: Springer.

Levin, B., and M. Rappaport Hovav (2014). Manner and result: A view from *clean*. In R. Pensalfini, M. Turpin, and D. Guillemin (eds), *Language Description Informed by Theory*, 337–58. Amsterdam: Benjamins.

Levinson, D. (2003). Probabilistic model-theoretic semantics for *want*. In R. B. Young and Y. Zhou (eds), *Semantics and Linguistic Theory (SALT) XIII*, 222–39. Ithaca, NY: CLC.

Lewis, D. (1973). *Counterfactuals*. Cambridge, Mass.: Harvard University Press.

Lewis, D. (1975). Adverbs of quantification. In E. Keenan (ed.), *Formal Semantics of Natural Language*, 3–15. Cambridge: Cambridge University Press.

Lewis, D. (1979). A problem about permission. In E. Saarinen, R. Hilpinen, I. Niiniluoto, and M. P. Hintikka (eds), *Essays in honour of Jaako Hintikka*, 163–75. Dordrecht: Reidel.

Lewis, D. (1981). Ordering semantics and premise semantics for counterfactuals. *Journal of Philosophical Logic* 10: 217–34.

Lewis, D., and R. Langton (1999). Defining 'intrinsic'. In D. K. Lewis, *Papers in Metaphysics and Epistemology*, 116–32. Cambridge: Cambridge University Press.

Lightfoot, D. W. (1979). *Principles of Diachronic Syntax*. Cambridge: Cambridge University Press.

Lim, D. (2010). Evidentials and interrogatives: a case study from Korean. Ph.D. thesis, University of Southern California.

Lin, J. (2006). Time in a language without tense: the case of Chinese. *Journal of Semantics* 23: 1–56.

Louie, M. (2013). Constraints on licensing if-clauses in Blackfoot. In S. Luo (ed.), *Actes du Congrès de l'ACL 2013/CLA Conference Proceedings*.

Louie, M. (2015). The temporal semantics of actions and circumstance in Blackfoot. Ph.D. thesis, University of British Columbia.

Lyons, J. (1977). *Semantics*. Cambridge: Cambridge University Press.

MacFarlane, J. (2004). Epistemic modalities and relative truth. MS. Available online at: http://johnmacfarlane.net/epistmod-2003.pdf

Maher, K. (2013). English *some* as an epistemic indefinite. Honors thesis, Stony Brook University.

Malamud, S. A., and T. Stephenson (2015). Three ways to avoid commitments. *Journal of Semantics* 32: 275–311.

Mari, A., and F. Martin (2009). On the Interaction between aspect and verbal polysemy: (im)-perfectivity and (non)-implicativity. MS, Institut Jean Nicod and University of Stuttgart.

Martin, F. (2006). Prédicats statifs, causatifs et résultatifs en discours: sémantique des adjectifs évaluatifs et des verbes psychologiques. Ph.D. thesis, Université libre de Bruxelles.

Martin, F. (2011). Epistemic modals in the past. In J. Berns, H. Jacobs, and T. Scheer (eds), *Romance Languages and Linguistic Theory*, 185–202. Amsterdam: Benjamins.

Martin, F. (2015). Explaining the link between agentivity and non-culminating causation. In S. D'Antonio, M. Moroney, and C. Little (eds), *Proceedings of Semantics and Linguistics Theory (SALT)* 25: 246–66.

Martin, F. (2016). Atypical agents and non-culminating events. Talk given to the workshop "Agentivity and event structure," DGFS 2016, Universität Konstanz, Feb.

Martin, F., and F. Schäfer (2012). The modality of 'offer' and other defeasible causatives. In N. Arnett and R. Bennett (eds), *Proceedings of WCCFL 30*, 248–58. Somerville, Mass.: Cascadilla Press.

Martin, F., and F. Schäfer (2013). On the argument structure of verbs with bi- and mono-eventive uses. In S. Keine and S. Sloggett (eds), *Proceedings of NELS 42*, 297–308. Amherst, Mass.: GLSA.

Martin, F., and F. Schäfer (2014). Causation at the syntax/semantics interface. In B. Copley and F. Martin (eds), *Causation in Grammatical Structures*, 209–43. Oxford: Oxford University Press.

Maslov, J. S. (1959). Glagol'nij vid v sovremennom bolgarskom literaturnom jazyke (znachenie i upotreblenie) [Verb aspect in modern literary Bulgarian (meaning and use). In *Voprosy grammatiki bolgarskogo literaturnogo jazika [Issues in Bulgarian Literary Grammar]*, 157–312. Moscow.

Matthewson, L. (2004). On the methodology of semantic fieldwork. *International Journal of American Linguistics* 70: 369–415.

Matthewson, L. (2006). Temporal semantics in a supposedly tenseless language. *Linguistics and Philosophy* 29: 673–713.

Matthewson, L. (2012). On the (non-)future orientation of modals. In A. Aguilar-Guevara et al. (eds), *Proceedings of Sinn und Bedeutung 16*, 431–46.

Matthewson, L. (2013). Gitksan modals. *International Journal of American Linguistics* 79: 349–94.

Matthewson, L., H. Davis, and H. Rullmann (2007). Evidentials as epistemic modals: evidence from St'át'imcets. *Linguistic Variation Yearbook* 7: 201–54.

Matthewson, L., and H. Rullmann (2012). Epistemic modality with a past temporal perspective. Paper presented at the Modality@OttawaU workshop, April.

Mazodier, C. (1998). "I must have read it in some article": instabilité qualitative de *some* + discontinu singulier. In *Cahiers de recherche en grammaire anglaise*, 111–26. Paris: Ophrys.

McCloskey, J. (1991). Clause structure, ellipsis and proper government in Irish. *Lingua* 85: 259–301.

McCready, E., and N. Ogata (2007). Evidentiality, modality and probability. *Linguistics and Philosophy* 30: 147–206.

McFadden, T. (2011). The Old English distribution and subsequent loss of preverbal *ge-*. Paper given at the 13th Diachronic Generative Syntax Conference, University of Pennsylvania, June 4.

MED (2002). *Middle English Dictionary*, electronic version: http://quod.lib.umich.edu/m/med/

Mezhevich, I. (2006). Featuring Russian tense: a feature-theoretic account of the Russian tense system. Ph.D. thesis, University of Calgary.

Mitchell, B. (1985). *Old English Syntax*. Oxford: Clarendon Press.

Moltmann, F. (2006). Presuppositions and quantifier domains. *Synthese* 149: 179–224.

Montague, R. (1974). The proper treatment of quantification in ordinary English. In R. H. Thomason (ed.), *Formal Philosophy: Selected Papers by Richard Montague*, 17–34. New Haven, Conn.: Yale University Press.

Montler, T. (1986). An outline of the morphology and phonology of Saanich, North Straits Salish. *Occasional Papers in Linguistics* 4. Missoula: Linguistics Laboratory, University of Montana.

Morris, R. (1880). *The Blickling Homilies of the Tenth Century from the Marquis of Lothian's Unique Manuscript, A. D. 971*. London: Trübner.

Munro, R., R. Ludwig, U. Sauerland, and D. W. Fleck (2012). Reported speech in Matses: perspective persistence and evidential narratives. *International Journal of American Linguistics* 78: 41–75.

Murray, S. E. (2010). Evidentiality and the structure of speech acts. Ph.D. thesis, Rutgers University.

Musan, R. (2002). *The German Perfect: Its Semantic Composition and its Interaction with Temporal Adverbials*. Berlin: Springer.

Nevalainen, T., and H. Raumolin-Brunberg (2003). *Historical Sociolinguistics: Language Change in Tudor and Stuart England*. Harlow: Longman.

Ngonyani, D. (1996). VP ellipsis in Ndendeule and Swahili applicatives. *UCLA Working Papers in Syntax and Semantics* 1: 109–28.

Nikolaeva, I. (1999). The semantics of Northern Ostyak evidentials. *Journal de la Société Finno-Ougrienne* 88: 131–59.

Nouwen, R. (2007). Predicates of (im)personal taste. MS, available online at: http://ricknouwen.org/rwfn/

OED (2013). *Oxford English Dictionary*, 3rd edn, online. http://www.oed.com

Ogawa, H. (1989). *Old English Modal Verbs: A Syntactical Study*. Copenhagen: Rosenkilde & Bagger.

Oehrle, R. (1976). The grammatical status of the English dative alternation. Ph.D. thesis, MIT.

Ono, S. (1958). Some notes on the auxiliary **motan*. *Anglica* 3: 64–80.

Palmer, F. R. (1986). *Mood and Modality*. Cambridge: Cambridge University Press.

Pancheva, R. (2003). The aspectual makeup of perfect participles and the interpretations of the perfect. In A. Alexiadou, M. Rathert, and A. von Stechow (eds), *Perfect Explorations*, 277–306. Berlin : Mouton de Gruyter.

Parsons, T. (1990). *Events in the Semantics of English: A Study in Subatomic Semantics*. Cambridge, Mass.: MIT Press.

Pašov, P. (1989). *Prakticeska bălgarska gramatika*. Sofia: Narodna prosveta.

Pašov, P. (2005). *Bălgarska Gramatika*. Sofia: Hermes.

PCEEC (2006). Parsed Corpus of Early English Correspondence. Annotated by A. Taylor, A. Nurmi, A. Warner, A. Pintzuk, and T. Nevalainen. Compiled by the CEEC Project Team. York: University of York and Helsinki: University of Helsinki. Distributed through the Oxford Text Archive.

Pearson, H. (2012). A judge-free semantics for predicates of personal taste. *Journal of Semantics* 30(1): 103–54.

Peterson, T. (2010). Epistemic modality and evidentiality in Gitksan at the semantics–pragmatics interface. Ph.D. thesis, University of British Columbia.

Piñón, C. (2014). Reconsidering defeasible causative verbs. Talk to the workshop "Agent control over non-culminating events," Chronos 11, Pisa, June.

Pintzuk, S. (1999). *Phrase Structures in Competition: Variation and Change in Old English word order*. New York: Routledge.

Pintzuk, S., and A. Taylor (2008). The loss of OV order in the history of English. In *The Handbook of the History of English*. Oxford: Wiley-Blackwell, 249–78.

Plank, F. (1984). The modal story retold. *Studies in Language* 8: 305–64.

Port, A. (2010). Epistemic specificity and knowledge. Talk presented at the workshop "Indefinites crosslinguistically" (DGfS), Berlin, Feb.

Portner, P. (1997). The semantics of mood, complementation, and conversational force. *Natural Language Semantics* 5: 167–212.

Portner, P. (2007). Imperatives and modals. *Natural Language Semantics* 15: 351–83.

Portner, P. (2009). *Modality*. Oxford: Oxford University Press.

Portner, P. (2012). Permission and choice. In G. Grewendorf and T. E. Zimmermann (eds), *Discourse and Grammar*, 43–68. Berlin: de Gruyter.

Potts, C. (2007). Conventional implicatures, a distinguished class of meanings. In G. Ramchand and C. Reiss (eds), *The Oxford Handbook of Linguistic Interfaces*, 475–501. Oxford: Oxford University Press.

Progovac, L. (1998). Structure for coordination, pt 1. *GLOT International* 3: 3–6.

Pylkkänen, L. (2008). *Introducing Arguments*. Cambridge, Mass.: MIT Press.

Rappaport Hovav, M. (2008). Lexicalized meaning and the internal temporal structure of events. In S. Rothstein (ed.), *Theoretical and Crosslinguistic Approaches to the Semantics of Aspect*, 13–42. Amsterdam: Benjamins.

Rappaport Hovav, M., and B. Levin (2008). The English dative alternation: the case for verb sensitivity. *Journal of Linguistics* 44(1): 29–167.

Rappaport Hovav, M., and B. Levin (2010). Reflections on manner/result complementarity. In E. Doron, M. Rappaport Hovav, and I. Sichel (eds), *Lexical Semantics, Syntax, and Event Structure*, 21–38. Oxford: Oxford University Press.

Rau, J. (2010). Semantic and syntactic differences between finite and infinitival complements in German. Ph.D. thesis, Universität Tübingen.

Raumolin-Brunberg, H. (2005). Language change in adulthood: historical letters as evidence. *European Journal of English Studies* 9: 37–51.

Récanati, F. (2007). It is raining (somewhere). *Linguistics and Philosophy* 30(1): 123–46.

Reis, M. (2001). Bilden Modalverben im Deutschen eine syntaktische Klasse? In R. Müller and M. Reis (eds), *Modalität und Modalverben im Deutschen*, 287–318. Hamburg: Buske.

Reis Silva, A., and L. Matthewson (2007). An instantaneous present tense in Blackfoot. In A. R. Deal (ed.), *Proceedings of SULA* 4, 191–214.
Ren, F. (2008). Futurity in Mandarin Chinese. Ph.D. thesis, University of Texas.
Reyle, U., A. Roßdeutscher, and H. Kamp (2007). Ups and downs in the theory of temporal reference. *Linguistics and Philosophy* 30: 565–635.
Rigsby, B. (1986). Gitksan grammar. MS, University of Queensland.
Ritter, E., and M. Wiltschko (2004). The lack of tense as a syntactic category: evidence from Blackfoot and Halkomelem. In J. C. Brown and T. Peterson (eds), *Proceedings of the 39th International Conference on Salish and Neighbouring Languages*, 341–70.
Ritter, E., and M. Wiltschko (2005). Anchoring events to utterances without tense. In J. Alderete, C-h. Han, and A. Kochetov (eds), *Proceedings of WCCFL*, 343–51.
Ritter, E., and M. Wiltschko (2009). Varieties of INFL: tense, location, and person. In H. Broekhuis, J. van Craenenbroeck, and H. van Riemsdijk (eds), *Alternatives to Cartography*, 153–201. Berlin: Mouton de Gruyter.
Ritter, E., and M. Wiltschko (2010). The composition of INFL: an exploration of tense, tenseless languages and tenseless constructions. Available online at: www.ling.auf.net/lingbuzz/001078
Rivero, M. L. (2005). Topics in Bulgarian morphology and syntax: a minimalist perspective. *Lingua* 115: 1083–1128.
Rivero, M. L. (2011a). *Cualquiera* posnominal: un desconocido *cualquiera*. *Cuadernos de la Asociación de lingüística y filología de la América Latina* 3: 60–80.
Rivero, M. L. (2011b). Un desconocido *cualquiera*. In M. V. Escandell Vidal, M. Leonetti, and C. Sánchez López (eds), *Problemas de gramática*, 54–61. Madrid: Editorial Akal.
Rivero, M. L. (2014). Spanish inferential and mirative futures and conditionals: an evidential gradable modal proposal. *Lingua* 151: 197–215.
Rivero, M. L. and N. Slavkov (2014). Imperfect(ive) variation: the case of Bulgarian. *Lingua* 150: 232–77.
Rivero, M. L., and A. Terzi (1995). Imperatives, V-movement and logical mood. *Journal of Linguistics* 31: 301–32.
Roberts, C. (1989). Modal subordination and pronominal anaphora in discourse. *Linguistics and Philosophy* 12: 683–721.
Roberts, I. G. (1985). Agreement parameters and the development of English modal auxiliaries. *Natural Language and Linguistic Theory* 3: 21–58.
Roberts, I. G. (1993). *Verbs and Diachronic Syntax: A Comparative History of English and French*. Dordrecht: Kluwer.
Roberts, I. G., and A. Roussou (2003). *Syntactic Change: A Minimalist Approach to Grammaticalization*. Cambridge: Cambridge University Press.
Robson, S. (2002). *Javanese Grammar for Students*, 2nd edn. Glen Waverley: Monash Papers on Southeast Asia.
Romero, M. (2005). Concealed questions and specificational subjects. *Linguistics and Philosophy* 28: 687–737.
Rooth, M. (1985). Association with focus. Ph.D. thesis, University of Massachusetts Amherst.
Roßdeutscher, A., and H. Kamp (2010). Syntactic and semantic constraints in the formation and interpretation of *ung-* nouns. In A. Alexiadou and M. Rathert (eds), *The Semantics of Nominalizations across Languages and Frameworks* 169–214. Berlin: Mouton de Gruyter.

Rubinstein, A. (2012). Roots of modality. Ph.D. thesis, University of Massachusetts Amherst.

Rubinstein, A. (2014). On necessity and comparison. *Pacific Philosophical Quarterly* 95: 512–54.

Rubinstein, A., D. Simonson, J. Chung, H. Harner, G. Katz, and P. Portner (2012). Developing a methodology for modality type annotations on a large scale. Paper presented at the Modality@Ottawa Workshop, University of Ottawa, April.

Rullmann, H., and L. Matthewson (2012). Epistemic modals can scope under past tense. Paper presented at the Texas Linguistic Society, June.

Rullmann, H., and L. Matthewson (2015). On the (in)dependence of tense and modality. MS, University of British Columbia.

Rullmann, H., L. Matthewson, and H. Davis (2008). Modals as distributive indefinites. *Natural Language Semantics* 16: 317–57.

Russell, B. (2007). Imperatives in conditional conjunction. *Natural Language Semantics* 15: 131–66.

Ruwet, N. (1994). Être ou ne pas être un verbe de sentiment. *Langue française* 103(1): 45–55.

Ruwet, N. (1995). Les verbes de sentiments peuvent-ils être agentifs? *Langue française* 105(1): 28–39.

Ryle, G. (1949). *The Concept of Mind*. London: Hutchinson.

Sæbø, K. J. (2009). Judgment ascriptions. *Linguistics and Philosophy* 32: 327–52.

Sag, I., and C. Pollard (1991). An integrated theory of complement control. *Language* 67(1): 63–113.

Salanova, A. (2007). Nominalizations and aspect. Ph.D. thesis, MIT.

Salanova, A. (2013). Event nominals in Mẽbengokre and the theory of nominalizations. *Canadian Journal of Linguistics* 58: 267–92.

Sauerland, U. (2004). Scalar implicatures in complex sentences. *Linguistics and Philosophy* 27(3): 367–91.

Sauerland, U., and M. Schenner (2007). Shifting evidentials in Bulgarian. *Sinn und Bedeutung* 11: 525–39.

Sauerland, U., and M. Schenner (2013). On embedding and evidentiality in Bulgarian *Contrastive Linguistics* 38(2–3): 131–52.

Scatton, E. (1983). *A Reference Grammar of Modern Bulgarian*. Columbus, OH: Slavica.

Scheffler, T. (2008). Semantic operators in different dimensions. Ph.D. thesis, University of Pennsylvania.

Schulz, K. (2014). Fake tense in conditional sentences: a modal approach. *Natural Language Semantics* 22: 117–44.

Schwarz, B., and J. Shimoyama (2011). Negative islands and obviation by *wa* in Japanese degree questions. In N. Lin and D. Lutz (eds), *Proceedings of the 20th Semantics and Linguistic Theory Conference*, 702–19. eLanguage.

Scontras, G., and E. Gibson (2011). A quantitative investigation of the imperative-and-declarative construction in English. *Language* 87: 817–29.

Searle, J. (1989). How performatives work. *Linguistics and Philosophy* 12(5): 535–58.

Silk, A. (2012). Modality, weights, and inconsistent premise sets. In A. Chereches (ed.), *Semantics and Linguistic Theory (SALT)* 22, 43–64. https://www.researchgate.net/publication/281213866

Skeat, W. W. (ed.) (1881). *Ælfric's Lives of Saints*. London: Trübner.

Slade, B. (2015). Sinhala indefinites with a certain *je ne sais quoi*. In L. Alonso-Ovalle and P. Menéndez-Benito (eds), *Epistemic Indefinites: Exploring Modality Beyond the Verbal Domain*, 82–100. Oxford: Oxford University Press.

Slobin, D. I., and A. A. Aksu (1982). Tense, aspect and modality in the use of the Turkish evidential. In P. J. Hopper (ed.), *Tense-Aspect: Between Semantics and Pragmatics*, 185–200. Amsterdam: Benjamins.

Smirnova, A. (2011). The meaning of the Bulgarian evidential and why it cannot express inferences about the future. *SALT* 21: 275–94.

Smirnova, A. (2013). Evidentiality in Bulgarian: temporality, epistemic modality, and information source. *Journal of Semantics* 30: 479–532.

Smith, C. S. (1991). *The Parameter of Aspect*. Dordrecht: Kluwer.

Smith, C., and M. Erbaugh (2005). Temporal interpretation in Mandarin Chinese. *Linguistics* 43: 713–56.

Soare, E. (2008). Perfect and imperfect modals in Romance: some syntactic remarks on the tense/modality interaction. *Bucharest Working Papers in Linguistics* 1: 39–55.

Speas, P. (2010). Evidentials as generalized functional heads. In A. M. Di Sciullo and V. Hill (eds), *Edges, Heads, and Projections*, 127–50. Amsterdam: Benjamins.

Stalnaker, R. (1968). A theory of conditionals. In N. Rescher (ed.), *Studies in Logical Theory*, 98–112. Oxford: Blackwell.

Stalnaker, R. (1984). *Inquiry*. Cambridge, Mass.: MIT Press.

Steele, S. (1975). Past and irrealis: just what does it all mean? *International Journal of American Linguistics* 41: 200–217.

Stephenson, T. (2007a). Judge dependence, epistemic modals, and predicates of personal taste. *Linguistics and Philosophy* 30: 487–525.

Stephenson, T. (2007b). Towards a subjective theory of meaning. Ph.D. thesis, MIT.

Sternefeld, W. (2006). *Syntax: Eine merkmalbasierte generative Analyse des Deutschen*. Tübingen: Stauffenburg.

Stowell, T. (2004). Tense and modals. In J. Guéron and A. Lecarme (eds), *The Syntax of Time*, 621–36. Cambridge, Mass.: The MIT Press.

Strawson, P. F. (1974). *Subject and Predicate in Logic and Grammar*. London: Methuen.

Stump, G. (1981). The interpretation of frequency adjectives. *Linguistics and Philosophy* 4: 221–57.

Sudo, Y. (2010). *Wh-ka* pronouns in Japanese and the semantics of indeterminate pronouns. Handout for talk at the Workshop on Epistemic Indefinites, University of Göttingen, June 2010.

Sun, H. (2014). Temporal construals of bare predicates in Mandarin Chinese. Ph.D. thesis, Université de Nantes/Universiteit Leiden.

Suttles, W. (2004). *Musqueam Reference Grammar*. Vancouver: UBC Press.

Szabolcsi, A. (2014). What do quantifier particles do? MS, New York University.

Szabolcsi, A., J. D. Whang, and V. Zu (2014). Quantifier words and their multi-functional(?) parts. *Language and Linguistics* 15(1): 115–55.

Taleghani, A. H. (2008). *Modality, Aspect, and Negation in Persian*. Amsterdam: Benjamins.

Talmy, L. (2000). *Toward a Cognitive Semantics*, vol. 1: *Concept Structuring Systems*, Cambridge, Mass.: MIT Press.

Tatevosov, S. and M. Ivanov (2009). Event structure of non-culminating accomplishments. In L. Hogeweg, H. de Hoop, and A. Malchukov (eds), *Cross-Linguistic Semantics of Tense, Aspect, and Modality*, 83–130. The Hague: Benjamins.

Taylor, A., A. Warner, S. Pintzuk, and F. Beths (2003). The York–Toronto–Helsinki Parsed Corpus of Old English Prose. York University. Available online at: www-users.york.ac.uk/~lang22/YCOE/YcoeHome.htm

TFS Working Group (2011a). Chore girl. *Totem Field Storyboards*. Retrieved from: http://totemfieldstoryboards.org/stories/chore_girl/

TFS Working Group (2011b). Sick girl. *Totem Field Storyboards*. Retrieved from: http://totemfieldstoryboards.org/stories/sick_girl/

TFS Working Group (2012). Feeding Fluffy. *Totem Field Storyboards*. Retrieved from: http://totemfieldstoryboards.org/stories/feeding_fluffy/

Thomas, G. (2014). Circumstantial modality and the diversity condition. In U. Etxeberria, A. Fălăuş, A. Irurtzun, and B. Leferman (eds), *Proceedings of Sinn und Bedeutung*, 18: 433–50.

Tonhauser, J. (2011). Temporal reference in Paraguayan Guaraní, a tenseless language. *Linguistics and Philosophy* 34: 257–303.

Traugott, E. (1972). *A History of English Syntax: A Transformational Approach to the History of English Sentence Structure*. New York: Holt, Rinehart & Winston.

Traugott, E. C. (1989). On the rise of epistemic meanings in English: an example of subjectification in semantic change. *Language* 65: 31–55.

Traugott, E. (1992). Syntax. In R. M. Hogg (ed.), *The Cambridge History of the English Language*, 168–289. Cambridge: Cambridge University Press.

Travis, C. E. (2006). Dizque: a Colombian evidentiality strategy. *Linguistics* 44: 1269–97.

Travis, L. (1984). *Parameters and Effects of Word Order Variation*. Cambridge, Mass.: MIT Press.

Trinh, T. (2009). A constraint on copy deletion. *Theoretical Linguistics* 35: 183–227.

Turner, C. K. (2011). Representing events in Saanich (SENĆOŦEN). Ph.D. thesis, University of Surrey.

Turner, C. K. (2013). Tense and type of modality in SENĆOŦEN and Hul'q'umi'num'. MS, University of British Columbia.

Txurruka, I. Gómez (2003). The natural language conjunction *and*. *Linguistics and Philosophy* 26: 255–85.

Ulutas, S. (2006). Conditional clauses and the architecture of the higher functional domain. MS, Harvard University.

van der Auwera, J., and V. Plungian (1998). Modality's semantic map. *Linguistic Typology* 2: 79–124.

Vander Klok, J. (2012). Tense, aspect, and modal markers in Paciran Javanese. Ph.D. thesis, McGill University.

Vander Klok, J. (2013). Pure possibility and pure necessity modals in Paciran Javanese. *Oceanic Linguistics* 52(2): 341–74.

van Eijk, J. (1997). *The Lillooet Language: Phonology, Morphology, Syntax*. Vancouver: UBC Press.

van Eijk, J. and L. Williams (1981). *Cuystwí Malh Ucwalmícwts: Lillooet Legends and Stories*. Mount Currie: Ts'zil.

van Gelderen, E. (2003). ASP(ect) in English modal complements. *Studia Linguistica* 57: 27–43.

Van Linden, A., and J.-C. Verstraete (2008). The nature and origins of counterfactuality in simple clauses: cross-linguistic evidence. *Journal of Pragmatics* 40: 1865–95.

Van Linden, A., J.-C. Verstraete, and H. Cuyckens (2008). The semantic development of *essential* and *crucial*: paths to deontic meaning. *English Studies* 89: 226–47.

van Rooij, R. (1999). Some analyses of pro-attitudes. In H. de Swart (ed.), *Logic, Game Theory, and Social Choice*, 534–8. Tilburg: Tilburg University Press.

Varasdi, K. (2014). Making progressives: necessary conditions are sufficient. *Journal of Semantics* 31(2): 179–207.

Villalta, E. (2000). Spanish subjunctive clauses require ordered alternatives. In B. Jackson and T. Matthews (eds), *Semantics and Linguistic Theory (SALT) X*, 239–56. Ithaca, NY: CLC.

Villalta, E. (2006). Context dependence in the interpretation of questions and subjunctives. Ph.D. thesis, Universität Tübingen.

Villalta, E. (2008). Mood and gradability: An investigation of the subjunctive mood in Spanish. *Linguistics and Philosophy* 31: 467–522.

Visser, F. T. (1963–73). *An Historical Syntax of the English Language*. Leiden: Brill.

von Stechow, A. (1999). Eine erweiterete Extended Now-Theorie für Perfekt und Futur. *Zeitschrift für Literaturwissenschaft und Linguistik* 113: 86–118.

von Stechow, A. (2009). Tenses in compositional semantics. In W. Klein and P. Li (eds), *The Expression of Time*, 129–66. Berlin: de Gruyter.

Warfel, Sam L. (1972). *Some*, reference, and description. In *Mid-America Linguistics Conference Papers*, 41–9. Oklahoma State University.

Warner, A. R. (1992). Elliptical and impersonal constructions: evidence for auxiliaries in Old English. In F. Colman (ed.), *Evidence from Old English: Material and Theoretical Bases for Reconstruction*, 178–210. Edinburgh: Donald.

Warner, A. R. (1993). *English Auxiliaries: Structure and History*. Cambridge: Cambridge University Press.

Weinreich, U., W. Labov, and M. Herzog (1968). Empirical foundations for a theory of language change. In W. P. Lehmann and Y. Malkiel (eds), *Directions for Historical Linguistics: A Symposium*, 95–195. Austin: University of Texas Press.

Weir, A. (2012). *Some*, speaker knowledge, and subkinds. In R. K. Rendsvig and S. Katenko (eds), *Proceedings of the European Summer School in Language, Logic and Information, Student Session Proceedings*, 180–90. University of Opole, Poland.

Willett, T. (1988). A cross-linguistic survey of the grammaticization of evidentiality. *Studies in Language* 12: 51–97.

Wilson, D., and D. Sperber (1988). Mood and the analysis of non-declarative sentences. In J. Dancy, J. M. E. Moravcsik, and C. C. W. Taylor (eds), *Human Agency: Language, Duty and Value*, 77–101. Stanford, Calif.: Stanford University Press.

Wiltschko, M. (2003). On the interpretability of tense on D and its consequences for case theory. *Lingua* 113: 659–96.

Wiltschko, M. (2009). The composition of INFL: an exploration of tense, tenseless languages and tenseless constructions. Handout, MIT colloquium.

Winkler, S. (2005). *Ellipsis and Focus in Generative Grammar*. Berlin: Mouton de Gruyter.

Wolf, L. (2012). Epistemic modality and the subjective–objective distinction. In M. van Koppen, E. Thrift, E. J. van der Torre, and M. Zimmermann (eds), *Proceedings of ConSOLE*, 19: 331–42.

Wolf, L. (2014). Degrees of assertion. Ph.D. thesis, Ben-Gurion University of the Negev.
Wurmbrand, S. (1999). Modal verbs must be raising verbs. *West Coast Conference on Formal Linguistics* 18: 599–612.
Wurmbrand, S. (2001). *Infinitives: Restructuring and Clause Structure*. Berlin: de Gruyter.
Yalcin, S. (2010). Probability operators. *Philosophy Compass* 5: 916–37.
Yanovich, I. (2013). Four pieces for modality, context and usage. Ph.D. thesis, MIT.
Yuqih, T., and A. Yupas (1991). *Pin'aras Ke' na Bnkis Tayal* (泰雅爾族傳說故事精選集 [Selected Atayal Legendary Stories]). Taipei: Promotion Committee of Native Languages, Presbyterian Christian Church.
Zabbal, Y. (2004). A compositional semantics of the French expression *n'importe*. MS, University of Massachusetts Amherst.
Zeijlstra, H. (2013). Not in the first place. *Natural Language and Linguistic Theory* 31: 865–900.
Zeitoun, E., L. M. Huang, M. M. Yeh, A. H. Chang, and J. J. Wu (1996). The temporal/aspectual and modal systems of some Formosan languages: a typological perspective. *Oceanic Linguistics* 35: 21–56.

Index

actuality entailments 93, 203–6
adnominal conditionals 49–69
agent
   oriented modality 45–7
   vs causer subjects 87, 95–100, 107
agentivity 92, 100, 102, 107
alethic 121–2, 125–6
algún 30, 33, 38–9, 42, 47–8
alternatives 109–11, 113–15, 117, 120
asking attitudes 139
Atayal 237, 239, 277–82, 282–3, 285–6
attitude
   holder 120, 129
   verb 109–10, 113, 119, 129–30

belief 110–13, 115–20
   reports 135
      adverbial modification of 136
Blackfoot 237, 239, 262–70, 282–3, 285–6
bouletic 116, 121, 124, 125, 127, 129, 130
Bulgarian 212, 213–23
   evidence acquisition time 221
   imperfective 216–19
   perfective 217, 220
   renarrated mood 214
   viewpoint aspect 215

can 144, 150
circumstantial modal base 98–101, 118
circumstantial modality 121–2, 127–8, 190–7
concealed questions 52–3
concessive clauses 152
conditional conjunctions 303, 305–8, 315–16
conditionals 60–3, 111–12, 119, 142, 192, 206
corpus
   evidence 137
   study 119, 123–4, 127
counterfactual conditionals
   dedicated (modal) operator in 174, 175–6
   marked by (fake) imperfective 169–73
   marked by (fake) past 159–69
   typology of 159, 160, 169, 172–3
counterfactuality 206

de dicto 85
defeasible causative verbs 87–108

deontic interpretation 125–9
deontic modality 121–3, 195, 197
desire
   reports 135
      adverbial modification of 136
   verb 109, 111
Diversity Condition 235–8, 261, 282–3
domain
   restrictions 19
   pragmatic competitors, based on 21
doxastic accessability 112, 116, 117
doxastic alternatives 112, 113, 114, 115, 117, 118
doxastic availability 112
doxastic possibility 134
Doxastic Problem 113, 115, 116, 117
doxastic uncertainty 135–6
Dutch 237, 240–6, 261, 285–6

Early Modern English 147–51
emotive doxastics 137
energetic modal base 98–9
English 119–21, 125, 127, 129, 157
entailment, cross-categorial 24
epistemics 121, 122, 125–9
epistemic effect 13–15, 18–22, 30, 35–6
   conceptual cover approach 13–15
   disappearance in downward entailing contexts 12–13, 19, 21
   disappearance in co-variation scenarios 13, 18–20, 21–2
   downward entailing environments, in 43–5
   implicature approach 20–1
   implicature, as an 43–5
   modal variation 41–3
   partial ignorance 39
   type vs tokens 36–7
epistemic modality 188–93, 195–8, 205, 213
epistemic verbs 70
evidence
   acquisition time 221–3, 227
   sources of 39–40
evidential modal 213
evidentiality 84

faultless disagreement 70
fearing attitudes 137
features, syntactic specification of 160–1, 163, 166–7, 169, 173, 177
French 161, 167–8
function
  property selection function 24
  subset selection function 20, 22

ge-prefixation 187–8
German 187–8, 204–5, 237, 240–6, 261, 285–6
Gitksan 237, 239, 246–9, 261, 285–6
goal-oriented modality see teleological modality
Greek 158

Halkomelem (Hul'q'umi'num') 237, 239, 270–7, 282–3, 283–5, 285–6
hedging 134–5
Hindi 170, 176
hope
  hopes about good health 143, 149, 150, 151–2
  hopes about the past 142, 149
  hoping attitudes 132–7
  presuppositions of 134–6

identification
  by description 14, 19
  by naming 19
  by ostension 14, 17–19
  methods of 13–15
ignorance
  about quantity 47–8
  partial ignorance 41–3
imperatives
  acquiescence 291
  Albanian 298, 304
  Catalan 311
  cross-linguistic variation 309
  French 298, 304
  German 294, 296
  Greek 289, 298, 304
  Hebrew 310
  imperative and declarative constructions (IaDs) 297–309, 315–18
    endorsing imperative and declarative constructions (e-IaDs) 299–303
    non-endorsing imperative and declarative constructions (n-IaDs) 303–5, 308–9
  indifference 291
  minimal semantics 291

  morphosyntax 289
  Palestinian Arabic 298, 304, 310
  permission 291
  Slovenian 294
  speech-act strength 312–14
  strong vs minimal theories 289–91
  syntax 289
  to-do lists (TDL) 290–1
  Turkish 298
  weak readings 291–7, 312–15
imperfective operator 214, 215
  event-in-progress 218
  generic/habitual 218–19
  inertia 219
  ongoing 217
indefinites
  anti-singleton 20
  modal indefinites 30
indeterminate pronouns 31–5
  restrictions of 33–4
inertia of use 141
inevitability 200–1
infinitival relative clauses 69
innovation 141
intentional vs non-intentional agents 102–4
iterated modality 68–9

Japanese 30–48
Javanese 237, 239, 251–4, 261, 285–6

Ktunaxa 237, 239, 259–61, 261, 285–6

limit assumption 60

Mandarin 237, 255–9, 261, 285–6
manner/result complementarity 95
Matses 212, 228
  aspect 228
  evidential 230
  inferentials 229
  resultative 231
  tense 228
may 144
  circumstantial 144, 150
  deontic 134, 144, 150
  epistemic 134, 150
  internal ability 144
  non-quantificational 133–4, 150–1, 153
meaning equations 151, 153
Mẽbengokre 212, 223–8
  conjectural 225
  evidentials 223, 226
  particles 223–4, 225
  temporal markers 225, 226

Index

Middle English 137–47
might 77–83, 144
modal adjectives 59, 63–4, 119, 121–2, 129
modal base 60–3

necessary 66–7, 109–10, 119–31
necessity 109–10, 119, 121–3, 127, 129, 130–1
non-culminating construals 88, 92, 107
non-intentional agent vs causer subjects 102
Northern Straits Salish (SENĆOŦEN) 237, 239, 270–7, 282–3, 283–5, 285–6

Old English 137–8
opinion verbs 70
ordering source 60–3

Palestinian Arabic 162, 166–7
past possibility 235–8, 285–6
perfective operator 216, 217
Persian 170–2, 176
politeness 141
polyfunctional modal 119, 122–3, 129–30
possible 65
prayers 152
predicates of personal taste 71
Present-Day English 145–6
presupposition 74–6
priority (modality, modals, interpretation) 121, 122, 125, 126, 130–1
properties
  identificational property 24–6
  intrinsic properties 24
  stable properties 24
purpose constructions 152

register 134–5
relative clauses 152
Russian 163–5, 176

scope
  of modal above tense 283–5

shall 141–2, 148
should 82, 142
Sinhala 40
Spanish 119, 131
speaker endorsement 312–15
St'át'imcets 237, 239, 249–51, 261, 285–6
stereotypical modal base 99–101
strong necessity 130–1
subjunctive 119, 131
  English inflectional subjunctive 142–4, 149, 152
sublexical modality 98–102
syntactic reanalysis 184

teleological modality 119, 121–31
temporal morphology
  underspecification of 158, 160–1, 163, 166–7, 173, 177
temporal orientation 235–8, 282–5, 285–6
temporal perspective 235–8, 261, 282–5, 285–6
topicalization 186–7
Turkish 175–6

un qualche 41
uno cualquiera 46
(un)tensed 121–2, 124–7

variable modal force 199–200
verb phrase ellipsis 185–6
vreun 41

want 109–20, 129–31
weak necessity 130–1
wh-*ka* indeterminates 31–5
will 140, 148
wishes 152
would 141

Zulu 162, 164–5

OXFORD STUDIES IN THEORETICAL LINGUISTICS

Published

1 The Syntax of Silence
Sluicing, Islands, and the Theory of Ellipsis
by Jason Merchant

2 Questions and Answers in Embedded Contexts
by Utpal Lahiri

3 Phonetics, Phonology, and Cognition
edited by Jacques Durand and Bernard Laks

4 At the Syntax–Pragmatics Interface
Concept Formation and Verbal Underspecification in Dynamic Syntax
by Lutz Marten

5 The Unaccusativity Puzzle
Explorations of the Syntax–Lexicon Interface
edited by Artemis Alexiadou, Elena Anagnostopoulou, and Martin Everaert

6 Beyond Morphology
Interface Conditions on Word Formation
by Peter Ackema and Ad Neeleman

7 The Logic of Conventional Implicatures
by Christopher Potts

8 Paradigms of Phonological Theory
edited by Laura Downing, T. Alan Hall, and Renate Raffelsiefen

9 The Verbal Complex in Romance
by Paola Monachesi

10 The Syntax of Aspect
Deriving Thematic and Aspectual Interpretation
Edited by Nomi Erteschik-Shir and Tova Rapoport

11 Aspects of the Theory of Clitics
by Stephen Anderson

12 Canonical Forms in Prosodic Morphology
by Laura J. Downing

13 Aspect and Reference Time
by Olga Borik

14 Direct Compositionality
edited by Chris Barker and Pauline Jacobson

15 A Natural History of Infixation
by Alan C. L. Yu

16 Phi-Theory
Phi-Features Across Interfaces and Modules
edited by Daniel Harbour, David Adger, and Susana Béjar

17 French Dislocation
Interpretation, Syntax, Acquisition
by Cécile De Cat

18 Inflectional Identity
edited by Asaf Bachrach and Andrew Nevins

19 Lexical Plurals
by Paolo Acquaviva

20 Adjectives and Adverbs
Syntax, Semantics, and Discourse
Edited by Louise McNally and Christopher Kennedy

21 InterPhases
Phase-Theoretic Investigations of Linguistic Interfaces
edited by Kleanthes Grohmann

22 Negation in Gapping
by Sophie Repp

23 A Derivational Syntax for Information Structure
by Luis López

24 Quantification, Definiteness, and Nominalization
edited by Anastasia Giannakidou and Monika Rathert

25 The Syntax of Sentential Stress
by Arsalan Kahnemuyipour

26 Tense, Aspect, and Indexicality
by James Higginbotham

27 Lexical Semantics, Syntax, and Event Structure
edited by Malka Rappaport Hovav, Edit Doron, and Ivy Sichel

28 About the Speaker
Towards a Syntax of Indexicality
by Alessandra Giorgi

29 The Sound Patterns of Syntax
edited by Nomi Erteschik-Shir and Lisa Rochman

30 The Complementizer Phase
edited by Phoevos Panagiotidis

31 Interfaces in Linguistics

New Research Perspectives
edited by Raffaella Folli and Christiane Ulbrich

32 Negative Indefinites
by Doris Penka

33 Events, Phrases, and Questions
by Robert Truswell

34 Dissolving Binding Theory
by Johan Rooryck and Guido Vanden Wyngaerd

35 The Logic of Pronominal Resumption
by Ash Asudeh

36 Modals and Conditionals
by Angelika Kratzer

37 The Theta System
Argument Structure at the Interface
edited by Martin Everaert, Marijana Marelj, and Tal Siloni

38 Sluicing
Cross-Linguistic Perspectives
edited by Jason Merchant and Andrew Simpson

39 Telicity, Change, and State
A Cross-Categorial View of Event Structure
edited by Violeta Demonte and Louise McNally

40 Ways of Structure Building
edited by Myriam Uribe-Etxebarria and Vidal Valmala

41 The Morphology and Phonology of Exponence
edited by Jochen Trommer

42 Count and Mass Across Languages
edited by Diane Massam

43 Genericity
edited by Alda Mari, Claire Beyssade, and Fabio Del Prete

44 Strategies of Quantification
edited by Kook-Hee Gil, Steve Harlow, and George Tsoulas

45 Nonverbal Predication
Copular Sentences at the Syntax–Semantics Interface
by Isabelle Roy

46 Diagnosing Syntax
edited by Lisa Lai-Shen Cheng and Norbert Corver

47 Pseudogapping and Ellipsis
by Kirsten Gengel

48 Syntax and its Limits
edited by Raffaella Folli, Christina Sevdali, and Robert Truswell

49 Phrase Structure and Argument Structure
A Case Study of the Syntax–Semantics Interface
by Terje Lohndal

50 Edges in Syntax
Scrambling and Cyclic Linearization
by Heejeong Ko

51 The Syntax of Roots and the Roots of Syntax
edited by Artemis Alexiadou, Hagit Borer, and Florian Schäfer

52 Causation in Grammatical Structures
edited by Bridget Copley and Fabienne Martin

53 Continuations and Natural Language
by Chris Barker and Chung-chieh Shan

54 The Semantics of Evaluativity
by Jessica Rett

55 External Arguments in Transitivity Alternations
by Artemis Alexiadou, Elena Anagnostopoulou, and Florian Schäfer

56 Control and Restructuring
by Thomas Grano

57 The Interaction of Focus, Givenness, and Prosody
A Study of Italian Clause Structure
by Vieri Samek-Lodovici

58 The Morphosyntax of Gender
by Ruth Kramer

59 The Morphosyntax of Imperatives
by Daniela Isac

60 Sentence and Discourse
edited by Jacqueline Guéron

61 Optimality-Theoretic Syntax, Semantics, and Pragmatics
From Uni- to Bidirectional Optimization
edited by Géraldine Legendre, Michael T. Putnam, Henriëtte de Swart, and Erin Zaroukian

62 The Morphosyntax of Transitions
A Case Study in Latin and Other Languages
by Víctor Acedo-Matellán

63 Modality Across Syntactic Categories
edited by Ana Arregui, María Luisa Rivero, and Andrés Salanova

Published in association with the series
The Oxford Handbook of Linguistic Interfaces
edited by Gillian Ramchand and Charles Reiss

In preparation
Phi Syntax
A Theory of Agreement
by Susana Béjar

Stratal Optimality Theory
by Ricardo Bermúdez Otero

Phonology in Phonetics
by Abigail Cohn

The Verbal Domain
edited by Roberta D'Alessandro, Irene Franco, and Ángel J. Gallego

Quantity Superlatives and Proportional Quantification
by Carmen Dobrovie-Sorin and Ion Giurgea

Concealed Questions
by Ilaria Frana

Lexical Semantics and Morphosyntactic Variation
by Itamar Francez and Andrew Koontz-Garboden

Generality and Exception
by Iván García-Álvarez

Computing Optimality
by Jason Riggle

Pragmatic Aspects of Scalar Modifiers
by Osamu Sawada

Gradience in Split Intransitivity
by Antonella Sorace

The Structure of Words at the Interfaces
edited by Lisa deMena Travis, Glyne L. Piggott, Heather Newell, and Máire Noonan